Preface

This was probably the first international conference on the integration of data and knowledge bases, although it was not planned as such. Our original objective was to provide a forum for academia and industry in the UK to discuss and debate the issues in data and knowledge base integration for industrial applications. But interest in the conference was such that very soon it was transformed into an international event with papers arriving from Australia, Japan and USA, as well as from Europe and Britain. We wanted to keep the size of the conference small, with only about 50 delegates, so that there would be a good atmosphere for discussion of issues—one of our main objectives. The final number of delegates was about 60. The whole proceedings were videotaped, and questions and answers eventually transcripted for publication.

The conference was organised by the DAKE Centre. It is an interdisciplinary centre at the University of Keele for research and development in Data and Knowledge Engineering (DAKE). The Centre draws most of its strength from the Department of Computer Science which also provides administrative support for the activities of the Centre, although its membership is spread over many departments. The Centre has three main streams of research activities, namely,

Large Knowledge Bases
Neural Networks
Software Engineering

The Large Knowledge Base group, which provided the main focus for this conference, is active in a number of research areas relating to data and knowledge bases, spanning from distributed databases to the interaction of data and knowledge bases. The current research topics include integration of data and knowledge bases, distributed knowledge bases, cooperating knowledge-based systems (with particular emphasis on multi-agent systems) and voice-operated database systems. The software engineering group has provided strong support to the conference and has a paper in the proceedings. The group is well-known for its work in logic-based software configuration management and software re-use. The neural network group specialises in speech and image recognition areas. The Centre is organising (October 1990) an international working conference on cooperating knowledge based systems.

To return to the current conference, we called it a 'working' conference to underline the special emphasis we placed on the discussion of ideas and exchange of views. To facilitate this, the conference was made residential, and plenty of time was allowed at the end of each presentation for a discussion. The results are recorded in the form of questions and answers at the end of each published paper in these proceedings.

The contributed papers for the conference were selected in two stages: an initial selection of draft papers for presentation at the conference and a final selection of the presented papers after the conference for publication. This book contains an invited paper followed by the 14 contributed papers, divided into five categories:

Integration languages (2 papers)
New directions (3 papers)
Prolog and databases (3 papers)
Design approaches (3 papers)
Applications and tools (3 papers)

The papers are published in order of these categories. I should, however, point out that this categorisation is somewhat artificial and not entirely fair, given the spread of the topics. I have nevertheless found it convenient for presentation in this book.

Professor Singh's invited paper, entitled Hybrid Knowledge Based Systems for Tactical Decision Making, describes how the different components of a decision support system can be combined with knowledge bases.

The two papers in the language category are Design and Implementation of DEAL by Banks, et al, and MPL/0: a Multi-paradigm Language Facility for Data/Knowledge Base Programming by Shyy and Su. DEAL is an enhancement of the relational model with some ideas borrowed from Prolog and functional languages, for a deductive and recursive capability and also extensibility—as needed for an integrated data/knowledge base processing; in contrast MPL/0 is a requirement specification of an object-oriented approach for the same purpose. The next group on new directions covers a number of divergent topics. The paper Knowledge-directed Mediation between Application Objects and Base Data by Barsalou and Wiederhold proposes a new technique based on the novel concept of a 'mediator' to integrate a heterogeneous collection of data and knowledge bases. The second paper there is on Constraints and Deduction—Convergent Evolution? by Bowers and Rawlings, who attempt to show data and knowledge base integration as a convergent evolutionary approach with examples drawn from their work on protein structures. The third paper on A Virtual Memory Support for Deductive Database Queries by Greco, et al is slightly different, and it proposes a new query processing strategy.

In Prolog and databases, the first paper, A Database Administration Tool Using a Prolog/ORACLE Coupling by Lucas and Yip, reviews their implementation of Prolog/ORACLE coupling and shows how this is used for a DBA tool written in Prolog, while the second paper, Combining Prolog with an RDBMS for Applications in Software Configuration Management by Singleton, et al, discusses algorithms for transitive closures in the Prolog interface to ORACLE, which they have implemented to handle problems of software configuration management. The last paper, Integration of Database Systems at the Navigational Level by Using Prolog by Takizawa and Katsumata, discusses how Prolog is used for both data and knowledge processing, as an interface language to a distributed database system.

We have three papers on design methods: the first paper presents an initial case study of a design approach, while the other two propose new techniques for integrated data/knowledge base design. The first paper, Integrating Expert Systems and Relational Databases: Results of an Initial Case Study Using a User/Task-

Data and Knowledge Base Integration

Proceedings of the Working Conference
on Data and Knowledge Base Integration
held at the University of Keele, England
on October 4–5, 1989

Edited by
S. M. Deen
G. P. Thomas

Pitman

PITMAN PUBLISHING
128 Long Acre, London WC2E 9AN

A Division of Longman Group UK Limited

First published in Great Britain 1990

British Library Cataloguing in Publication Data
Working Conference on Data and Knowledge Base Integration
(1989: University of Keele)
Data & knowledge base integration.
1. Databases
I. Title II. Deen, S.M. (S Misbah) III. Thomas, G.P.
005.74

ISBN 0-273-08826-2

ISBN 0 273 08826 2

Printed and bound in Great Britain by
Richard Clay Ltd, Bungay, Suffolk

oriented Design Framework by Brayshaw, et al, discusses the findings of the group on their proposed design methodology. The second paper, A Knowledge Assistant for the Design of Information Systems by Ip and Holden, proposes a methodology based on several layers of abstraction, whereas the third paper Knowledge-based Applications = Knowledge Base + Mappings + Applications by Pun and Kahn, concentrates on mapping between applications and knowledge bases.

The three papers in the application category are A Graphical Knowledge Base for Large Industrial Domains by Butler, et al, The Generis Knowledge Base Management System: an Exploratory Review by Kennedy and Crerar, and Quantitative Evaluation Method for Intelligent Interface to a Document Database by Kinoshita, et al. Butler, et al, propose a graphical representational technique for digital switches, whereas Kennedy presents an evaluation study of the Generis system based on a Library application. In the final paper, Kinoshita, et al, propose an evaluation method for a natural language interface to a document retrieval database.

Each of the papers presented are interesting in their own way, and I hope you the reader will find them as interesting as the conference delegates did. The edited samples of the questions and answers attached at the end of each paper convey part of the conference atmosphere.

Finally, I would like to thank a number of people, without whose support this conference could not have taken place: among them the members of the organising committee, particularly Dr Glan Thomas, the members of the Programme Committee, the sponsors, and a number of individuals whose names do not appear elsewhere. The last group include three research students: Mike Green, Atula Herath and Jonathan Knight; and my two secretaries: Jayne Beardmore and Kendal Allen. Thanks to all of them.

S. Misbah Deen, the Conference Chairman

Contents

A Working Conference on Data and Knowledge Base Integration

Programme Committee

Prof. S. M. Deen (Chairman)
Dr. T. Barsalou (Stanford University)
Dr. O. P. Brereton (University of Keele)
Dr. R. J. Lucas (University of Aberdeen)
Dr. C. J. Rawlings (Imperial Cancer Research Fund, UK)
Prof M. Singh (UMIST)
Dr. W. Staniszkis (CRAI, Italy)
Prof M. Takizawa (Tokyo Denki University)

Organising Committee

Prof S. M. Deen (Keele)
Dr. G. P. Thomas (Keele)
Dr. O. P. Brereton (Keele)
Ms. J. Mabon (BCS)

Sponsors

The conference was organised by the DAKE Centre of the University of Keele, and supported by the BCS Specialist Groups in Data Management and Expert Systems. Financial contributions were received with thanks from the Information Engineering Directorate of the UK Department of Trade and Industry.

1 Hybrid Knowledge Based Systems for Tactical Decision Making

M. Singh

Abstract

In this paper we describe how the major components of Decision Support Systems (i.e. Dialog Generation and Management System, Database Management System and Model Base Management System) can be combined with knowledge bases and control mechanisms of Expert Systems in order to develop a new class of Knowledge Support Systems called Hybrid Knowledge Based Systems. Hybrid Knowledge Based Systems are of particular value as Knowledge Support Tools for tactical managerial decision making issues. In this paper we provide a detailed practical case study of the use of the Hybrid Knowledge Based System TAPS (Targetting and Allocation of Promotional Spend) within the context of an international bank to illustrate the main concepts described.

1. Introduction

Knowledge Support Systems is a generic term to describe computerised aids for helping knowledge workers in their performance of cognitive tasks. Examples of Knowledge Support Systems for managerial decision making would be: Expert Systems, Decision Support Systems, Group Decision Support Systems, Hybrid Knowledge Based Systems, etc. In this paper, we will focus on Hybrid Knowledge Based Systems as an important class of aids for tactical decision making in organisations. Since, in the field of helping managers to take "smarter" decisions, the real proof of the pudding is in the eating, our concerns will be very much applications orientated. In this context, we will describe a real life resource allocation case study where the author's Hybrid Knowledge Based System TAPS (Targetting and Allocation of Promotional Spend) was used (and is currently in routine use) by a leading international bank to determine its promotional budget and its targetting across products, market segments and media types.

We will begin by describing Managerial Decision Making Problems, their information needs and the kinds of Knowledge Support tools which are best suited for different problems.

2. Managerial Decision Making Problems

Vast numbers of interrelated decisions are made by organisations. It is possible to group these in various ways e.g. through a hierarchy of impact, time horizon of interest, data needs, degree of structure, etc.

Anthony (1965)[1] describe four levels of Decision Making (Figure 1).

- ***Strategic Plannning Decisions:*** These are related to choosing the highest level policies and objectives and associated resource allocations

- ***Management Control Decisions:*** These are decisions made for the purpose of assuring effectiveness in the acquisition and use of resources

- ***Operational Control Decisions:*** These are decisions made for the purpose of assuring effectiveness in the ***performance of operations*** and

- ***Operational Performance Decisions:*** which are the day to

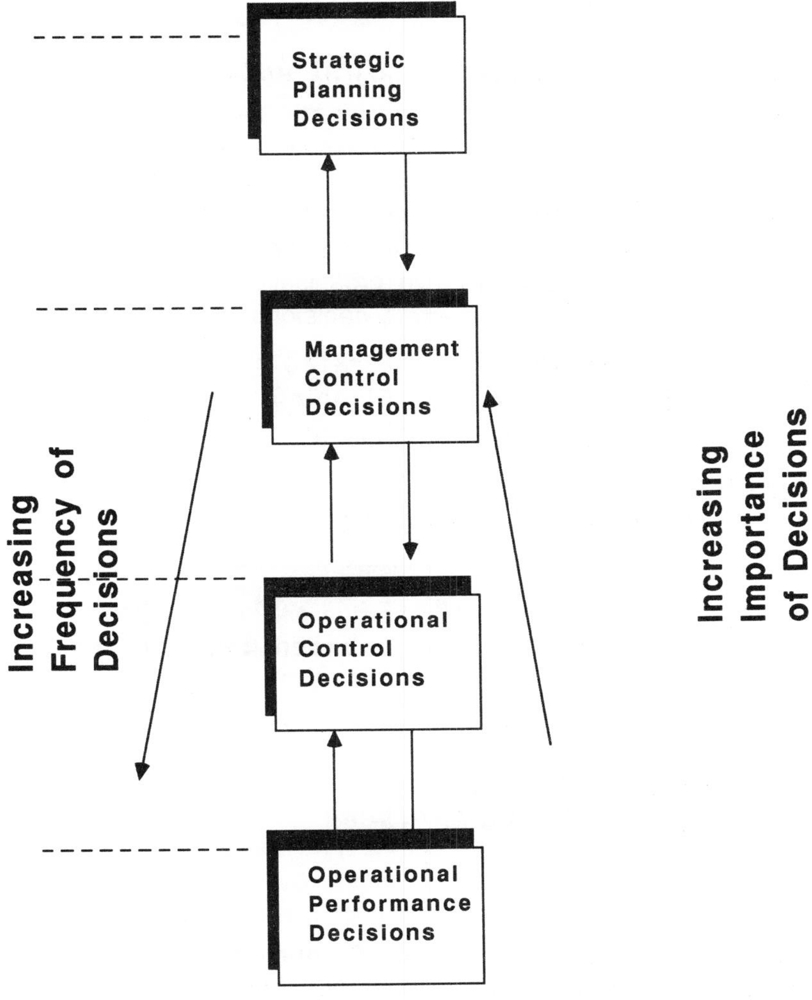

FIGURE 1 ANTHONY'S DECISION HIERARCHY

day decisions made while performing operations

Simon (1960) has described decisions as ***structured*** or ***unstructured*** depending on whether the Decision Making Process can be explicitly described prior to the time when it is necessary to make a decision. Generally, as Sage points out (Sage 1987)[2] operational performance decisions are more likely than strategic planning decisions to be prestructured. Thus,

- ***Expert Systems*** can usually be expected to be more appropriate for ***operational perfomance*** and ***operational control decisions*** than they are for ***strategic planning*** and ***management control decisions.***

Environment	Structured	Unstructured
Decision Making Process	Can be pre specified	Can't be pre-specified
Spectrum	Operational Performance Decisions Expert Systems D.S.S. ←——————→ ↑ Hybrid Knowledge based Syst.	Strategic Planning Decisions

FIGURE 2 SIMON'S tAXONOMY OF CORPORATE DECISIONS

- ***DSS*** will be more appropriate for ***Strategic Planning and Management Control*** than for operational control and operational performance.

Note, however, that ***expertise*** is a relative term which depends upon familiarity with the task and the operational environment into which it is embedded. Since decision environments do change and since novices become experts through learning and feedback, clearly there will exist many areas where the proper form of Knowledge Base Support is a Hybrid of a Decision Support System and an Expert System. Figure 2 depicts this notion.

Hybrid Knowledge Based Systems represent a new generation of Business Decision Technologies for tactical and, to some extent, Strategic Decision Making. They bring together ideas from Systems Engineering, Operations Research, Management Science and Cognitive Psychology.

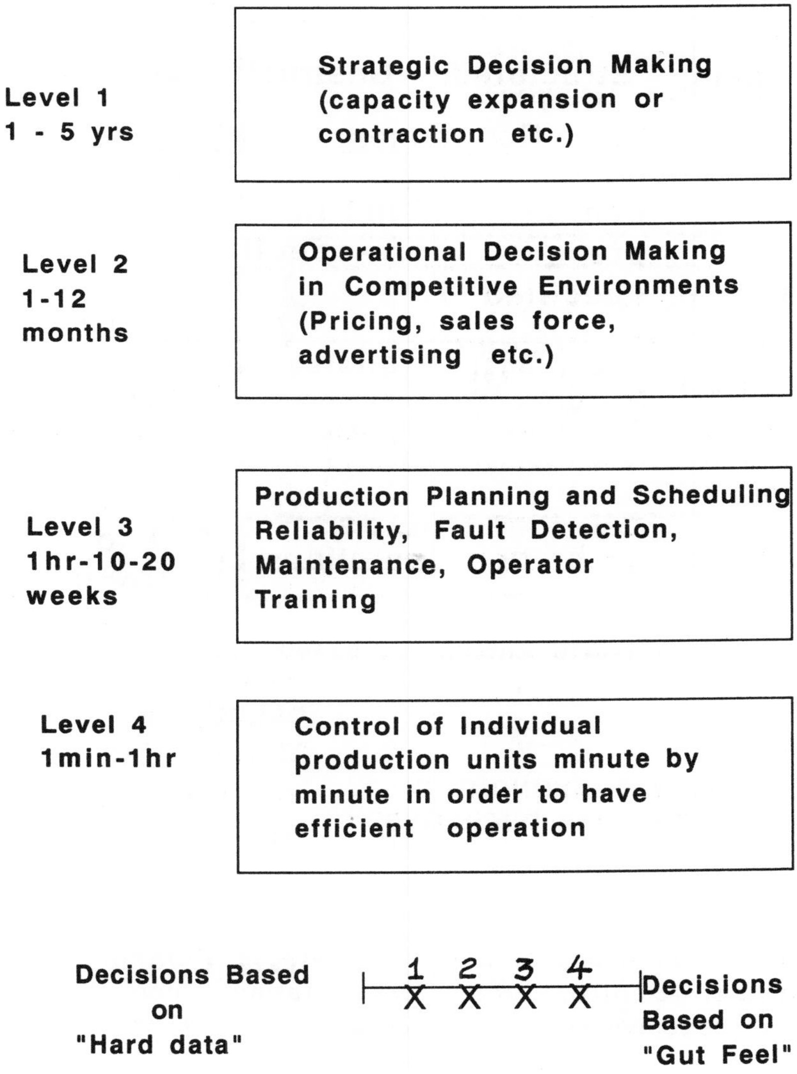

Level 1 1 - 5 yrs	Strategic Decision Making (capacity expansion or contraction etc.)
Level 2 1-12 months	Operational Decision Making in Competitive Environments (Pricing, sales force, advertising etc.)
Level 3 1hr-10-20 weeks	Production Planning and Scheduling Reliability, Fault Detection, Maintenance, Operator Training
Level 4 1min-1hr	Control of Individual production units minute by minute in order to have efficient operation

Decisions Based on "Hard data" — 1 X, 2 X, 3 X, 4 X — Decisions Based on "Gut Feel"

FIGURE 3 DECISION MAKING HIERARCHY IN MANUFACTURING

To understand the precise nature of the decisions for which one is seeking knowledge support, let us consider a typical manufacturing hierarchy as shown in Figure 3. Hybrid Knowledge Based Systems would have a major role to play at the Tactical Decision Making level in order to help with issues like:

- Product Pricing
- Sales Force Allocation
- Marketing Budget Allocation

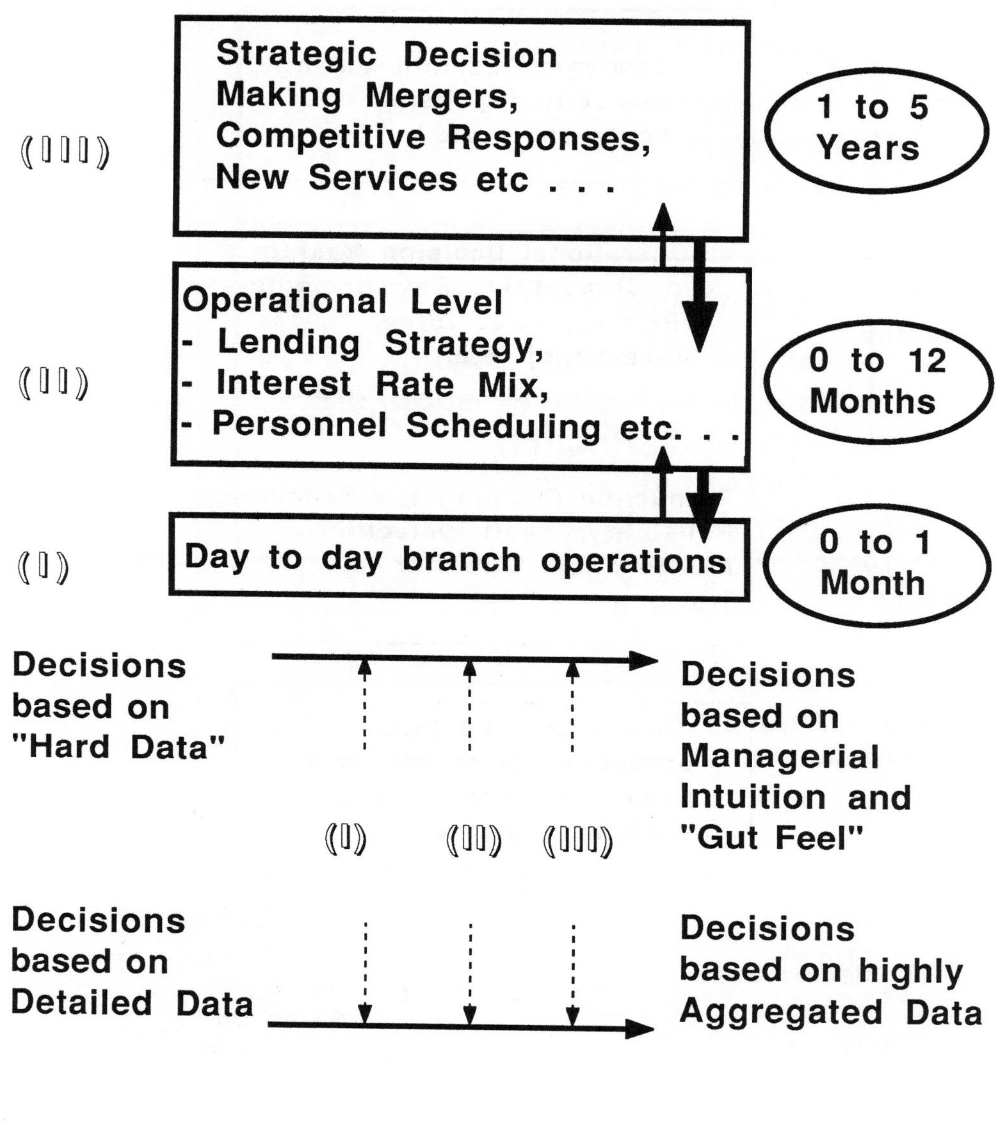

FIGURE 4 DECISION MAKING HIERARCHY IN RETAIL BANKING

Figure 4 shows a similiar hierarchy in the Retail Banking Sector. Here, Hybrid Systems would have a major role to play at the operational or tactical Decision Making levels in order to help with issues like:

- Interest Rate Mixes for Savings and Lending Products
- Pricing of Services
- Marketing Budget Allocation

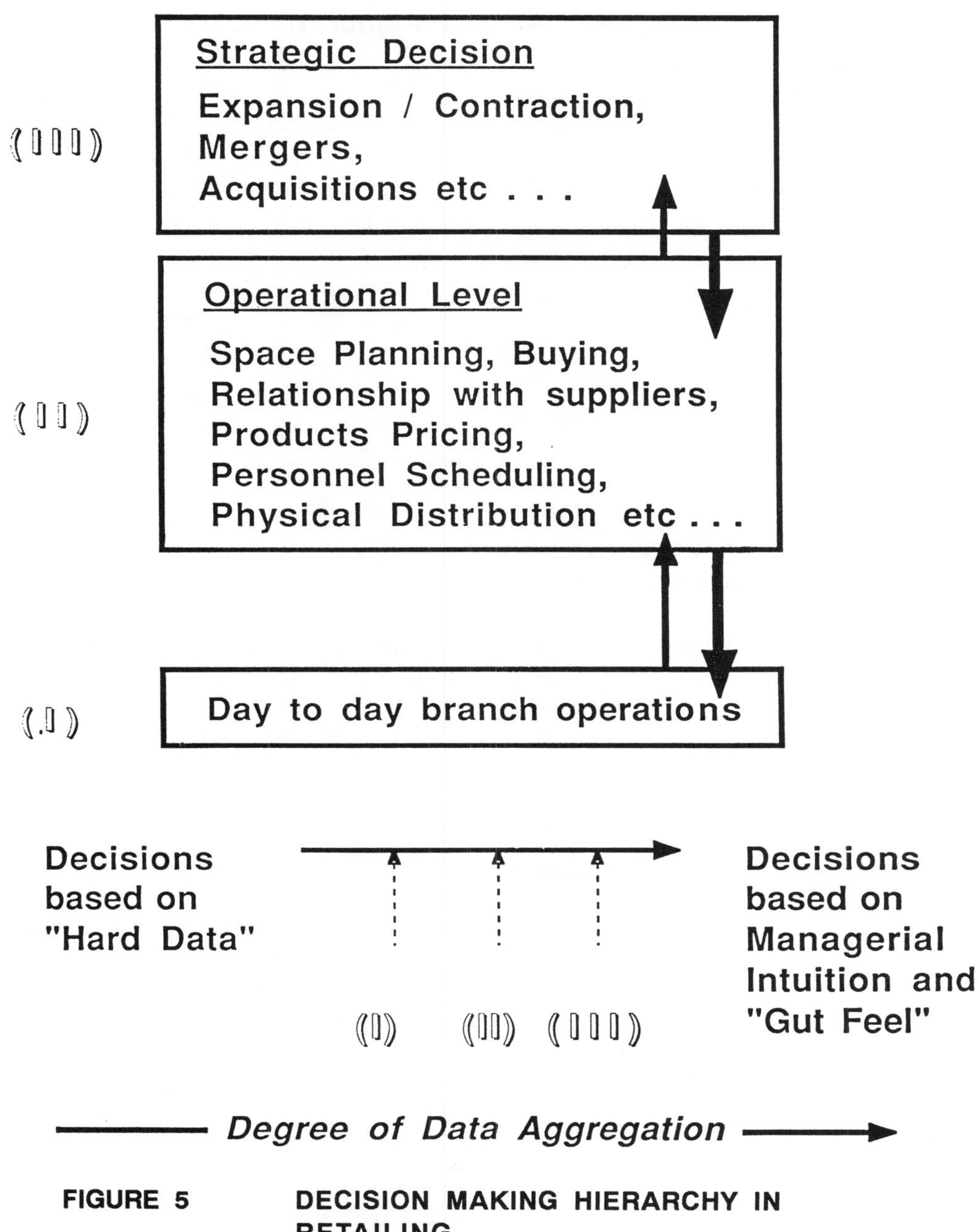

FIGURE 5 DECISION MAKING HIERARCHY IN RETAILING

Similar hierarchies can be developed for any other industry. Figure 5 shows a hierarchy of this kind for retailing.

We note that at the tactical decision making level, the key issues of concern are those which relate to the allocation of resources or to pricing.

3 Decision Technologies for the Higher Decision Making Tasks

3.1 Expert systems and decision support systems

So far we have highlighted the various kinds of decisions which Senior Managers make and pointed out that there is a Spectrum of Decision aids to help the manager which go from Expert Systems to Decision Support Systems as we go up the managerial decision making hierarchy. Figure 6 shows the generic structure of an Expert System and Figure 7 for a Decision Support System. We note that:

(a) In the case of Expert Systems:

- The user is generally a novice
- Such systems are primarily of value in diagnostic types of applications

(b) In the case of Decision Support Systems, the user is assumed to be a Senior Manager or a group of Senior Managers who might be assisted by a facilitator.

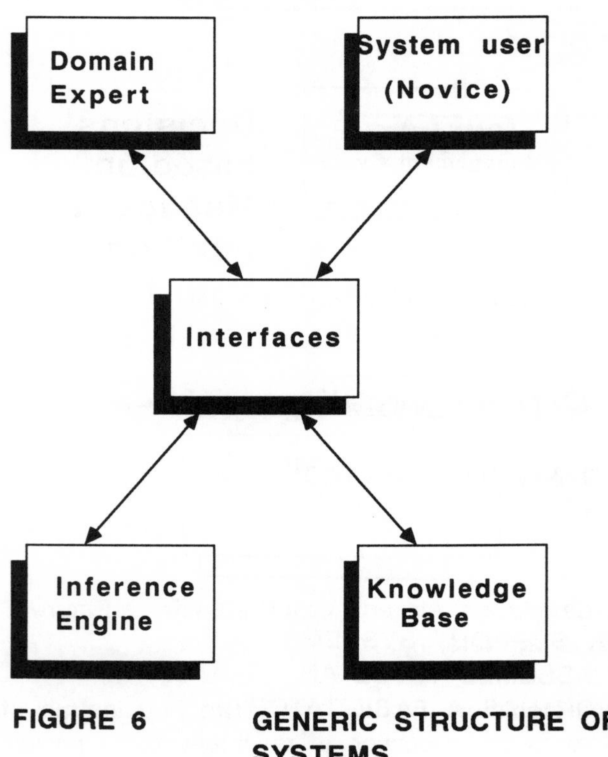

FIGURE 6 GENERIC STRUCTURE OF EXPERT SYSTEMS

Figure 8 shows the structure of Hybrid Knowledge Based Systems which attempt to marry together Expert Systems and Decision Support Systems.

Hybrid Knowledge Based Systems

A number of Hybrid Knowledge Based Systems have been developed in UMIST by the author to help companies to tackle key specific problems in different industries e.g.

- ***Price-Strat:*** A System for helping companies to price their

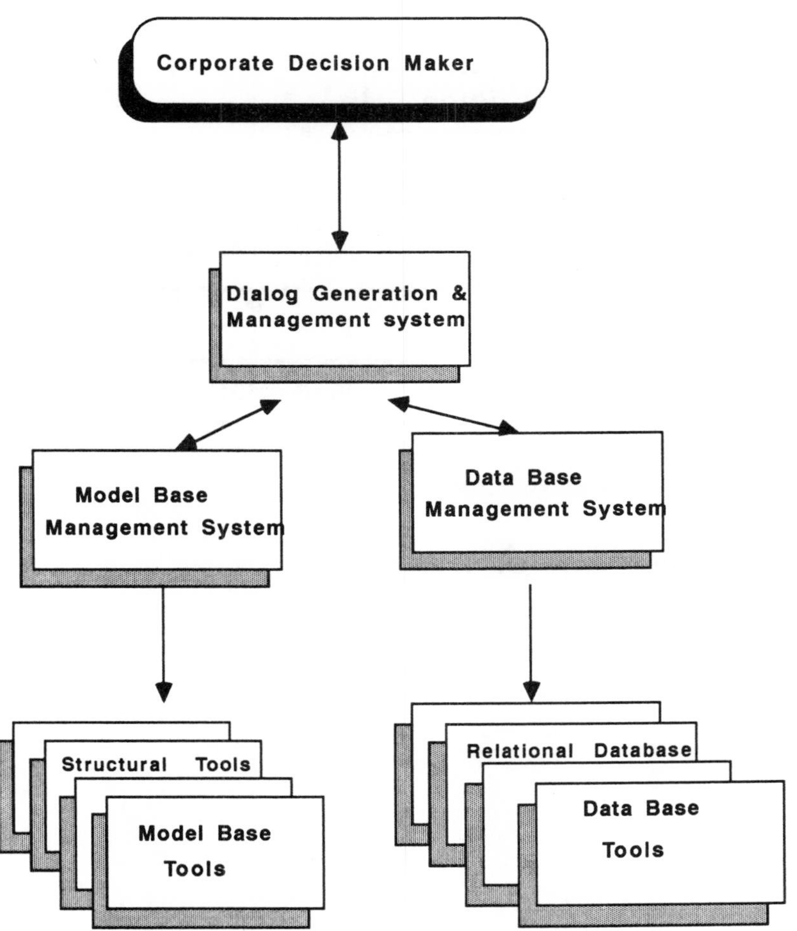

FIGURE 7 DECISION SUPPORT SYSTEMS: USER IS ASSUMED TO BE AN EXPERT OR HAS A FACILITATOR

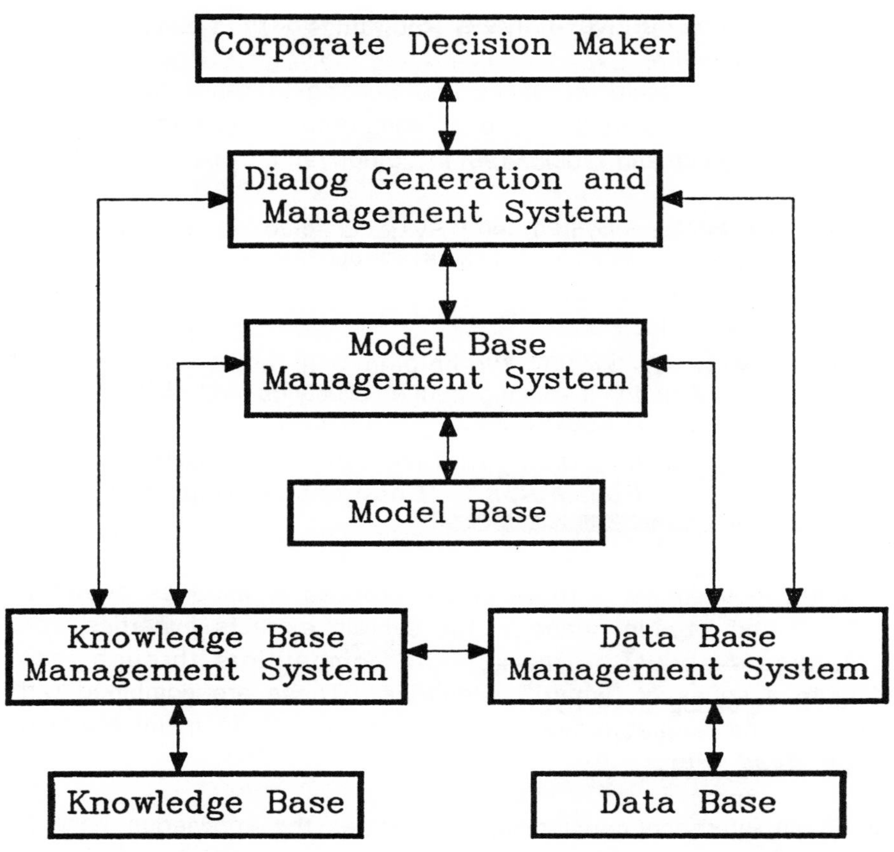

FIGURE 8 **STRUCTURE OF HYBRID KNOWLEDGE BASED SYSTEMS (HKBS)**

products in competitive markets [Singh (1988)][7]

- ***BS-opt:*** A System for Banks and Building Societies to determine interest rate mixes in the face of competitors. [Singh and Cook (1986)[3], Singh and Cook (1987)[4], Singh and Cook (1988)][6]

- ***Resource-opt:*** A System for

    - Retail Space Allocation
    - Sales Force Allocation

    Singh, Cook and Corstjens (1988)[5]
- ***TAPS:*** A System for marketing budget allocation and sizing,

and for Strategic Decision Making:(***Mark-opt*** [Singh, Bhondi and Corstjens (1985)][8] ***Pharmplan*** [Corstjens, Bhondi and Singh (1986)]

In each of these systems, a three phase process is used as shown in Figures 9, 10 and 11. In phase 1, the system extracts expertise from Senior Managers about the market and competitiors through their responding to a series of "what-if" scenarios. These are combined with historical data and market research data to make up an initial ***Market Knowledge Base*** (Figure 9).

In phase 2, an inference mechanism interrogates the knowledge base to determine the profit maximising decisions and their sensitivity. Sales and profit forecasts are also provided (Figure 10).

In phase 3 (Figure 11), new data which emerges after the application of the profit maximising decisions is used as a reality check and the systems uses this to learn about the environment and to enrich its knowledge base. Thus, decision making is improved over time.

Finally, we provide a detailed description of Hybrid Knowledge Based System for the Targetting and Allocation of Promotional Spend (TAPS) in order to illustrate the concepts .

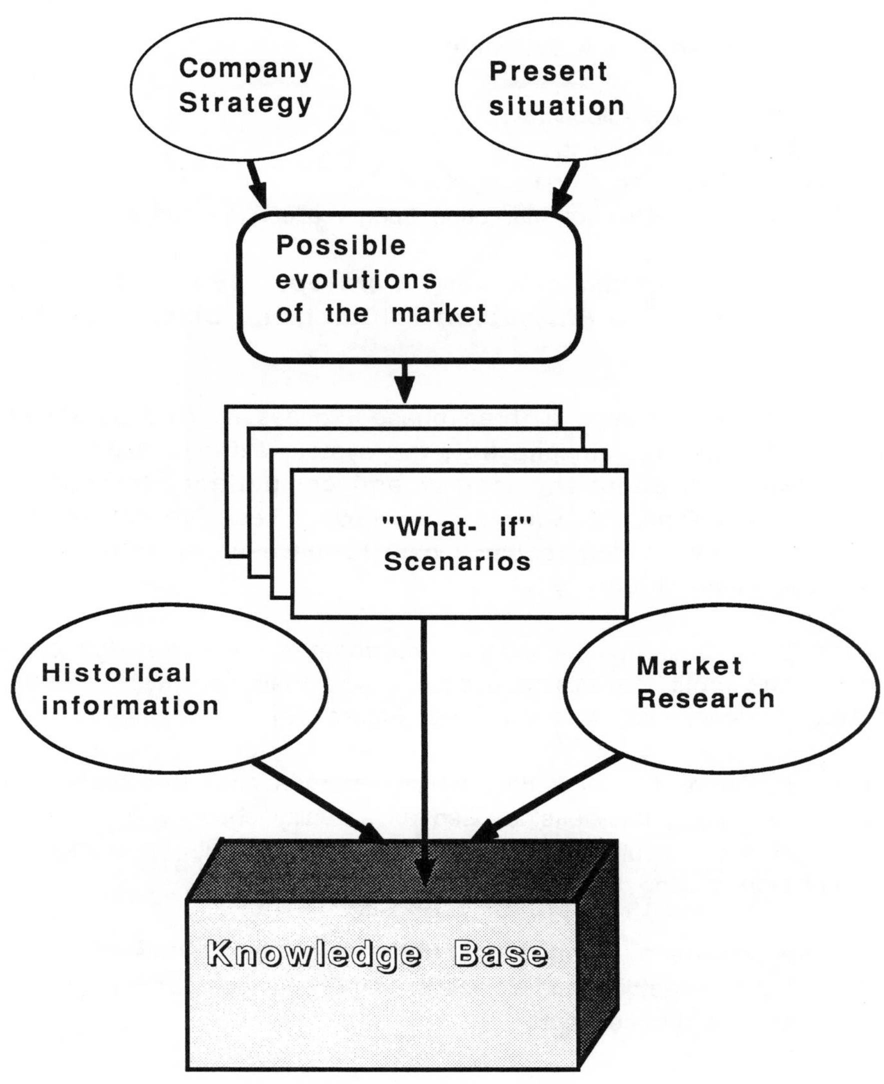

FIGURE 9 1ST PHASE: CONSTRUCTING THE MARKET KNOWLEDGE BASE

2nd Phase :
Finding the optimal decision & its sensitivity

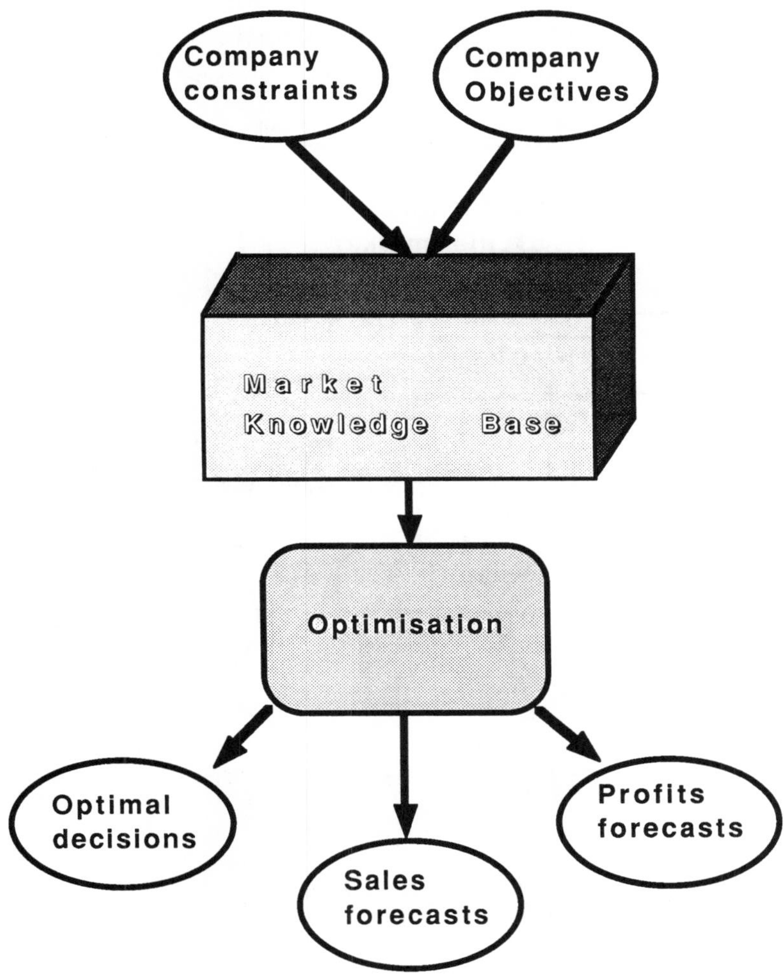

FIGURE 10 2ND PHASE: FINDING THE OPTIMAL DECISION AND ITS SENSITIVITY

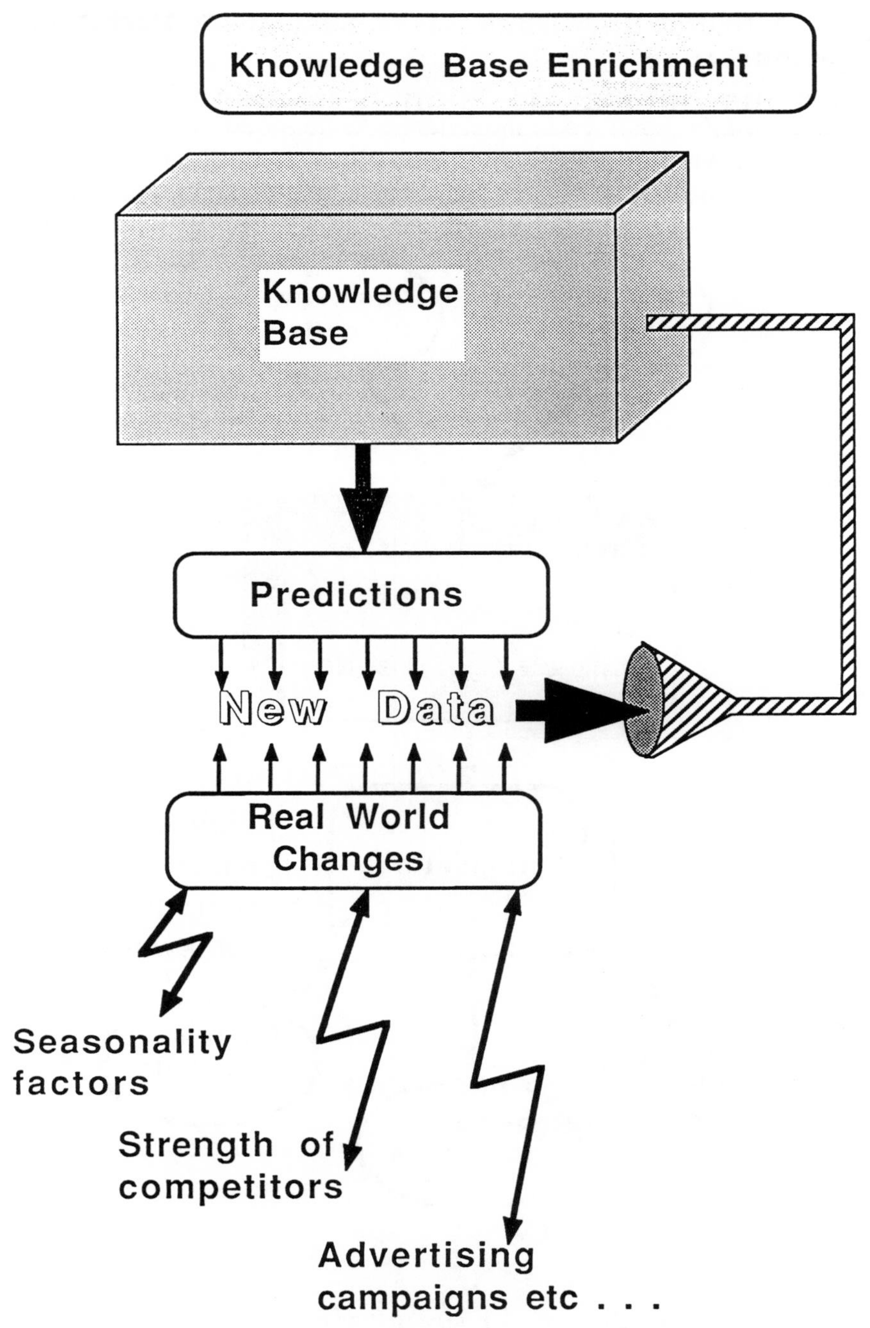

FIGURE 11 KNOWLEDGE BASE ENRICHMENT

4 TAPS: A Hybrid Knowledge Based System for Marketing Budget Allocation

Before the begining of each year most large firms need to draw up a promotional spend budget to be allocated across media types and distributed between products. Figure 12 shows a typical budget for a bank. The unknowns in the rows and columns in Figure 12 need to be

	TV/ CINEMA/ RADIO	PRESS	------	
YOUTH	?	?	?	?
SMALL BUSINESS	?	?	?	?
PENSIONS	?	?	?	?
-------	?	?	?	?
	?	?	?	?

MAX IMPACT ON

SALES OR Image Within Longer term strategic framework

FIGURE 12 BUDGETING OF PROMOTIONAL EXPENDITURE

chosen so as to maximise the impact on sales and/or maximise the impact on the firm's image or some combination of the two. It is part of the folk wisdom particularly in Retail Banking, for example, that the expenditure mix which maximises sales may well be a poor one as far as impact on the image is concerned and vice-versa. There is therefore significant interest in attempting a quantitative trade-off analysis between the image and the sales dimensions.

The budgeting problem as depicted in Figure 12 is quite a complex one and it is typically resolved within the organisation by considering a two level hierarchy as depicted in Figure 13. Here individual product/market segment managers propose a budget to more senior management (Head of Products and Head of Communications) and provide an allocation of it between media and the Senior Managers adjudicate between these proposals to arrive at an overall budget split, as depicted in Figure 12, after some interaction with the product/market segment managers.

The TAPS System follows the same path as the organisational hierarchy depicted in Figure 13 or the alternative hierarchy shown in Figure 14.

4.1 The TAPS Methodology

The TAPS methodology also follows the structure given in Figures 9, 10, 11. The keystep occurs in phase 1 where the expert knowledge of a number of managers is extracted through their responding to a series of "what-if" spend scenarios and their expected impact on Sales and on the Image dimensions.

The spend scenarios themselves are set within a long term strategic framework which comes into play through the fixing of the minmax boundaries on each spend variable.

The "what-if' responses of the managers are combined with any historical information available as well as any market research information in order to make up the initial Market Knowledge Base.

In phase 2, the market knowledge base is interrogated to yield optimal spend decisions for each Manager's view as well as for a consensus view. The optimisation is done separately for the Sales and Image objectives.

Experience shows that it is often possible to obtain a reasonable consensus view through the optimisation analysis. Trade-off studies can also be carried out between the Sales and Image dimensions on the individual or

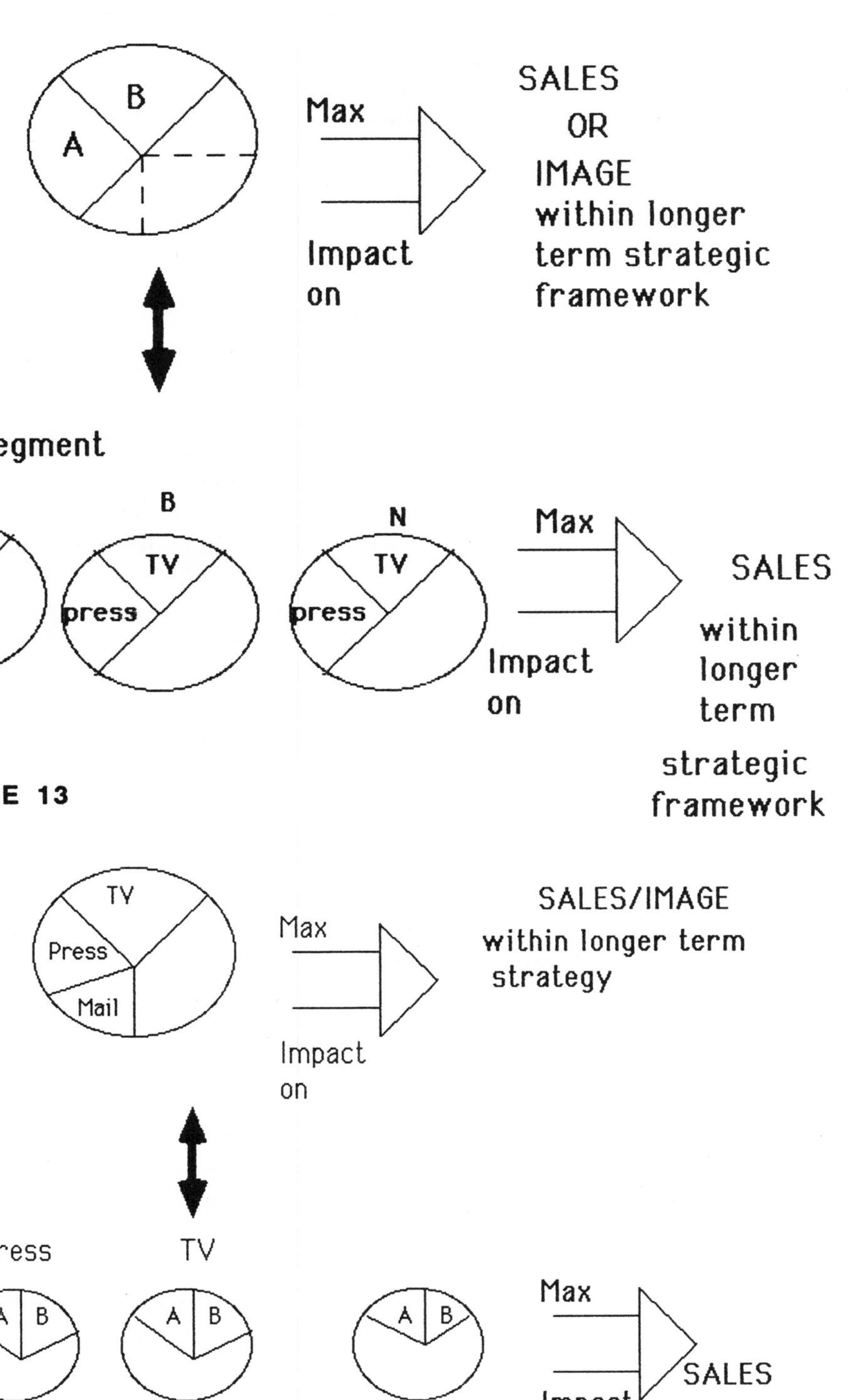
A
B
Max
Impact on
SALES
OR
IMAGE
within longer term strategic framework
product/segment
A
B
N
TV
press
Max
Impact on
SALES
within longer term
strategic framework

FIGURE 13

TV
Press
Mail
Max
Impact on
SALES/IMAGE
within longer term strategy
Press
TV
A
B
Max
Impact on
SALES
Products/ segments

FIGURE 14

consensus view.

The TAPS System which incorporates the TAPS methodology is a complex piece of software (≈ 20,000 lines of code) written in PASCAL which is currently being upgraded into an even more user friendly form through a complete rewrite in C and the fourth generation language Clipper. The system has facilities for:

- Generation of the "what-if" spend scenarios once the number of products/media have been provided by the user along with the min-max values for each spend variable. The scenarios are generated using an experimental design procedure so as to uniformly cover the decision space using a reasonably small number of scenarios. The number of scenarios generated is a user option and this enables the user to do a trade-off between the need of getting a sufficient number of scenarios to build good quality models and managerial fatigue which limits this number considerably.

- Managing the databases and ensuring their consistency and integrity as views of different managers are fed in or modified on-line. The database with the historical data and market research data are also managed by the data base management component in the TAPS System.

- Building different models from the "what-if" spend scenarios and/or from the "hard" data or the market research data and managing these. Standard errors are also calculated.

- The non-linear model forms used would appear to provide an excellent fit for the budget allocation problems either at the overall level between products or at the lower level between media.

- An optimisation facility for finding the budgetary mix which maximises sales or the image index for any of the models also forms a part of the TAPS System.

- Various "Help" facilities are also provided for the user.

- Facilities for carrying out the phase 3 in Figure 11 are also provided.

Next, we illustrate the use of the approach for the marketing budget allocation and sizing problem for a leading Retail Bank. To protect the confidentiality of the client, the results provided do not show the product/market segment names.

5 Example: Marketing Budget Allocation for a Retail Bank

For this Bank, the field trial involved the allocation of a budget of £39 million between 7 market segments (P1, P2,...P7) each one of which had a number of specific products. At the lower level, a single product with an initially planned budget of £4.2 million was to be allocated across 6 media types (TV, Press, displays, publications, direct mail and Staff Training).

In the way of criteria, the sales measure used was the expected number of new accounts generated with weights supplied by the Bank to specify the perceived relative importance of the accounts from each market segment. The image index used was the Milward Brown awareness index as a surrogate variable for the Bank's "image".

Senior Management of the Bank also provided the minimum and maximum values for expenditure on each segment/media which satisfied their longer term strategic objectives as well as expected impact of their initially planned budget. Based on all this information, the TAPS system generated 42 "what-if" spend scenarios on allocation between the 7 market segments and their expected impact on new accounts generated and the Image Index.

Each of the 42 market segment spend scenarios were completed independently by 7 Expert Managers (Product Managers, Head of Products, Head of Communications).

For allocation between media for one of the 7 segments, 35 "what-if" spend scenarios were generated and these were also completed independently by the same seven managers.

Based on the judgemental responses of the 7 managers, 7 individual models were built relating expenditure between market segments and the Sales dimension. A further 7 individual models were built relating the expenditure between market segments and the Milward Brown Index. Seven individual models were also built relating the expenditure between media to the sales dimension.

5.1 Results

Although the individual models showed immense variations, on optimisation, it was found that virtually all the models gave identical results. These results correspond to those of the AOP models where, for each scenario, the extreme values had been rejected by TAPS and the remaining managerial views averaged. Thus the AOP model was used for further study.

Optimisation on the sales dimension showed that a different mix of expenditure than the currently planned one would yield **13.4% more sales!** Next, the size of the spend pie was varied between £33 million and £39 million in steps of £1million and at each step the sales maximising expenditure mix was calculated. Figure 15 shows the resulting curve from which the mix for achieving the current planned impact was determined. This was found to cost **£8.4 million less!**

Figure 16 shows the resulting sales maximising mix as compared to the currently planned mix.

Next, the image maximising mix was calculated for the AOP model and this turned out to be very different from the sales maximising mix shown in Figure 16. In order to study the trade offs between the image and sales dimensions, the image maximising mix was calculated for the same value of expenditure as in Figure 15 and the resulting sales were plotted for comparison. Figures 17 and 18 show these results.

We note that at the currently planned level of expenditure (£39 million), image maximising spend could lose the Bank 17.7% of potential sales!

Finally for the single market segment, optimisation studies showed that the same impact as that which is currently planned could be achieved by an expenditure of £3.6 million as opposed to the planned £4.2 million. Figure 19 shows the optimum mix as compared to the currently planned one.

Conclusions

In this paper we have given an overview of the approaches which are being developed to help Senior Decision Makers in industry and commerce to take better decisions. After outlining the Decision problems facing managers and the Technological tools available to help them, we highlighted one area of special interest, i.e. tactical decision making within a competitive environment where the proper form of decision support was a hybrid of Decision Support Systems and Expert Systems. The methodology behind a number of these Hybrid Knowledge Based Systems developed by the author was outlined and the approach has been illustrated on a key problem i.e. Promotional Budget Allocation.

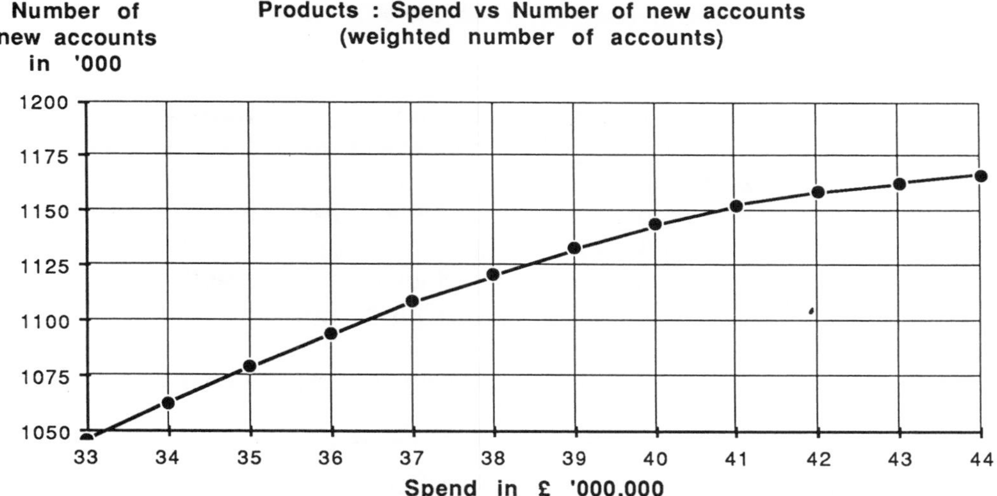
Number of
new accounts
in '000
Products : Spend vs Number of new accounts
(weighted number of accounts)
1200
1175
1150
1125
1100
1075
1050
33
34
35
36
37
38
39
40
41
42
43
44
Spend in £ '000,000

FIGURE 15

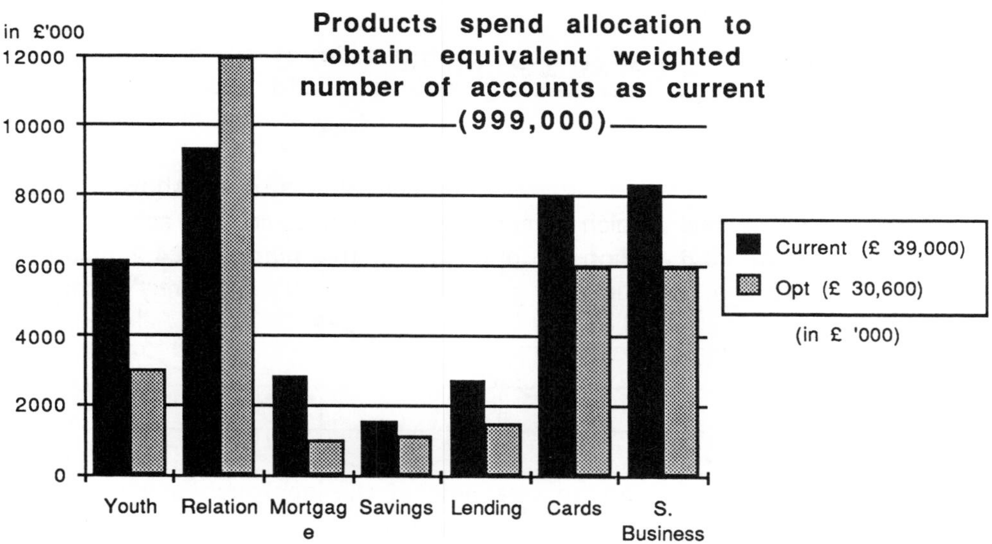
in £'000
Products spend allocation to
obtain equivalent weighted
number of accounts as current
(999,000)
12000
10000
8000
6000
4000
2000
0
Youth
Relation
Mortgag
e
Savings
Lending
Cards
S.
Business
Current (£ 39,000)
Opt (£ 30,600)
(in £ '000)

FIGURE 16

Spend vs Sales

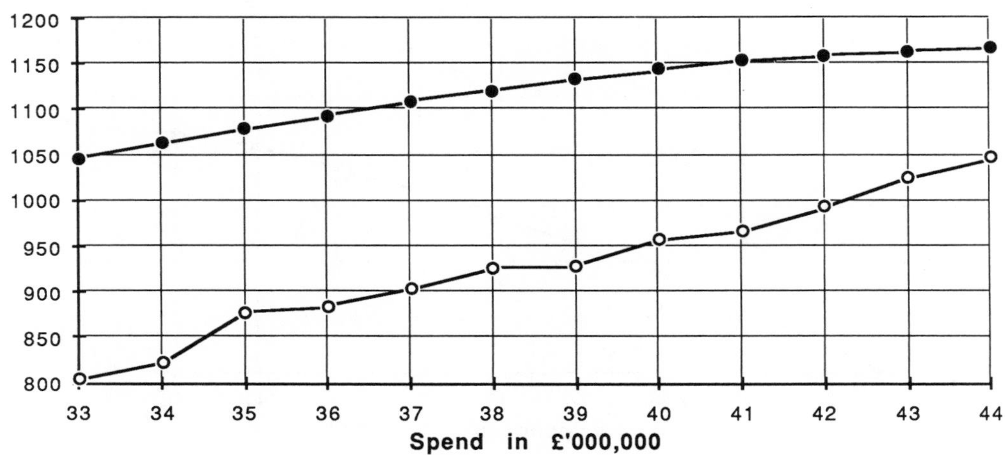

—●— Max sales for expenditure show (A.O.P. model)

—o— Sales achieved when the shown expenditure allocated to maximise image

FIGURE 17 SPEND VS. SALES

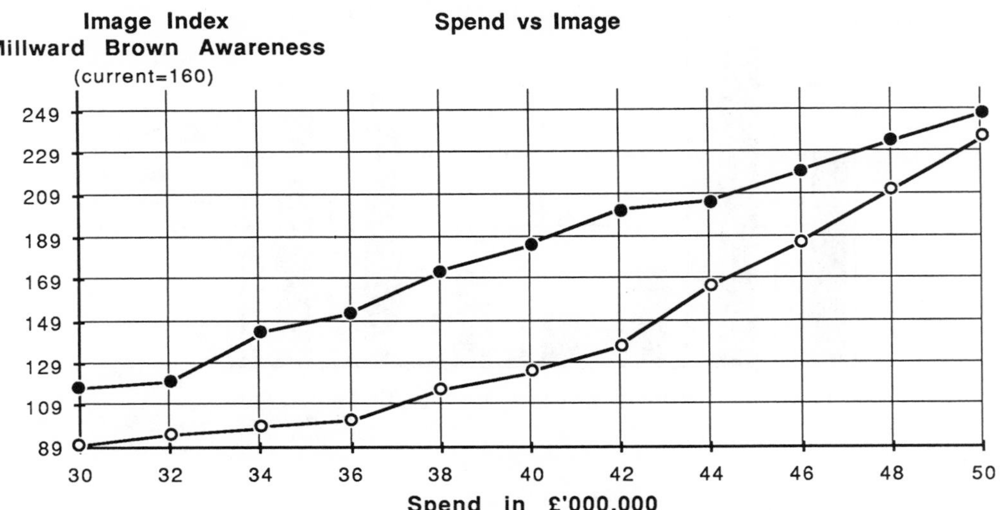

—●— Max image for expenditure shown

—o— Image achieved when the shown expenditure allocated to maximising sales

FIGURE 18 SPEND VS. IMAGE

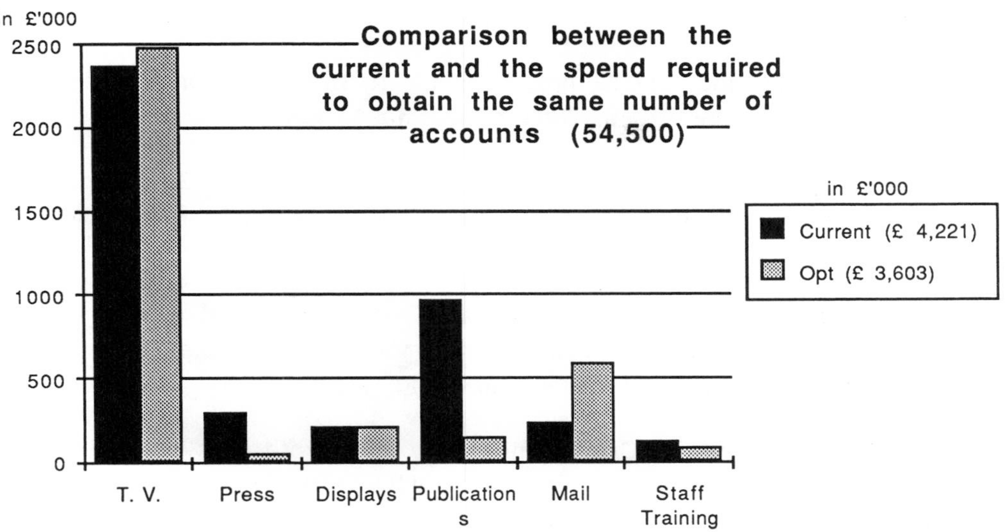

FIGURE 19

Decision Technologies, like HKBS, Expert Systems, Decision Support Systems, etc, are being increasingly used by go-ahead companies to improve their profitability in a competitive environment.

References

1. Anthony, "Planning and Control Systems: a framework for analysis" Harvard University Press, Cambridge, Mass, 1965.

2. A. P. Sage "Decision Support Systems" in Singh M. G. (editor) Encyclopedia of Systems and Control, Volumes 1-8, Pergamon Books Ltd. (1987).

3. M. G. Singh and R. Cook "Price-Strat: a decision support system for determining Bank and Building Society Interest Rate Mixes" International Journal of Bank Marketing, (1986).

4. M. G. Singh and R. Cook "Improving the Profitability of Bank lending in a Competitive Environment" International Journal of Bank Marketing, Vol. 5.3 (1987).

5. M.G. Singh, R. Cook and M Corstjens "A Hybrid Knowledge Based System for Retail Space and Other Allocation Problems" Interfaces (1988).

6. M. G. Singh and R. Cook "Decision Support Systems for Assets and Liability Management in Retail Banking". Quarterly Journal of the Girocentrale Bank Austria, (1988).

7. M.G Singh "Price-Strat: A Hybrid Knowledge Based System for Competitive Pricing", Proceedings IX Euro TIMS, Paris, (1988).

8. M.G. Singh, J. Bhondi and M. Corstjens "Mark -opt: A Negotiating Tool for Manufacturers and Retailers" IEEE Trans SMC, Vol. 15, 14, (1988), pp. 483-495.

QUESTIONS

Mr C. Church (Hitachi Europe Ltd.).

CC. When do you leave your post in UMIST to become marketing director of Marks and Spencer?

(Laughter)

It seems that what you've done is you've actually taken a body of knowledge and you've actually added to it constructively. You mentioned some words, for example, you talked about "gut feel". We won't agonize too much about what this is, but what you seem to have gone in and done is you've provided a way to utilize this "gut feel", whatever it is.

You also said, on one of your slides, that you've taken the knowledge of the existing experts and incorporated it into your system. To what extent did you personally integrate into those organisations? How much knowledge was created by you for them?

Prof. M. Singh.

MS. Let me start with the last part of the question first. As far as implementing the knowledge of the organisation is concerned. The point I'm making there, is that in many of these situations there is an historical knowledge base, or data-base for that matter, in which managers have sufficient confidence. So I'm saying because we don't have this confidence, let's try to extract the intuition of managers as a starting point.

CC. What do you mean by "intuition"?

MS. Intuition, let me give you an example. "If I were to increase my price by a little bit how much sales would I lose?". "If more money were put into a TV campaign for 'Orchard', how much more sales would I make?" That's market knowledge, intuition. The point is that one doesn't know this, one doesn't know the answer to that one until its actually done, but managers have a feel for it.

Now, the next issue is, given the manager's theory of how the market works, I can get managers to give me that knowledge. And it might not be easy, because managers often try to look at it each little bit of legislation. In other words, they don't look at the whole pattern and say, "With that I look at that". They say, "My analyses in the past, I expect......" or "I can't answer this question".

So the first thing that I point out to each of these managers is to take a broad view and not say to themselves "Am I getting it right in each one of these scenarios?" (I give them about thirty or forty scenarios). I say to them, "Don't worry if you get them all wrong. The key issue that I want is your gut feel, just the surface of your solution." And although I give them the scenarios on pieces of paper, I stress that I don't want them to spend more than an hour on them. What knowledge can I get in an hour? Twenty years knowledge absolutely at the surface. And I actually find that further refinement of the test doesn't improve it so much.

That said, there is another enhancement that you can build in to the TAPS approach. I get the managers to do the scenarios and I get some statistical measures of goodness-of-fit on the curves that have been generated. Having got these statistical measures of goodness-of-fit, I can then pick out which of the scenarios are the furthest out from the view of a particular manager coming through the rest. And I can present these back to the manager, interactively on the computer, and say to him or her "Do you really mean what you said?" "Is there any special reason for what you said?" Or, "would you like to change your mind?" And, of course, in doing this, I can improve the goodness-of-fits quite dramatically. If one is doing this interactively in a group, the group can then discuss why some of these are different. Interactivity is, in fact, very, very important, because between this kind of analysis and then going on to actually make real decisions people might say, "I hadn't really thought about that, but having looked at some of the elasticities, I believe I can do better than that." So I can tune these. So it's a very interactive kind of thing.

And the final, or rather first, question on my role in either academia and industry. There is a lot of science still to be discovered. But another part of it is that this kind of science cannot be discovered solely in my university laboratory. It needs to be put into practice.

Dr. B. Papegaaij (Erasmus University).

P. Do you need knowledge engineering to get this kind of information out of managers or can the company do it by itself?

MS. No, the company does it all by itself. That's the issue, I've simply pointed the problem out. If you remember, I had those response curves and I have reason to believe that that is the shape of these kind of curves. Given that that's the shape of the curves I can now automate the process of knowledge acquisition because I know precisely what knowledge I require in order to fit these kinds of curves. Now, if for any reason, these curves are rubbish, then, of course, it's a different ball game. But then I don't know how to solve this problem.

BP. So, in fact, the introduction of the system into the company needs a couple of weeks' work from you?

MS. The first unique feature of this system is that it does only take a couple of weeks to set it up, so you don't have to hang around for six months before the consultants come back.

The second feature is that in this kind of budgetary process, there are lots of revisions that have to be done, and that's a matter of an interactive session on the computer.

The next feature I consider very important. Lord Leverhulme, about fifty years ago, said that half of what you spend on advertising has no impact, The question has always been, which half? Now that's an important issue, because world expenditure on the above the line advertising is estimated at 200 billion dollars. A lot of money. So, in that kind of case, if you want to spend 10, 15, 20 million pounds on things, senior managers need to be reassured that there has been some thought gone into this. If you ask yourselves, when you go to your boss, (I don't, not in academia, we don't have the same structure), but in a company, when you go to a boss and say, "I want to spend £100,000," you'd have to make long cases. Now here, if you're spending £50 million on mainly intangible things, you have to try to convince a whole lot of people, and we find that this kind of analysis helps managers make more robust cases to their management. The involvement of the managers is fairly minimal in the sense that I can extract their knowledge in a couple of hours. And then I can go away and play with the data and so on. At the end of the day, the system provides a structured framework for decision-making. In other words, even though they might have been doing the same thing before, it now asks very specific questions, and they need to answer these questions.

I'm a firm believer in the notion that the important thing about any of these kinds of aids is not in the technology, it is how it's implemented within the organisation; and how our rules and procedures changed in order to make sure that this can improve the effectiveness of knowledge workers.

Dr. S Bennett (Sheffield University).

SB. How easy is it to change the TAPS system to respond to new media becoming available, say, the sponsorship of TV programmes?

MS. No problem. At the moment, the way it's been structured, we can deal with up to 12 media types.

SB. How sensitive is the system to changes in the historical data? For example, can it cope with one particular campaign in one particular medium which may have been disastrous? Can it deal with situations like this?

MS. Oh yes. I think the thing I didn't emphasise was that there's a learning loop in here. What that means is that at the end of each campaign, as you get real sales data back, you put that data back in and it improves the elasticity coefficients. And the result of that is, that, over time, it does get better.

2 Design and Implementation of DEAL

B. J. Banks, S. M. Deen, L. A. Garcia, S. M. Harding, A. C. Herath

ABSTRACT

DEAL, which stands for *De*ductive *Al*gebra, is an intelligent database language based on SQL and aspects of Prolog. Instead of adding new constructs to SQL, it examines the basic structure of SQL and strengthens it with the deductive power of Prolog and the recursive capacity of Lisp. DEAL supports deductions, functions, recursion, molecular objects and virtual attributes. It can also be used in the processing of lists.

A subset of DEAL has been implemented on the top of ORACLE in C with a view to building a research prototype for experimentation. Further implementation is in progress.

1. INTRODUCTION

Until very recently, research in databases and expert systems followed a divergent path, without any common focus; this has now changed with the growing realisation that the industrial application of knowledge based systems requires the integration of traditional data and knowledge bases. As a result, there are now many research groups working on this area; their approaches may broadly be divided into the following categories:

(i) Logic based approach
(ii) AI frame interfaces to databases
(iii) Object-oriented approach
(iv) Extended relational approach

Most of these systems deal with relational databases, although there are some exceptions [1]. Many of the logic based systems [2,3] provide Prolog interfaces to databases; some of them are tightly-coupled, in the sense that one can update a relational database from a Prolog interface [4]. The LDL of MCC[5] is a Prolog-like database language, which has been implemented as an autonomous system, rather than as an interface to a DBMS. In some basic queries LDL and Prolog are similar, but they diverge on more complex queries.

A typical example of an AI frame interface to databases is the KEE interface to relational databases [6]. This is a loosely-coupled interface which creates control problems since the database cannot be updated for the KEE interface. There is also a serious impedance mismatch between the two.

Object-oriented database systems come in various shapes and guises. In one extreme, researchers are developing new object-oriented database languages [7], based on the idea of Smalltalk; and at the other extreme, some object-oriented interfaces [8] are built on the top of the relational systems, much like the C++ on the top of C. Since there is no formal definition of an object-oriented data model, every research group defines its own, resulting in a plethora of models. Additionally there is no common algebra which can be used as a basis for optimisation in object-oriented languages.

There are several groups working on the extension of the relational model to provide a knowledge processing capability. The NF2 of IBM Heidelberg [9] supports repeating groups within an extended SQL construct, while both POSTQUEL[10,11] and Hydrogen[12,13] add a new facility on the top of QUEL and SQL respectively, in a manner similar to C++ interface to C. Both POSTQUEL and Hydrogen support externally defined complex data structures and operations (as functions), which can be used within their respective languages QUEL and SQL. Some of these developments are inseparable from object-oriented interfaces to relational systems.

Language DEAL [14] is also an extended relational approach; and although it is capable of supporting externally defined data structures and operations, its main thrust has been the redesign of the basic SQL constructs with a view to enriching it with the deductive capability of Prolog and the recursive capability of Lisp. In this respect, DEAL is fundamentally different from those other works, and it provides a far greater expressive power.

The areas where relational languages are particularly deficient are:

Deduction
Functions
Recursion
Molecular attributes
List processing

DEAL supports these activities directly through its constructs, except for list processing which can be achieved indirectly through a set of built-in sequential functions which in turn can be used to define other functions. During the design of DEAL, we tried to avoid ad hoc constructs, always favouring simple basic constructs, for instance the GROUP BY construct is unnecessary in DEAL. The basic construct of DEAL is

```
ANON [attribute-space]
FROM base-expression
WHERE tuple predicates
```

corresponding to the SELECT, FROM and WHERE clause of SQL. The ANON clause may be viewed as generating an anonymous relation with an attribute list, analogous to the SELECT clause. The base-expression can be a relational expression, which can in turn be a full DEAL query, thus permitting nested expressions. However, the FROM clause is unnecessary for most queries as will be shown below. The WHERE clause uses tuple predicates which are Prolog-like, and more powerful than the traditional relational predicates as will be shown shortly below.

The relational view facility is extended in DEAL with statically bound (compile-time) and dynamically bound (execution-time) views, known as stat and dyn relations, more generally stat and dyn variables. Both can be parameterised. Stat relations are like macros, but more powerful, and can support Prolog-like rules. Dynamic views are functions, and can be recursive. One can also define external functions to be used in DEAL queries. In addition DEAL also supports a number of built-in functions, which can be used to provide other facilities. An attribute in DEAL can be atomic or molecular (repeating group), and each in turn can be actual or virtual. A virtual attribute is a function, which can be parameterised.

We shall explain the facilities described above with some examples. The plan of the paper is as follows. In Section 2 we shall describe the basic DEAL constructs, followed by virtual relations in Section 3 and functions in Section 4. The capability of DEAL to support List processing is covered in Section 5, with Section 6 devoted to molecular attributes. Implementation issues are discussed in section 7 followed by a conclusion in Section 8.

2. BASIC DEAL CONSTRUCTS

We begin with a basic SQL query (in the ORACLE version) to find the salaries of programmers earning more than 25k, and at the same time to change attribute names to EMPNAME and SALARY.

```
SELECT  ENAME 'EMPNAME', SAL 'SALARY'
FROM    EMP
WHERE SAL > 25  AND JOB = 'Programmer'
```

The DEAL version of this query, without a FROM clause, is

```
ANON[EMPNAME :=E, SALARY := S]
WHERE EMP [ ENAME = E, SAL = S, S>25, JOB = 'Programmer']
```

where the expression in the WHERE clause is a tuple predicate, E and S are link attributes (cf. example elements of QBE). The attribute-specs in the ANON clause are a list of attribute-elements, each of which is defined as

outer-attribute := inner-attribute

An inner attribute can be an attribute from the base-expression, a link attribute or a suitable function. The outer-attribute is optional; for instance ANON [E,S] will be treated as ANON [E := E, S := S]. Observe that a lone expression

```
ANON[EMPNAME :=E, SALARY := S]
```

without a following WHERE clause will generate an unnamed binary relation of a single tuple, with attribute EMPNAME and SALARY, with values taken from E and S respectively; E and S will be assumed to be suitable scalars.

Tuple predicates are very powerful and can be used in first-order deduction. In DEAL a deduction rule defines a virtual variable; for instance to deduce tuples using a rule "Paul likes anyone who likes car", we can write:

```
S == ANON [PNAME := 'PAUL', OBJECT := X]
    WHERE LIKE [PNAME = X, OBJECT = 'CAR']
```

where S represents the tuples deduced from LIKE and can be added to LIKE by a union operation such as LIKE := LIKE ++ S. The Prolog equivalent of this query is

```
? like (paul, X) :- like (X, car)
```

The advantages of the DEAL representations are that DEAL is strongly typed, unnecessary attributes can be dropped from the tuple predicates and the order of appearance of attributes in the predicates can be different. Thus for complex queries DEAL will be simpler, while for simpler queries Prolog looks neater. However, attribute names can be dropped in an option of DEAL which produces a more Prolog-like syntax:

```
? LIKE ['PAUL', X] : LIKE [X, 'CAR']
```

In this version, the positions of attributes in the predicate become significant. As before, the result ? ['PAUL', X] can be added to LIKE by a union operation.

Consider the following query to find part number (PNO), description (DES) and supplier number (SNO) from inventory (INV) relation and price from quotation (QUOT) relation for part number with the least price. (The different suppliers charge a different price for the same part number). This query cannot be formulated easily in conventional SQL, but in Hydrogen of the Starburst project [12,13] it can be written as:

```
SELECT Q1.PNO, Q2.DES, Q3.SNO
FROM INV Q1, QUOT Q2
WHERE Q1.PNO = Q2.PNO
  AND Q2.PRICE <= ALL (SELECT Q3.PRICE
                       FROM QUOT Q3
                       WHERE Q2.PNO = Q3.PNO)
```

In DEAL we can formulate this query more simply as

```
ANON [PNO:=P, DES:=D, SNO:=S]
WHERE INV [PNO=P, DES=D]
  AND QUOT [PNO=P, PRICE = MIN(PRICE), SNO=S]
```

The relative position of a statistical function (AVG, SUM, COUNT, MAX, MIN) is important in a tuple predicate. In the above query MIN(PRICE) will be calculated for PNO = P, thus effectively providing a GROUP BY facility. If we rewrite the predicate above as QUOT [PRICE = MIN(PRICE), PNO = P], then MIN will range over the whole relation.

A tuple predicate permits the universal quantifier ALL, a special quantifier ONLY, and a non-existential quantifier FAIL. The quantifier ONLY is more restrictive than ALL, and will be satisfied, only if there is an exact number of matches. For instance if we wish to find the students who have taken course C1 and C2 only, then we must use the quantifier ONLY, since a predicate with quantifier ALL will be satisfied also by the students who have taken C1, C2 and C3. Consider a query to find the student number (SNO) of all students who have taken exactly the same majors (MAJNAME) as student S10 from relation MAJOR (SNO, MAJNAME), where a student may take several majors:

```
ANON [SNO := X]
WHERE MAJOR [SNO = X, MAJNAME = ONLY Y]
    AND MAJOR [SNO = 'S10', MAJNAME = Y]
```

The quantifier ONLY is stricter than ALL, and ensures the exactly the same majors. Compare this with POSTQUEL [13] formulation of the same query:

```
retrieve (MAJ.SNO)
from MAJ in MAJOR
where {(X.MAJNAME) from X in MAJOR
                   where X.SNO = MAJ.SNO}
     = { (X.MAJNAME) from X in MAJOR
                    where X.SNO = 'S10' }
```

This query is less natural to formulate and less easy to understand. The quantifier FAIL can be used to define an outer join, for example,

```
ANON [ENAME := EN, DNAME := DN]
WHERE (EMP [ENAME = EN, EDN = X] AND DEPT [DNO = X, DNAME = DN])
   OR (EMP [ENAME = EN, EDN = X] AND DEPT [DNO = FAIL X])
   OR (DEPT [DNO = X, DNAME = DN] AND (EMP [EDN = FAIL X])
```

where DNO = FAIL X will be True if there are no tuples with DNO = X (that is, no tuples with DNO = EDN, since X is a link-element). Similarly, EDN = FAIL X will be True if there are no tuples with EDN = X. Thus this query will join all tuples which have matching department numbers, and also create tuples with null employee name or null department name in the absence of a match.

Before we leave this section, we shall briefly explain the facilities of the base-expression. The earlier query on employee salary can be written with a FROM clause as:

```
ANON[EMPNAME := ENAME, SALARY := SAL]
FROM EMP
WHERE [SAL >25, JOB = 'Programmer']
```

This "headless" tuple predicate applies to the evaluated base expression in the FROM clause. This is not a very interesting formulation since the base-expression is a named relation. The FROM clause is needed only when a base expression is a relational expression or a DEAL query (which can be nested). As a relational expression, the base-expression can have union (++), difference (--), Cartesian product (**), equi-join (*=) and outer-join (*?) operations. Functions (see later) are also allowed. Some simple examples of such base expressions are:

(i) EMP1 ++ EMP2
(ii) EMP (EDN) *= (DNO) DEPT
(iii) EMP (EDN) *? (DNO) DEPT

Where (i) is a union of two union-compatible relations EMP1 and EMP2, (ii) is an equi-join of relations of EMP and DEPT with join attributes EDN, DNO, and (iii) is an outer-join. Needless to say that tuple predicates can be used to formulate both equi-join and outer-join operations, and therefore it is not necessary to allow them in the base expression. However joins can often be formulated more easily in the base expression than in the WHERE clause, and therefore we have left the choice to the user. Next, consider the following three expressions:

(i) base-expression [A, B]
(ii) ANON [ALL]
FROM base-expression
(iii) base-expression

In (i) attributes A and B are projected from the base-expression, e.g. EMP [ENO, ENAME]. In (ii) all attributes of the base-expression are retrieved. This ALL should not be confused with the universal quantifier in tuple predicates. Expression (iii) is a short-hand form of (ii).

3. VIRTUAL RELATIONS

The concept of views has been generalised in DEAL as virtual variables, which are of two types: stat variables and dyn variables. A stat variable is bound statically (i.e. compile-time), whereas a dyn variable is bound dynamically (i.e. execution-time). A virtual variable can be a scalar or a relation. Thus a stat relation is a view, except that a stat relation can be parameterised. For instance we can define a stat relation V(X) with parameter X as

```
V(X) == ANON [ENO := E1, ENAME := E2]
        WHERE  EMP [ENO = E1, ENAME := E2, EDN = X]
```

where the symbol == implies static binding. V(X) will be evaluated when assigned to a suitably defined relation, say T, as

```
T := V('D25')
```

whereupon T will hold employee number and the name of those in department 'D25'. It should be stressed that a stat variable disappears after compilation, and is replaced by the right hand side of the == symbol. However, a stat variable is not a macro, as it is not strictly a text replacement mechanism; a stat variable is syntactically checked and the resultant query optimised during compilation. That is, if a query has many stat relations, it can be optimised into a single efficient expression.

A dyn variable, again optionally parameterised, can act as a function; for instance, we can define a dyn relation D with argument X as:

```
D(X) <- ANON [ENO := E1, ENAME := E2]
          WHERE  EMP [ENO = E1, ENAME := E2, EDN = X]
```

where the symbol <- implies dynamic binding. Now D(X) can be treated as a function and held in a function library, that is D(X) will out live the compilation process. It can be executed at any time, again by assigning it to a relation:

```
T := D ('D25')
```

Since a dyn variable must survive the compilation process, it cannot be removed by a compile-time optimiser. A function will be recursive if the function name appears on the right hand side.

The advantage of stat variables are that they can not only serve as handy notation (like a macro), but they can - as already stated - also be optimised easily during compilation, although they cannot define recursive operations for which functions are needed. Stat variables can be used very effectively to represent Prolog-like deductive rules; as shown below.

Consider some simplified rules to define Voter (Name, Doe) for British election. A person is a voter if he/she is a British citizen of age 18 or over, on the day of election (Doe). We may use the following relations in the definition.

Permanent relation

Birth (Name, Dad, Mum, Cob, Dob)
where Cob is the country of birth and Dob the date of birth.

Virtual relations

```
Citizen (Name)
Over18 (Name, Doe)
Marriage (Husb, Wife)
Qualmum (Mum)            /* Qualified mother */
Qualdad (Dad, Mum)       /* Qualified father */
```

We can now state the rules in Prolog as

```
voter (X, Edate):- over18(X, Edate),
                   citizen(X)
over18 (X, Edate) :- birth(X, _, _, Bdate),
                     (Bdate - Edate) > 18
```

Now a person born in the UK is a British citizen if either the father or the mother was also born in the UK, except that in the case of the father, he has to be the legitimate father We assume a father is legitimate if he was, or is, the husband of the mother. So we can write:

```
citizen (X) :- birth (X, -, Z, uk, _),
               qualmum (Z)

citizen (X) :- birth (X, Y, Z, uk, _),
               qualdad (Y, Z)

qualmum (Z)     :- birth (Z, _, _, uk, _)

qualdad (Y, Z)  :- birth (Y, _, _, uk, _),

               marriage (Y, Z)
```

These rules can be defined in DEAL in a similar fashion:

```
Voter := ANON[Name := x, Doe := Edate]
     WHERE Over18[Name=x, Doe=Edate]
     AND Citizen [Name=x]

Over18 == ANON[Name := x, Doe := Edate]
     WHERE Birth [Name=x, Dob=Bdate]
```

```
        AND [(Bdate-Edate) > 18]

Citizen == ANON[Name :=x]
         WHERE Birth [Name=x, Dad=y, Mum=z, Cob='uk']
         AND (Qualmum[Mum=z]
           OR Qualdad [Dad=y, Mum=z])
Qualmum == ANON [Mum := z]
        WHERE Birth [Name=z, Cob='uk']

Qualdad == ANON[Dad := y, Mum := z]
        WHERE Birth [Name=y, Cob='uk']
        AND Marriage [Husb=y, Wife=z]
```

Note that in these DEAL formulations, the unnecessary attribute names are avoided. Since these are written in stat relations, they can be optimised following some simple rules to be elaborated in a later paper. However the optimised version of the above query is

```
Voter := ANON[Name := x, Doe:=Edate]
      WHERE Birth[Name=x, Dad=y, Mum=z, Cob='uk', Dob=Bdate]
      AND  (Birth[Name=z, Cob='uk']
        OR  (Birth[Name=y, Cob='uk']
          AND  Marriage[Husb=y, Wife=z]  ) )
      AND  [ (Bdate-Edate) > 18]
```

Thus stat relations can be used to specify non-recursive rules which are optimised for efficient execution. For recursive rules we can use dyn relations, but they are not so amenable to compile-time optimisation.

Three optimisation rules used in the compilation of stat relations are:

(i) Replace the stat relations at the head of tuple predicates, gradually from the lowest levels upwards, dropping the unnecessary ANON clause in each lower-level stat relation.

(ii) If the join attribute of a self-join is unique, then combine the two predicates into a single one, provided these is no conflict in the other attributes. Above, we have combined Birth[Name = x, Dob = Bdate] and Birth [Name=x, Dad=y, Mum=z, Cob='uk'] into a single one Birth [Name=x, Dad=y, Mum=z, Cob='uk', Dob=Bdate], as x is unique and the other attributes are complementary.

(iii) Free conditions should be merged; for instance [(Bdate-Edate)>18] should replace Dob=Bdate in the first tuple predicate in the WHERE clause as (DOB-Edate)>18.

4. DEAL FUNCTIONS

A DEAL function must have its appropriate Type declaration, which we did not mention when we introduced functions earlier. Let us define here a slightly different function, complete with Type, to find the father of X as:

```
F(X:CHAR):CHAR <- PARENT [DAD]
                  WHERE [PNAME = X]
```

Observe that both function F and its argument X are declared as character variables, and that there will be a Type coercion in this function, which projects attribute DAD from PARENT, subject to the WHERE clause. A multi-statement function is bounded by keywords DYN and ENDDYN, as shown in the example below. DEAL permits both iterative and recursive functions. Compared to a recursive function, an iterative function is less powerful, but generally more efficient in execution, and therefore whenever possible iterative functions should be used. Although a recursive function can in principle be converted into an equivalent iterative form [15], conversion algorithms such as those available do not often produce the most efficient transformation [16]; a human being does much better. To prevent infinite looping in iterative functions, we support explicitly a WHILE construct. For instance to derive all the known paternal ancestors (successive fathers) of X, we can define a function PAT as:

```
PAT(X:CHAR):REL <-
DYN
     TYPE (F:CHAR, R:REL, PT(DAD:CHAR):REL)

     R := PARENT [DAD] WHERE [PNAME = X]
     F := R [DAD]
     PT := EMPTY

     WHILE (F != NULL)
       PT := PT ++ R
       R := PARENT [DAD] WHERE [PNAME = F]
       F := R[DAD]
     ENDWHILE
     PAT := PT
ENDDYN
```

Note F above is declared as a character string, and relation PARENT is treated as global data. The TYPE statement is used to declare the Types of intermediate variables; however, in the absence of such a declaration the system will attempt to work out the Types of these variables from the assignments, wherever possible. The first assignment of R selects those tuples with PNAME equal to the parameter X; the second assignment of R selects tuples with PNAME equal to F, which is the name of the father most recently found. The statement PT := EMPTY initialises PT to an EMPTY relation; i.e. a relation with no tuples. The WHILE loop is terminated by the ENDWHILE.

Recursion

For recursion, consider the following statement:

```
ANC <- ANC ++ R
```

Strictly speaking this a recursive function since ANC appears on the right hand side as well. However the problem with such recursive functions are that they can become uncontrolled. We therefore provide an explicit IF..THEN..ELSE facility for recursion control. It may be noted that even LDL which tried to avoid such ugly things as explicit constructs for controls, have eventually succumbed to them [17]. As database researchers we wish to be pragmatic, that is we prefer the efficiency of execution to the elegance of constructs. We can define a recursive dyn function which will return all known paternal ancestors of X:

```
ANC(X:CHAR):REL <-
DYN
  TYPE (F:CHAR, R:REL)

    R := PARENT [DAD] WHERE [PNAME = X]
    F := R [DAD]

    IF (F != NULL)
    THEN ANC := R ++ ANC(F)
    ENDIF
ENDDYN
```

This is a simple recursive function, which can be easily rewritten in an iterative form. A more complex recursive function is required in the part explosion problem described below.

Assume two relations, PART (PN COST QST) and LINK (SUP INF QTY), where a part can be made up of many other parts, and the same part can be a component of several other parts. A PART record contains part number (PN), its assembly cost (COST) excluding the cost of its inferior parts, and quantity in stock (QST). There is a LINK record for each superior/inferior pair, each record containing a superior part number (SUP), its immediately inferior part number (INF) and the quantity (QTY) of the inferior part number in that superior part number. We can define a recursive dyn scalar SUPCOST to find the cost of a superior part X as

```
SUPCOST (X:CHAR) :REAL <-
DYN
TYPE (R:REL)

    R := LINK WHERE [SUP = X]

    IF (R = EMPTY)
    THEN SUPCOST := PART [COST]
                    WHERE [PN = X]
    ELSE SUPCOST := CONV (PART[COST]
                    WHERE [PN = X]) +
          CONV (R [SUM (QTY * SUPCOST(INF))])
ENDDYN
```

Observe that in this function, we have treated relations PART and LINK as global data; we could have instead passed them as parameters. CONV is a built-in function (see below) which converts a unary relation of a single tuple into a scalar.

The incremental cost of any part X can be obtained from PART [COST] where [PN = X]. Since a basic part does not have any lower level, it produces an empty relation R; its cost is given by the incremental cost as shown above. A part which has inferior parts produces a non-empty relation R.

The total cost of all the immediately inferior parts of a given type in a superior part is derived by the expression (QTY * SUPCOST(INF)) which is the quantity times the total cost of an inferior part. The incremental cost of a superior part is added to the sum (SUM) of the total costs of all its immediately inferior parts; this recursive process continues for all successive lower levels, terminating at basic parts. SUPCOST can be evaluated for any part X, including a basic part. SUM is a built-in function as in SQL.

A function in DEAL can have output arguments which return output values, when the function is called. It may be noted that a DEAL function permits C code (in the form of a C function) within it, although not shown here. In general DEAL functions can be divided into three classes:

External
Internal
Built-in

Both external and internal functions are user-defined, but external functions can be defined in a host language for operations on user-defined data structures, as in Hydrogen, while internal functions are dyn variables, defined within DEAL. Built-in functions are those supported by the system, and can be used in DEAL or to define other dyn variables.

DEAL provides two special attributes SEQ and LEVEL for each relation (or sub-relation), and several built-in functions.

Attributes SEQ and LEVEL are automatically defined by the system for each relation in DEAL. Attribute SEQ holds the stored position of tuples (in a system-defined order) and LEVEL is the level number of a relation. If a relation is a sub-relation (i.e. a repeating group), then its SEQ is defined separately for each set of the tuples belonging to a parent tuple (see section 6). If a relation is not a subrelation, then its level number is zero. The LEVEL of a relation is interpreted as the LEVEL of its tuples, and is thus held in each tuple, although it is same for all the tuples of a relation. SEQ and LEVEL number may not necessarily be stored physically, but generated when needed. Both are treated like ordinary attributes, although cannot be directly updated.

The built-in functions include:

(i) CARD(SEQ) which gives the cardinality of the relation or subrelation concerned.
(ii) CONC (y) which concatenates attribute list y, but y may itself include a CONC function.
(iii) Standard statistical functions (COUNT, AVG, SUM, MAX, MIN).
(iv) ORDER (R(y)) to order tuples of R in order of attribute list y.
(v) Piping functions: FIRST, NEXT and LAST for sequential processing of tuples. Their general form is X(R(y)) where X is the function name, R is the relation and y is the attribute list. Default of X(R(SEQ)) is X(R) which returns only one tuple at a time. Since the operation is relational, the piped out set is a relation with one or more tuples, as the case may be. The piping function FIRST (R(y)) retrieves the set of tuples from R which matches the first value of y (in system defined order). The piping functions can be used to provide a list processing capability as shown in section 5.

(vi) CONV(R) which converts a unary relation R of a single tuple into a scalar; the scalar inherits the Type of the attribute of R.

5. LIST PROCESSING

A major objective in DEAL is to add new facilities by user-defined functions, rather than by defining new constructs. This capability of DEAL can be tested in list processing where traditional relational facilities are weak. A list can be declared in DEAL as a unary relation with the system-defined SEQ field providing the relative positions. Consider for instance some examples from protein chemistry, where a polypeptide is made up of up to 20 different amino-acids in sequence. In analysing protein sequences, one often has to find out if a given subsequence (sometimes with wild cards) matches a known sequence. Let us consider a simple polypeptide of 5 items (amino-acids):

```
POLY(AA)
        ala
        leu
        val
        trp
        tyr
```

where the entries are amino-acids (AA) in standard abbreviations; assume also a subsequence of 3 items: ala, any and val, where "any" means any amino-acid (i.e. wild card). To ascertain if the subsequence matches, we can write:

```
ANON [POS := P]
WHERE POLY [AA = 'ala', SEQ = P]
    AND POLY [AA = 'val', SEQ = P+2]
```

where the system-defined attribute SEQ gives the stored order of tuples in a relation (or sub-relation - see in molecular attributes later), POS yields the starting position of the match, if true. This example is rather simple. More often than not, the user has to compare a variable length subsequence, which we assume is held in relation SUB(AA). For this general problem of string matching, with wild cards, we can write a function MATCH as described below:

```
MATCH (POLY (AA:CHAR):REL, SUB(AA:CHAR):REL):REL <-
DYN
   TYPE (GR (RES_AA:CHAR, SUB_AA:INT, POS:INT, SDIFF:INT):REL)
```

```
GR := ANON [RES_AA:= W, SUB_AA:= X, POS:= Y, SDIFF := Y - Z ]
      WHERE POLY [AA = W, SEQ = Y]
         AND SUB [ AA = X, (AA = W | AA = 'any'), SEQ = Z]
         AND Y >= Z

MATCH := ANON [POS := P]
            WHERE GR [ SDIFF = X, COUNT (SUB_AA) = C, POS = P]
               AND SUB [CARD(SEQ) = C ]
ENDDYN
```

GR contains one tuple for each tuple in POLY which matches a tuple in the subsequence SUB (joining on amino acid AA). If AA in the SUB tuple is "any", then it will match all POLY tuples. POS holds the starting position in POLY for the match. (The subsequence SUB may match POLY in more than one place; if so, MATCH will hold the starting position for each match). SDIFF holds the difference between the positions of AA in POLY and SUB; SDIFF will therefore have the same value for each matching group. The condition Y >= Z prevents subsequences in the reverse order being matched.

MATCH groups the tuples by SDIFF, and selects only those tuples where the number of items (COUNT(SUB_AA)) in the group is the same as the number of tuples in SUB (CARD(SEQ)), so that incomplete groups are ignored. Thus the attribute POS in MATCH will contain the starting positions of all matches in the POLY sequence.

However, the user may need to process the items of the matched group individually; in that case, one can use piping functions, as shown below:

```
GR := ANON [RES_AA:= W, SUB_AA:= X, POS:= Y, SDIFF := Y - Z ]
      WHERE POLY [AA = W, SEQ = Y]
         AND SUB [ AA = X, (AA = W | AA = 'any'), SEQ = Z]
         AND Y >= Z

R := FIRST (GR(SDIFF))
WHILE R = NOT EMPTY
      MATCH := ANON [POS := P]
                  WHERE R [CARD(SEQ) = C, POS = P]
                     AND SUB [CARD(SEQ) = C ]
      IF MATCH != EMPTY
      THEN
      { do processing, say to find out the counterparts of
                  "any"s, their positions in the sequence, and their
                  other characteristics:

        ANON [ AA := X, SQ := Y]
```

```
            WHERE R [ RES_AA = X, SEQ = Y]

            Further processings such as to find their properties
                    can be carried out in C, if preferred, and results
                    returned with suitable output parameters.

            C code in the form of a C function is allowed in DEAL
                    functions
        }
        ENDIF
        R := NEXT(GR(SDIFF))
    ENDWHILE
```

However, if piping functions are used, it may be adequate to define MATCH as a scalar rather than a relation. Once written, this function can be used for any match operation of this type.

6. MOLECULAR ATTRIBUTES

An attribute in DEAL can be atomic or molecular, and each in turn can be actual or virtual. An actual attribute is physically stored, while a virtual attributed is derived. A virtual attribute is fact a function. Consider a non-first-normal (*non-normal* for short) relation BOSS for company bosses which includes a repeating group of salary for each year of employment:

```
BOSS (BNAME COMPANY PROFIT CAPITAL SALS(SAL))
```

Profit and capital are shown for the current year only, to keep the example simple. With the two system-defined attributes LEVEL and SEQ described above, this non-normal relation may be seen as:

```
BOSS (BNAME COMPANY PROFIT CAPITAL LEVEL SEQ
        SALS(SAL LEVEL SEQ))
```

The value of attribute BOSS.LEVEL is 0 and that of BOSS.SALS.LEVEL (qualifier BOSS is redundant if we assume subrelation name SALS to be unique) is 1, as explained in the Appendix. Attribute BOSS.SEQ gives the ordinal number of the non-normal tuples and SALS.SEQ the ordinal number of each SALS tuple for each boss separately. Thus the maximum value of SALS.SEQ will be 5 for a boss if the boss has only 5 salary tuples.

To find the boss-name, company name, current salary C_SAL (in K pounds sterling), percentage salary rise (S_RISE) and percentage company profit-rise (P_RISE) for those who got more than 20% salary rise this year.

```
ANON [BNAME := B, CNAME := C, C_SAL := X, S_RISE := R, P_RISE := P]
WHERE BOSS [BNAME = B, COMPANY = C,
        SALS [SAL = X, SEQ = CARD (SEQ))
        SALS [SAL = Y, SEQ = (CARD(SEQ)-1)
        AND [R = (X-Y)/Y*100 ,R > 20, P = PROFIT/CAPITAL]
```

Built-in function CARD(SEQ) within each SALS returns the maximum value of SALS.SEQ for that employee, and therefore the SALS tuple with SALS.SEQ = CARD(SEQ) holds the current salary, and the one with SALS.SEQ = (CARD(SEQ) - 1) the previous salary. The reader may be curious to look at a sample result of this query in 1989 (Source: Sunday Times):

(BNAME	CNAME	C-SAL	S-RISE	P-RISE)
T. Rowland	Lonrho	1015	54	12
Sir Walters	B.P.	515	48	-13
C. Southgate	Thorne EMI	481	52	28
Sir Henderson	ICI	478	20	12
Lord Rayner	M&S	424	21	5
Lord King	British Airways	386	116	18

All relational operations are permitted in non-normal form, based on the principle that an operation in non-normal form is equivalent to the same operation on the normalised version of the operand relation(s). A relational operation may be assumed to proceed as follows:

(i) Convert operand non-normal relation(s) into normalised (i.e first normal) form.
(ii) Carry out the operation on the normalised operands.
(iii) Convert the resultant normalised relation into non-normal form depending on the attribute specification.

Actual implementation may be carried out differently for improved performance, but the principle remains valid. In other words, a complex object can be viewed as a single entity at a higher level, and as a set of normalised relations at a lower level, thus combining the advantages of the object concept with the flexibility of the relational model.

Consider another example of solids bounded by plane faces; a given solid may be part of other solids (super solids), and may itself in turn be made up of some other solids (sub solids), as graphical representations. A face has straight-line edges (boundaries) each edge having two end points, each end point being represented by Cartesian coordinates.

Solids may share faces, edges and points. A non-normal representation of this structure is:

```
SOLIDS (SOL-NO DESCRIPTION DIMENSION
        SUPER(SOL-NO) SUB(SOL-NO)
        FACES(FACE-NO EDGES(EDGE-NO
        POINT1(X Y Z) POINT2(X Y Z))))
```

An interesting question is to find overlapping edges. This would require a mathematical function to determine if an overlap exists. This query may look like this:

```
ANON  [SOLID1 := S1, FACE1 := F1, EDGE1 := E1,
       SOLID2 := S2, FACE2 := F2, EDGE2 :=E2]
WHERE SOLIDS [SOL-NO = S1,
        FACES [FACE-NO = F1,
       EDGES [EDGE-NO = E1,
          POINT1 [X = X1, Y = Y1, Z = Z1],
          POINT2 [X = X2, Y = Y2, Z = Z2]]]]
AND SOLIDS [SOL-NO = S2,
       FACES [FACE-NO = F2,
       EDGES [EDGE-NO = E2,
         POINT1 [X = X3, Y = Y3, Z = Z3],
         POINT2 [ X = X4, Y = Y4, Z = Z4]]]]

AND OVERLAP (X1, Y1, Z1, X2, Y2, Z2,
             X3, Y3, Z3, X4, Y4, Z4)
```

where OVERLAP is a user-defined external function which returns True if an overlap exists, and False otherwise. Recall symbol | (vertical bar) implies logical OR.

7. IMPLEMENTATION

A subset of DEAL is being implemented over ORACLE within its C interface in what is called Pro* C. The ORACLE interface looks like that in figure 1.

ORACLE provides a set of lower-level functions called ORACLE Call Interface (OCI) which supports SQL Plus (interactive SQL) and a number of programming language interfaces such as Pro* C, Pro* Cobol etc. Although the programs written in OCI are more efficient they are less portable, and therefore we decided to implement DEAL in Pro* C, so that the resultant codes can also be used for DB2.

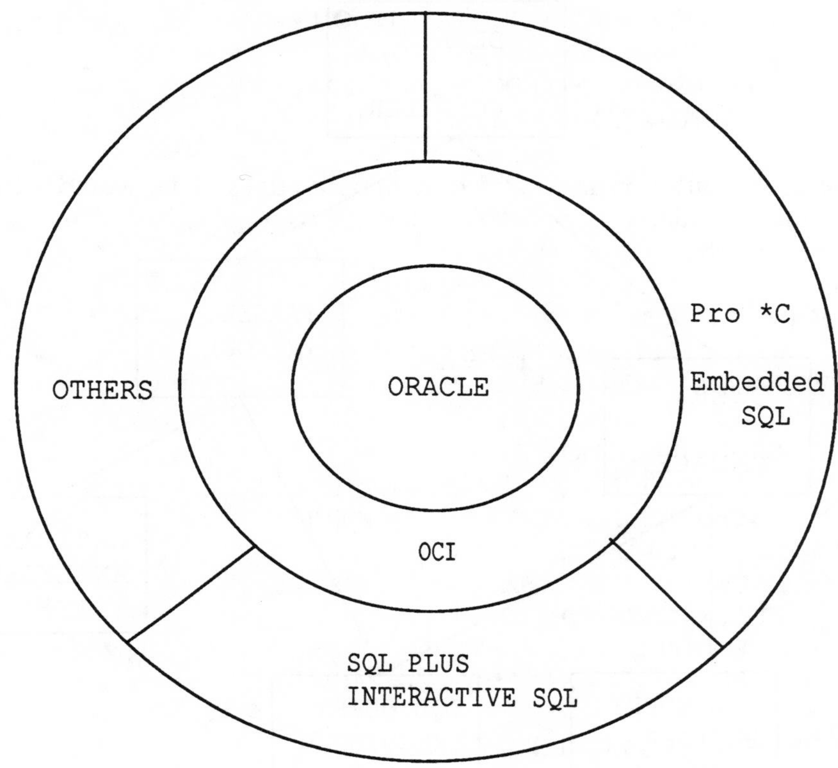

Pro*C - Host Language Interface - 'C'

OCI - Oracle Call Interface.

OTHERS - Other Host Language Interfaces and Application Tools.

Figure - 1.

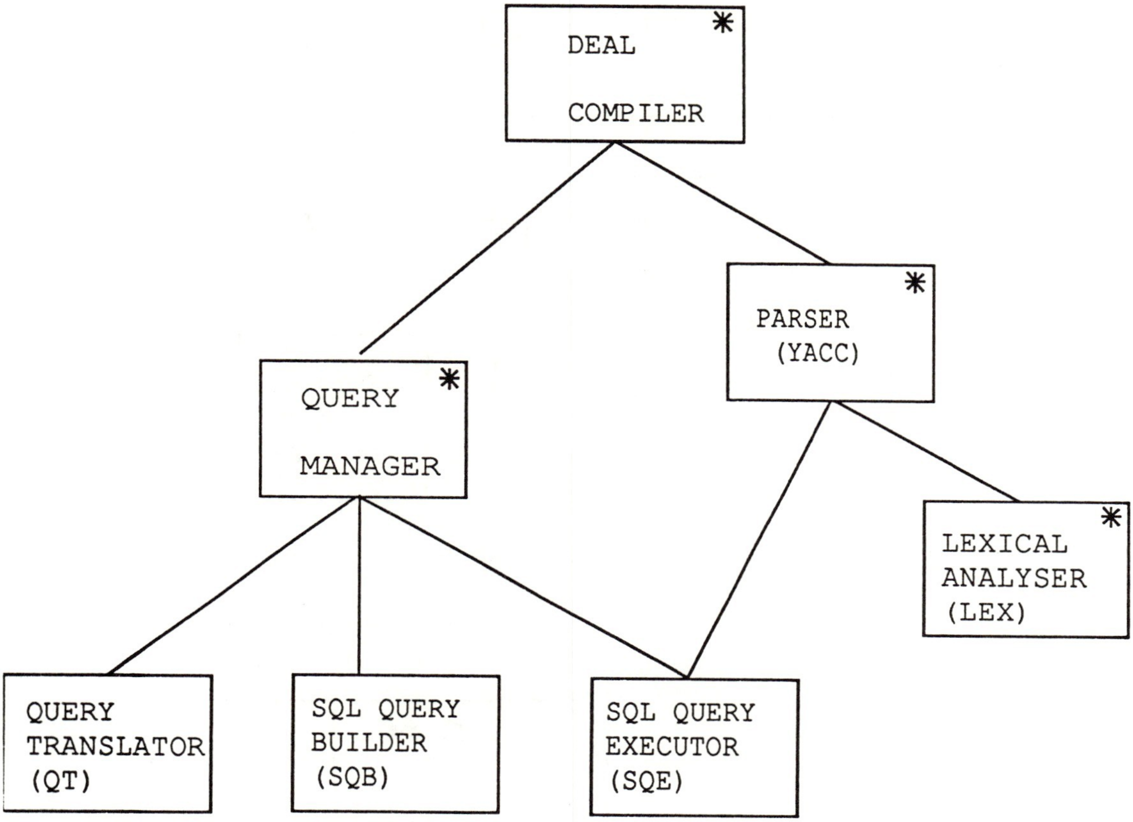

DEAL COMPILER *

QUERY MANAGER *

PARSER (YACC) *

LEXICAL ANALYSER (LEX) *

QUERY TRANSLATOR (QT)

SQL QUERY BUILDER (SQB)

SQL QUERY EXECUTOR (SQE)

JSP DIAGRAM OF THE DEAL COMPILER

Figure - 2.

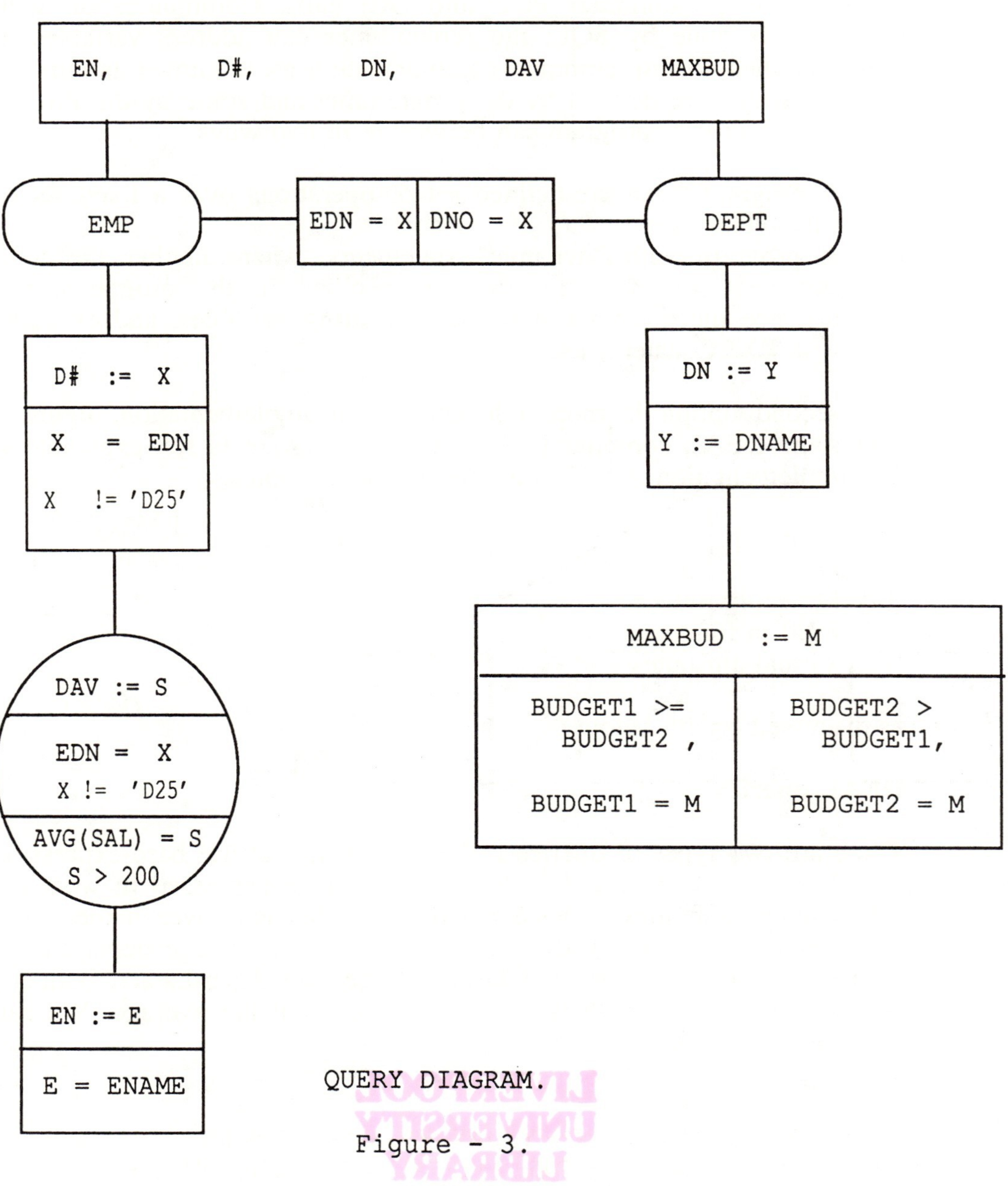

QUERY DIAGRAM.

Figure - 3.

A Pro* C program is basically a C program with embedded SQL. Each SQL statement is prefixed by a EXEC SQL statement; which is compiled by the pre-compiler PCC into OCI calls. Communication with ORACLE is done by SQL; the programmer can address variables in SQL statements using common communication areas known as cursors, some of which are defined by the programmer and some by the Pro* C interface. A Pro* C program can be written in two ways.

(i) A program for a pre-defined set of operations over a fixed set of base relations
(ii) A program with "dynamic" statements, where neither the SQL statement, nor its structure are specified in the programs. For instance the queries can be held in string variables, and executed with EXEC statements.

The second option is more relevant to our implementation, figure 2 shows the DEAL compiler in Pro* C. The diagram is self-explanatory. The implementation itself has the following six topics:

(i) DEAL queries
(ii) Data definition
(iii) Molecular DEAL
(iv) Built-in functions
(v) Virtual attributes

as discussed briefly below.

DEAL queries

There are two types of queries in DEAL; those that use base-expression and those that do not, and both of them can be expressed in what are called query diagrams. Consider a query to list employee name (EN), department number (D#), department name (DN), average departmental salary (DAV) over 200K and larger of the two departmental budgets; however department D25 is to be excluded from the average. We can write this query as

```
ANON [EN := E, D# := X, DN := Y, DAV := S, MAXBUD := M]
WHERE EMP[EDN = X, X !='D25', AVG(SAL) = S, S > 200, ENAME= E]
  AND DEPT [DNO = X, DNAME = Y, (BUDGET1 >= BUDGET2, BUDGET1 = M |
                              BUDGET2 > BUDGET1, BUDGET2 = M)
```

This can be expressed in a query diagram as shown in figure 3. All conditions relevant to an aggregation box are included in that box, irrespective of whether they appear outside as well. All attributes to be projected are shown separately.

We make the following observation about the query diagram: The aggregate function (vertical ellipse) includes all its evaluation conditions, and therefore can be evaluated in isolation, thus freeing it from its relation position in the tuple predicate. For instance, the diagram can now be redrawn with the EN:=E box first as required in the ANON clause. The inter-relational links (EDN = X, DNO = X) can include other conditions; for instance in the earlier query on students taking majors, the condition will be (MAJNAME = ONLY Y, MAJNAME = Y), while in the query on protein sequences, it will be (AA = X, (AA = W | AA = 'any')). Finally the condition box for MAXBUD := M can be extended to support more alternative conditions and levels if needed. In particular it can be re-drawn to support if ..then.. else type assignment, optionally nested, as follows

<table>
<tr><td>MAXBUD : = M</td><td></td><td></td><td></td></tr>
<tr><td>IF condition</td><td></td><td></td><td></td></tr>
<tr><td>then</td><td>else if condition</td><td></td><td></td></tr>
<tr><td></td><td>then</td><td>else if condition</td><td></td></tr>
<tr><td></td><td></td><td>then</td><td>else</td></tr>
</table>

A query with a base-expression will also produce a similar diagram, with the base-expression to be evaluated before the ANON clause is executed.

Returning to the query diagram, it is first redrawn with the following changes

(i) aggregate functions and new attribute clauses are brought forward
(ii) the order of attributes and associated conditions in the diagram are altered to conform to the order in the ANON clause.

The query is then processed with the following rules:

(i) Every aggregate function and new attribute clause is made into a separate query.
(ii) These are then joined appropriately with the parent relations
(iii) The inter-relational link box is then examined.
    (a) equi-join is invoked if specified
    (b) Quantifier ALL is replaced by its SQL equivalent

(c) Quantifier ONLY is replaced by a combination of quantifier ALL and a COUNT; for instance, the query on students will be transformed as:

```
ANON [SNO := X]
WHERE MAJOR [SNO = X, COUNT (MAJNAME) = C, MAJNAME = ALL Y]
AND MAJOR [SNO = 'S10', COUNT (MAJNAME) = C, MAJNAME = Y]
```

(d) Quantifier FAIL is replaced by quantifier DOES NOT EXIST of SQL.

(e) More complex conditions and actions require a general procedure which we have not yet finalised; but it will be written as a function in the C interface.

The application of these rules will result in the following subqueries:

(1) Evaluate the aggregate function

```
CREATE VIEW V1 (D#, DAV) AS
SELECT EDN, AVG(SAL)
FROM EMP
GROUP BY EDN
HAVING AVG(SAL) > 200
WHERE EDN!= 'D25';
```

(2) Join the aggregate function with the rest of the relation

```
CREATE VIEW V2 (EN, D#, DAV) AS
SELECT ENAME, D#, DAV
FROM EMP, V1
WHERE EDN = D# AND EDN != 'D25'
```

3. Create new attribute in V3 from DEPT

```
CREATE VIEW V3 (DNO, DN MAXBUD BUDGET2) AS
SELECT DNO DNAME BUDGET1, BUDGET2
FROM DEPT;
```

4. Evaluate the new attribute MAXBUD using the C interface. Change the new attribute condition to

```
(MAXBUD >= BUDGET2, MAXBUD = M | BUDGET2> MAXBUD, BUDGET2 = M)
```

It may be possible to reduce it to IF (BUDGET2 > MAXBUD) THEN MAXBUD = BUDGET2 for the C function.

The C interface produces V4

V4 (DNO DN MAXBUD)

5. The final inter-relational link

```
SELECT EN D# DAV DN MAXBUD
FROM V2, V4
WHERE V2.D# = V4.DNO
```

Data definition and Molecular attributes

In order to maintain compatibility with ORACLE, we have used ORACLE data definitions, with suitable extensions for molecular DEAL which permits repeating groups. All definitions and operations of molecular DEAL are resolved into atomic counterparts, and stored and processed as such. There are a number of system tables held in the form of relations which are used to aid the process. Outer-join operations are used to recreate the molecular versions from the atomic relations, but whenever possible molecular queries are optimised into atomic ones; for example consider the non-normal relation.

BOSS (BNAME, COMPANY, PROFIT, CAPITAL, LEVEL, SEQ
SALS (SAL, LEVEL, SEQ))

where boss names are unique. This relation is resolved into:

BOSS* (BNAME, COMPANY, PROFIT, CAPITAL, LEVEL, SEQ)
SALS* (BNAME, SAL, LEVEL, SEQ)

where BOSS* and SALS* are internal names and SEQ in SALS* is defined separately for each BNAME value. In case some bosses do not earn any salary, an outer-join is needed to create the original relation. A query such as

ANON [BNAME := B, CSAL := S] WHERE BOSS [BNAME = B, SALS [SAL = S, SEQ = CARD (SEQ)]]

will be transferred into

ANON [BNAME := B, CSAL := S] WHERE SALS* [BNAME = B, SAL = S, SEQ = CARD (SEQ)]

Built-in functions and virtual relations

All the built-in functions have been implemented in the C interface in a straight-forward manner except for the piping function X(R(y)) where X can be FIRST, NEXT or LAST. Since a piping function retrieves tuples of R
in order of attribute list y, the access is faster if R is ordered in y, and is accessed by an appropriate cursor.

```
EXEC SQL DECLARE C1 CURSOR FOR
SELECT ....
FROM ....
ORDER BY y
```

The cursor will allow tuple at a time retrieval. This works well if y is unique (for instance if it is SEQ), since in this case each piping- function call, say NEXT (R(y)), will produce only a single tuple. However if y is non-unique, then a NEXT (R(y)) may generally produce more than one tuple, and this creates two problems, since the cursor produces only one tuple at a time.

(a) Each tuple has to be examined to check the end of the current y value. If so checked the tuple will disappear from the buffer. This can be solved by creating a private buffer, as we do.

(b) Since by our definition NEXT (R(y) returns a relation, this output relation has to be defined by the SQL CREATE table command and populated by the SQL INSERT command by inserting each matched tuple retrieved by the cursor in the SQL interface. This operation is not necessarily cheap.

One can produce an alternative solution for non-unique y. In this case create a copy RC of R, create an index for y on RC, and hold the distinct y values (in the correct order) in a list in the C interface. Then access RC for each NEXT as

```
SELECT * FROM RC WHERE y = n
```

where n is the next value in the list. However this may not necessarily be more efficient than the cursor approach.

We have implemented the cursor approach for y =SEQ and the index approach for other values of y. We plan to implement the cursor approach for non-unique y as well, in order to compare performance.

We do not anticipate any problem in implementing external functions (such as OVERLAP in the query on box) in the C interface, since C code in the form of a C function can be used within dyn variables. The implementation of dyn variables is in progress, but without any optimisation for the recursive functions. Parameterised stat variables with compile-time binding have been implemented, with an optimiser which eliminates unnecessary intermediate operations.

The system maintains a list of built-in functions, which is copied for each user in a function-stack. All virtual relations defined by the user are added on the top, without any duplication check. When a function is called, the list is searched from the top. This allows a user to define a new function to replace a synonymous old one.

8. CONCLUSION

As indicated earlier DEAL is designed as an intelligent database language for the processing of both facts and rules. It explores the basic structure of SQL and enriches it with a Prolog-like deduction capability, within a relational framework.

DEAL is not designed as a stand-alone and full blown AI language; its objective is more modest - to provide a single integrated facility for the high-level processing of both relations and rules with a relational framework. It can be hosted in a lower level language such as C for an additional processing capability. DEAL can be used not only for integrated data and knowledge processing, it can also serve as the high-level common language in heterogeneous distributed knowledge bases. We chose SQL as our base language because of our belief that this language, given the current industrial commitment to it, will remain a potent force for a while. Our intention was to examine the basic SQL structure, and to explore if it can be improved suitably for deductive and recursive capabilities.

DEAL implementation over ORACLE highlights the problem of interfacing an intelligent language over SQL, arising out of SQL's rigid structure and the inability of the implementor to access lower-level ORACLE codes. The resultant implementation is necessarily inefficient, although good enough as a research prototype for experimentation.

While DEAL supports externally defined functions (e.g. function OVERLAP in the query on solids), it does not as yet incorporate the other features of extensibilty, such as abstract data types with method inheritance. These features are expected to be added later. DEAL is currently being used for statistical databases and protein structure study.

REFERENCES

[1]. Dayal, U. and Smith, J.M., "PROBE: A knowledge-oriented Database Management System", Knowledge Base Management Systems : Integrating AI and DB Technologies, edited by M. Brodie, and J. Mylopoulos, Springer-Verlag, 1986.

[2]. Bocca J., "A marriage of Convenience: Prolog and relational DBMS'. 1986 The third IEEE symposium on Logic Programming (Sep 1986).

[3]. Ceri S., Gottlob G., Wiederhold G., "Interfacing Relational Databases and Prolog efficiently", Expert Database Systems, L. Kerschberg (ed.), Benjamin/Cumming, 1987.

[4]. Lucas R., et al : "A Prolog-relational database interface" Prolog and Databases, edited by Gray and Lucas, Ellis Horwood (1988) p67.

[5].

(a) Chimenti D., et al. "An overview of the LDL system", Data Engineering, Vol 10, no. 4, September 1987.

(b) Chimenti D., et al. "Towards an open architecture for LDL", 15th VLDB Conf, 1989, p195.

[6]. KEE Interface to ORACLE DBMS, 1986. Intellicorp, 707 Laurel St., Menlo Park, Calif. 94025 - 3445.

[7].

(a) Agrawal R., and Gehani N.H., "ODE - The language and Data Model", ACM SIGMOD Conf., 1989, p 36-45.

(b) Velez F., et al: "The O2 Object Manager - an Overview, 15th VLDB Conf, 1989, p357.

(c) Alashqur A.M., et al : "OQL - a query language for manipulating object-oriented databases", 15th VLDB Conf, 1989, p433.

[8]. Gardarin G., et al. "Managing Complex Objects in an extensible relational DBMS" 15th VLDB Conf, 1989, p55.

[9]. Pistor P., and Andersen F., "Designing a generalised NF2 model with an SQL-type language interface", Proc. 12th VLDB Conference, Kyoto, 1986, p278.

[10]. Rowe L.A., Stonebraker M. R., "The POSTGRES data model", Proc. 13th VLDB Conference, Brighton, 1987, p83.

[11]. Stonebraker M., "The design of the POSTGRES Storage System", Proc. 13th VLDB Conference, Brighton, 1987, p289.

[12]. McPherson J., and Pirahesh H., "An overview of the Extensibility in Starburst", IEEE Databases Engineering, June 1987, Vol 10, no.2, pp 32-39.

[13]. Chang W., and Schek H-J., "A signature access method for the Starburst Data-base System", 15th VLDB Conference, Amsterdam, August 1989, p145.

[14]. Deen S.M., "A Relational Language with Deductions, Functions and Recursions", Data and Knowledge Engineering, Vol, 1985, pp 139-154.

[15]. Henschen L.J., and Naqvi S.A., "On Compiling queries in recursive first-order databases", JACM, 31, 1, 1984 p 47-85.

[16]. Beeri C., and Ramakrishanan R., "On the Power of Magic", Proc. of 6th ACM PODS 1987.

[17]. Zaniolo C., "Design and implementation of a logic based language for data intensive applications", Proc. of the Int. Conference in Logic Programming, Seattle, 1988.

QUESTIONS

Prof. M. Takizawa (Tokyo Denki University).

MT. What is the relationship between SQL and DEAL in the context of expressive power?

A. C. Herath.

AH. Basic query structure of both languages are similar. But the expressive power differs significantly. In SQL, FROM clause and WHERE clauses are simple. Whereas in DEAL, we can include complex relational expressions in the from clause and user defined functions in both places.

The ability to define user defined functions is very important, especially since we allow complex objects in DEAL. One cannot support every possible function to manipulate such complex objects in a query language. So the user can define functions for manipulating complex objects. The ability to use these functions as a part of the query language (which is totally absent in SQL) is a major difference. DEAL also supports deductions and recursions.

Dr. J. Zelezinkow (La Trobe University).

JZ. What facilities of SQL do you use; for example do you have your own optimization mechanism etc?

AH. We are working on query optimization in DEAL now. But our present implementation is a prototype, built on top of ORACLE (SQL). The DEAL queries are translated into SQL at the moment. We cannot do much about the optimization of SQL queries (we assume that ORACLE does such a thing). Certainly we can introduce the optimization in translation of DEAL queries to SQL. We are working on that at the moment.

Prof. S.M. Deen (University of Keele).

One student has been working on optimization. The automatic translation of DEAL queries into SQL results in some unnecessary intermediate steps. We can certainly introduce a mechanism to identify such unnecessary intermediate steps and remove them. We are currently looking at such algorithms.

JZ. Is there anything you lose which we have in SQL ?

SMD.In terms of expressive power, in DEAL you get whatever you have in SQL. Yet it is more powerful than SQL and has more facilities. The nature of the DEAL query structure makes some SQL structures obsolete (for example GROUP BY clause is unnecessary in DEAL.)

Certain things like the concept of ordered set of tuples, are absent in SQL. This is a necessity in manipulating complex objects. We provide this facility in DEAL but its implementation over ORACLE caused us lots of problems since ORACLE does not support it.

Mr. P. Singleton (University of Keele).
PS. Do you store your complex objects as flat tables?

AH. Yes, complex objects would be broken down into a set of normalised (flat) relations, with some extra attributes in order to establish the hierarchy of the object. This is a consequence of implementing over ORACLE.

PS. What about the impedance mismatch ? (Refering to Prof. Deen's highlighting of impedance mismatch in the tutorial session).

*SMD.*Impedance mismatch would be there as much as it is in SQL. To match that we provide ability to define and manipulate complex objects. Which are absent in SQL.

PS. But PROLOG can represent lists and other constructs as they are.

*SMD.*Such impedance mismatch is the price we pay when try to implement a language like DEAL which supports complex objects on top of a traditional relational database like ORACLE. Ideally we would like to implement DEAL from scratch, but this is only a prototype just to try out our ideas.

Q. Is there any way you can negate the quantifier?

AH. There are three quantifiers ALL, FAIL and ONLY.

Q. But can you negate them ?

AH. Yes one can use the **not** construct to negate them.

Ms. R. Kerry (CCTA).
RK. Have you had any discussions with the company ORACLE or SQL standards body about adding functions to SQL?

AH. Well, not specifically, we talked to ORACLE about getting details about the ORACLE database. No we didn't speak to SQL standardisation body.

RK. Would you make your proposals available to the Standards body ?

AH. Yes we would.

Dr. R. Moore (Software Sciences Ltd.).
RM. Are there any facilities in DEAL to perform simple calculations?

AH. Yes, we allow external functions as a part of DEAL, so computations can be performed as external function and can be done in DEAL. Apart from that there are facilities in DEAL like DYN functions which can be used to perform simple computations. But for more complex computations the external functions is the way.

RM. The reason why I asked this question is, the unavailabilty of such facilities in SQL. If there is such a facility available in DEAL, not necessarily efficient, then I think it is a way forward.

AH. We do have facilities in DEAL. DYN functions for computations and control structures like

```
if .. then .. else
endif

and

while ..
endwhile
```

are available in DEAL. Apart from that we allow variables of several types in DYN functions (like scalars, relations etc). But the computations inside DEAL may not be as efficient as they are in external functions. These external functions are supposed to be written in high level languages like C or FORTRAN.

Mr. S. Kinoshita (ATR Interpreting Telephony Labs.).
SK. How do you manage the knowledge about database? I mean do you have complex things like virtual relations, user defined functions etc?

AH. At the moment we are implementing functions. The knowledge about the databases are kept as tables (including virtualrelations) but we keep them away from the database due to the problem of efficiency. But we would exploit the possibility of putting them in the database. Our main concern is the efficiency. We do quite a few things, like translation of DEAL queries into SQL. So if we put these informations in the database we may have to have access to the database to retrieve this information. That may be inefficient, that's why we keep them separate from the database.

RM. Do you have any indexing mechanisms in DEAL?

AH. No, not specific to DEAL. We use the existing indexing mechanisms in SQL (ORACLE), specially when we decompose the complex objects into flat tables, we exploit this in depth, by using clustering and indexing.

RM. How about integrity constraints?

AH. No, not at the moment. But we are looking at the possibilities of introducing integrity constraints, specially Prof. Deen is looking at implementation of Triggers and implementing some integrity constraints via this.

RM. Do you think that this is the way of introducing integrity constraints?

AH. Yes, this is a way for some complex constraints.

3 MPL/0: a Multi-paradigm Language Facility for Data/Knowledge Base Programming

Y. M. Shyy and S. Y. W. Su

ABSTRACT

This paper presents the preliminary design of a multi-paradigm language facility called MPL/0 which is designed for the next generation data/knowledge base programming in advanced application domains such as artificial intelligence, computer-aided design and manufacturing, office information systems, and software engineering. By integrating the concepts introduced in semantic data models, knowledge representations, object-oriented paradigms of programming language, object-oriented design methodology, and rule-based deduction into a single knowledge model, MPL/0 not only captures the structural and behavioral aspects of the application domain, but also enforces modern software development principles, such as reusability and modularity. To achieve powerful expressiveness of rules and associative access, the conventional predicate calculus is extended to include new concepts of O-term, context, and extended dot form which facilitate multi-valued parallel navigation, bi-directional navigation, and parallel selection. The computation model of MPL/0 is an integration of message passing, sequential and parallel computations, imperative and declarative programming styles, goal-directed method invocation and data-directed rule invocation.

1. INTRODUCTION

A database model is a formalism to model the real world. In general, the *semantics* of an application domain can be described by its (1) structural properties, (2) operational properties that consist of both specification and implementation of operations, and (3) knowledge rules that model constraints, deductive rules, and production rules to keep the system in a consistent state [SU86, SU89a]. While the conventional hierarchical, network, and relational models capture only the structural properties, operational properties and knowledge rules are implemented in application programs. The so-called *semantic data model* [HK87, PM88] captures both structural properties and the specification part of operational properties and leaves the rest of semantics properties to application programs. Besides, influenced by the need of managing large scaled knowledge bases, the capability of incorporating *knowledge rules* is becoming an important requirement for any modern database model [BBMR89, SU89b], in which more powerful expressiveness of the *behavioral* aspects can be achieved with the combination of operations and rules. We can see that the trend is to relieve the burden of writing application programs by incorporating more expressiveness in the data/knowledge model and the data/knowledge base programming language. We believe that the next generation *intelligent database systems* must have an integrated data/knowledge model which provides (1) a framework to integrate the key concepts of semantic data models, object-oriented paradigms of programming language [BZ87, DT88, GR83, MSO86, RS88, TD89, WP89, ZM86], knowledge representation [BL85], rule-based deduction [GMN78, GMN84, GN87, JP85, MJ88, NN80], and software development [BG86, BG87], and (2) a data/knowledge base programming language facility for the system designers, application programmers, and end-users to specify and manipulate such systems. In this paper, we present the preliminary design of a multi-paradigm language facility called MPL/0 along with its integrated data/knowledge model and control structure that are aimed at serving this purpose.

Specifically, the design of MPL/0 is guided by the following principles:

(1) Data and knowledge rules should be *tightly coupled*. This reflects the goal of MPL/0 and is achieved by taking an object-oriented approach where data and knowledge rules are treated in the same way as objects. In the rest of this paper, the term "knowledge" in "knowledge model" and "knowledge base" stands for both data and knowledge rules.

(2) The language should provide facilities for (a) the knowledge base designers to specify the structural and behavioral aspects of an application domain, (b) the application programmers to implement the system and to write application programs, and (c) the end-users to query the system.

(3) The semantics should be as rich as possible. By integrating rich semantics directly into the language, the users could have more expressive power while the burden of coding semantics into application programs can be relieved from the application programmers [SU89b].

(4) The knowledge model should be *extensible*. As the need of database for use in nontraditional application domains such as Computer Aided Design and Manufacturing, Office Information Systems, Artificial Intelligence, and Software Engineering is becoming the trend for the future database design, the user should be able to specify special-purpose operations, new data types, and even new type constructors, and to integrate them into an existing model easily [BLW88].

(5) The language should be *strongly-typed*, i.e., it should prevent an operation from being applied to a value of an inappropriate type. To achieve this goal, *early-binding* [TD89] is necessary to facilitate type checking and debugging.

(6) The language should be *multi-paradigm*. By integrating different paradigms into a single framework, the language can take advantage of all these paradigms and provides the users with more flexibility and expressive power.

(7) The language should enforce software development principles such as *modularity* and *reusability* to facilitate the modeling and implementation of large-scaled application systems. Besides, since each program is also treated as an object, data persistency and software evolution can be managed by the underlying knowledge base management system.

The rest of this paper is organized as follows: Section 2 gives an overview of the underlying knowledge model of MPL/0 in terms of set and associations. In Section 3, we introduce an extended predicate calculus which includes the concepts of O-term, context, and extended dot form. We use examples to illustrate the unique features of bi-directional navigation, parallel navigation, and parallel selection. In Section 4, we illustrate the multi-paradigm aspects of MPL/0 by describing its control structure. Finally, Section 5 presents the comparison with other related works, our conclusions and future research direction.

2. MPL/0 KNOWLEDGE MODEL

The OSAM* knowledge model [SU89a] is extended with generic units from Ada [BG86], typing from database programming language [AB87, BZ87, DT88], and behavioral associations. We strive to develop a uniform knowledge model [SH89] that provides an abstraction mechanism to organize objects and a conceptual basis for capturing structural and behavioral knowledge of any application domain. The basic knowledge model is shown in Figure 1.

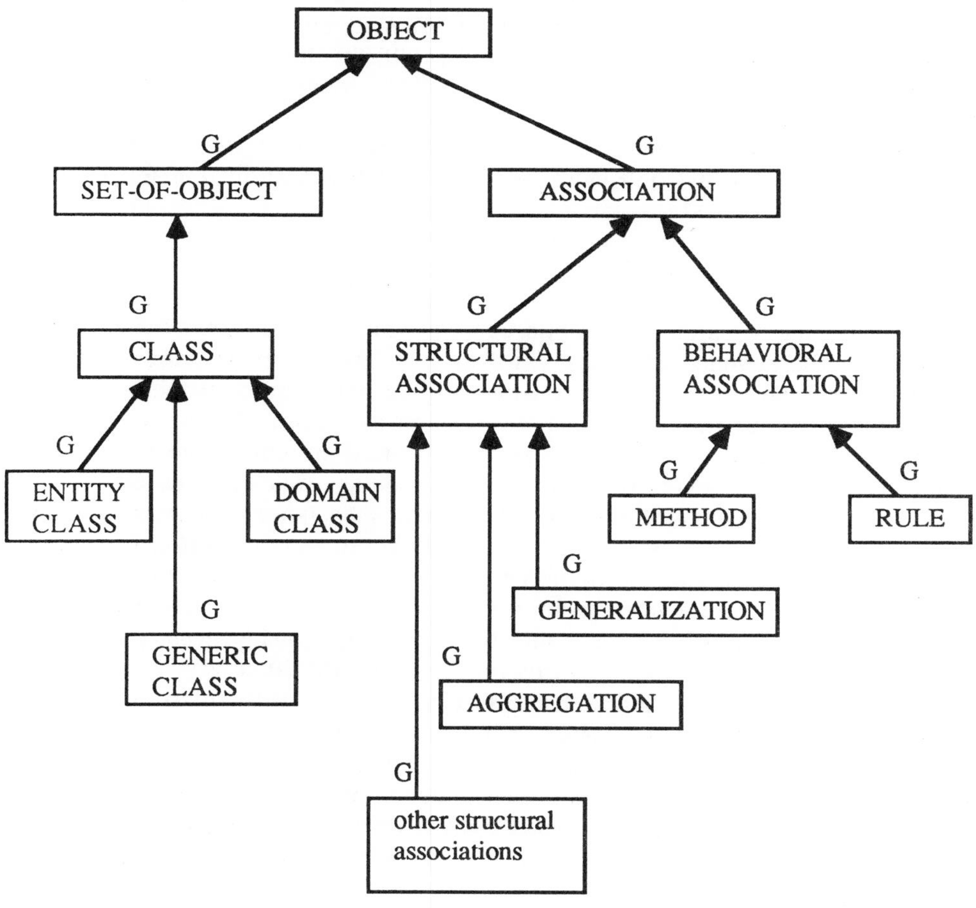

Figure 1. The Basic Reflective Knowledge Model of MPL/0

2.1 Basic Concept

Object, set, and association are the three basic components of MPL/0 knowledge model. Everything in the application domain can be thought of as an object. Structurally, each object is associated with a private *state* described by a set of *attributes*. The value of an attribute is itself an object, which is in turn described by its own attributes. All the object states consititute the system state. Behaviorally, each object state can only be changed through the application of *methods*, and the changes must comply with some *rules* which govern the system state *evolution*. Objects communicate with one another through *messages*. An object reacts to a message by executing a corresponding method or retrieving an attribute value, and returning an object in response.

The general grouping mechanism in MPL/0 is *multiset* (set whose elements do not have to be unique). In this paper, we use the conventional term "set" to stand for multiset. *Class* and *List* are two special types of set in MPL/0. Objects are categorized into classes according to their common structural and behavioral properties, and classes are related to one another through associations. Objects of the same class are called *instances* of this class. For any given class, the attributes, methods, and rules applicable to all its instances can be thought of as *associations* with those classes defined by the corresponding STRUCTURAL ASSOCIATION class instances, METHOD class instances, and RULE class instances, respectively. We will discuss different types of associations in detail in Section 2.3.

2.2 Class Classification and Type

There are three categories of classes in MPL/0: *Entity Class*, *Domain Class*, and *Generic Class*, which are represented as rectangular, circular, and triangular nodes in the graphic notation, respectively. Objects in the application domain that can be accessed independly are categorized as entity classes. The instances of an entity class X are either (1) explicitly created by the user with system-given object identifiers (OIDs), or (2) derived from another entity class by some association such as generalization association and crossproduct association that we will discuss in Section 2.3.1. We call instances in case (1) *local instances* of that class. A class is defined to be a *base class* if the user can populate new objects for this class by instantiation. A class is defined to be a *derived class* if the user should never try to populate a new object. In case (1), the user can explicitly declare an entity class instance to be *persistent* at its creation time. In MPL/0, a class is defined as a derived class by the crossproduct association and composition association implicitly, or by the keyword "**derived**" in the class definition explicitly for defining a *view* [PG86, ZW85] or a *selection* [CA89]. Every entity class object must be an instance of precisely one base class which is called the *type* of this object. In other words, an entity class object is of type X if and only if it is a member of the set of local instances of base class X. This corresponds to the concept of *type-as-a-set* [WP89].

A domain class is a class that specifies a finite or infinite domain of possible atomic or non-atomic objects that could be entered into the knowledge base as method parameters or the attribute values of other objects. The OID of a domain class object is its own value for an atomic object, or its attribute-value tuple for a non-atomic object. For example, [month 1 day 23 year 89] is an instance of a non-atomic domain class DATE; DIGIT = '(0 1 2 3 4 5 6 7 8 9) is a finite atomic domain class; and INTEGER is an infinite atomic domain class. A domain class instance is created and persistently stored in the database only if it serves as the attribute value of some persistent entity class instance. Every domain class X is defined with a membership predicate p such that p is true for all instances of X. A domain class object is of type X if it satisfies the membership predicate defined by class X. This corresponds to the concept of *type-as-a-predicate* [WP89]. The use of entity class and domain class provides a more clear and accurate semantics than the traditional non-primitive and primitive object classes.

A generic class in MPL/0 is similar to that in Ada [BG86] as a *template* or *parameteralized class* to construct actual classes by instantiating its *generic attributes*. Generic classes can be thought of as *data structure* class constructors for the users to build new classes out of existing ones. It is possible to build a library of generic classes as *reusable* data structure components, such as SET, LIST, STACK, QUEUE, TREE, ARRAY, and VECTOR [BG87]. Generic classes in MPL/0 serve as an extension to traditional object-oriented programming paradigms to achieve *type polymorphism* and *software reusability* to a greater extent.

2.3 Associations

Each association is a tuple R(a1 a2...an) defined over classes A1 to An (represented as R: A1xA2x...xAn), where each ai is an instance of set Ai. A1xA2x...xAk is called the *domain* and Ak+1xAk+2x...xAn is called the *range* of this association for some integer k such that 1<= k <= n. The set of all tuples is called the *extension* of this association. An association is called unary if n=1, binary if n=2, and n-ary if n>2, respectively. An association with domain A1xA2x...xAn-1 and range An is mono-valued if for any pair of tuples (x1 x2...xn-1) = (y1 y2...yn-1), we have xn = yn. Otherwise it is multi-valued. For any given class, all the common structural and behavioral properties among its instances can be thought of as *structural associations* and *behavioral associations* with other classes. Each type of association can be thought of as a set of rules that govern the knowledge base manipulation operations on the instances of those classes that are defined by the association. One interesting observation about the reflective property of MPL/0 is that each type of association itself is also an object class, and can be defined in the same way as any other class. Consequently, the user can define new types of associations in addition to the primitive associations described in Section 2.3.1 and 2.3.2. All the different types of associations are defined as classes in our class system. Therefore, they can serve as the types of the attributes defined in any user-defined classes.

2.3.1 Structural Associations

A structural association is a binary mono-valued or multi-valued association. To capture the structural properties, MPL/0 provides the following primitive associations:

(1) *Generalization (G) Association*: [G: {**superclass** | **subclass**} (<class>+)]. Class A is said to be a *superclass* of class B, or equivalently B is a *subclass* of A, if there is a generalization association from B to A so that all the instances of B are also instances of A. All the associations such as attributes, methods, and rules defined by class A are *inherited* by class B. *Multiple inheritance* is allowed in MPL/0 as each class could have more than one *immediate superclass*. The *name conflict* problem [ORION87] is handled by requiring the definer to resolve the conflict via renaming.

Note that (1) if we define B is a subclass of A, the system will automatically assert that A is a superclass of B, and vice versa. (2) Generic classes can be organized through the generalization association just like any other classs, and all the attributes, methods, and rules defined by a generic class and its superclasss are automatically possessed by the classs constructed from it. (3) For every entity class or domain class X, the system will implicitly construct from the generic class SET a domain class (setof X). This implies that the elements of a set in MPL/0 must be instances of the same entity class or domain class. The class (setof X) is a subclass of (setof Y) if and only if X is a subclass of Y. The user can also explicitly specify *cardinality* constraint with generic attributes "atleast" and "atmost".

(2) *Aggregation (A) Association*: [A: (<attribute-declaration>)+]. For each class X, we use the aggregation associations to define a set of common attributes shared by all its instances. Each attribute can be thought of as a binary mono-valued or multi-valued association. An attribute is assumed to be *changable* for every instance unless the user declares it to be *read_only*, i.e. once given a value, the value can not be changed. For each attribute definition, we have to give its range and other optional attributes such as default value, procedure attachment, and constraints. Note that all these attributes themselves are defined for the class AGGREGATION-ASSOCIATION as aggregation associations with other classes in a reflective manner. For a multi-valued attribute R: AxB of class A, the range is expressed as (setof B). For example, we can define attribute "enrolled" for class STUDENT with the constraint that each student must take at least one course but no more than six courses with [A: (**attribute** enrolled **range** (**setof** COURSE **atleast** 1 **atmost** 6))]. In the S-diagram, if no name is specified, the attribute is assumed to be of the same name as the range class with lower-case letters.

(3) *Crossproduct (X) Association*: [X: **group** <class> **by** (<attribute>+)]. Crossproduct association is used to define a derived entity class A by grouping the instances of an existing entity class B according to the given attribute(s). The cross product of these attributes serves as the composite identifier for the instances of A which are the resulting groups of instances of B. We can also use the normal aggregation association to define other attributes for the instances of A. For example, [**define entity-class** PART_CATEGORY **with** [X: **group** PART **by** (p# country)] [A: (**attribute** avg_cost **range** INTEGER)]] defines class PART_CATEGORY by grouping instances of class PART with attributes p# and country, which has attribute avg_cost for each resulting group. The crossproduct

association has shown to be very useful for statistical database [SU86]. As mentioned in Section 2.1, selection association and crossproduct association specify a derived class. Note that any subclass of a derived class must also be a derived class.

(4) *Interaction (I) Association*: [I: (<attribute-declaration>)+]. Interaction association is a special case of aggregation association, corresponding to the *part-of* relation in object-oriented language [TD89], and is used to form composite attributes. For example, [I: (**attribute** day **range** DAY) (**attribute** month **range** MONTH) (**attribute** year **range** YEAR)] specifies that the three attributes day, month, and year forms a composite identifier which can be thought of as an attribute whose range is the cross product of classes DAY, MONTH, and YEAR. Note that interaction association can be used to enforce the *referential constraint* [SU86, SU89a]. For example, if class WORK_FOR has [I: (**attribute** emp **range** EMPLOYEE) (**attribute** proj **range** PROJECT)], then when any particular employee or project is deleted from the database, all the instances of WORK_FOR that has an occurrence of that deleted employee or project as value of emp or proj will also be deleted. Besides, we can attach cardinality to specify 1:1, 1:N, N:1, and M:N constraints of an interaction association. For example, we can redefine WORK_FOR with [I: (**attribute** emp **range** EMPLOYEE) (**attribute** proj **range** PROJECT) **mapping** n:1] to specify the N:1 constraint that each project can have more than one employee working for it, and each employee can work for only one project.

(5) *Composition (C) Association*: [C: **instance** (<class>+)] or [C: **class** (<class>+)]. Composition association captures the concept of *metaclass* in [MBW80]. A metaclass is a class whose instances are classes with common *class-properties* which apply to each constituent class as a whole instead of each instance of this class. For example, we can define WORKING-GROUP as a metaclass by [**define entity-class** WORKING-GROUP **with** [C: **instance** (DOCTOR LAWER)] [A: (**attribute** avg_sal **range** INTEGER **derived-by** self.compute-avg-sal)]], which has two instances DOCTOR and LAWER, and attribute "average-age" that is associated with classes DOCTOR and LAWER instead of each individual doctor and lawer.

(6) *Derivation (D) Association*: [D: **from** <generic-class> **with** <generic-attribute>+]. Derivation association specifies the construction of a new class from a generic class by instaniating the generic attributes. For example, we can define STACK with [**define generic-class** STACK **with** [A: (**attribute** item **range** CLASS) (**attribute** lower_bound **range** INTEGER) (**attribute** upper_bound **range** INTEGER)]]. Then we can construct a new domain class STACK_OF_BOOKS by the instantiation [**define domain-class** STACK_OF_BOOKS [D: **from** STACK **with** item BOOK lowerbound 0 upperbound 20]].

For any application domain, the structural properties can be represented with a S-diagram in the same way as OSAM*[SU89a]. A simplified University scheme is shown in Figure 2.

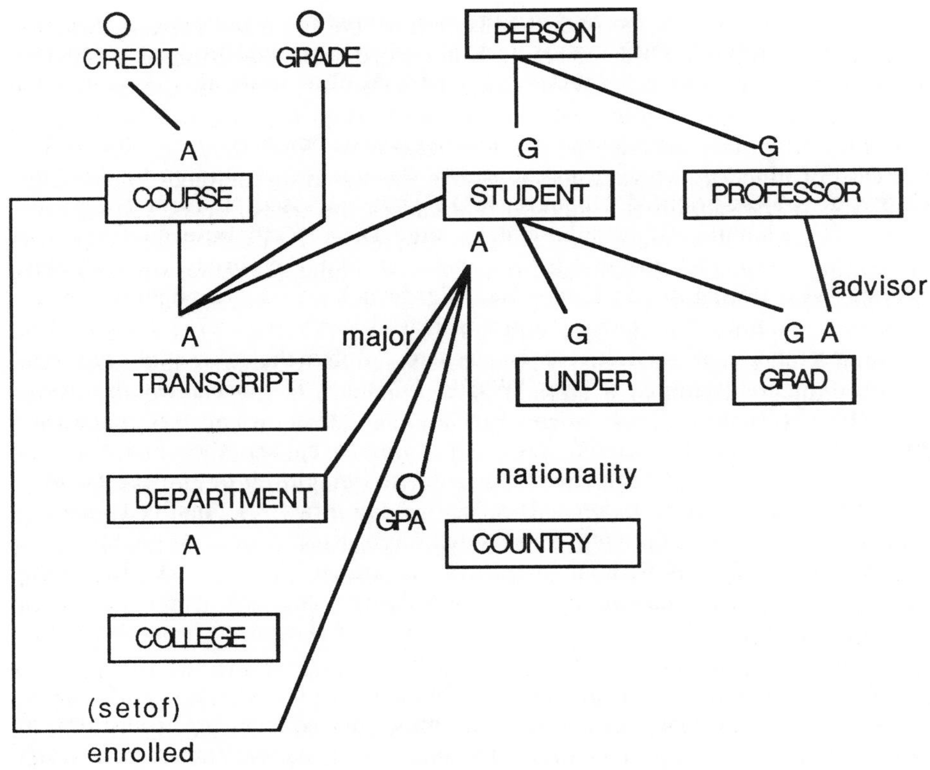

Figure 2. Structural Diagram for a Sample University Scheme

2.3.2 Behavioral Associations

The behavioral properties of an object is captured by the behavioral associations: method and rule. A method association is defined as a mono-valued N-ary association f: A1xA2x...xAn. Similar to Ada [BG86], a method expression can be one of the following: (1) *positional* notation of message passing <receiver>.(method <argument>+) or <receiver>.<method>, and (2) *named parameter* notation of message passing <receiver>.(<method> (<name> := <argument>)+). The receiver is an instance of domain A1, and each argument is an instance of the corresponding co-domain. For example, 3.(+ 2).(* 4) is equivalent to ((3 + 2) * 4), and 3.(+ 2.(* 4)) is equivalent to (3 + (2 * 4)) in conventional programming language.

There are two types of method in MPL/0: *function* and *transaction*. A function is a method which has no side-effect. In other words, the execution of a function is not allowed to change the current state of any entity class in the knowledge base. For example, no attribute value of an entity class instance can be updated, nor can an entity class instance be created or deleted. Note that a predicate is a special case of function, whose range is always the system-predefined domain class BOOLEAN. A transaction is a method that causes the transition of system state. A method is declared within a class definition by giving its method-type (function or transaction), name, co-domain and range. For example, [**function** square **return** INTEGER] and [**function** add **with** (adder : INTEGER) **return** INTEGER] declare two functions square and add for class INTEGER. For a transaction declaration, if no return class is specified, it is assumed to be system-defined class NIL. The implementation of a method is seperated from the class definition to achieve data abstraction. A sample program for the definition and implementation of class STUDENT is given in Figure 3 and Figure 4. The notations used will be explained in the following sections. The control structure for methods will be discussed in Section 4.1. Rules are *invariants* that govern the system state evolution. Each rule association R:A1xA2x...xAn is defined over a particular subset of the knowledge base by a context, i.e. the extension of this rule association, which is to be governed by this invariant. The rule expression will be described in detail in Section 4.2.

Finally, note that the MPL/0 knowledge model as shown in Figure 1. is *reflective* in the sense that it uses the same class and association notations to describe itself. For example, the class OBJECT which contains all the objects in the knowledge base is itself an entity class, and the class ENTITY-CLASS which has all the entity classes as its instances has a generalization (G) association with the class CLASS which has all the classes as its instances.

2.4 Type Concept

Objects and variables in MPL/0 are strongly-typed, i.e. we can determine the type of an object at compile time as described in Section 2.2, and each variable must be declared to have a type. MPL/0 is strongly-typed in the sense that the type compatability can be determined at compile time.

A class defines the type of an attribute value, a formal parameter of a method, or the return value of a method by specifying a class as the *range* of that attribute, parameter, or method. For each expression <receiver>.<attribute> or <receiver>.<method-expression>, we check at compile time whether the attribute/method is defined by the type of <receiver> and the type compatibility between the type of each argument and the type of each formal parameter. We say argument type X is compatible with formal parameter type Y in one of the two cases: (1) if Y is a base class, then X must be either Y or a subclass of Y, and (2) if Y is a derived class, X must be either Y, a subclass of Y, or a superclass of Y. In case (2), a run-time check is necessary when the argument is bound to see if the argument can be derived to be an instance of class Y.

```
[define entity-class STUDENT with
   [G: superclass (PERSON)]
   [A: [attribute major range DEPARTMENT read-only yes]
       [attribute nationality range COUNTRY default USA]
       [attribute enrolled range [setof COURSE atleast 1 atmost 6]]
       [attribute GPA range GPA derived-by self.compute-GPA]]
   [Method: [function straight-A-student range BOOLEAN]]]
```

Figure 3. Sample Class Definition for STUDENT

```
[implement STUDENT with
  [function straight-A-student
     [context self * TRANSCRIPT * (g : GRADE)]
     [if [forall g  g.(= 4.0)]
         then [return true] else [return false]]]

   [function compute-GPA
     [context self * TRANSCRIPT * AND
                  ((grade : GRADE),
                   COURSE * (credit : CREDIT))]
     [var (s1 : REAL) (s2 : REAL)]
     [parado [s1 := [all credit.(* grade)].sum]
             [s2 := [all credit].sum]]
     [return s1.(div s2)]]]
```

Figure 4. Sample Class Implementation for STUDENT

Also note that by using the class system, we can solve the untyped attribute problem as discussed in [ORION87]. For example, if the value of attribute vehicleID of class VEHICLE could be either an integer or a string, then we can declare a derived class VID with subclasses INTEGER and STRING, and declare the type of vehicleID to be VID. This corresponds to the *union-type* concept in programming language. To ensure strongly-typed, however, MPL/0 requires that to access such a variable, the user must use a case statement similar to CLU [CLU77] to exhaust all the possible base classes so that no type mismatch can occur at run time except applying a method which is defined by the derived class. For example, if variable x is declared as [var (x : X)] referring Figure 5 where class X is a derived class with three base classes A, B, and C as subclasses, then x.p is legal but x.q1 and x.a are not. Instead, a case statement [case x type [A : ...x.q1...] [B : ...x.q2...] [C :...x.q1...]] must be used.

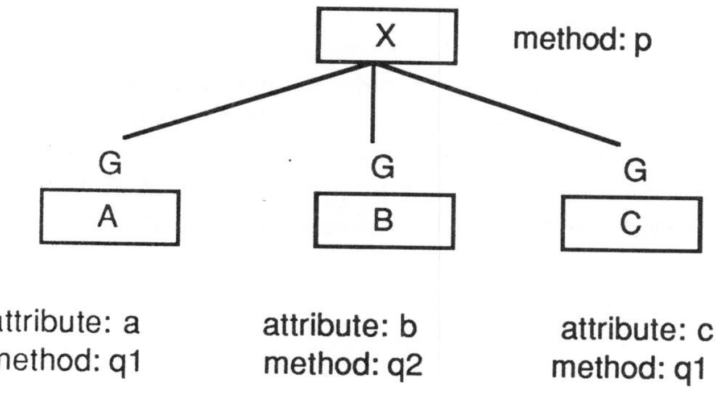

Figure 5. A Sample Union-type Class Structure

3. EXTENDED PREDICATE CALCULUS

In this Section, we present the ideas of an extended predicate calculus. The proposed O-term is an extension of traditional term, extended dot form is an extension of the traditional function composition, and context is an extension of the traditional relation composition.

3.1 O-term and Well-Formed Formulas

In MPL/0, the basic expression representing a value (which itself is an object) is called *O-term*. An O-term is defined as one of the following:

(1) *OID*: the system-given identifier for an entity class instance or the value of a domain class instance.

(2) *Type variable*: a variable standing for some instance of a given type. A type variable can be (i) the system defined variable "self" for each class definition as in SMALLTALK[GR83], or (ii) declared in the form (X : Y), where X is the variable and Y is a class name. A type variable could be either *bound* to some object or *unbound*.

(3) *Navigation expression*: a navigation expression corresponds to a function composition in traditional predicate calculus, which returns an object. As the conventional dot form [BZ87,KC86] can not handle multi-valued attribute properly and can be only in one direction, we propose the extended dot form with the capabilities of *bi-directional navigation*, *parallel navigation*, and *parallel selection*. A detailed description will be given in Section 3.2.

(4) *Context variable*: the variable standing for some object of some type in a specified context. A context expression is similar to the extended dot form except that only structural associations can be composed to form the navigation. For each

context expression, the user can declare a context variable for each class along the association links. For example, (g : GRADE) in the context self * TRANSCRIPT * (g : GRADE) as shown in Figure 4 declares a context variable g which will be bound to some object of class GRADE that satisfies the context expression. The conceptual difference between a navigation expression and a context is similar to the difference between a function and a relation in predicate calculus. In other words, the former only retrieves the final value of navigation while the latter keeps the whole subdatabase along the navigation path.

Based on O-term, we can define *well-formed formula* (wff) as one of the following:
(1) *atomic formula* : a predicate call or a context expression that returns true or false. Predicates are called in the same message passing notation as method. For example, 2.(> 3) returns false and 2.(< 3) returns true. Note that t1.(= t2) returns true only if t1 and t2 refer to the same object. A context expression is regarded as true if its extension is not empty.
(2) *logical formula* : if P1 to Pn are all wffs, then [**not** p1], [**and** P1...Pn], [**or** P1...Pn], [P1 ==> P2], and [P1 <== P2] are logical formula where '==>' stands for 'implies'.
(3) *quantified formula* : if P is a wff, then [**forall** {<context-variable> | (<type-variable> in <set>)}+ P] and [**exist** {<context-variable> | (<type-variable> in <set>)}+ P] are quantified formulas. For example, [forall g g.(= 4.0)] as shown in Figure 4 is a quantified formula which states that every binding for context variable g makes g equals to 4.0.

3.2 Extended Dot Form

In general, a MPL/0 navigation is an O-term recursively defined in one of the forms: <receiver><op><attribute>,<receiver><op><function-expression>,and <receiver>[<selection>]. Note that <receiver> itself is an O-term, <selection> is a well-formed formula as selection criterion, and <function-expression> could be <function>, (<function> <argument>+), or (<function> (<name> := <argument>)+) as described in Section 2.3.2, where each <argument> is itself an O-term. Note that a transaction is not allowed in a navigation expression because it will change the system state and effect other O-term unexpectedly. The dot operator <op> could be '.' (do), '||' (parado), and '!' (non-association). In the following we will illustrate the unique features of extended dot form by giving some examples drawn from the University domain shown in Figure 2.

Example 1. *Bi-directional Parallel Navigation*: Find the maximal average student GPA of all the departments of college c. Assume c is a variable bound to a college object.
Sol: the extended dot form c . (college DEPARTMENT) || (major STUDENT) || GPA || avg . max stands for the desired result in a straight forward manner. The navigation is shown in Figure 6. Note that (1) the do operator '.' applies the following attribute or method directly to the receiver, (2) the receiver of a parado operator || must be of type (setof X), where X itself could be (setof Y)

recursively to form a nested set of any depth, (3) the parado operator '||' has the property that it can *penetrate* the nested set boundaries until it finds the proper type of objects to which it could apply the attribute or function, and (4) while the user does not have to specify the range class normally, he/she can also achieve navigation in the reverse direction by specifying the attribute and the domain class in a pair. For example, as there is no association defined from DEPARTMENT to STUDENT, we can use (major STUDENT) to tell the system reverse the navigation direction. Conceptually, d1.(major STUDENT) = {x | x is a student and x.major = d1}.

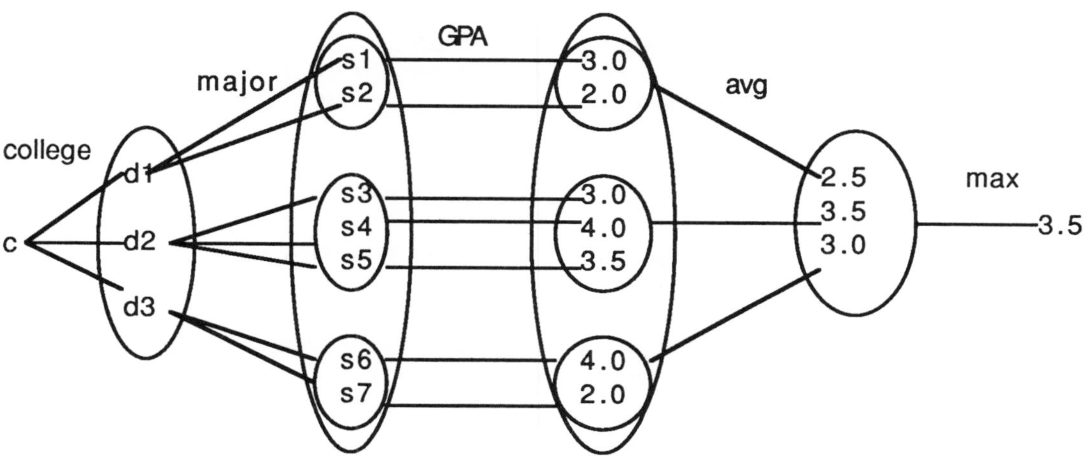

Figure 6. A Sample Knowledge Base Navigation

Example 2. *Parallel Selection*: Find the average age of all the female students majoring in CS department.
Sol: the expression DEPARTMENT [**self**.name = "CS"] || (major STUDENT) [**self**.sex = "female")] || age . avg stands for the desired result. The first selection selects the department whose name is "CS", for each such department, the inverse association and the second selection find the female students major in this department.

Example 3. *the use of "non-association" operator*. Find the professors that are not serving as advisor of some graduate students.
Sol: the expression PROFESSOR ! (advisor GRAD) retrieves the desired answer. Note that the "!" operator is implicitly a parallel selection operator that selects from a set those objects which do not have a specified association. Conceptually, this example is equavelent to PROFESSOR -(GRAD || advisor).

4. CONTROL STRUCTURE

As we mentioned before, the behavioral aspects of the application domain are captured by methods and rules. The overall control structure of MPL/0 can thus be divided into two parts: *goal-directed* computation for methods and *data-directed* computation for rules.

4.1 Goal-directed Computation

In MPL/0, a method could be a function or a transaction. The execution of a method is goal-directed in the sense that we first set a highest level method call as the *goal*, which will in turn invoke other methods as the *subgoals*. The goal is achieved only when all the subgoals are achieved.

4.1.1 Basic Structure

A MPL/0 program for a method consists of a sequence of *statements*. Each statement is placed in a block [...]. A statement could be (1) variable declaration: [**var** <type-variable declaration>+], (2) an assignment statement [<variable> := <value>] or [<variable>.<attribute> := <value>], (3) a return statement [**return** <value>] where <value> is an O-term, (4) a transaction call [<O-term>.<method-expression>], (5) an I/O function call. MPL/0 currently supports only the function "print" in the form [<O-term>**.print**] or (6) a compound statement constructed by one of the following statement constructors:
(1) *Table lookup*: similar to the STORED function in [IRIS87], we can define a function by giving its extension in a [**table** <value tuple>+] block. The table lookup constructor is useful for fast prototyping when the detailed implementation of a function is not known yet. The user can use this constructor to model such a function as a blackbox by giving its input(s) and output and use these information to test the functionality of the whole system.
(2) *Context retrieve*: as stated in Section 3.1, a context declares a set of context variables over a subdatabase, and the statement [**context** <context>] retrieve the subdatabase from which context variables can draw their value. The statement [**all** <context-variable>] returns the set of all possible values that the context variable could take. We also define a *tuple* of a context to be a set of bindings of context variables that satisfy the context pattern. The statement [**all** <statement>] is an implicit for loop where the <statement> will be executed for each tuple of the context, and all the return values for each tuple will be returned as a set. For example, each tuple generated from the context retrieve statement shown in the implementation of compute-GPA of Figure 4 will be a set of values for the variables (self grade credit) such as (s1 4.0 3) and (s1 3.5 3). The statement [all credit.(* grade)] will calculate the product of credit value and grade value for each tuple and group all the results as a set, e.g., {4.0*3 3.5*3} = {12 10.5}. The statement [all credit.(* grade)].sum will thus sum up all the values in this set, e.g. 12+10.5 = 22.5. The reader can verify the whole function similarily.

(3) *Block*: [**do** <statement>+] or [**parado** <statement>+]. The "do" specifies a sequential execution of following statements while [parado...] specifies a parallel processing.
(4) *Conditional selection*: [**if** <test> **then** <statement> {**else-if** <test> **then** <statement>}* {} | {**else** <statement>}] where <test> is a wff.
(5) *Conditional Repetition*: [**while** <test> **do** <statement>] where the test condition is a wff. It is easy to see that the for-loop described as "for(<variable-initialization>;<terminate-condition>;<variable-update>)<statement>" in C can be expressed with this "while-do" statement. Consequently, We do not include "for-loop" for the sake of simplicity and making the language more close to natural language.
(6) *For loop over a set*: [**for** <variable> **in** <set> **do** <statement>]. The for loop will automatically apply the statement to all the members of the set in sequence. For example, [**for** x **in** e1.dept.employees **do** [x.name.print]] will print all the names of employees working in the same department as e1. We can also use [parafor...] block to explicitly express parallel processing.
(7) *Case statement*: [**case** <derived-class-variable> **type** (<class> <statement>)+ {} | (**else** <statement>)].

4.1.2 Transaction

A transaction is a method that can change the system state and/or call other transactions while a function can't. Every transaction is *atomic* in the sense that the execution is committed only if the change in the system state does not violate any constraint associated with those instances whose states are modified by this transaction execution.

MPL/0 provides the following facilities for basic object manipulation:
(1) *Create an instance of class X*: this operation can be thought of sending a create instance message to class object X, which will return an OID. In MPL/0, we can express it in the block [<create>] or [<var> := <create>] where <create> is of the form [**create** <class> **with** <attribute-value>+]. After the execution, <var> will be bound to the OID of this object. For example, [p1 := [**create** PERSON **with** name "Smith John" age 24]] creates a PERSON object p1.
(2) *Delete an object*: To delete an attribute value, we just set it to NIL. To delete an instance of some class, we use the block [**delete** <var>] where <var> is the variable bound to the OID of this object.
(3) *Define a class*: [**define** {{**derived**} **entity-class** | **domain-class** | **generic-class**} <class-name> **with** <association-declaration>+].
(4) *Implement a class*: [**implement** <class> **with** <method-code>+]. This is the implementation part of a class. Note that in addition to the public methods declared in class definition, those functions that are used to derive attribute values are implemented as private methods. We can also take a *functional* approach by decomposing the public methods with smaller private methods. A private method is hidden from the outside world which can only send a message to invoke a public method. Referring Figure 3 and Figure 4, for example, the function "straight-A-student" is a public method and the function "compute-GPA" is a private method used only by the system to derive the attribute GPA.

4.2 Data-directed Computation

The invocation of MPL/0 rules is data-directed in the sense that the rule plays a passive role listening to the data and getting triggered when the "cause" is satisfied or the constraint is violated by the data in the application domain. In general, there are two types of rules, i.e. *static invariant* and *differential invariant*: (1) a static invariant **[create rule** {{} | <name>} **with context** <context> **behavior [maintain** <wff>]] defines a constraint that the subdatabase specified as the context of this rule must always maintain. In other words, for any tuple of this context, the <wff> must always be true. For example, we can specify a rule that in any department, the salary of an employee can not be greater than that of his department manager as shown in Figure 7, and (2) a differential invariant **[create rule** {{} | <name>} **with context** <context> **behavior [if** <wff> **then** <statement>]] defines a rule over a context in the sense that for any tuple of this context, if <wff> is true, then the <statement> must be executed to keep the system in a consistent state. See [AS90] for more examples.

Note that (1) deduction rules are not explicitly declared as rules because they have been captured as either predicates, part of the derived class definition, or derived attribute definition, (2) each rule is associated with a context so that the rule checking task can be reduced to only the specified context instead of the whole knowledge base. Only changes in the specified subdatabase will cause the rule to be checked, (3) rules are stored as part of a class definition and managed by the inheritance mechanism of MPL/0. For a rule defined over a context of a single class, it is included as part of the class definition. For a rule defined over a context of several classes, the system creates a class as the superclass of these classes, and includes the rule as part of the class definition, and (4) we can capture the concept of *exceptions* in form of rules. For example, if we have constraint P and exception handler E, then we can write it as the rule **[create rule with context** <context> **if** [not P] **then** E]. Besides, while those globally defined exceptions and exception handlers can be defined as rules of class OBJECT, we can also define local exceptions and exception handlers, or even define a local handler for a global exception.

5. CONCLUSION

The design of MPL/0 has been influenced by different areas of research. We borrow the ideas of (1) data types and generic units from programming language, especially Ada, (2) encapsulation, inheritance, and message passing from object-oriented programming language and semantic data models, and (3) predicate calculus, frame, and rule-based system from knowledge representation. We integrate all the above concepts in a uniform object-oriented framework.

The research works most related to the design of MPL/0 is LAURE [CA89], which is also a multi-paradigm language based on a reflective model of set and relation. The current syntax of MPL/0 is also based on a similar natural-language-like notation as LAURE. The major difference between LAURE and MPL/0 is that the former is based on an algebraic knowledge model, while the latter is developed in the framework of OSAM* [SU89a]. Based on OSAM* and its query language OQL[ASL89], we extend its knowledge model to incorporate behavioral associations, generic classes, and typing. We propose the extended dot form notation for declarative, parallel, and set-oriented data access. It also has the capability to express bi-directional navigation and selection. The expressive power of predicate calculus is greatly enhanced when function is extended with extended dot form, and relation is extended with context. We also provide traditional control structure of programming language such as for loop and if-then-else. Combined with the extended predicate calculus, the control structure processes the flexibility of allowing both declarative and imperative programming styles.

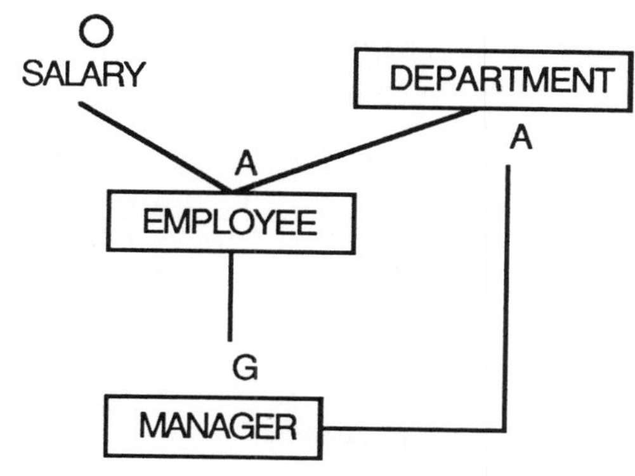


```
[create rule with
   context EMPLOYEE * ((s1:SALARY) AND
                              DEPARTMENT * MANAGER * (s2:SALARY))
    behavior [maintain s1.(<= s2)]
]
```

Figure 7. A Sample Rule Definition over a Company Domain

The rule expression is based on [AS90]. As each rules is declared separately outside class definition to facilitate incremental knowledge acquisition, the system automatically associate each rule to a proper class so that data and knowledge are managed in the same framework. High reusability and modularity of methods and rules can be achieved through the inheritance mechanism. Both goal-directed invocation of methods and data-directed rule invocation are supported.

The other related works are TAXIS [MBW80], DEPLEX [SD81], IRIS [IRIS87], and GALILEO [ACO85]. TAXIS is one of the earliest database programming languages, and it is notable for introducing semantic network to build ISA hierarchies of data, transaction, and exception. DAPLEX and IRIS are both based on functional data model, where both structural and behavioral properties are represented as functions. GALILEO is a strongly-typed database programming language. MPL/0 is different from these languages in its association-based knowledge model, explicit notation of parallism, and multi-paradigm programming styles. Besides, contrary to most other database models and database programming languages, MPL/0 directly supports *data structure* aspects through generic classes.

In the future, we have the following research directions:

(1) a formal specification of the syntax and semantics of MPL/0 is needed. As this paper provides the basic ideas of the preliminary design of MPL/0, a formal study from the programming language point of view is needed.

(2) we are going to incorporate *temporal predicates* into MPL/0 to model the time and history aspects of an application domain. For example, instead of being activated all the time as in MPL/0, a rule can be activated only by some special event for some specified period of time. We would like to improve the data model of MPL/0 to incorporate this aspect of time.

(3) in addition to the name conflict resolution mechanism in traditional object-oriented database, a *rule conflict* resolution mechanism is also needed for the underlying knowledge base management system supporting MPL/0.

(4) in order to support parallel computation and data-directed rule invocation efficiently, a computation model is needed. Currently, we intend to use IC* rule-based parallel computation model [CV88] as the low level computation model, and the IC* language as the target language at the assembly language level. In other words, all the associations (structural properties, methods, and rules) will be translated into rules and be executed with the IC* computation model. Hopefully with the development of IC* machine hardware, we can achieve high efficiency by executing MPL/0 directly on top of the IC* machine.

ACKNOWLEDGEMENT

This research is supported by NSF grants number DMC-8814989 and DDM-8814989, and Florida High Technology and Industry Council grant number UPN 88040802.

REFERENCES

[AB87] Atkinson, M.P., Buneman, P.O., "Types and Persistance in Database Programming Languages", *ACM Computing Survey*, July 1987.

[ACO85] Albano, A., Cardelli, L., Orsini, R., "Galileo: A Strongly-typed, Interactive Conceptual Language", *ACM Transaction on Database Systems*, Vol.10, No.2, June 1985.

[AH187] Abiteboul, S., Hull, R., "IFO: A Formal Semantic Database Model", *ACM Transaction on Database Systems*, Vol.12, No.4, December, 1987.

[AN86] Ait-Kaci, H., Nasr, R., "LOGIN: A Logic Programming Language with Built-in Inheritance", *The Journal of Logic Programming*, 3(3), October 1986.

[ASL89] Alashqur, A., Su, S., Lam, H., "OQL--A Query Language for Manipulating Object-oriented Databases", *Proceedings of VLDB89*, August, 1989.

[AS90] Alashqur, A., Su, S.Y.W. "Deductive Object-Oriented Databases", to appear in *Proc. 1990 COMPDEC Conference*, Los Angeles, 1990.

[BBMR89] Borgida, A., Brachman, R., McGuinness, D., Resnick, L., "CLASSIC: A Structural Data Model for Objects", *Proc. 1989 ACM SIGMOD International Conference on Management of Data*, May, 1989.

[BG86] Booch, G., *Software Engineering with Ada*, Benjamin/Cummings, 1986.

[BG87] Booch, G., *Software Components with Ada*, Benjamin/Cummings, 1987.

[BL85] Brachman, R.J., Levesque, H.J., *Readings in Knowledge Representation*, Morgan Kaufmann Publishers, Inc., 1985.

[BLW88] Batory, D.S., Leung, T.Y., Wise, T.E., "Implementation Concepts for an Extensible Data Model and Data Language", *ACM Transaction on Database Systems*, 13(3), September 1988.

[BZ87] Bloom, T., Zdonik, S.B., "Issues in the Design of Object-oriented database Programming Languages", *OOPSLA '87 Proceedings*, October 1987.

[CA89] Caseau, Y., "A Model for a Reflective Object-Oriented Language", *SIGPLAN Notice, Special Issue on Concurrent Object-Oriented Programming*, March 1989.

[CP76] Chen, P.P., "The entity-relationship model-Toward a unified view of data", *ACM Transaction on database Systems*, March 1976.

[CLU77] Liskov, B., Snyder, A., Atkinson, R., Schaffert, C., "Abstraction Mechanisms in CLU", *CACM*, 20(8), August 1977.

[CV88] Cameron, E.J., Cohen, D.M., Gopinath, B., Keese, W.M., Ness, L., Uppaluru, P.V., and Vollaro, J.R., "The IC* Model of Parallel Computation and Programming Environment", *IEEE Transaction on Software Engineering*, March 1988, Vol 14, No 3.

[DK79] Deliyanni, G., Kowalski, R.A., "Logic and Semantic Networks", *CACA*, 22(3), 1979.

[DT88] Danforth, D., Tomlinson, C., "Type Theories and Object-Oriented Programming", *ACM Computing Survey*, March 1988.

[GMN78] Gallaire, H., Minker, J., Nicolas, J.M., "An Overview and Introduction to Logic and Data Bases", in: Gallaire, H., and Minker, J.,(eds.) *Logic and Data Bases*, Plenum 1978.

[GMN84] Gallaire, H., Minker, J., Nicolas, J. M., "Logic and Databases: A Deductive Approach", *ACM Computing Surveys*, June 1984.

[GN87] Genesereth, M.R., Nilsson, N.J., *Logical Foundations of Artificial Intelligence*, Morgan Kaufmann, 1987.

[GR83] Goldberg, A., Robson, D., *SMALLTALK-80 The Language and its Implementation*, 1983.

[HK87] Hull, R., King, R., "Semantic Database Modeling: Survey, Application, and Research Issues", *ACM Computing Survey*, 19(3), September 1987.

[HM81] Hammer, M., McLeod, D., "Database Description with SDM: A Semantic Database Model", *ACM Transaction on Database Systems*, 6(3), September 1981.

[HO87] Halbert, D.C., O'Brien, P.D., "Using Types and Inheritance in Object-Oriented Programming", *IEEE Software*, September 1987.

[HP79] Hayes, P., "The Logic of Frames", appeared in *Frame Conceptions and Text Understanding*, 46-61, edited by D. Metzing, 1979.

[IRIS87] Fishman, D., etc., "IRIS: An Object-Oriented Database Management Systems", *ACM Transaction on Office Information Systems*, Vol. 5, No.1, January 1987.

[JP85] Jackson, P., *Introduction to Expert Systems*, Addison-Wesley, 1985.

[KBG89] Kim, W., Bertino, E., Garza, J.F., "Composite Objects Revisted", *Proc. 1989 ACM SIGMOD International Conference on Management of Data*, May, 1989.

[KC86] Khoshafian, S.N., Copeland G.P., "Object Identity", *OOPSLA '86 Proceedings*, September 1986.

[KG87] Kaiser, G., Garlan, D., "Melding Software Systems from Reusable Building Blocks", *IEEE Software*, July 1987.

[MBW80] Mylopoulos,J., Bernstein, P.A., Wong, H.K.T., "A Language Facility for Designing Database-Intensive Applications", *ACM Transaction on Database Systems*, Vol.5, No.2, June 1980.

[MJ88] Minker, J., "Perspectives in Deductive Database", *The Journal of Logic Programming*, March 1988.

[MSO86] Maier, D., Stein, J., Otis, A., Purdy, A., "Development of an Object-Oriented DBMS", *OOPSLA '86 Proceedings*, September 1986.

[NN80] Nilsson, N.J., *Principles of Artificial Intelligence*, Morgan Kaufmann, 1980.

[OBB89] Ohori, A., Buneman, P., Breazu-Tannen, V., "Database Programming in Machiavelli - A Polymorphic Language with Static Type Inference", *Proc. 1989 ACM SIGMOD International Conference on Management of Data*, May, 1989.

[ORION87] Banerjee, J. etc., "Data Model Issues for Object-Oriented Applications", *ACM Transaction on Office Information Systems*, Vol. 5, No.1, January, 1987.

[PG86] Pascoe, G.A., "Elements of Object-Oriented Programming", *BYTE*, August 1986.

[PM88] Peckham, J., Maryanski, F., "Semantic Data Models", *ACM Computing Survey*, 20(3), September 1988.

[RS88] Ramamoorthy, C.V., Sheu, P.C., "Object-Oriented Systems", *IEEE Expert*, fall 1988.

[SD81] Shipman, D.W., The Functional data Model and the Data Language DAPLEX", *ACM Transaction on Database Systems*, 6(3), September 1981.

[SH89] Shyy, Y.M., "KM*: A Knowledge Model Based on Set, Association, and Extended Predicate Calculus", extended abstract in *Proc. The Second Florida Conference on Productivity through Computer Integrated Engineering and Manufacturing*, November, 1989.

[SU86] Su, S.Y.W., "SAM*: A Semantic Association Model for Corporate and Scientific-Statistical Databases", *Journal of Information Sciences*, 29, 1983, pp. 151-199.

[SU89a] Su, S.Y.W., Krishnamurthy, V., Lam. H., "An Object-Oriented Semantic Association Model OSAM*", in *Artificial Intelligence Manufacturing Theory and Practice*, S. Kumara et. al. (eds.), American Inst. of Indus. Engr., 1989, Chap. 17, pp. 463-494.

[SU89b] Su, S.Y.W., "Extensions to the Object-Oriented Paradigm", *Proc. 13th International Computer Software & Applications Conference (COMPSAC)*, October, 1989.

[TD89] Thomas, D., "What's in an Object", *BYTE*, March, 1989.

[WP89] Wegner, P., "Learning the Language", *BYTE*, March 1989.

[ZM86] Zaniolo, C., Ait-Kaci, H., Beech, D., Cammarata, S., Kerschberg L., Maier, D., "Object-oriented Database Systems and Knowledge Systems", in: Kerschberg, L.(ed.) *Proceedings of the first International Workshop on Expert Database Systems*, 1986.

4 Knowledge-directed Mediation between Application Objects and Base Data

T. Barsalou and G. Wiederhold

Abstract

Integration of database and artificial-intelligence methods is critical for the next generation of information systems. In this paper, we offer a conceptual framework for such systems. We envision a partitioned architecture where multiple applications residing on distributed workstations exploit multiple remote data resources. Central to the model is an intermediate layer of mediators that perform the knowledge-based task of transforming data into information needed by the workstation applications. To illustrate this notion, we introduce a specific mediator, implemented in the PENGUIN system, that defines an object-based layer on top of relational database systems.

1. Introduction

It is clear that most future information systems will require both the problem-solving capabilities of expert systems and the data-handling capabilities of database management systems. Indeed, combining database and expert-system techniques is a growing research area. There is great potential in bringing together the two domains, as knowledge-based systems try to move toward solving real-world problems and database systems try to manipulate and exploit more effectively the huge volumes of data at hand. The intent of this paper is twofold. First, we propose a three-layer model for future information systems that takes advantage of both technologies and in which components are distributed over high-speed networks and work cooperatively. We assign a crucial role in those systems to modules that mediate between data resources and decision-making processes. Second, we demonstrate the validity of the concept by presenting an instance of such modules—an object-based layer on top of a relational database system capable of selecting and aggregating relational tuples into object instances.

In Section 2, we elaborate on the concepts of data, knowledge, and information, and we describe a model for future information systems that uses those definitions. In Section 3, we introduce mediators, a critical component of the model. In Section 4, we discuss the design and implementation of a prototype mediator that generates complex objects from database relations. In Section 5, we demonstrate the functionalities of that mediator in the context of a biomedical application. We conclude in Section 6 with a discussion of the strengths and weaknesses of our approach.

2. A Model of Information Systems

Before we discuss the structure of information systems, it is useful to state explicitly the distinctions that we make among the notions of *data*, *knowledge*, and *information*, and to describe how those notions fit into a consistent model of information systems.

2.1 Data, knowledge, and information

Wiederhold, in [13], gives an informal litmus test to distinguish data from knowledge; if a clerk can handle (for instance, can acquire or update) some item, then that item probably consists of data; on the other hand, if an expert is required to handle the item, then the item is probably knowledge. More formally, we use the term *data* to refer to raw facts—facts that are usually objective and verifiable, and that can be acquired automatically. We therefore do not attach any *meaning* or *interpretation* to data. In contrast, *knowledge* comes from experts. It is typically acquired through the lengthy processes of education and experience, and includes abstractions, generalizations, theories, models, and strategies to use all of these concepts (metaknowledge). Knowledge is often not verifiable (in the way that data is), and is associated with uncertainty and subjective beliefs. These conceptual differences between data and knowledge are reflected in the computational contrast that exists between databases and knowledge bases. Databases take an extensional view of the world—a class is defined by the enumeration of its members; in contrast, knowledge bases take an intensional view—membership in a class is determined by rules and criteria.

Admittedly, this distinction between knowledge and data is somewhat arbitrary and certainly is not clear cut. Facts that are considered data by some application may be seen as knowledge by another application that deals at a different level of abstraction. The distinction is therefore, to some extent, context-dependent. It provides us, however, with a useful framework in which to classify information systems.

Information theory allows us to investigate the average information content of a message. Although it has been developed as a mathematical language for communications engineering, information theory can be applied to a variety of domains. Shannon defined *information* as facts that convey material previously unknown to the receiver [10]; information is thus measured by the extent of "surprise" it causes to its recipient. In all professional environments, information is required for making appropriate decisions and for subsequently following a specific course of action. As Drucker observed recently [6], "information is data endowed with relevance and purpose." The generation of information then lies at the confluence of knowledge and data. Combining knowledge and data produces information on which the decision maker will act. In turn, actions (such as conducting a scientific experiment) probably will yield new data, the analysis and generalization of which can lead to new insights and additional knowledge. We therefore have a closed-loop model for information systems where data, knowledge, and information each have a distinct role, as summarized in Figure 1.

2.2 Toward future information systems

Information systems that are now available are beginning to reach the capabilities envisioned by Vannevar Bush in 1945 [5]. Let us look more closely at two important classes of such systems—database management systems (DBMSs) and expert systems (ESs). Those two classes share a common goal (generating useful information for action), but accomplish their tasks separately, using different principles; that is, they combine data and knowledge in different ways to produce information. Database systems use mostly *external* knowledge (knowledge

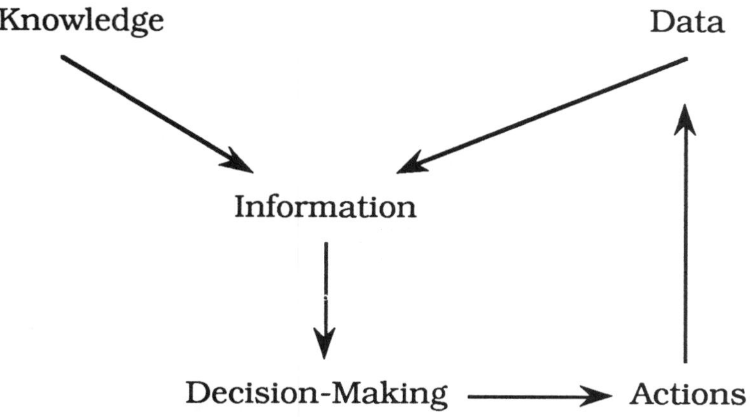

Figure 1: The combination of data and knowledge generates information that leads to actions. Feedback takes place when an action yields new data, from which additional knowledge can be extracted.

not explicitly stored in and directly exploitable by the DBMS) provided by application programs and end users to manipulate data stored in databases and to generate information. In contrast, most knowledge-based systems treat data no differently from knowledge, thus ignoring issues of storing and managing large volumes of facts, and offer no general-purpose ways of tapping into external databases, thus requiring manual data input.

A logical direction of research emerges from this analysis. We can combine database and artificial-intelligence techniques into new information systems where both data and knowledge are encoded in computer-readable form and are used to create information. We must be very careful, however, in intermingling database and knowledge-base concepts, to avoid creating a combination that reflects the weaknesses, rather than the strengths, of both fields.

We see these future systems supporting decision makers through a two-phase process:

1. Location and selection of relevant factual data, followed by aggregation according to the decision alternatives

2. Processing and reduction of the data, so that the number of alternatives to be chosen from is small, and the parameters for each choice are aggregated at a high conceptual level

Today, most of these support tasks are carried out by human experts who mediate between the data sources and the decision makers. For many tasks in medicine, warfare, emergency relief, and other areas requiring rapid actions, dependence on human intermediaries introduces an intolerable delay. Future information systems will increasingly take over these support processes.

In summary, information is created at the confluence of knowledge and data. Note, however, that communication is indispensable to achieving this confluence, as data and knowledge reside on large numbers of heterogeneous, distributed resources. Such communication may occur not only over space but also over time. Therefore, the information systems that we consider must support *both* communication and combination of data and knowledge.

It is clear that no single system can or will accomodate the great variety of tasks that is required to support today's complex decision making. Instead, the current trend toward distributed computing will lead to a modular architecture, where multiple heterogeneous components cooperate through standardized interfaces. We now characterize the components of such partitioned information systems.

2.3 Conceptual components

There are two dimensions to the partitioning of the information systems we foresee [18]. Horizontal partitioning divides the architecture into three main layers—an application layer, an interface layer, and a data-server layer. Obviously, these layers cannot be monolithic entities, and each will be further partitioned vertically. The data-server layer may contain multiple autonomous databases managed by distinct DBMSs; similarly, multiple applications will exist, sharing and accessing the underlying databases through a variety of interfaces.

Data resources

There is a wide variety of data resources. We might classify them by a measure of closeness to the source. Raw data obtained from sensors, such as purchase records obtained by point-of-sale scanners, or, on a different scale, images recorded by earth satellites, are at the factual extreme. Census and stock reports contain data that have been somewhat processed, but are still considered as facts by most users.

At the other extreme are textual representations of knowledge. Books, research reports, and library material, in general, contain knowledge, contributed by the writers and their colleagues. The text, tables, and figures contained in such documents is data as well. Unfortunately, from our processing-oriented view, that knowledge is not exploitable without a human mediator. If we store document information in bibliographic systems, such as MEDLINE [9], we can only perform selection operations; the machine representation of that information does not currently lend itself well to automated analysis, abstraction, and generalization.

Workstation applications

The environment where most decision-making activity will be performed is the emerging generation of workstations. Following the trend toward systems' interoperability, the user will employ a suite of applications that can not only communicate but also cooperate to solve complex problems. In corporate planning, for instance, the user needs to generate competing hypotheses, to analyze intermediate results, and to display the alternate projections over time to gain the necessary insights that will lead to a decision.

By removing issues of managing hardware resources, current systems already simplify the users' tasks. The envisioned architecture will go further by addressing the management of information resources. We want to provide seamless access to and manipulation of facts scattered across multiple data repositories. An interface layer is required to fulfill such a goal.

Interfaces

Networking standards can now interface heterogeneous computers and allow those systems to exchange data. Yet, communication of data alone does not guarantee that the data will be correctly understood for processing by the receiver. Differences often exist in the *meaning* assigned to the bits stored; for example, an integer can be encoded as an integer, as a string, or as a floating-point number. Such differences may not cause a problem for human interpreters, but must be resolved before automatic processing can manipulate the data.

We see then a need for interfaces that take on an active role, going beyond the setting of static standards. We will refer to such a dynamic interface function as *mediation*, and to the agents performing that function as *mediators*. Mediation includes the processing that makes the interfaces work, the knowledge structures that drive the transformation of data into information, and any intermediate storage and data structures that are used by the mediators.

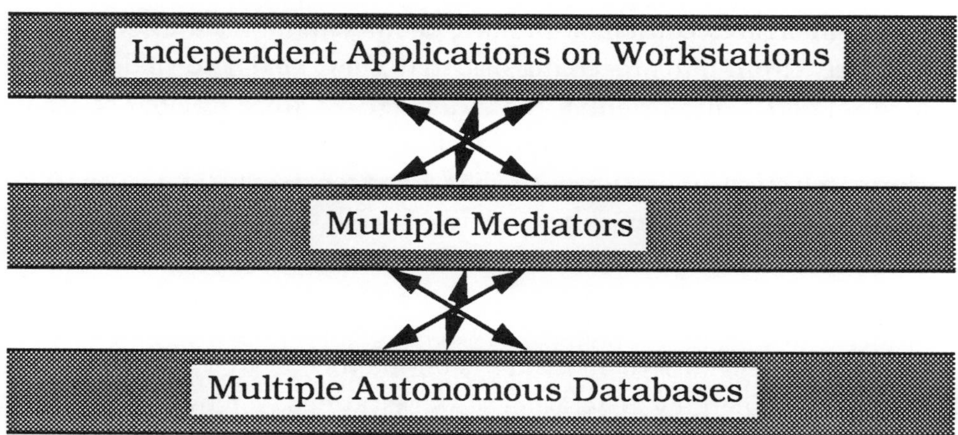

Figure 2: A three-layer architecture for future information systems.

As we have mentioned, the databases, the mediators, and the applications will all reside on nodes of powerful networks. The resulting layered architecture is summarized in Figure 2.

3. Mediators

To support the demands of intelligent interfaces, we envision software modules that mediate between the workstation applications and the databases. A recent paper discusses the reasons for introducing this independent mediation layer and surveys a number of projects, tools, and approaches that can be seen as examples of mediators [15].

3.1 Definition and requirements

We use the term *mediator* to capture the general concept of a knowledge layer between the user and the data. A more general definition follows:

> *A mediator is a software module that exploits encoded knowledge about some sets or subsets of data to create information.*

We place the same requirements on a mediation module that we place on any software module: A mediator should be sufficiently small and simple so that it can be maintained by one expert or by at most a coherent group of experts.

An important, although perhaps not essential, requirement we would like to place on mediators is that they be *inspectable* by the potential users. Since eventually there will be a great number of mediators, the users have to be able to choose among them. Inspectability enables that task. For instance, distinct mediators that can provide the 10 best consultants in database design may use different criteria; one may use the number of publications, another may use the number of clients.

Since the databases being accessed are largely autonomous, it is important that only a limited and recognizable set of mediators depend on them. This requirement provides the *independence* that is necessary to permit databases to evolve. Currently, compatibility constraints are hindering growth of databases in terms of breadth, since many users will be affected. As the number of users and the automation of access increases, the importance of indirect access via mediators will increase.

Each mediator should have *a consistent structure* imposed on it; we expect that this structure often will be hierarchical. Changes in knowledge (or the underlying facts that led to a piece of knowledge) can then be accommodated with secondary changes of limited and predictable scope. Finally, mediators should deal with *one constrained set of base data*, so that updates to the underlying data and data structures can be handled effectively and unambiguously.

3.2 Distribution of mediators

We have mentioned throughout that mediators are distinct modules, distributed over the network. Distribution can be motivated by greater economy for access, by better locality for maintenance, and by issues of modularity. We believe that the latter two forces are those inciting distribution.

Why should such mediators not be attached to the database? In many cases, such attachment may be feasible; in the general case, however, it is not appropriate. Some of the reasons why it is not are

- The mediator contains knowledge that is beyond the scope of the database per se
- Intelligent processing of data often involves dealing with uncertainty, adding excessive complexity to database technology

- Many mediators access multiple databases to perform appropriate fusion

Similarily we can argue that the mediators should not be attached to the users' workstation applications. Again, the functions provided by mediators are of a scope different from that of the tasks being performed on the workstations. Workstation applications may use a variety of mediators to explore a variety of data resources.

4. An Object-Based Layer for Relational Databases

In the remainder of the paper, we present our work in developing an object-based layer on top of a relational DBMS—a layer that constitutes a concrete example of a mediator and that fits well in our model of future information systems.

Objects offer the appropriate level of abstraction for many applications. In addition, object-oriented presentations of information can be clearer and more concise than can long tables of voluminous text. Storing information in the form of complex objects, however, can seriously inhibit flexibility and sharing, since persistent objects bind application-dependent knowledge to the data [14]; that is, different applications will assign different object boundaries to the same information. A desirable compromise is then to provide an object-oriented interface to relational data, combining many of the better features of each representation. Such an interface serves as an effective mapping from databases to applications, translating relational tuples into object instances. We have implemented this concept in a system called PENGUIN [1,16].

4.1 The PENGUIN system

PENGUIN's architecture calls not for storing objects explicitly in the database, but rather for generating and manipulating temporary object instances by binding data from base relations to predefined object templates. The three components of the object interface are as follows:

1. The **object generator** maps relations into object templates, where each template can be a complex combination of join (combining two relations through shared attributes) and projection (restricting the

set of attributes of a relation) operations on the base relations. In addition, an *object network* groups together related templates, thereby identifying different object views of the same database. The whole process is knowledge-driven, using the semantics of the database structure. We define the *object schema* as the set of object networks constructed over a given database. Like the data schema for a relational database, the object schema represents the domain-specific information needed to gain access to PENGUIN's objects; this information enables us to combine well-organized, regular tabular structures (the relations) into complex, heterogeneous entities (the objects).

2. The **object instantiator** provides nonprocedural access to the actual object instances. First, a declarative query (e.g., `Select instances of template` x `where attribute` y $<$ 0.5) specifies the template of interest. Combining the database-access function (stored in the template), and the specific selection criteria (e.g., $y < 0.5$), PENGUIN automatically generates the relational query and transmits it to the DBMS, which in turn transmits back the set of matching relational tuples. In addition to performing the database-access function, the object template specifies the structure and linkage of the data elements within the object. This information is necessary for the tuples to be correctly assembled into the desired instances. Those instances are then made available to the application program directly, or to the user through a graphic interface.

3. The **object decomposer** implements the inverse function; that is, it maps the object instances back to the base relations. This component is invoked when changes to some object instances (e.g., deletion of an instance, update of some attributes) need to be made persistent at the database level. An object instance is generated by collapsing (potentially) many tuples from several relations. By the same token, one update operation on an object may result in a number of update operations that need to be performed on the base relations. Results of our group's previous research, which deals with updating through relational views [7], can be applied here.

In summary, an object template represents a complex view of the database. Instantiation selects, retrieves, and aggregates relevant data into object instances that can now be manipulated further by an end

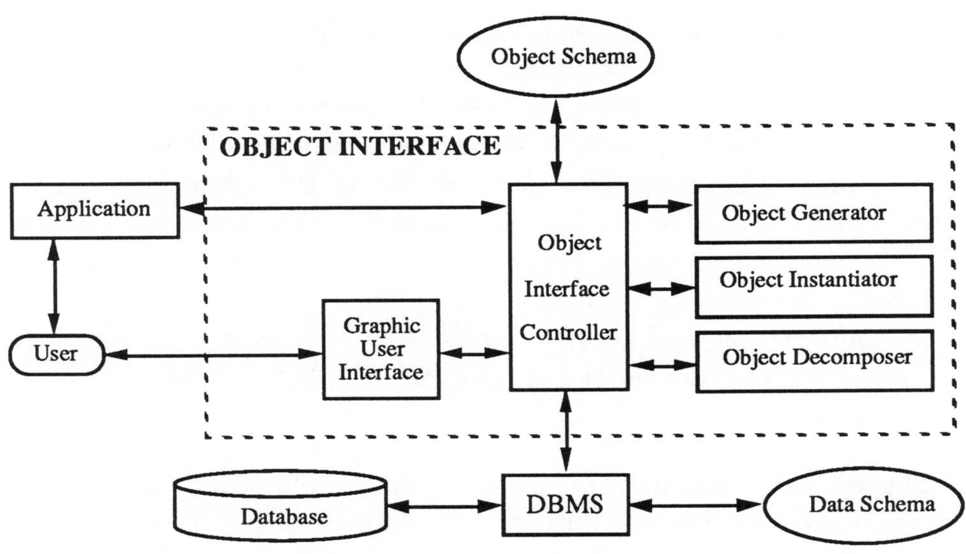

Figure 3: The architecture of the PENGUIN system.

user or by an application. Figure 3 shows the resulting architecture and illustrates the interactions among the relational database, the application, the object layer, and the user—interactions orchestrated by a controller unit within the object interface.

We now explain the decisions we made when designing PENGUIN before demonstrating some of its functionalities.

4.2 Design Decisions

Despite the current trend toward object-oriented DBMSs [8], PENGUIN keeps a relational database system as its underlying data repository. Indeed, we believe that the relational model should be extended, rather than replaced. The relational model has become a de facto standard, and thus some degree of upward compatibility should be kept between the relational format and any next-generation model.

Unfortunately, the relational model lacks a rich set of modeling constructs, with which more meaning could be represented in the database. The consequence of that lack of semantics of the relational model is twofold:

1. The absence of an explicit concept of an abstract object, because an object instance is usually described by tuples in various relations,

which share identical values for common attributes

2. The inability to distinguish different semantic types of relationships, because the database relation describing a specific relationship carries only the relationship's extension, not its intension (that is, its meaning)

Consequently, the use of the relational model provides for the expression of only a restricted part of the application's semantics. In other words, the relational model does not offer a logical structure that is close enough to the domain structure that is being represented in the database.

To address those problems, we apply a *structural model* of the database that augments the relational model [12]. The structural model uses relations and *connections* to describe relationships between pairs of relations. These connections capture the knowledge about constraints and dependencies among relations in the database [17]. In contrast with other semantic data models, this relatively simple and compact model can be implemented easily on top of any standard relational DBMS. Most important, the structural model not only provides the semantics sufficient for the design of the object-based interface, but also can enhance traditional relational transactions in several ways. For instance, structural knowledge adds the concepts of aggregation, categorization, and generalization to the relational model [11]. It also allows us to define *dynamic* integrity constraints that state how the database consistency is to be maintained when an update process requires associated changes [3].

PENGUIN's object template generator uses the structural model together with the traditional data schema to define the *object schema.* In turn, the object schema drives the two processes of object instantiation and object decomposition.

We already alluded to the fact that we do not store the objects explicitly in the relational database. Several factors motivated this choice:

- Different users require different *views* of the information included in an object. Update anomalies and problems of redundancy would arise if the objects corresponding to the different views were stored as such in the database.

- In early stages of any project development, changes to the set of classes and to the inheritance network are made frequently. If the objects were stored explicitly in the database, the database schema would have to be changed accordingly.

- Because we expect the descriptions of the objects—the object templates—to be relatively small when compared to the large number of data in the database, those templates can be kept in main memory.

For all these reasons, our proposal is not to store the objects directly in persistent form but rather to generate their descriptions, which are later instantiated as needed. We think that this approach will provide more flexibility.

5. A Demonstration

We are collaborating with the department of genetics at our institution to develop a system that will assist biomedical researchers in designing immunologic-experiment protocols [2]. This system requires combining database and expert-system technologies to fulfill both the data- and knowledge-intensive tasks of planning an experiment. It then serves as the ideal testbed for the PENGUIN architecture. Figure 4 shows a partial schema for the immunology database, where the links among relations correspond to connections of the structural model. We now use this medical application to demonstrate the processes of object generation and object instantiation.

5.1 Object generation

The object-generation module defines new object templates using semantic information provided by the structural model. Each template is organized around (or "anchored on") one *pivot relation* in the underlying database, so that every object instance can be uniquely identified by its values for the pivot-relation key attribute(s). Obviously, not every relation in the database schema has to be part of a given new template. We have thus defined rules to determine, once the pivot relation has been specified, which other relations are valid candidates for inclusion in the template. Using those rules, an algorithm we designed can derive a unique tree, where the root is the pivot relation and all

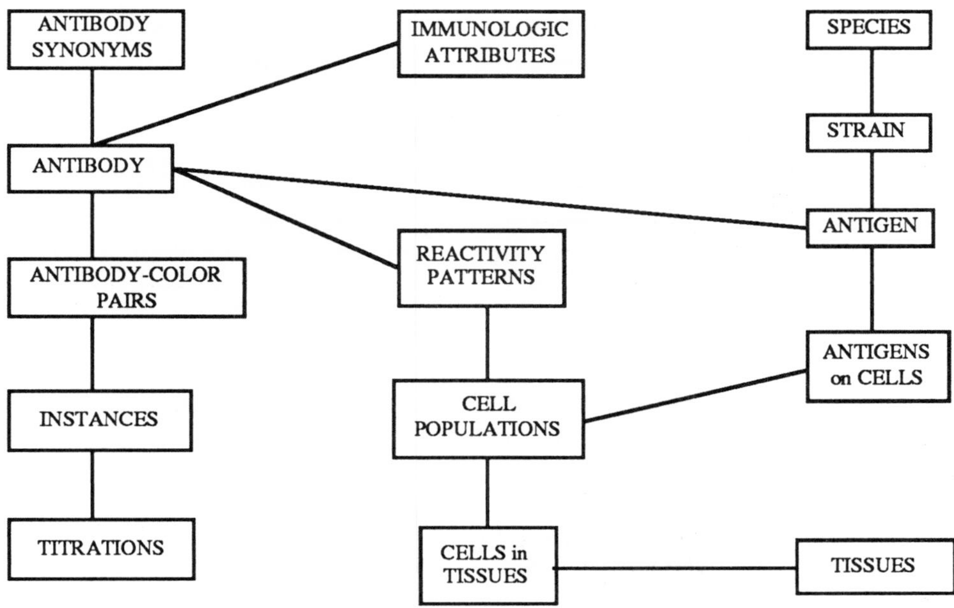

Figure 4: Partial structural model of an immunology database.

other nodes are valid candidate relations. We can then choose from that tree any number of relations to be included in the new template.

The generation process is driven by information from the structural model, which allows automatic generation of much of the internal structure of an object template. The user specifies only the pivot relation, as well as any number of secondary relations and attributes of these relations, through a direct-manipulation, graphical interface. Based on this input, PENGUIN will automatically (1) derive the database-access function and the linkage of the various data elements within the object, (2) include compulsory attributes (e.g., the attributes that implement the joins on the selected relations), and (3) insert the newly created template into an object network by connecting it to other object templates already defined in the network (thereby updating the object schema).

Figure 5 illustrates the object-generation process. Using the immunology database of Figure 4, the user creates a template anchored on the ANTIBODY relation. From this pivot relation and from the structural model, PENGUIN derives the candidate tree that is specific to the new template. Using this tree, the user chooses to include relations

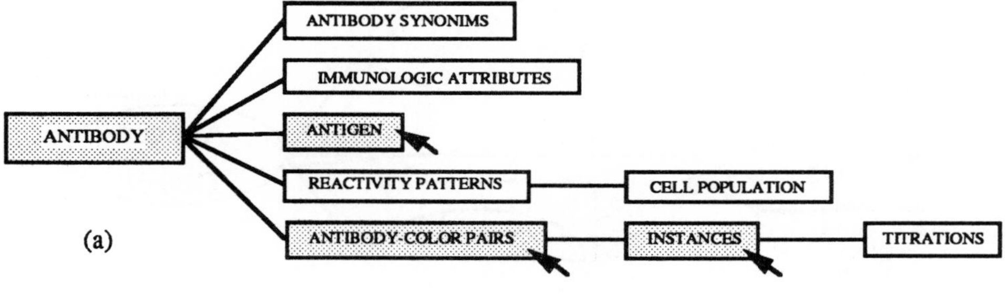

(a)

(ANTIBODY OBJECT
(Hierarchical-Structure
(**ANTIBODY** *clone-name fine-specificity brightness*)
(**ANTIGEN** *antigen-name antigen-species strain*)
(**ANTIBODY-COLOR PAIRS** *color-name f-to-p-ratio*
(**INSTANCES** *batch-number date-creation*)))

(Data-Access-Function
(antibody.antigen-name = antigen.antigen-name and
antibody.antigen-species = antigen.antigen-species and
antibody.clone-name = antibody-color-pairs.clone-name and
antibody.clone-name = instance.clone-name)))

(b)

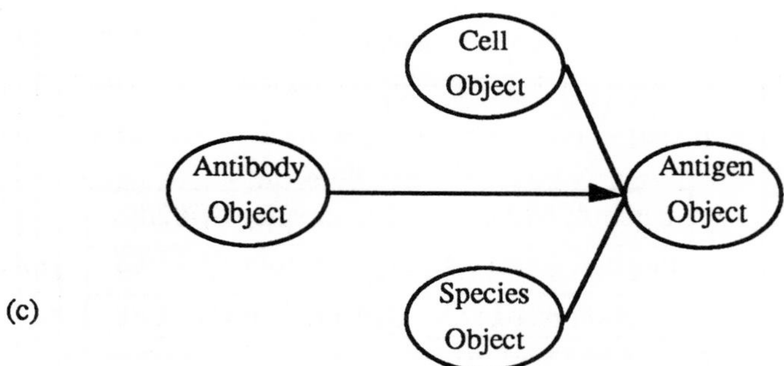

(c)

Figure 5: The object-generation process. (a) The candidate tree derived from the structural model; (b) partial internal structure of the new template; (c) insertion of the new template in an object network.

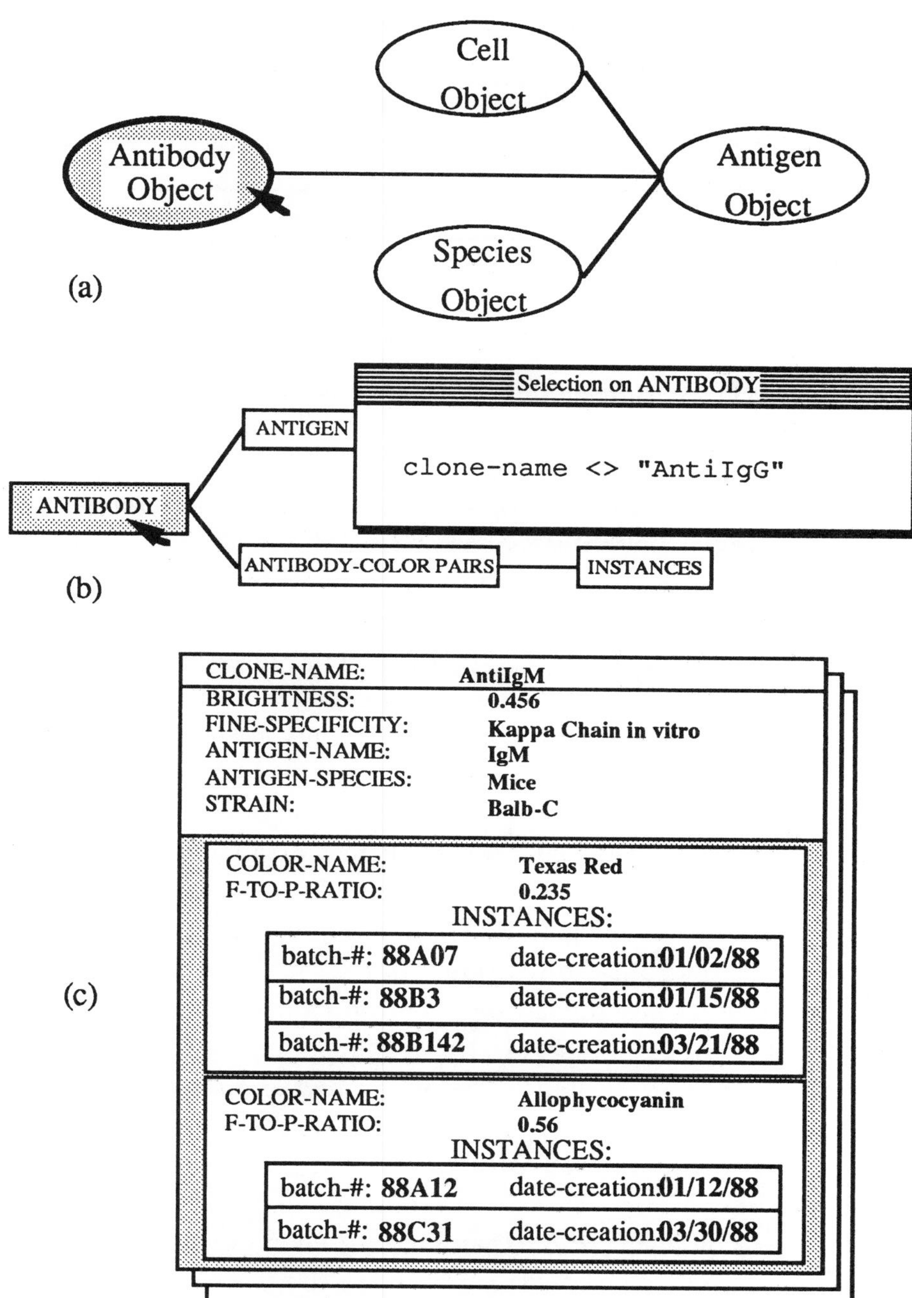

Figure 6: An instance of the ANTIBODY OBJECT template. (a) Choosing a template in an object network; (b) defining the selection clause; (c) displaying the set of new instances.

ANTIGEN, ANTIBODY-COLOR PAIRS, and INSTANCES (Figure 5a). PENGUIN now generates the data-access function and the default structure of the various data elements for the template (Figure 5b, where relations are set in boldface type and attributes are in italic type) before inserting it in an object network through a new link with the ANTIGEN OBJECT template (Figure 5c). The resulting template is a complex unit, incorporating many attributes from various relations.

5.2 Object instantiation

Our goal was to provide *nonprocedural* access to data in a fashion similar to the declarative approach offered by relational query languages. Since an object template contains both the access function to retrieve all the base tuples and the structural information to merge those tuples into complex, heterogeneous entities, we need only to specify a selection clause to retrieve the desired set of instances.

Based on this selection information and on the database-access function, PENGUIN dynamically builds a relational query that is executed by the DBMS. Note that the set of relational tuples returned by the DBMS may contain more than one tuple for any given instance. Therefore, an algorithm (the details of which are presented in [4]) ensures that each tuple in the answer set can be traced back to the proper instance. This algorithm guarantees correct arrangement of the data elements for each newly created instance within the object structure; it also supports the generation of *multivalued* attributes that are, by definition, absent from the relational model but often critical to symbolic reasoning. The application program can now manipulate those instances directly. Alternatively, the graphic interface can display them in a separate window, using the template's hierarchical structure as the default presentation format. However, additional formats for different presentations can be stored with any object template. The user can then switch her perspective on the information contained in the instances (e.g., collapsing and expanding nested subunits).

As an example, consider the ANTIBODY OBJECT template created in Figure 5. To generate instances of this object, the user first selects the correct node in the object network (Figure 6a); she then uses the template's tree of relations to specify the selection clause—here only one attribute is involved: `clone-name <> "AntiIgG"` (Figure 6b). PENGUIN now assembles the set of resulting tuples into several AN-

TIBODY OBJECT instances, which are displayed using a hierarchical format (Figure 6c).

6. Discussion

The formal design of our system is domain-independent. It is our belief that the ideas, principles, and programs developed in PENGUIN offer a promising demonstration of the mediator concept and will be applicable to other knowledge-based interface approaches. PENGUIN's object-based layer indeed satisfies many of the requirements imposed on the mediators.

The layer provides a clear separation between storage and working representations. The application and the end user are able to interact at a level of abstraction higher than that of the information explicitly stored in the database. Indeed, an application now retrieves declaratively a single object, usually represented by many base tuples over various relations, without having to generate complex SQL statements, and handles it as though it were a single unit. Moreover, the same real-world entity can have different descriptions for different purposes, ranging from a high-level, black-box template, to a low-level, detailed one.

Providing **multiple views** of the same database information is a necessity for numerous applications. Our approach, which relies on the definition of object networks, significantly enhances the view mechanism found in relational DBMSs. As previously noted, a template network comprises all the related objects to which a group of users has access. Different views then correspond to separate template networks, although a given object can be in as many networks as are defined for the specific application. This approach provides a compact representation, since an object is stored only once but can be shared by many views.

This architecture provides **sharing of information** contained in the database. Any application-specific structure is imposed at the interface level, not at the database level. Further, the basic distinction between an object and its instances should support a multiple-granularity approach to concurrency control, where locking could include any one of a single instance, an object and its instances, or a set of objects.

Growth of the system and **flexibility** are accomodated easily.

The database administrator can augment the underlying database with new attributes or relations without affecting work on existing templates and object networks. Conversely, the addition, modification, or reorganization of objects does not require that the database schema be modified accordingly.

The main problem that we have encountered is a loss of performance that was to be anticipated. We believe, however, that the overhead incurred by the object-based layer could be offset by the combined use of the following methods:

- Faster relational DBMSs
- Caching techniques for frequently accessed data
- Database reorganizations that follow dominant access patterns
- The ability to abandon inefficient object bindings

In conclusion, we have presented a model of future information systems that combine database and artificial-intelligence techniques. We have assigned a central role to modules that mediate between application programs and data resources; those mediators contain the administrative and technical knowledge needed to create information from factual data. We have implemented in PENGUIN a prototype mediator that enables users to define and manipulate complex objects, the components of which are stored in relational databases. PENGUIN therefore remedies the lack of structural abstraction that exists in the relational model. Research is now underway to specify more elaborate types of mediators that perform more sophisticated operations on data, using domain-dependent, declarative knowledge.

Acknowledgments. We thank Lyn Dupré for her editorial comments. This work was supported by the National Library of Medicine under Grant R01 LM04836, by DARPA under contract N39-84-C-211, and by DEC under the Quantum project. Additional computer facilities were provided by the SUMEX-AIM resource under NIH grant RR-00785.

References

[1] T. Barsalou. An object-based architecture for biomedical expert database systems. In R.A. Greenes, editor, *Proceedings of the*

Twelfth Symposium on Computer Applications in Medical Care, pages 572–578, Washington, D.C., November 1988. IEEE Computer Society Press. Reprinted in *Computer Methods and Programs in Biomedicine*, 30(2/3):157–168, 1989.

[2] T. Barsalou, W.A. Moore, L.A. Herzenberg, and G. Wiederhold. A database system to facilitate the design of FACS experiment protocols (abstract). *Cytometry*, page 97, August 1987.

[3] T. Barsalou and G. Wiederhold. Applying a semantic model to an immunology database. In W.W. Stead, editor, *Proceedings of the Eleventh Symposium on Computer Applications in Medical Care*, pages 871–877, Washington, D.C., November 1987. IEEE Computer Society Press.

[4] T. Barsalou and G. Wiederhold. Knowledge-based mapping of relations into objects. To appear in *Computer-Aided Design*, 1989.

[5] V. Bush. As we may think. *Atlantic Monthly*, 176(1):101–108, 1945.

[6] P.F. Drucker. The coming of the new organization. *Harvard Business Review*, January–February:45–53, 1988.

[7] A.M. Keller. The role of semantics in translating view updates. *IEEE Computer*, 19(1):63–73, January 1986.

[8] D. Maier, J. Stein, A. Otis, and A. Purdy. Development of an object-oriented DBMS. In N. Meyrowitz, editor, *Proceedings of OOPSLA 86*, pages 472–482, New York, 1986. Association for Computing Machinery.

[9] W. Sewell and S. Teitelbaum. Observations of end-user online searching behavior over eleven years. *Journal of the American Association of Information Sciences*, 37(4):234–245, 1986.

[10] C.E. Shannon and W. Weaver. The mathematical theory of computation. 1948, reprinted by The University of Illinois Press, 1962, 80pp.

[11] J.M. Smith and D.C.P. Smith. Database abstraction: Aggregation and generalization. *ACM Transactions on Database Systems*, 2(2):105–133, 1977.

[12] G. Wiederhold. *Database Design*, 2d edition. Computer Science Series. McGraw Hill, New York, 1983.

[13] G. Wiederhold. Knowledge bases. In *Proceedings of the International Symposium on Fifth Generation and Super Computers*, Chapter 1, pages 110–122, 1984.

[14] G. Wiederhold. Views, objects and databases. *IEEE Computer*, 19(12):37–44, December 1986.

[15] G. Wiederhold. The architecture of future information systems (abstract). In *Proceedings of the International Symposium on Database Systems for Advanced Applications*, KISS and IPSJ, Seoul, Korea, 1989.

[16] G. Wiederhold, T. Barsalou, and S. Chaudhuri. Object management in a relational framework. Technical report No. STAN-CS-89-1245, Computer Science Department, Stanford University, January 1989.

[17] G. Wiederhold and R. El Masri. The structural model for database design. In *Entity-Relationship Approach to System Analysis and Design*, pages 237–257. North-Holland, 1980.

[18] G. Wiederhold, P.K. Rathmann, T. Barsalou, B.S. Lee, and D. Quass. Partitioning and composing knowledge. To appear in *Information Systems*, 1989.

QUESTIONS

Dr. B. Papegaaij (Erasmus University).

BP. In the system you presented, how much of the functionality can you find in already existing systems, for example, KEECONNECTION, and what are the differences?

Dr. T. Barsalou.

TB. There are two main differences.

First of all, KEECONNECTION is still pretty much a one-to-one mapping. You have one frame in KEE corresponding to one relation in the database.

The second main difference is that you cannot update the frames that you get from the database unless you write the complete program to handle all the updates. Our system copes with updates.

Dr. J. Zeleznikow (La Trobe University).

JZ. You seem to do all your work on medical applications. Why have you chosen this sort of approach to medical applications? Also, might there be other applications where you want to go directly to an object-oriented approach?

TB. Several answers. First of all, I don't want to imply that object-oriented systems have no usefulness. I think that eventually there is going to be room for relational databases side-by-side with object-oriented databases. But, before we actually see an object-oriented database handling the masses of data that conventional databases do handle on a daily basis, much research and work is needed to add a lot more features. Along this line of the two models co-existing, I can mention that people have started working on an SQL interface for object-oriented databases, much as we provide object-orientation for relational databases.

Secondly, for one of the specific applications I showed you, we didn't want to go object-oriented directly because we knew that we also wanted to offer the data-access and manipulation capabilities of a relational database.

Dr. S. Bennett (Sheffield University).

SB. Can you tell me something about the implementation?

TB. The machine the database is on is a VAX. It's currently running on a MICROVAX. The mediator system is running on a MACINTOSH II and the two are connected over a network. On the

MACINTOSH side, it's OBJECT PASCAL which is an object-oriented version of PASCAL from APPLE.

5 Constraints and Deduction —Convergent Evolution?

D. S. Bowers and C. J. Rawlings

ABSTRACT

Present day knowledge base management systems and AI programming languages do not adequately deal with the problem of very large data volumes nor offer any particular design methodology for their construction. These aspects are, however, relatively well-developed in the database community. Although early databases were relatively weak in the areas of view management and deduction, recent developments have extended the mechanisms for storing and managing virtual relations and for constraining the types of data and relationships between them in relational database management systems.

The duality between goal-driven (deductive) and data-driven (extensional) paradigms is considered, and it is shown that, as the sophistication of logic programming systems on the one hand and database constraint mechanisms on the other develops, so their evolution may be converging towards a common paradigm appropriate for the representation of knowledge. Given such convergent evolution, the choice of paradigm becomes a question of performance rather than of expressive power.

1. Introduction

A distinction which is often drawn between a *database* and a *knowledge base* is that the former is concerned with (very) large volumes of data but with few inferences being drawn from that data, whereas the latter draws many inferences from a rather smaller base of facts and a relatively large set of rules. Thus, a database is regarded as being primarily *extensive*, and a knowledge base *intensive*.

Clearly, this is a gross over-simplification. Many database management systems provide a sophisticated view mechanism, which can form the basis of an elementary deductive system, and knowledge bases are increasingly being developed which can manipulate fact-bases of significant proportions. Further, there is not a simple dichotomy between the two extremes. Rather, depending on the relative proportions of intension and extension in any given system, there is, in effect, a complete spectrum from knowledge-base to database, as indicated in figure 1. However, it is still generally true that there must be tradeoff, particularly in terms of performance, between the ability to handle large volumes of data and an efficient deductive mechanism.

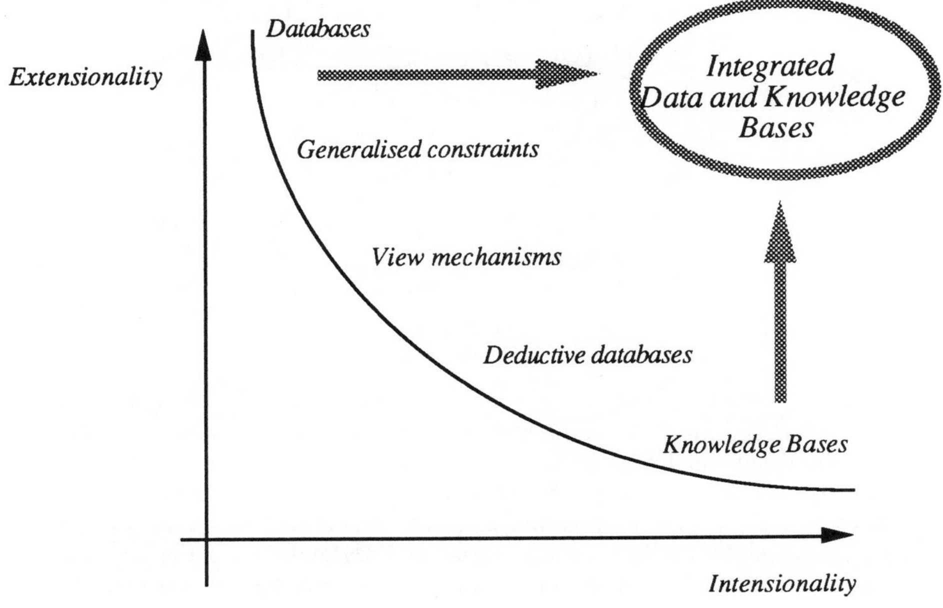

Figure 1: The Database / Knowledge Base Spectrum

The performance tradeoff is well-known in 'database' applications, in which derived data (views) can either be deduced dynamically or physically stored and constrained, by a sophisticated integrity mechanism, to be consistent with the data from which it could have been derived. The use of triggered updates can allow for such derivations to be performed automatically whenever the 'base' data is updated, effectively allowing for pre-computed views. In effect, a constraint mechanism can be regarded as a 'dual' of a view mechanism, in the sense that each can support the same *information* content in a database for given base data.

An alternative view of the spectrum is shown in figure 2, in which the two approaches of view mechanism and constraints are depicted as disjoint circles in a quasi-Venn diagram. Thus, the idea that a view mechanism is a subset of logical deduction is shown in the standard Venn notation, as is the relative insignificance within a generalised constraint mechanism of the notion of referential integrity. Traditional 'database' concepts correspond (loosely) to the 'data driven' approaches depicted at the right hand side of the figure, with the 'goal-driven' approaches on the left being closer to those of logic languages such as Prolog. Within this spectrum, knowledge-oriented concepts occur nearer the centre.

Triggered procedures are essentially pro-active constraints, corresponding to a 'data driven' strategy in deduction, and extend the concept of constraint management towards a view-based paradigm. Similarly, deductive databases are based fundamentally on view mechanisms, and extend that paradigm towards the 'knowledge' area of the spectrum. The two extremes are also bridged, in different ways, by programming language concepts such as Constraint Logic Programming and Truth Maintenance.

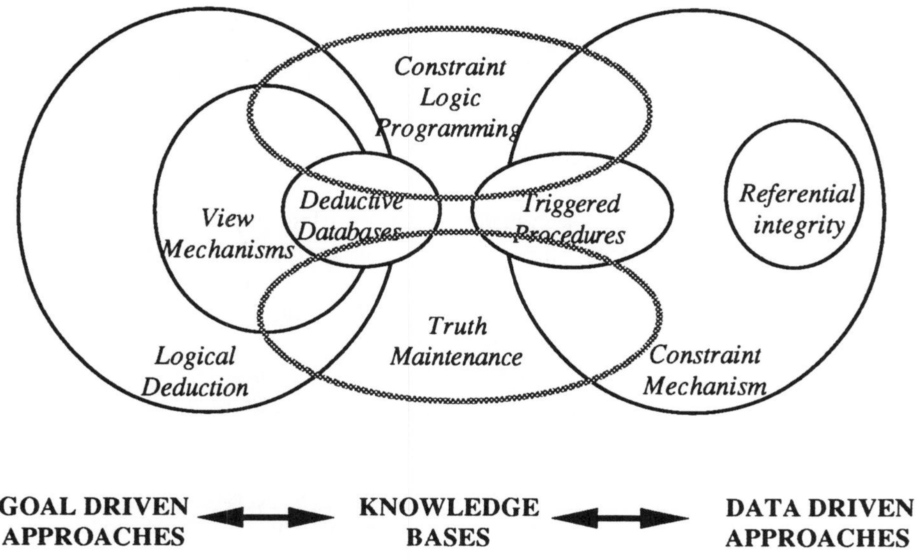

GOAL DRIVEN APPROACHES ⟷ **KNOWLEDGE BASES** ⟷ **DATA DRIVEN APPROACHES**

Figure 2: Goal Driven and Data Driven Paradigms

Despite the apparent convergence of the two extreme paradigms - data-driven and goal-driven - there seems as yet to be little general appreciation of the duality of constraint-based systems and deductive systems. This paper explores the duality by considering in detail the implementations of models based on a variety of paradigms for two specific applications. The expression of specific concepts within each paradigm is compared, and it is shown that the principal differences between the means of expression are more stylistic than conceptual.

The paradigms concerned were logical deduction , a (rudimentary) deductive database and a fully-constrained extensional database. The first paradigm was represented by Prolog, whereas the second and third were implemented using VAX-RDB, DEC's relational database system, which supports both a VIEW mechanism (for the 'deductive' system) and generalised integrity constraints.

The two applications were (i) the TILES puzzle problem, and (ii) a very restricted subset of the domain of protein topology. The former is considered because, although it is a common example in AI, it is considered 'hard' in the database world. It was in the context of the more complex second application that the authors have been collaborating, and the views expressed in this paper developed.

The basic modelling constructs which were employed are outlined in section 2, and the two applications are discussed in sections 3 and 4. The similarities between the implementations are then discussed in section 5.

2. Modelling and Implementation

This section provides a brief overview of the techniques and paradigms utilised in this study. Readers are referred to the appropriate references for more complete descriptions.

2.1 Extended Entity Relationship Analysis

When designing any database or knowledge base, the first step is to express, in an appropriate manner, the concepts which are to be captured in the system. The set of concepts, or conceptual model, is independent of the final implementation paradigm, and, in particular, of any subsequent choice which is to be made between, say, a Prolog implementation or one based on a relational database.

The modelling approach and notation adopted within the context of this study were essentially those of Entity-Relationship Analysis, as described, for example, in Bowers[3]. Although the notation is graphical, it is sufficiently formal to imply many of the constraints which are discussed in this study. However, two extensions are necessary to represent *sub-types* and the *intersection* of disjoint subtype categorisations.

For example, the categorisation of an entity type 'person' into 'male' and 'female' simultaneously with an independent categorisation into 'hourly paid' and 'salaried' would be represented thus:

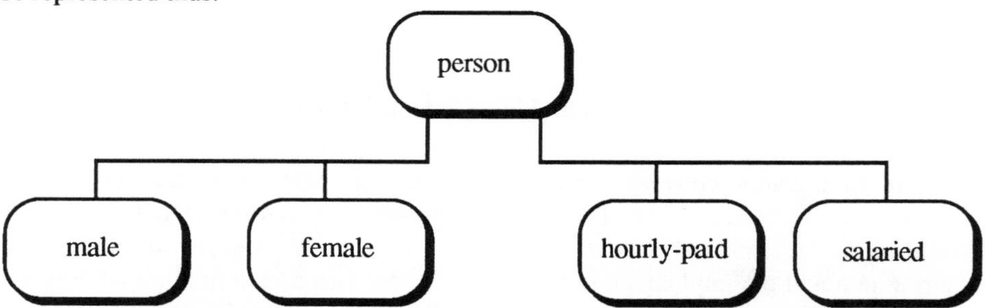

By extension, a subset relationship (= incomplete categorisation) can be represented in an analogous manner:

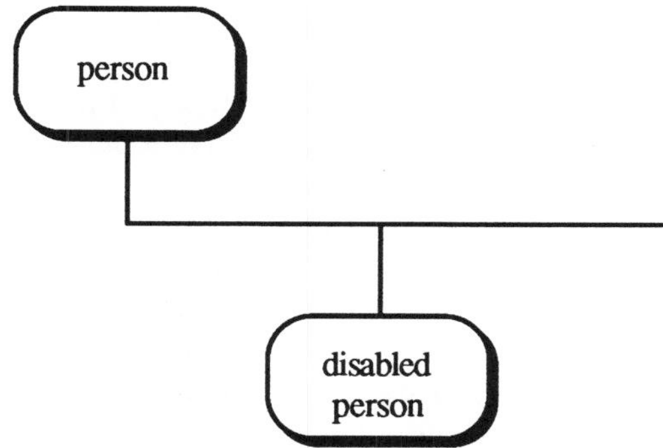

Once independent sub-type categorisations such as that above are permitted, it is necessary to be able to represent the *intersection* of subtypes. The notation used for this is due, in part, to the work associated with Addis[2]. The intersection of 'female' and 'salaried', in the above example, would be depicted thus:

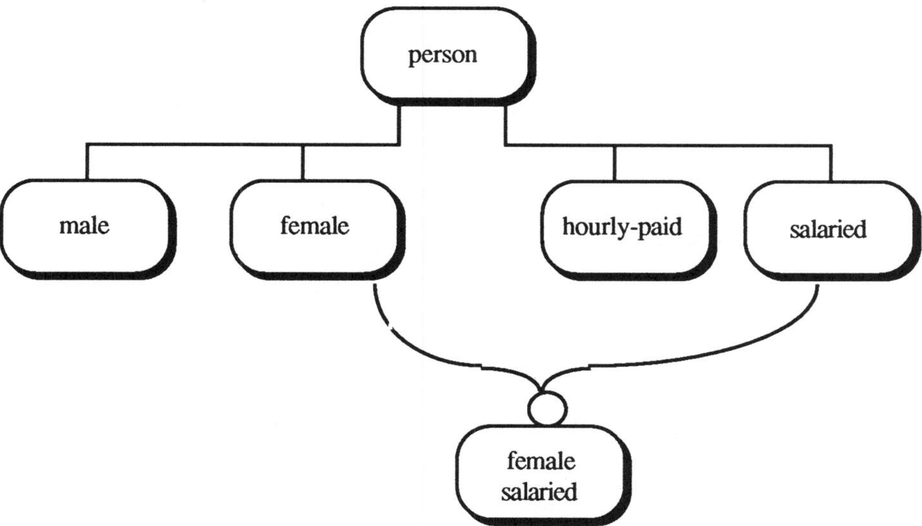

Incidentally, it is interesting to note that it is largely in the area of subtypes and their intersections that there is a choice between goal-driven and data-driven approaches.

These extensions to standard entity relationship analysis permit the expression of most of the concepts which relate to deduction and constraints as discussed in this paper. However, modelling the applications at this level does not prejudge the implementation technique. Hence, by comparing implementations in different paradigms derived from a single conceptual model, it should be possible to compare the paradigms rather than specific implementations.

2.2 RDB

Rdb is DEC's Relational Database Management System which runs under VAX/VMS. Although Rdb has a standard SQL interface, the alternative RDO interface was used for this study, since the expressive power of the latter is considerably greater. RDO is a cursor-based language founded on relational calculus, although expressed in a quasi-procedural manner. There is an associated data definition language which supports the specification of both views and general constraints, which are essential to this study.

A fundamental concept in RDO is that of a *context variable*, which corresponds to a tuple variable in relational calculus. A context variable is normally declared by part of an RDO command such as,

```
for P in POSITION
    ....
```

where 'position' is the name of a relation and 'p' is the context (tuple) variable. Fields (domains) of the context variable are the referenced by the variable name, a dot and the field name, thus:

```
P.LABEL
```

Whilst, given these basic concepts, the definitions presented later in this paper should be intelligible, readers are referred to the appropriate manual[5] for a complete description of the language if required.

2.2.1 RDB constraints

Constraints in Rdb are static predicates which must be satisfied by tuples in specified relations. The conditions to be enforced can involve database queries of arbitrary complexity, involving any number of relations and expressions; thus they are considerably more powerful than the mechanisms proposed for standard SQL. The predicates can be checked either at update or at commit time.

2.2.2 RDB Views

Rdb views are single virtual relations which result from applying specified queries to the database. Views can reference any number of relations, and be of arbitrary complexity, but only views based on a single relation, and with no removal of duplicates (e.g., following projection) can be updated.

View definitions are stored as text in system relations, and interpreted dynamically; thus, the performance of a view based system is not all that it might be. In particular, where a given view occurs more than once in a query, or in another view definition, it seems that the view query is evaluated completely for each reference - hence the diabolical performance of the view based implementations considered in this study. However, Rdb was being used to explore the concepts of a view-based system, and its performance, which could in principle be optimised, was not at issue.

2.3 Prolog

The logic programming language Prolog[17] from Quintus Computer Systems was used to develop the Prolog implementations of the example data models. A logic programming style was adopted and neither side effects nor extra-logical constructs (e.g. the cut operator) were used.

3. The Study

Two example models were chosen to illustrate the features common to deductive and constraint-based approaches to implementing a data model. The examples have been built from common conceptual models and E-R diagrams are presented for the tiles puzzle (derived from Addis[1]) in Figure 4 and for a subset of the domain of protein topology which we refer to as the 'meanders' model in Figure 5. The RDB implementation was built by DSB, who did not have any extensive prior knowledge of Prolog. Conversely, the Prolog implementation was built by CJR who did not have any extensive knowledge of RDB.

In our discussion we will be limiting most of our comments to issues of relation integrity constraints. Our justification for doing this is that most of the complexity of data models comes from defining constraints over relations rather than enforcing domain integrity. The mechanisms for expressing relation integrity constraints in VAX/RDB and rules of deduction in Prolog are approximately equivalent in terms of the concepts they are meant to capture and a comparison is thus appropriate.

By contrast, the methods for representing issues relating to domain integrity are very different in RDBMS and Prolog. Contemporary implementations of relational database management systems and the SQL standard restrict the expression of domain integrity constraints to little more than datatype definitions. Prolog, on the other hand, is a monotyped language with a type construction mechanism and Prolog extensions have been implemented[19] to include a polymorphic type system with compile-time type checking analogous to that available in functional and object-oriented programming languages. Until the methods for representing and reasoning about domains and types in relational database and Prolog or other deductive system are more equivalent a comparison of this type would probably not be instructive. It might be more appropriate to compare these aspects using an object-oriented or functional data model.

3.1 TILES

The tiles puzzle is commonly used as a sample application in computer science as a relief from the ubiquitous "Blocks World" problem and we use it here in order to provide a comparison with other approaches that have been presented previously[1].

3.2 System Description

Eight tiles (identified by integers 1 to 8 and labelled A to H) are placed in a grid with nine positions (labelled 1 to 9) arranged in three rows of three columns, as in figure 3. One space in the grid is empty and therefore only one tile may be moved at a time. Each tile may only move to occupy the empty space when it is 'up', 'down' 'left' or 'right' from it. The puzzle consists of moving the tiles into some arbitrarily interesting sequence from a random starting arrangement.

E(5) 1	F(6) 2	G(7) 3
D(4) 4	5	H(8) 6
C(3) 7	B(2) 8	A(1) 9

Figure 3: The TILES Puzzle

Table 1 Relations in TILES database

Relation	*Domains*
TILE	id, pattern, position
POSITIONS	coord
PAIRS	direction, first, second
OPPOS	direction, converse

3.3 Comparative Implementation - Prolog vs. RDB Constraints

The tiles puzzle has been implemented in Prolog and as a fully constrained RDB database. The schema for the database is shown in table 1. Using the same model as the starting point means that a considerable amount of commonality exists between the implementations. For example, the model dictates that relations are needed to represent the legal grid positions (POSITIONS) and the spatial relationships that exist between each pair of grid positions (PAIRS). In RDB, The PAIRS relation has three fields: the DIRECTION, and the FIRST and SECOND grid positions. The semantics of this relation are that it describes all legal pairs of positions together with the direction of movement required to get from the FIRST position to the SECOND. Directions and their opposites, such as 'left' and 'right', are represented by a binary relation, OPPOS.

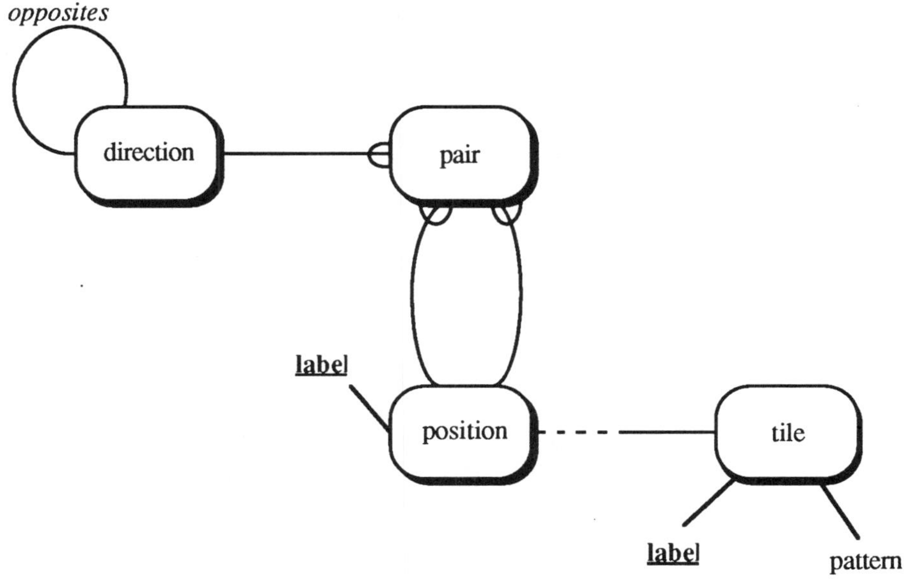

Figure 4: Data Structure for TILES model

In RDB, what constitutes a legal grid is defined and enforced by three RDB integrity constraints "POSITIONS_IN_PAIRS", "PAIRS_IN_POSITIONS" and "REQ_BOTH_PAIRS".

```
define constraint POSITIONS_IN_PAIRS
    description is /* a grid position must be defined in
       both parts of a pair */
    for PO in POSITION require
       any PR in PAIRS with
           PO.COORD = PR.FIRST
    and any PA in PAIRS with
           PO.COORD = PA.SECOND
  check on commit.

define constraint PAIRS_IN_POSITIONS
    description is /* pairs contain only values which are
       legal positions */
    for PR in PAIRS require
       unique P1 in POSITION with
           PR.FIRST = P1.COORD
    and    unique P2 in POSITION with
              PR.SECOND = P2.COORD
check on commit.
```

```
define constraint REQ_BOTH_PAIRS
description is /* both expressions of pair must exist */
    for P in PAIRS require                                    3.1
       unique Q in PAIRS with                                 3.2
           P.FIRST = Q.SECOND                                 3.3
       and Q.FIRST = P.SECOND                                 3.4
    and    any O in OPPOS with
           P.DIRECTION = O.DIRECTION                          3.5
       and O.CONVERSE = Q.DIRECTION                           3.6
check on commit.
```

The constraint "POSITIONS_IN_PAIRS" says that every legal position in POSITIONS must be represented in both the FIRST (1.3) and SECOND (1.5) field of the PAIRS relation. That is, every position on the board must be accompanied by the definition of the legal position that a move might take a tile and the direction that the tile must travel in. The "PAIRS_IN_POSITIONS" constraint says that the only legal possible movements listed in the pairs relation must come from the POSITIONS relation. These two constraints are typical of the constraints seen in RDB implementations, in that they are a "caring pair". The "PAIRS_IN_POSITIONS" and "POSITIONS_IN_PAIRS" correspond to the constraints for referential integrity and closure respectively for the mapping between PAIRS and POSITIONS. The third "REQ_BOTH_PAIRS" definition expresses the constraint that for every tuple in the PAIRS relation each grid position pair must be accompanied by a unique tuple in the PAIRS relation with the FIRST and SECOND positions in the reverse order (3.3, 3.4) and that there is a tuple in the OPPOS relation such that the DIRECTION of the first PAIRS tuple is listed as the opposite to the DIRECTION of that in the second PAIRS tuple (3.5, 3.6). The integrity of the OPPOS relation is in turn constrained by a group of constraints.

The way that the information equivalent to this was encoded in Prolog was 3 Prolog rules.

```
       pairs(Pos,Neigh,Dir) :-
       half_pairs(Pos,Neigh,Dir).                    4.1


    pairs(Pos,Neigh,Dir) :-
       half_pairs(Neigh,Pos,Con),                    5.1
       oppos(Con,Dir).                               5.2


    half_pairs(Pos,Neigh,Dir) :-
       position(Pos),
       position(Neigh),
       grid_pairs(Pos,Neigh,Dir).
```

```
grid_pairs(1,2,right).          grid_pairs(1,4,down).
grid_pairs(2,3,right).          grid_pairs(2,5,down).
grid_pairs(4,5,right).          grid_pairs(3,6,down).
grid_pairs(5,6,right).          grid_pairs(4,7,down).
grid_pairs(7,8,right).          grid_pairs(5,8,down).
grid_pairs(8,9,right).          grid_pairs(6,9,down).


position(1).   position(2).   position(3).
position(4).   position(5).   position(6).
position(7).   position(8).   position(9).

oppos(left,right).              oppos(right,left).
oppos(up,down).                 oppos(down,up).
```

These need a little explaining. The major difference between the two implementations is largely stylistic and comes from the ease with which it is possible to deduce relationships in Prolog. We have chosen, for reasons of economy, to derive the full extension of the Prolog "pairs" relation from the symmetrical nature of the definition of the legal moves on the grid. The extension of "grid_pairs" simply lists the legal moves in one direction only. The rules defining the "half_pairs" and "pairs" relations specify how to deduce these relations and furthermore capture the semantic constraints for the model.

The "half_pairs" rule in English states that all pairs of entities represented by variable Pos and Neigh have a direction relationship (Dir) between them if Pos and Neigh are both defined in the "position" relationship and Pos, Neigh and Dir are related according to the "grid_pairs" relation. The "pairs" rule uses the "oppos" relation to complete the extension of "pairs". The two "pairs" rules are disjunctive and the first simply defines "pairs" as either the same as "half_pairs" (4.1) or the inverse; the inversion of the first two fields/arguments (a projection) is achieved by swapping the positions of the var variable names Pos and Neigh in the second "half_pairs" subgoal (5.1) and the inverse direction is achieved by looking up the opposite direction in the binary relation "oppos" (5.2).

The similarity between the two implementations can be seen by comparing the purpose of the two RDB PAIRS/POSITIONS constraints with the Prolog definition of "half_pairs". In the closed world of this example, the purpose of the PAIRS/POSITIONS constraints is to prevent inconsistent updating of either the RDB PAIRS or POSITIONS relations. Other constraints (or derived relationships) may then be defined knowing that the integrity of these data are assured. In this example we only build on the PAIRS relation. The definition of the "half_pairs" rule achieves the same end. It permits only logically valid conjunctions of data from the "positions" and "grid_pairs" relations from being used. Similarly, the RDB definition of "REQ_BOTH_PAIRS" can be compared with the Prolog definition of "pairs". Both ensure that each tuple defining a pair of positions and direction of movement is accompanied by its inverse and that inverse is constrained/deduced using the definition of "oppos".

4. The MEANDERS application

This model (Figure 5) is of a restricted subset of the domain of protein topology. This domain was selected as an example because it was familiar to one of the authors (CJR), has been implemented using logic programming techniques as a knowledge based system[22] and is being developed further at ICRF. It is also a representative example of a complex application from the biological sciences.

It must be emphasised that this description represents only a small part of the protein topology domain. The MEANDERS subset has been chosen to illustrate some of the fundamental characteristics of the domain. The model we developed and present as an E-R diagram in Figure 5 is similar to that developed by Paton and Gray using the functional data model[20].

The MEANDERS model has been implemented using three methods: in Prolog, using the view mechanism of VAX RDB and as a fully constrained RDB database. The relational schema is depicted in table 2.

4.1 System Description

The MEANDERS domain can be described as follows. A number of structural regularities can be observed in X-ray crystallographic structures of the amino acid chain which forms the primary structure of a protein molecule.. Each of these secondary structures comprises a short section (usually less than 20 amino acids), and can be shown to be thermodynamically stable. The secondary structure elements are alpha-helices and beta-strands, with the latter grouped together to form beta-sheets. The relative positions and orientations of these structures within a protein molecule are termed its topology. (See, for example, Ptitsyn[21].) Secondary structures do not overlap, and are separated by sections of the primary sequence termed loops. Throughout the sequence, there is a concept of direction, from one end of the primary structure to the other.

The linear sequence is folded in space so that beta-strands lie in sheets. Such beta-sheets contain only beta-strands, other connecting sections of the primary sequence lying outside the sheet. Strands are labelled by single lower-case letters. The protein itself has a name and an abbreviated identifier.

A protein may potentially contain any number of beta-sheets (though typically the number is small). Within a sheet, adjacent strands are either parallel or antiparallel, depending on the direction the sequence takes in the two strands. Strands which are consecutive in the primary structure need be neither adjacent nor parallel in the three-dimensional structure, nor even in the same sheet. Consecutive strands are connected either by a simple loop or by an alpha-connection, which is itself an alternating sequence of alpha-helices and loops.

A number of motifs, or super-secondary structures, have been observed as combinations of secondary structure components. These motifs provide a higher level of abstraction which has helped to clarify and aid understanding of protein structure and function. The motifs discussed here include the beta-hairpin which comprises two consecutive beta-strands which are also antiparallel and physically adjacent, although not necessarily in the same sheet. The beta-meander motif can be considered as two hairpins with a common strand. Hairpins and meanders are labelled by the ordered labels of their constituent strands.

A protein whose structure has been determined and which we frequently use to

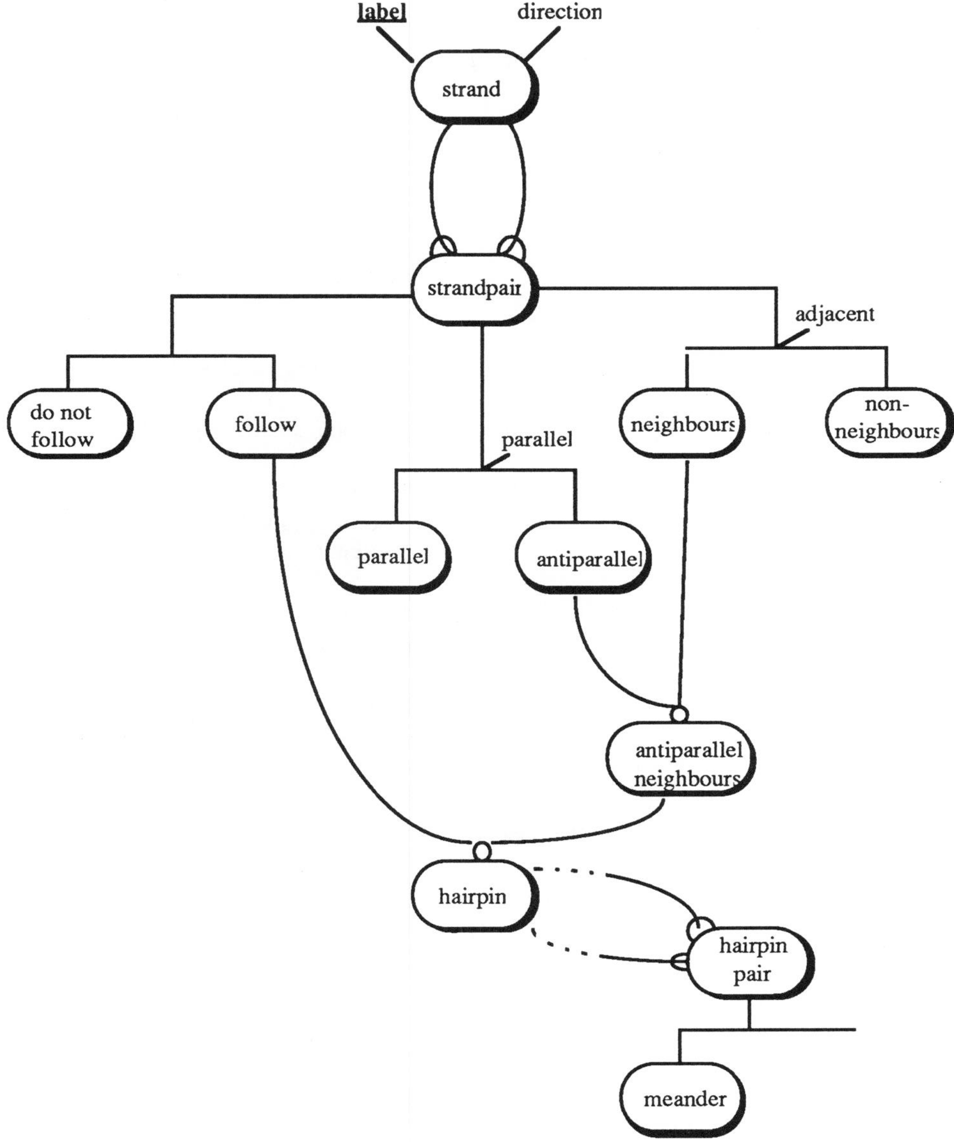

Figure 5: Data Structure for protein topology (MEANDER) database using extended ER analysis

illustrate the principles of protein topology is the human blood plasma protein, prealbumin, p2pab. Figure 6 shows two diagrammatic representations of the three-dimensional structure of p2pab. The protein contains eight beta-strands arranged in two beta sheets, and a single alpha-helix. The first diagram is an 'ends-on' view of the strands in the two beta-sheets, whilst in the second, the supersecondary structure has been 'flattened' into a quasi-2-dimensional form. Within the restricted topological world adopted in this study, the super-secondary motifs present in p2pab are a meander formed of strands b, c and d, and hairpins (b,c), (c,d), (g,h) and (e,f).

Table 2 Relations in MEANDERS database

Relation	*Domains*
STRAND	strand_id, next_strand, orientation
STRANDPAIR	first_strand, second_strand, adjacent
* FOLLOWS	first_strand, second_strand
* ANTIPARALLEL	first_strand, second_strand
* NEIGHBOURS	first_strand, second_strand
* ANTIPARALLEL_NEIGHBOURS	first_strand, second_strand
* HAIRPINS	left_strand, right_strand
* HAIRPIN_PAIRS	left_1, right_1, left_2, right_2
* MEANDERS	first_strand, second_strand, third_strand

* *indicates VIEW in view-based implementation*

(a)

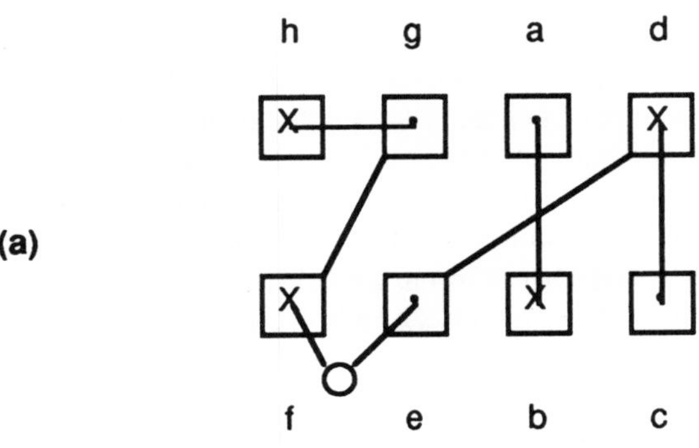

(b)

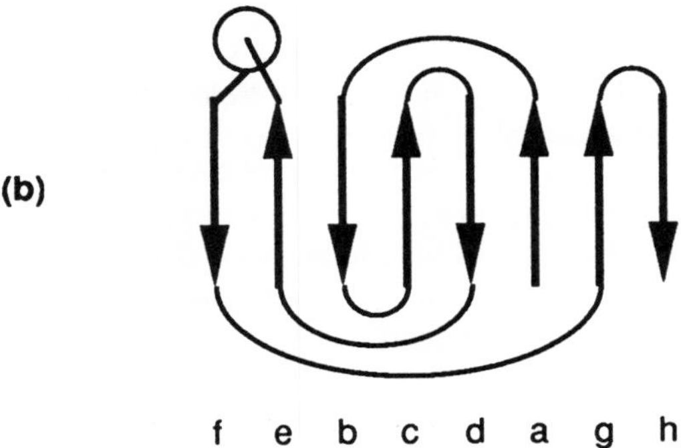

Figure 6 - Secondary Structure of Prealbumine p2pab

letters signify strand labels.

(a) 'edge' view - boxes are strands, the circle a helix; direction of strand (into or out of paper) shown by • or X

(b) 'flattened' view - arrows are strands, arcs loops, and circle helix

4.2 Prolog vs. RDB Views

The approach to using a view (virtual relation) mechanism is similar to developing a Prolog application. The base relationships are established, their extensions provided and then all remaining relationships are derived on demand from a description of the links between either the base relations or views of those relations. The difference between Prolog and a relational database is the language used to describe the links between relations and the computational model of the engine which derives the virtual relations. In the case of Prolog the language is the Horn clause subset of the predicate calculus and the computational model is SLD resolution[15]. In the case of RDB the language is based on a relational calculus[4].

The contrasts and similarities between Prolog and relational databases have been dealt with extensively elsewhere [10,11] and it would be inappropriate to recapitulate them here. An example from the MEANDERS domain should, however, serve to illustrate the major points we wish to make. The base relations for these implementations are STRANDS and STRANDPAIRS. The STRANDS relation has three fields which define the order of beta-strands along the protein sequence with the NEXT field being the successor strand to that in the ID field and ORIENTATION being the orientation (up or down) of the strand called ID. The STRANDPAIRS relation contains the Cartesian product of STRANDS with STRANDS where the two fields FIRST and SECOND identify a member of the pair. (Tuples in which the FIRST and SECOND strands are identical are excluded.) The third field ADJACENT contains a boolean value which flags whether the pair of strands in that tuple are physically adjacent in a beta-sheet.

The following RDB command defines a view for the virtual relation ANTIPARALLEL_NEIGHBOURS. It uses the relations ANTIPARALLEL and NEIGHBOURS, both of which are also views of base relations.

```
define view ANTIPARALLEL_NEIGHBOURS
   description is /*intersection of antiparallel and
      neighbours */
   of ap in ANTIPARALLEL                                 6.1
   cross n in NEIGHBOURS                                 6.2
      with AP.FIRST = N.FIRST                            6.3
      and AP.SECOND= N.SECOND.                           6.4
         AP.FIRST.                                       6.5
         AP.SECOND.                                      6.6
end ANTIPARALLEL_NEIGHBOURS view.
```

The ANTIPARALLEL relation is a selection from the STRANDPAIRS relation (7.1) where the orientation of the two strands are opposite as defined in the STRANDS relation (7.2,7.3,7.4).

```
define view ANTIPARALLEL
    description is /* strands which are antiparallel */
       of sp in STRANDPAIRS                                   7.1
          cross S1 in STRAND                                  7.2
          cross S2 in STRAND                                  7.3
          with S1.ID = SP.FIRST
          and S2.ID = SP.SECOND
          and S1.ORIENTATION <> S2.ORIENTATION.               7.4
       SP.FIRST.
       SP.SECOND.
end ANTIPARALLEL view.
```

The NEIGHBOURS relation is a selection from the STRANDPAIRS relation where the third field (ADJACENT) is set to true, i.e., the strands are adjacent in the same beta-sheet.

The PROLOG rule representing the same relationship is read as: A and B are antiparallel_neighbours IF (:-) A is a neighbour of B and A is antiparallel to B:

```
antiparallel_neighbours(A,B) :-            8.0
   neighbours(A,B),                        8.1
   antiparallel(A,B).                      8.2
```

It is clear that the Prolog definition is somewhat simpler than the RDB view definition; but that essentially they are the same. The simplification that Prolog provides is that unification of logical variables provides the mechanisms both for defining the structure of the arguments in the relation (8.0) (cf 6.5, 6.6) and the test for equality (cf 6.3, 6.4). The conjunctive subgoals of antiparallel_neighbours (8.1, 8.2) with shared logical variables provides the equivalent mechanism to the relational JOIN or "cross" in the RDB definition (6.1, 6.2) though there is no requirement for set union compatibility.

The remaining definitions of the RDB view implementation are all very similar to the Prolog program. An additional feature of the RDB database is that the integrity of base relations is maintained by RDB constraints (see later).

4.3 Prolog+Views vs. RDB Constraints

When implementing the MEANDERS model using RDB constraints and employing a fully extended database, similarities were observed between the integrity constraints and the Prolog deductive rules and RDB view definitions.

We again use the example of defining the antiparallel relationship between two beta-strands. In a fully constrained database there must be a constraint that requires that for every pair of strands that is defined as being antiparallel, the orientations of the two strands must not be the same (assuming that the orientation is either 'up' or 'down') (constraint NOT_ANTIPARALLEL).

```
define constraint NOT_ANTIPARALLEL
    description is /* antiparallel strands must be
       oriented in opposite directions */
    for A in ANTIPARALLEL require
       unique S1 in STRAND
           with S1.ID = A.FIRST
    and unique S2 in STRAND
           with S2.ID = A.SECOND
           and S1.ORIENTATION <> S2.ORIENTATION
check on update.
```

Conversely, it is also necessary to say that every pair of strands that have opposite directions must be defined as antiparallel (constraint SHOULD_BE_ANTIPARALLEL):

```
define constraint SHOULD_BE_ANTIPARALLEL
   description is /* strand pairs with opposite
      orientations are antiparallel */
   for S in STRANDPAIR with
      unique S1 in STRAND with
         S1.ID = S.FIRST
   and unique S2 in STRAND with
         S2.ID = S.SECOND
   and S1.ORIENTATION <> S2.ORIENTATION
require
   unique A in ANTIPARALLEL with
      A.FIRST = S.FIRST
   and A.SECOND = S.SECOND
check on commit.
```

The above constraints form the familiar "caring-pair" between the referential integrity constraint (NOT_ANTIPARALLEL) and the closure constraint (SHOULD_BE_ANTIPARALLEL) that we observed before in the TILES model. These constraints can be compared with the RDB view definition of antiparallel in 7.0 and the following simple Prolog rule:

```
antiparallel(A,B) :-    strands(A,_,OA),
                        strands(B,_,OB),
                        OA \== OB.
```

which in English states that strands A and B are antiparallel IF strand A has an orientation OA and strand B has an orientation OB and OB and OA are not equal (\==).

4.4 Sequences

A characteristic requirement for databases in molecular biology, and we would argue for databases in other domains, is the need to model and implement the semantics of a sequence of entities. In the MEANDERS model the only sequences represented in the database are the sequence of strands along the amino acid sequence and the sequence of segments within alpha-connections. One property which is important for sequences in molecular biology is that they - or, rather, the application of the operator 'next' to a sequence - must exhibit transitive closure. That is, a sequential traversal of the elements of a sequence must include every component exactly once. The following RDB commands constrain the FOLLOWS relation to be a description of a linear sequence of strands.

```
define constraint DOESNT_FOLLOW
   description is /* strands which 'follow' must be
       related by 'next' */
   for F in FOLLOWS require
       unique S in STRANDS with
           S.ID = F.FIRST
       and S.NEXT = F.SECOND
   and unique S2 in STRANDS with                        9.5
           S2.ID = F.SECOND                             9.6
check on commit.

define constraint SHOULD_FOLLOW
description is /* next strand must follow this one */
   for S in STRANDS with S.NEXT <> '$'                  10.1
   require unique F in FOLLOWS with
       F.FIRST = S.ID
   and F.SECOND = S.NEXT
check on commit.

define constraint INCOMPLETE_SEQUENCE
   description is /* there must be only one strand in
       the sequence with no successor */
   for S in strand with S.NEXT = '$'
   require unique F in FOLLOWS with
       F.SECOND = S.ID                                  11.3
   and not any S1 in STRANDS with
       S1.NEXT = '$'                                    11.5
   and S1.ID <> S.ID
check on commit.
```

The two constraints DOESNT_FOLLOW and SHOULD_FOLLOW form the usual caring-pair that deal with the fact that FOLLOW is selection and projection of the STRANDS relation. The '$' symbol is used in the STRANDS relation to signify the end of the sequence. Additionally DOESNT_FOLLOW contains the referential integrity constraint (9.5, 9.6). The third constraint INCOMPLETE_SEQUENCE is the transitive closure constraint. It ensures that there is only one end strand that has no successor (11.5) and that that strand must the successor of another (11.3).

Unfortunately, these are not a complete set of constraints for a sequence relation since they do not preclude the sequence from containing loops; nor do they allow for singleton sequences. It would seem that some special features are required in order to deal with transitive relations that represent sequences or plexes. In the case of sequences it should be possible to constrain the FOLLOWS relation so that:

- every strand is either a predecessor or a successor or both;
- no strand is its own (transitive) successor;
- there is exactly one strand with no successor (& one with no predecessor).

The constraints above express the first and third (almost), but not the second.

It is not actually possible to make a direct comparison with these constraints and the Prolog and RDB view implementations since these implementations do not use the transitivity of the relation. In the full Prolog implementation of the ICRF programs which reason about protein topology (TOPOL) the FOLLOWS sequence is:

<segment>-<loop>-<segment>-<loop> ...

where segment can be either a beta-strand or an alpha-helix segment. The simplest transitive use of the FOLLOWS relationship is to deduce the segment_follows relation which skips over loops.

```
segment_follows(A,B) :-                          12.0
   follows(A,loop(X)),
   follows(loop(X),B).
```

segment_follows is then used in the recursive definition of helices_between which constructs a list of the helices lying between two strands in the FOLLOWS sequence:

```
helices_between(A,B,[]) :-                       13.0
   segment_follows(B,A).

helices_between(A,B,[helix(H)|T]) :-             14.0
   segment_follows(helix(H),A),
   helices_between(helix(H),B,T).
```

The '[]' symbol signifies the empty list and the '[helix(H)|T]' term in 14.0 constructs the helix list whose head is helix(H) and whose tail is T.

It is clearly important for both the segment_follows rule (12.0) and the helices_between rules (13.0,14.0) that the underlying data in the FOLLOWS relation is correct and complete.

5. Discussion

5.1 DEDUCTION: RDB Views and Prolog

If we look at the composition of the Prolog and RDB view implementations of the MEANDERS model we can see that they contain approximately similar amounts of information in the intensional part and the extensional parts of the database. The RDB version has in addition 2 constraints that maintain the integrity of the two base relations.

Table 3: View and Prolog Implementations

		MEANDERS RDB View	
	Intension		**Extension**
Definitions			
No.of Relations	*No. of Views*	*No. of RDB Constraints*	*No.of Tuples*
9	7	2	72
		MEANDERS Prolog	
No.of Predicates	*No.of Rules*		*No.of Tuples*
9	7		72

Since both implement the same domain model and both have the same relative distribution of information in their intension and extensional parts they, can for the purposes of this study be considered as equivalent. The examples in the previous sections have provided a comparison between the representation languages. The outstanding difference in the implementations was actual performance. The RDB view mechanism took minutes to derive the top level view (MEANDERS), whereas Prolog was virtually instantaneous. Clearly, a direct comparison of performances is not really appropriate because of the radically different assumptions behind how data is stored and manipulated by a disk-based database management system and a programming language that keeps all data memory-resident. Given ideal implementations of both systems, their performance should be equivalent since they execute the same ratio of deductions to retrievals.

Accepting that Prolog and RDB View mechanisms are essentially equivalent means that we can combine the TILE and MEANDERS model implementations to compare fully constrained with deductive approaches.

5.2 Constraints versus Deduction

The following table summarises the contents of the Prolog or RDB view implementations of the TILES model and presents them together with the fully-constrained RDB implementations of the same models.

Table 4 Views and Constraints

	RDB View/Prolog			
	Intension			Extension
	Definitions			
	No.of Relations	*No. of Views/ Rules*	*No. of RDB Constraints*	*No.of Tuples*
TILES	9	6		25
MEANDERS	9	7	2	72
	RDB Constraints			
TILES	5	0	12	45
MEANDERS	9	0	14	160

There are clear differences in the composition of the two implementations. In the fully constrained versions, the intensional component is restricted entirely to the constraint definitions and on average it takes about 2 constraints to replace one view definition or Prolog rule in the deductive approach. Furthermore, because the constraint implementation must store all the database extension the number of tuples maintained by the database is also (probably coincidentally) also nearly twice as many as in the deductive approaches.

A superficial assessment of this comparison might easily conclude that the constraint implementation is inferior to the Prolog/View implementation, however, there are advantages to using constraints. First of all, in addition to the space-time trade off there is also a trade-off between cost of update and cost of retrieval. View/Prolog systems are cheap to update (at least for the base data - updating derived data is, of course, an unresolved problem), but (potentially) costly for retrieval. The converse is true for constraint-based systems. They are costly to update, but retrieval is cheap. Secondly, using integrity constraints seems to encourage a more thorough approach to the defining the intension. It is common practise conveniently to forget parts of a view definition or aspects of a Prolog rule assuming that the database will contain the correct data. This can prove acceptable when the database is relatively static (as logic databases are often assumed to be) and the use of the system is envisaged as primarily goal- (query-) driven, but when the database is changing frequently, inadequately defined rules can easily lead to unsound inferences.

In the examples presented from our study we have stressed the similarity of purpose in the use of constraints in a data-driven (extensional) approach and the definition of rules or view definitions for a deductive approach. The two approaches also have essentially equivalent expressive power and thus their differences are reduced to issues of performance.

5.3 Constraints in Knowledge Based Systems

Practical knowledge-based systems are rarely purely goal-driven or purely data-driven; they generally use some of both of these techniques. This is coming to be acknowledged by the developers of knowledge representation languages and AI languages and many systems now admit a mixed programming style (e.g. PROPS [8,9,16]). Most knowledge based systems use a rule-based approach for their knowledge representation, however, constraints are becoming viewed as an increasingly important way of programming. Some knowledge base developers view constraints as the most natural way to develop an application[13] whereas others have proposed a constraint-based language as a complete knowledge representation system (CL) [2]. The CL system provides a language for defining integrity constraints using set theoretic techniques and relational algebra. The constraints are managed as a network which is used to enforce global consistency of the knowledge base. Updating any relation in the network triggers the system to propagate the appropriate updates to other relations to bring the system back to a consistent state.

Recent developments in logic programming have also looked to constraints and a data-driven approach to complement the deductive power of Prolog. The most general use of constraints within a logic programming language is in the CHIP language developed at ECRC [6]. CHIP allows constraints to be defined over finite domains including arithmetic and set membership constraints. It is also possible to specify constraints over boolean terms, rational arithmetic expressions and develop user-specified constraints. CHIP embodies a data-driven technique (demons) to drive constraint propagation and consistency maintenance.

Finally, although constraints as such are not used explicitly, knowledge base systems that employ belief revision or truth-maintenance (after Doyle [7]) need to keep their database of propositions and justifications in a consistent state as their world models changes. This is clearly a related issue to that of maintaining a consistent database by use of integrity constraints.

6. Conclusions

For practical reasons of exploiting existing databases or as part of developing approaches to managing large knowledge based systems a variety of approaches to interfacing database systems to knowledge bases have been proposed [12,14] and numerous system architectures proposed to support large knowledge based systems[24]. The majority of these concentrate on interfacing to the deductive aspects and retrieval of data from databases rather than using integrity constraints to represent parts of the knowledge base and allowing the database to manage issues of consistency as well as data storage.

Our study has highlighted how closely related are the ideas and methods for building (data-driven) databases using integrity constraints and deductive (goal-driven) data and knowledge bases using relational view mechanisms or rule-based programming. We believe that developments in AI languages and database architectures are converging to accommodate both integrity constraints and deduction[23,18]. This convergent evolution is not generally appreciated, but will be an important requirement for the development of languages and data and knowledge base design methods that can cater for the next generation of very large knowledge bases.

References

1. T. R. Addis, *Designing Knowledge-Based Systems*, Kogan Page, London, (1985).

2. T. R. Addis, and S. P. Bull , A Concept Language for Knowledge Elicitation, *Proceedings of the European Knowledge Acquisition Workshop (EKAW'88)*, GMD-Studien report, no. 143, Bonn , (1988).

3. D.S. Bowers, *From Data to Database*, Van Nosrand Reinhold, (1988)

4. E.F. Codd, A relational model of data for large shared data banks, *Comm. Association of Computing Machinery*, vol. 13, pp. 377-387, (1970).

5. DEC, *VAX-RDB Reference Manual*

6. M. Dincbas, P. Van Hentenryk, Simonis, A. Aggoun, T. Graf, F. Berthier, The Constraint Logic Programming Language CHIP, *Proceedings of the International Conference on Fifth Generation Computer Systems*, p. 693, ICOT Press, Japan, (1988).

7. A. Doyle, A truth maintenance system, *Artificial Intelligence*, vol. 12, pp. 231-272, (1979).

8. T. Duncan, PROPS 2 Reference Manual, BCU-TR-PROPS-e, Imperial Cancer Research Fund, Biomedical Computing Unit, (1986).

9. J. Fox, D. Frost, T. Duncan, N. Preston, The PROPS 2 Primer, BCU-TR-PROPS-e, Imperial Cancer Research Fund, Biomedical Computing Unit, (1986).

10. P.M.D. Gray, *Logic, Algebra and Databases*, Ellis Horwood, Chichester, (1984).

11. P.M.D. Gray, R.J. Lucas, (editors) *Prolog and Databases*, Ellis Horwood, Chichester, (1988).

12. P.M.D. Gray, Expert systems and object-oriented databases: evolving a new software architecture , in *Research and Development in Expert Systems V*, ed. B. Kelly and A.L. Rector, Cambridge University Press, Cambridge, (1988).

13. B. Hayes-Roth, B.G. Buchanan, O. Lichtarge, M. Hewett, R. Altman, J. Brinkley, C. Cornelius, B. Duncan, O. Jardetsky, PROTEAN: Deriving Protein Structure from Constraints, *Proceedings of American Association of Artificial Intelligence*, vol. 5, pp. 904-909, (1986).

14. L. Kerschberg, (editor), *Expert Database Systems*, Database Systems and Applications, Benjamin/Cummings, (1986).

15. R. Kowalski, Predicate logic as a programming language, *Proceedings of IFIP-74*, pp. 569-574, North Holland Press, Amsterdam, (1974).

16. J.C. Kunz, T.P. Kehler, M.D. Williams, Applications development using a hybrid AI development system, in *Artificial Intelligence Programming Environments*, ed. Robert Hawley, pp. 177-196, Ellis Horwood Ltd., Chichester, (1987).

17. C.S. Mellish, W.F. Clocksin, *Programming in Prolog*, Springer-Verlag, Berlin, (1981).

18. M. Morgenstern, The role of constraints in databases, expert systems and knowledge representation, in *Expert Database Systems*, ed. L. Kerschberg, Database Systems and Applications, p. 351, Benjamin/Cummings, (1986).

19. A. Mycroft, R.A. O'Keefe, A Polymorphic Type System for Prolog, *Artificial Intelligence*, vol. 23, pp. 295-307, (1984).

20. N.W. Paton, and P.M.D Gray, An object-oriented database for storage and analysis of protein structure data, in *Prolog and Databases*, ed. P.M.D. Gray, R.J. Lucas, Ellis Horwood, Chichester, (1988).

21. O.B. Ptitsyn, A.V. Finkelstein, Similarities of protein topologies: evolutionary divergence - functional convergence or principles of folding?, *Annual Reviews of Biophysics*, vol.13, pp. 339-386, 1980.

22. C.J. Rawlings, W.R.T. Taylor, J. Nyakairu, J. Fox, M.J.E. Sternberg, Reasoning about protein topology using the programming language Prolog, *Journal of Molecular Graphics*, vol 1, #1, 1985

23. A. Shepherd, L. Kerschberg, Constraint management in expert database systems , in *Expert Database Systems*, ed. L. Kerschberg, Database Systems and Applications, p. 309, Benjamin/Cummings, 1986.

24. D. Shin, P.B. Berra, Computer Architectures for logic-oriented data/knowledge bases, *Knowledge Engineering Review*, 1989. In press

QUESTIONS

Mr. P Singleton (University of Keele).

PS. I was a bit surprised that your TILES problem didn't exploit its two dimensional nature. There's a certain symmetry in it, especially as you've labelled the positions (1,1), (1,2), etc. using a cartesian system.

Dr. C. Rawlings.

CR. The comparison is slightly rigged, I guess, because we wanted to keep the spirit of the implementations fairly equivalent. We didn't want to exploit unification any more than was necessary in order to give database-like search and selection to the PROLOG example.

PS. What do you mean by "set union compatibility"?

CR. In PROLOG, you can have duplicates in your database, whereas in a normalized database, you don't.

PS. You said, "Who cares about efficiency?" Well I expect most of us here do. Do you plan to continue developing what you've presented in this paper to cover efficiency?

CR. The comment was facetious. Of course we are concerned too, but this study was restricted to comparisons of representational adequacy. So I think the answer at the moment is, no. I can't see us using RDB as a back-end to our PROLOG database system, although I don't know of any other database product that handles integrity constraints in such a nice way.

PS. You're not going to use RDB for what reason?

CR. Well, it's on VAX. There's a serious performance problem with RDB. Really, I guess we chose RDB because it was a good example of a database that allowed us to have nicely described integrity constraints. And basically, we could, if we wanted to, go forward with RDB to build a fully constrained database and have it maintained dynamically. We chose not to go down that route, partly because of the efficiency reasons, partly because of the engineering involved which isn't really our line of work.

6 A Virtual Memory Support for Deductive Database Queries

S. Greco, N. Leone, W. Staniszkis

ABSTRACT

An approach to query processing in the deductive database system based on a dedicated virtual memory subsystem is presented. The general architecture of the Logic Query Language (LQL) subsystem integrated with the Epsilon KBMS is discussed. The principal parts of the presentation concentrate on the execution strategies and the virtual storage structure in the context of the recursive query processing. The potential for parallel processing of the logic queries as well as the intra-query run-time optimization techniques are presented.

1. INTRODUCTION

A Logic Query Language (LQL), to be used as a vehicle for specification of database theories in the Epsilon system, is to provide a powerful (recursion) and efficient access mechanism to SQL-based relational databases. It is to be fully integrated with the Epsilon environment to facilitate definition of collections of LQL rules as theories to be comprised within the Epsilon knowledge base. Efficient execution of LQL queries against the corresponding theories requires sophisticated optimization techniques to be applied both on the term rewriting as well as on the logic query execution levels. The LQL queries are to be compiled into the Relational Algebra (RA) proposed as the target execution language. The proposed LQL support software environment is to include also a dedicated storage environment, called the RA Virtual Storage, to support efficient execution of the RA programs.

Epsilon [15] is a prototype of a knowledge base management system developed within the ESPRIT Project 530. Epsilon is built on top of a commercial PROLOG and it provides an interface from PROLOG to relational database management systems. A theory is a basic component of the Epsilon database. It is considered to be a chunk of knowledge associated with a specific inference engine (called the theory processor). The theory processor contains operations to query the theory, to update and search the theory, and to load/unload the theory as a separate atomic object. The principal theory classes currently available within Epsilon are the extended (with theory features) PROLOG theories and the Data Base theories.

The objective of our work is to propose a run-time software subsystem supporting efficient execution of the LQL queries issued against a relational database in the Epsilon environment. LQL is a Datalog type language [26] with arithmetics and negation. The completeness of LQL as well as the LQL query termination must be guaranteed. It is required that LQL theories are stratified [1] and the safety of logic queries is enforced at the compilation time. The base predicates of LQL must refer to relations (derived or base) of a SQL-based relational database. Both intentional and extensional rules may be stored within a LQL theory. However, no update operations against the database relations are currently allowed within the language. It is assumed that the source relational databases are updated via the host database management systems by their respective applications.

The research on interfacing logic programming with relational databases is motivated by the belief that data intensive applications represent a natural application domain with great growth potential. Many systems coupling PROLOG with relational databases have already been proposed [7,8,13,14]. The principal problem of the straightforward coupling of PROLOG with relational databases is heavy interaction (in terms of the number of queries) between the logic program and the relational DBMS. Reducing the number of interactions by caching intermediate results based on pre-analysis of the PROLOG programs has been proposed in [8]. An alternative approach based on the bottom up evaluation of logic programs compiled into relational algebra [4,5,18,19,21,25] has been proposed to facilitate the use of the logic programming paradigm in the data intensive applications. The main thrust of the research went in the direction of optimization of logic programs by term rewriting techniques. Examples of this approach are results of the LDL project at MCC [9,27], the KIWI project at CRAI [20], and the Nail project at the Stanford University [16]. Another research direction was to propose efficient algorithms for bottom up evaluation of recursive predicates. The representative results in the area of the recursive query processing algorithms include the Henschen-Naqvi algorithm [11], the Query/Subquery algorithm [24], as well as the Naive [22] and Semi-Naive Evaluation [3] algorithms. A survey of recursive query processing methods together with the assessment of their relative performance characteristics may be found in [4].

Our approach is to combine the term rewriting optimization of LQL programs with a dedicated storage organization supporting efficient execution of the RA operations. The LQL programs are to be compiled into the RA programs, represented as Petri nets of the RA operations, and into complex SQL queries. Base predicates will be materialized into the RA Virtual Storage and all remaining operations will be supported by the physical data structures determined by the LQL program optimizer. We present the general architecture of the LQL subsystem in the following section, and subsequently we discuss the LQL query execution strategy, in particular as applied to the recursive rules, and finally we present the LQL virtual storage model.

2. GENERAL ARCHITECTURE OF THE LQL SUBSYSTEM

The LQL subsystem is to be integrated with Epsilon in the sense that all its functions are to be accessible via the Epsilon user interface. The general architecture of the subsystem is shown in figure 1. The shaded boxes represent software external to the LQL subsystem. We assume that any relational DBMS supporting SQL as the embedded query language will be accessible from the LQL subsystem. In fact one of the possible development directions is to allow accessing preexisting heterogeneous databases supporting other data models (network, hierarchical) via the multidatabase management system DQS [6].

The information flow between the LQL subsystem components consists of control information, at the query compilation and optimization level, and of data coming out of the relational database(s) at the execution level. The LQL theory is specified as a collection of LQL rules to be stored in the LQL Data Dictionary. The theory rules are to be analyzed by the LQL Rule Analyzer to enforce stratification and safety. The result of the analysis is the dependency graph (DAG) of the LQL theory rules. The intermediate steps comprise construction of the cyclic dependency graph, in the case of recursive programs, identification of recursive clusters consisting of rules comprising the mutually recursive predicates, and collapsing the recursive clusters into single dependency graph nodes to obtain an acyclic dependency graph (DAG). The theory may comprise both intentional and extensional (facts) LQL rules.

The LQL Program Optimizer performs the analysis of the binding propagation resulting from constants appearing in the query predicates according to the approach presented in [18], and subsequently performs program optimization based on the constant pushing [17] as well as the term rewriting methods [18]. The final optimization step generates the Relational Algebra (RA) program pertaining to the query as well as all control blocks describing the required storage object types.

The RA program is submitted for execution by placing is in the query queue. We discuss the representation of the RA programs as well as the scheduling and execution strategies in the ensuing sections.

3. EXECUTION OF THE LQL QUERIES

The LQL queries are submitted via the Epsilon User Interface to be analyzed by the LQL Rule Analyzer. The query Q is expanded into a triple <G,LP,D> derived from the corresponding LQL theory, where G is the LQL program goal, LP is the set of LQL rules reachable from the query and D is the set of predicates corresponding to relational database relations. The relational database relations may either be derived relations, defined as SQL views, or base relations, defined as SQL tables. The LQL Rule Analyzer retrieve from the LQL Data Dictionary the dependency graph of LP (DAG_{LP}) and passes DAG_{LP} and the triple <G,LP,D> to the LQL Program Optimizer.

The LQL program optimization comprises two distinct levels, namely the term rewriting optimization, utilizing methods based on the compilation of recursive logic programs [4,5,18], and the execution level optimization. The execution level optimization generates the RA program to be executed by the RA Program Executor, and the physical representation control blocks determining the storage

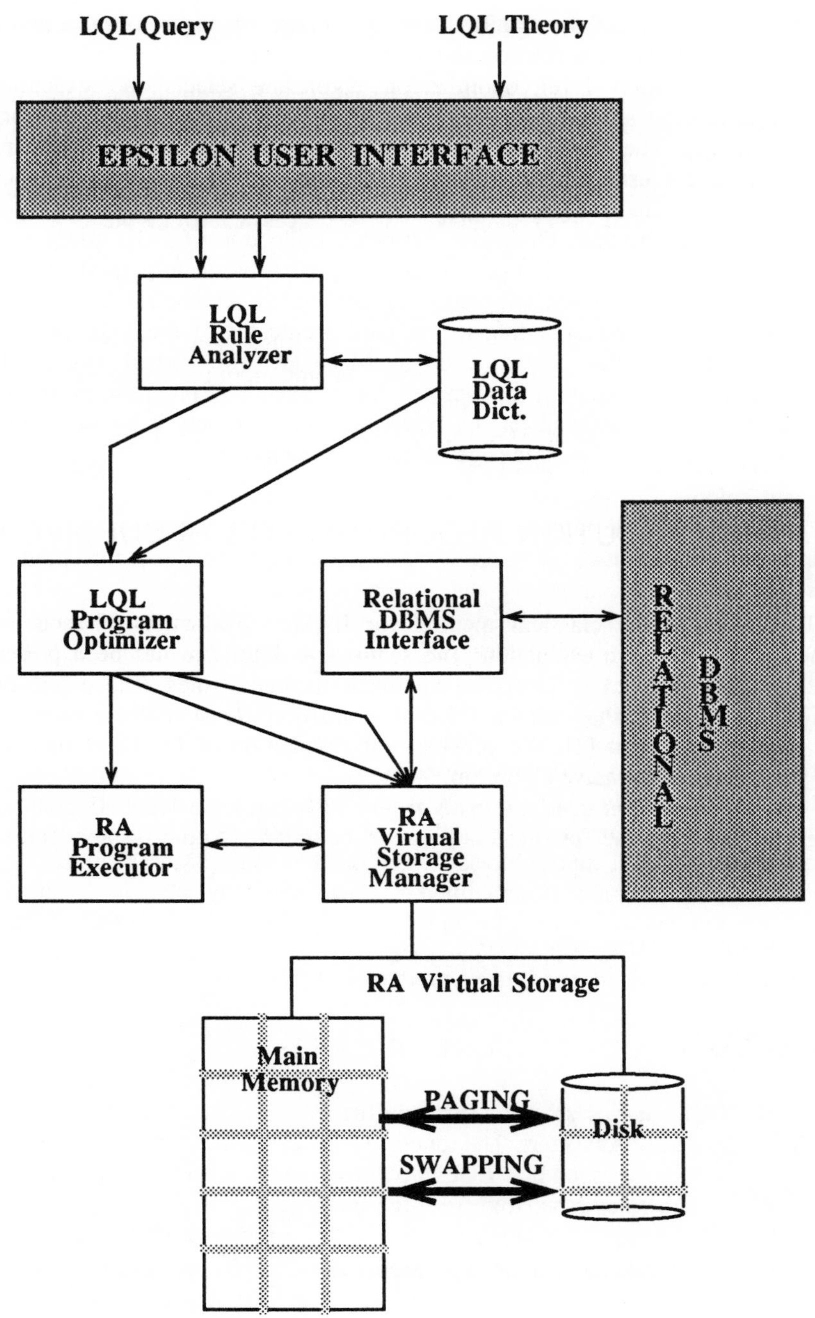

Figure 1. Architecture of the LQL; subsystem

strategies to be utilized by the RA Virtual Storage Manager to store and manipulate the argument database relation and intermediate results.

The execution level optimization algorithm selects the execution algorithms and storage strategies on the basis of the cost model formulated for the RA Virtual Storage. The cardinalities of RA operation arguments (base and intermediate relations) are established on the basis of the quantitative characteristics of the source relational database obtained from the LQL Data Dictionary.

The LQL Program Optimizer defines a collection of SQL query parameters, passed to the RA Virtual Storage Manager, to be subsequently used in calls to the Relational DBMS Interface triggering the embedded parametric SQL queries. The resulting relations, corresponding to the base predicates of the LQL program rules, are passed to the RA Virtual Storage Manager. The virtual storage functions according to control strategy determined for a given RA program by the optimizer and determining the demand paging behaviour, the swapping behaviour and the proportion of fixed versus dynamic pages in the main memory.

3.1. THE EXECUTION ALGORITHM FOR RECURSIVE CLUSTERS

We adopt the classical method for fixpoint evaluation of recursive rules, namely the semi-naive evaluation. The semi-naive algorithm has been presented and exhaustively discussed in [3,4] for the linear recursive rules. The extension of the semi-naive method, that allows fixpoint evaluation for non-linear recursive rules, has been presented in [2]. We propose implementation of the latter method, called the generalized, semi-naive algorithm.

The *Concurrent semi-naive algorithm* computes the least fixpoint of a subprogram defining the predicates $p_1, \ldots, p_n$ belonging to the same recursive cluster.

algorithm *Concurrent_semi-naive*

    par [$\Delta p_1 := eval\_pred(p_1, norecursive);\ P_1 := \Delta p_1$

        || $\Delta p_2 := eval\_pred(p_2, norecursive);\ P_2 := \Delta p_2$

        ...

        ...

        || $\Delta p_n := eval\_pred(p_n, norecursive);\ P_n := \Delta p_n$

        ];

    repeat

        par [$\Delta p_1 := eval\_pred(p_1, recursive) - P_1;\ P_1 := \Delta p_1 \cup P_1$

            || $\Delta p_2 := eval\_pred(p_2, recursive) - P_2;\ P_2 := \Delta p_2 \cup P_2$

            ...

            ...

            || $\Delta p_n := eval\_pred(p_n, recursive) - P_n;\ P_n := \Delta p_n \cup P_n$

            ];

    until $\bigcup_{1 \leq i \leq n} \Delta p_n = \emptyset$

where:

- P_i denotes the global relation for predicate symbol p_i;
- *eval_pred* is the function that computes the relation for a derived predicate.

function *eval_pred(p,t)*

```
    par [ T^1 := eval_rule( r_t^1 )
        || T^2 := eval_rule( r_t^2 )
           ...
           ...
        || T^{m_t} := eval_rule( r_t^{m_t} )
        ]
    return ( ∪_{1≤i≤m_t} T^i )
```

where:

- $r_t^1, \ldots, r_t^{m_t}$ are the rule defining the predicate p; they are either recursive or non-recursive rule according with the value of the parameter t;
- *eval_rule* is the function that computes the relation for the relational algebra expression associated to a logical rule [1].

function *eval_rule*$(p \leftarrow c_1,\ldots,c_h,q_1,\ldots,q_k)$

```
    C := C_1 ⋈ C_2 ⋈ ,..., ⋈ C_h;
    if k=0 then
        return (C)   /* the rule is non-recursive */
    else
        par [ T_1 := C ⋈ Δq_1 ⋈ Q_2 ,..., ⋈ Q_k
            || T_2 := C ⋈ Q_1 ⋈ Δq_2 ,..., ⋈ Q_k
               ...
               ...
            || T_k := C ⋈ Q_1 ⋈ Q_2 ,..., ⋈ Δq_k
            ]
        return ( ∪_{1≤i≤k} T_i )
    end_if
```

where:

- $c_1,\ldots,c_h$ are either base or derived predicates non-recursive with respect to p;
- C_i is the global relation for c_i; if c_i is a derived predicate it has to be already computed by recursively applying the algorithm;
- $q_1, \ldots, q_k$ are derived predicates recursive w.r.t. p;

---

1 notice that for the sake of simplicity we assume that the rule contains positive, non-comparison constant free predicates only. A general mapping from a Datalog rule to an equivalent relational expression can be found in [26].

- Δq_i is the differential relation for q_i (i.e. the set of tuples added to Q_i at the previous step of the semi-naive algorithm).

Implementation of the semi-naive algorithm requires the following relational algebra operations:

Equi-join($\bowtie$) The equi-join operation is to be implemented as a nested loop multijoin, where the outer loop is controlled by the differential relation.

Union ($\cup$) Two stage hashing function is to be used to eliminate duplicate tuples, where the first stage is a bit map, and the second stage is the hashing synonym table.

Difference(-) Two stage hashing function is to be used to eliminate the intersectiontuples, where the first stage is a bit map, and the second stage is the hashing synonym table.

A more detailed description of the use of the two stage hashing functions, applied to distributed query processing, operations may be found in [6]. The *equi-join* operation algorithm is determined by organization of the LQL virtual storage. Therefore, the nested loop multiway join algorithm is presented in the following section.

3.2 CONTROL OF THE RA PROGRAM EXECUTION

An instance of the LQL program, after having undergone the appropriate optimization steps, is transformed into a relational algebra program. The RA programs are composed of *cluster procedures* evaluating the corresponding clusters of the LQL program. A *cluster procedures* may correspond to the semi-naive recursive cluster evaluation presented above, may be an external query materializing an external predicate, or may be an evaluation procedure for a non-recursive predicate. Dependencies between the *cluster procedures* within a program are derived from the LQL program dependency graph. In order to exhibit the dependencies and to detect the potential parallelism we represent the relational algebra program as a Condition-Event (C-E) Petri net.
Internally the relational algebra program is represented as an ordered triple $<A,F,S>$, where:

A is a dynamic precedence matrix representing the cluster procedure dependencies expressed by the C-E Petri net representation.

F is the sequence of the cluster procedure specifications.

S is the symbol table providing linkage between the symbolic cluster procedure arguments and their physical representations.

The dynamic precedence matrix *A* is a square matrix of order *n* over the domain (0,1), where *n* is the number of cluster procedures comprised in the relational algebra program. An element $a_{ij}=1$ means that the *j-th* cluster procedure involves post-conditions, which are also preconditions of the *i-th* cluster procedure. Hence, the execution of the *i-th* cluster procedure is conditioned on termination of the *j-th* cluster procedure. Elements of the dynamic precedence matrix are to be updated appropriately by the application tasks executing the corresponding cluster procedures. The application tasks are presented in more detail in the following section.

The above control scheme allows for many concurrent application tasks asynchronously processing the independent cluster procedures. Integrity of the matrix *A* is maintained with the use of a locking policy, that enforces locks on the entire matrix *A* during the matrix update operation. The concurrent application tasks independently process cluster procedures taking the arguments from and storing the results in the virtual storage. The application task scheduling algorithm looks for the first unlocked dynamic precedence matrix *A* in the queue of the relational algebra programs, locks it, and selects the *i-th* row such that $\forall_{1 \leq j \leq n}\ a_{ij}=0$, sets $a_{ii}=1$, unlocks the matrix *A*, and initiates the application task.

4 THE RELATIONAL ALGEBRA VIRTUAL STORAGE MODEL

The virtual storage model represents the central part of our approach to interfacing LQL with relational databases. The principal problem of the bottom up approach represented by LQL, already optimized by simulation of the top down, SLD-like resolution based on the rule rewriting optimization techniques, is the lack of efficient recursive query mechanisms within the current relational database management systems. Hence, processing of recursive queries must be done outside of the relational DBMS and we believe that the dedicated storage structures coupled with intelligent memory management algorithms may greatly increase efficiency of the recursive query processing.

Our approach is to support the classical semi-naive fixpoint evaluation algorithm with the two level storage organization. The upper level comprises dedicated storage objects generated ad hoc in the context of the particular query and the relevant subset of the logic program rules. The lower level is the virtual storage consisting of the fixed number of pages, either residing in the main memory or stored on disk. Operations on the storage objects are available to implement the relational algebra equations generated from the logic program rules.

We present the physical organization of the LQL virtual storage discussing the proposed classes of storage objects and the associated operations. Then we explain the virtual storage control algorithm concentrating in particular on the semantic aspects pertaining to a particular logic program context.

The salient characteristic of the iterative evaluation of fixpoints of the relational algebra equations is the repetitive execution of the equi-join operations on the monotonically growing recursive relations and the base relations. It is obvious that the performance gain may be realized by the dedicated storage structure support for such a regular and predictable behaviour of the semi-naive algorithm. In particular, equations implementing transitive closure of relations may be implemented in much more efficient way than currently possible with the use of the standard relational DBMS features.

4.1. STORAGE OBJECTS

The principal observation underlying the proposed selection of the storage objects is that the implementation of the equi-join operations on a sequence of relations specified in the body of a relational algebra expression requires supporting of the *constant → surrogate set* and the *functional dependencies* mappings. Note, that we follow the standard logic programming terminology referring to the attribute value as a constant. The mappings may be defined in the following way:

constant → surrogate se mapping:

$$v{:}C \rightarrow 2^{I}$$
$$v_{R.A_j}(c) = \{\, i \mid \pi_{A_j}(r_i) = c \,\}$$

functional dependency mapping:

$$f{:}I \rightarrow C$$
$$f_{R.A_j}(i) = \pi_{A_j}(r_i)$$

where:

- C — is the set of constants belonging to the domain $(R.A_j)$
- I — is the set of integers
- $R.A_j$ — is the *j-th* attribute of the relation R
- r_i — is the *i-th* tuple of the relation R
- i — is the integer denoting the ordinal number used as the surrogate key of the relation R
- c — is the constant such that $c \in C$

Note, that the functional dependency mapping represents the usual (1 NF) fact that all attributes are functionally dependent on the surrogate key [11].

Example 4.1

Let us consider the following relations $A(a_1,a_2)$, $B(b_1,b_2)$, and $C(c_1,c_2)$ participating in the following recursive relational algebra equation:

$$B(a_1,c_1) = A(a_1,a_2) \underset{a_2=b_1}{\bowtie} B(b_1,b_2) \underset{b_2=c_2}{\bowtie} C(c_1,c_2)$$

We can view the above join operations as the series of nested loop equi-joins, the first returning a series of tuples for each realization of the join predicate $a_2{=}b_1$, and the second also returning several tuples for each value of the attribute b_2 such that $b_2{=}c_2$. Notice, that these two operations correspond to the *constant → surrogate set* mapping, since for each value of the left-hand side join argument we may reference several tuples comprising the right-hand side argument value (hence referencing several surrogate key values). For each tuple of the relation B, represented by the surrogate key value, we take the new value of the attribute b_2 to perform the second equi-join operation. This corresponds to the *functional dependencies* mapping.

Due to the functional dependency mapping, the above multi-join result could unambiguously be represented as $B(s_A,s_C)$. Note, that s_A and s_C are the surrogate keys referring to tuples of the relations A and C respectively comprising the corresponding values of attributes a_1 and c_1. If we assume that the original order of the above relations remains unchanged, we can always retrieve the required attribute values.

The above example also indicates that different attributes, playing diverse roles in the relational algebra equations, may require application of different mappings during the equi-join operations. In order to establish the roles of attributes and to construct the appropriate physical objects supporting the corresponding mappings, we represent the collection of attributes as a labelled directed graph G, where for each $<a,n> \in G$, an arc $a \in V \cup F$ and a vertex $n \in A$. V, F are the families of the *constant* $\rightarrow$ *surrogate set* (v-type) and *functional dependency* (f-type) mappings, and A is the set of attributes.

The *attribute role graph* for the example 4.1 is shown in figure 2. The arcs must also be labelled with cluster identifiers to associate the roles with the logic program clusters. The arcs linking the attributes a_2 and a_1 as well as c_2 and c_1 reflect the functional dependency mappings necessary to collect all attribute values in the result relation tuples. The *attribute role graph* has a dual function; to provide information about required storage objects pertaining to particular mappings, and to provide control information for the virtual storage manager. We discuss the latter function in more detail in the following subsection.

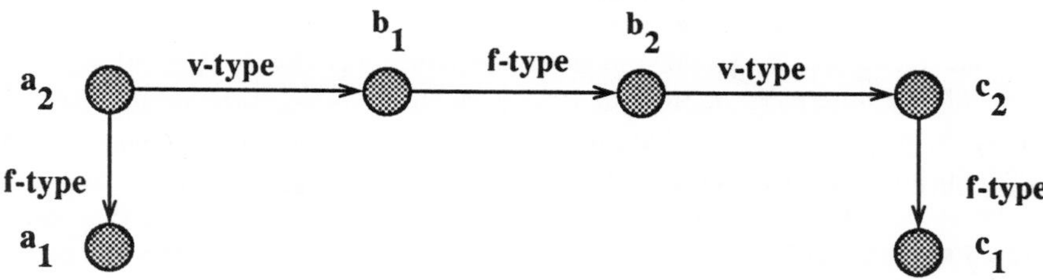

Figure 2. The attribute role graph

The *attribute role graph* imposes the following classification on th set of attributes:

Active attribute	all attributes that are reachable via the v-type arcs.
Relevant attribute	all attributes that are reachable via the f-type arc.

All other attributes of the corresponding base as well as derived relations are not represented in the *attribute role graph* and consequently have no supporting storage objects. In the case of the derived relations, the storage objects that are not longer used are logically deleted from the virtual storage.

The following three classes of the storage objects are proposed to support the above attribute role classes and the mapping families:

Inverted list	$I^{x}_{R.A_j} = \{ i \mid \pi_{A_j}(r_i) = x \}$
Transposed attribute	$T_{R.A_j} = \pi_{A_j}(R)$
Multi-transposed attribute	$T_{R.A_1,\ldots,R.A_k} = \pi_{A_1,\ldots,A_k}(R)$

where:

C_R	is the number of tuples in R.
i	is the surrogate key of the relation R such that $1 \le i \le C_R$
N_R	is the arity of the relation R
j,k	are the attribute numbers within R such that $1 \le j,k \le N_R$
x	is a constant such that $x \in R.A_j$

The above storage objects are considered to be the first class objects in the sense that they may be stored, retrieved and manipulated in their entirety by the appropriate Virtual Storage Manager operations. They are stored on virtual storage pages and their unique identification is supported by the physical address being the combination of the virtual page/page index number. We discuss the virtual storage address translation in the subsequent subsection.

We impose the partial order by the relation $\le$ in each of the inverted list structures to be retained throughout the life span of the storage object. The range of the surrogate key may vary depending on the storage strategy generated by the optimizer. In the case of the base relation being retained in the database, meaning that the relevant but inactive attributes are not brought into the LQL storage, the range of the surrogate key is delimited by the cardinality of the original database relation. Otherwise, when the relation is brought into the virtual storage, in its projected and restricted form, the range of the surrogate key is determined by the cardinality of the internally represented base relation. Note, that in the first case we must impose the restriction that the original order of the base relation remains unchanged during execution of the logic program. This implies locking entire relations in the source database, which may not always be feasible. Hence, the optimizer storage structure strategy decisions are also influenced by the external processing constraints. The inverted list storage objects support the v-type mappings from a constant (attribute value) to the set of tuple identifiers (surrogate keys).

The transposed attribute storage objects provide support for the functional dependency mapping from the surrogate key value to the transposed attribute value. The mapping is implemented by the following address function:

$$addr_{R.A_j}(i) = (i - 1) \times l_j$$

where l_j is the length (in bytes) of the attribute $R.A_j$.

The multi-transposed attribute storage objects are used to retain all attributes that are relevant to the given logic program instance (LP/query combination), but are not participating as arguments of any equi-join predicate. As we pointed out above, the multi-transposed objects are optional, since they may always be reconstructed from the original base relation with the use of the corresponding surrogate key value set. The mapping is implemented by the following address function:

$$m\text{-}addr_{R.A_j,\ldots,R.A_k}(i) = (i - 1) \times \sum_{i=j}^{h} l_i$$

where l_i is the length (in bytes) of the attribute $R.A_i$.

4.2 THE VIRTUAL STORAGE

Design of the LQL virtual storage has two principal objectives, namely maximization of the system throughput, which may be achieved by concurrent execution of queries, and minimization of the I/O activity, achieved by the global optimization of task scheduling and by efficient support of storage object sharing. We illustrate how we propose to attain the above objectives presenting the main aspects of the LQL virtual storage organization, namely the architecture of the virtual storage subsystem, mapping of storage objects into the page structure, allocation of virtual storage pages to application tasks supporting the LQL queries and the task scheduling strategy, as well as the support for object sharing.

The proposed virtual storage subsystem is very similar to the classical virtual memory subsystems of large computer systems. The main difference lying in the control algorithms, which in our case make use of prior knowledge regarding behaviour of the application tasks servicing the LQL queries. The main memory is allocated to accommodate 4 kbyte physical pages, that are read in or written to a direct access paging file on disk. While in main memory, the physical pages are identified by their offsets.

The physical pages contain storage objects currently residing in the main memory and their usage depends on the type of object. In the case of shared objects, a single physical page may be "seen" by many application tasks through the virtual pages comprised in their address space. The number of storage pages depends on the number of page slots available within the paging file on disk.

The main memory comprises the system control block area (a standard feature in any system), the common object area, and the application area. Additionally, some memory is reserved for emergency actions and we call such memory the safety cushion. Note, that the above areas represent the logical rather than physical division of the main memory, and that they do not represent contiguous memory ranges. They may be thought of as collection of physical pages characterized by the common usage e.g. to store shared objects.

The disk memory is divided into two principal parts, namely the page slot area and the swap area. The first is to be used for all paging activity and the latter, organized to support fast chained I/O operations is to be used to swap in and out entire working sets.

The application tasks are scheduled to service the LQL queries. The granularity of a typical application task corresponds to the logic program clusters. For example, a fixpoint evaluation for a recursive cluster will be considered to be an application task. In order to exploit the inherent concurrency below the above granularity level, we propose control algorithms that allow spawning concurrent subtasks within an single task. The storage objects utilized by a given task occupy the page slots on disk, the number of page slots must be sufficient to accommodate all required objects, and a number of main memory pages are also allocated to accommodate the working set of the task. The working set of a task is a collection of virtual storage pages residing in main memory allocated to that task. The size and composition of a working set is determined by the appropriate virtual storage control algorithms. The virtual storage page may contain many storage objects, as well as many pages may be used to store a single object. The page header contains the allocation information, time stamps (last read, last written), update flag, and the pointer to the corresponding working set control block of a given application task. The page indexes store byte offsets, from the beginning of the data area of a page, to the first byte of the storage object. Since the physical address of a storage object is the virtual storage page number and the page index number, we may freely move objects within a page. Note, that we are using the virtual page number allocated within each task address space, rather than the actual physical page numbers (the disk slot numbers). Each storage object commences with an object header comprising the object length information within the given page and the continuation pointer, if the object is continues on other pages. The chain of continuation pointers allows arbitrary length objects to be stored within the virtual storage subsystem.

The application tasks are scheduled in such a way as to maximize the system throughput and in the same time to satisfy the memory requirements, established as the minimum working set size, of each individual task. Tasks that share objects tend to be scheduled for concurrent execution, if no task dependency constraint precludes such schedule.

The shared objects are excluded from working sets of individual tasks, and they are stored in the common object area. Note, that the addressing scheme constraining the references to each individual task address space may lead to a situation that the same shared object residing in a given physical page may be addressed with different virtual page numbers by distinct application tasks. The side effect is the object sharing transparency that exemplifies our approach based on separation of the storage object manipulation and the virtual storage control.

5 THE RA VIRTUAL STORAGE CONTROL ALGORITHMS

Due to the space limitation we only present the virtual storage control algorithms that are considered fundamental to our approach. We view these algorithms in the context of the iterative fixpoint computation, namely the generalized seminaive method as presented in [2], since this is the hardest problem from the performance point of view in the recursive query processing. The complete presentation of the virtual storage control strategy may be found in [10]. In the following we discuss the virtual storage page management, in particular the physical page allocation strategies and address translation, management of the task working sets, object sharing control, and application task scheduling.

5.1 VIRTUAL STORAGE PAGE MANAGEMENT

The Virtual Storage Manager (VSM) allocates an address space to each initiated application task containing sufficient number of pages to accommodate the input storage objects, the intermediate objects, and the resulting output objects. The output storage objects, or rather their pages are subsequently allocated to the succeeding tasks, or if appropriate they may become shared objects. Each address space is defined by the Virtual Storage Control Block (VSCB) stored as a relation comprising the following information:

Virtual-Page-Number The virtual pages allocated to a single address space are numbered contiguously from 1 to *N*, where *N* is the number of pages allocated to the address space. The virtual page number is to be used for internal reference within the application task, and its sub-tasks, to provide the mapping between the local view of the address space and the actual physical page allocation. For example, the virtual page may only exist as a pointer to a physical page storing a shared object seen from several active address spaces.

Page-Slot-Number The page umber represents the physical address of a page on disk. It corresponds to the physical block number in the direct access file organization. A physical page is always paged in/out from the same slot (physical block) in the secondary memory. Only in the case of swapping operations the page may be also written (redundantly) into the swapping area. This approach accommodates fast chained input/output techniques.

Physical Page Offset The physical page offset indicates the first byte of the main memory space allocated to this area. The offset value is the base for the pointer addressing scheme underlying our address translation approach. The offset value also indicates whether the physical page is currently in the main memory or it has been paged out (written to disk or simply overwritten by a new page). In the latter case the offset value is equal to zero.

Virtual Page Status The virtual page status indicates the type of current usage. For example, the virtual page may be local updatable, indicating a 1:1 mapping between the virtual and the physical page, or shared, thus implying the N:1 mapping. The status information may also indicate, for local virtual pages only, the current paging priority. For example, the working set control algorithm may fix some pages in main memory, due to the high probability (or certainty) of immediate reference.

The VSCB provides means for direct address translation scheme. The address translation function maps directly the virtual page numbers into the corresponding main memory offsets or the paging file slot number. The second address may be required, if the page fault occurs and the page read operation must be effected. The VSCB is stored on the local virtual page (or pages) of the address space and its paging status is "fixed". It may be written to disk only when the entire address space (or rather the working set of an address space) is swapped out.

The address translation function of the type *addr* : $O \rightarrow$ P, where O is the set of storage object addresses defined as ordered pairs *<virtual page number, page index number>* and P is the set of physical page addresses defined alternatively as ordered pairs *<physical page offset, byte offset within page>* or *<page slot number, byte offset within page>*. The second alternative is used when the page fault occurs. The value of the byte offset within page is stored as the value of the corresponding page index. Note, that the VSCB stores the extension of the *addr* function for a given address space.

5.2 MANAGEMENT OF APPLICATION TASK WORKING SETS

The application task working set is the subset of the address space that currently resides in main memory. It may be viewed as a window moving across the address space pages and containing a fixed number of pages at any time. Whenever a reference is made to a page that is not currently included in the working set, the set fault occurs and the required page must be read (paged-in) from the secondary storage. The page-in operation implies overwriting of one of the existing working set pages, possibly preceded by the write operation, if an updatable page is being paged out. The problem at hand is to establish the optimal size, in terms of the number of pages, of the working set for the application task, and to establish a paging discipline matching the processing requirements of the application task. The processing requirements may be expressed in terms of the storage object occurrences accessed by the application task, the common objects shared with other tasks, as well as the page access patterns, in particular any possible cyclicity, during the execution of the application task. Obviously, our goal is to set up such a working set configuration as to minimize the number of page faults for a given application task execution.

Before looking at the possible options, let us discuss the usage modes of the various storage object types. As before our underlying context is the semi-naive evaluation of the recursive relational algebra equations and first of all we concentrate on the equi-join operation with differential relations.

Example 5.2

Let us discuss the following recursive relational algebra equation:

$$B(a_1,c_1) = B(b_1,b_2) \underset{b_1=a_2}{\bowtie} A(a_1,a_2) \underset{a_1=c_2}{\bowtie} C(c_1,c_2)$$

Supposing that relations A and C are base relations, or relations derived before and given as input to the application task resolving the above recursive cluster, we can rewrite the above equation (keeping in mind the iterative semi-naive algorithm) in the following way:

$$B(a_1,c_1) = \Delta B(b_1,b_2) \underset{b_1=a_2}{\bowtie} A(a_1,a_2) \underset{a_1=c_2}{\bowtie} C(c_1,c_2)$$

where ΔB is the differential relation.

We assume that the optimizer has generated the nested loop multi-join execution strategy for the above recursive equation, where the outer loop is controlled by the differential relation ΔB. Let us suppose that all appropriate storage objects exist. In particular to implement the above multi-join we need the following storage object types:

1. The inverted list type on values of the attribute a_2 denoted I_{a_2}
2. The transposed attribute for the attribute a_1 denoted T_{a_1}
3. The inverted list type on values of the attribute c_2 denoted I_{c_2}

Note, that we ignore the tuple construction phase of the multi-join concentrating only on the actual equi-join arguments. The operation may be implemented by the following algorithm:

The nested loop multi-join algorithm

for each $b \in \Delta B$ **do**
    address($I_{a_2}^{b_1}$ *) := hash(* b_1 *)*
    for each $i \in$ $I_{a_2}^{b_1}$ **do**
        $a_i = t_i$ such that t_i is the i-th element of the transposed file T_{a_1}
        asdresses($I_{c_2}^{a_1}$) := *hash(* a_1 *)*
    end_for;
end_for;

The above algorithm gets an inverted list of the attribute a_2 for each value of the attribute b_1, and for each value of the surrogate key in the inverted list it gets a value of the attribute a_1 from the transposed attribute T_{a_1} and it uses that value to get the inverted list of the attribute c_2. This completes the navigation of the nested loop multi-join.

So far we saw that it is not worthwhile to keep more than one occurrence of each inverted list type needed in the join operation plus one page per each transposed argument. Hence, we may have to read in new occurrences of inverted lists for each new value in the differential relation and for each left hand join predicate argument value down the nesting level. It may be worthwhile to optimize I/O operations by analyzing the value bindings, e.g. magic sets, differential relation to establish what is the value reference pattern with respect to the inverted lists. It is feasible, considering the possible size of the main memory allocated to a working set, to fix in memory some working set pages containing referenced storage objects. Another performance gain may be realized by management of shared objects. This problem and the related task scheduling problems are discussed in the subsequent subsections.

5.3 OBJECT SHARING CONTROL

Let us first of all see which storage objects may be shared among the concurrent application tasks, or better which storage objects are worthwhile sharing. Naturally the sharing granularity is the occurrence, rather than the storage object class, level. However, there are salient characteristics of some object classes that preclude object sharing. The transposed attribute objects are one such class. We have already established in the previous subsection, that maintaining more than one transposed attribute page in the working set does not result in significant performance gain. The current page of such an object may be viewed as a window moved sequentially across a series of values. Apart from the clustering effect, that results in accessing the current page a number of times, there is no referencing of pages storing the transposed attribute objects. Hence, each of the concurrent application tasks moves its own individual window at its own pace and no significant gain from object sharing may be materialized.

On the other hand, the prime candidates for object sharing are the inverted list storage objects. The principal reason for eligibility to be shared efficiently is the fact that the inverted lists are not updatable objects, and that they offer significant performance gain while kept entirely in the main memory.

Let us have the set $P = (p_1, p_2, \ldots, p_M)$ of application tasks that are either executing (we call them active), or waiting in a queue to be scheduled for execution (we call them ready). We assume a backlog of processes and consequently the ready application tasks may either be the swapped out address spaces waiting to resume processing, or new tasks that wait to commence processing. We assume that in the case of bound queries we may pass binding information into the application task, so that we can identify occurrences, or a restricted subset of occurrences, of the inverted list storage objects pertaining to the bound attributes.

Let us have a matrix O_{ij}, where $1 \leq i \leq M$, and $1 \leq i \leq N$, N being the number of the allocated or identified for allocation storage objects. We call the matrix O_{ij} the allocation matrix. An element o_{ij} of the matrix O_{ij} has the value equal to 1, if the corresponding storage object is allocated or scheduled for allocation to the i-th application task. Otherwise the value of such element is equal to 0. We impose the integrity constraint on the matrix saying, that an object must be allocated or scheduled for allocation to at least one application tasks. Objects that become free (all zeros in the corresponding column) do not participate in the allocation matrix. We also have a function *count(j)* that produces a sum $count(j) = \sum_{i=1}^{M} O_{ij}$. If for the *j-th* storage object in the allocation matrix the condition *count(j)*>1 is true, then we call such an object a shared storage object.

We have already stated that a special class of pages exists that collectively represents the shared object memory. The main memory is not allocated in contiguous blocks, and the shared pages are identified through a main memory directory. The shared object control algorithm fixes the shared pages in main memory. The fixed pages may not be subject to paging operations and must stay intact, unless an exception condition arises, in the main memory. The application tasks sharing a given page (main memory offset), view that page through the virtual page listed in its address space VSCB.

5.4 APPLICATION TASK SCHEDULING

The heuristic of our task scheduling approach is to privilege application tasks with the maximum number of shared storage objects. Notice, that such tasks may avail of large working sets without actually consuming as much main memory. Thus, if such tasks prevail, the sum of working set sizes may substantially exceed the size of the available main memory. On the other hand, tasks, that are low on our priority ladder, are those that have large working sets and few shared pages. Such tasks, if an application dependent value of processing time is exceeded, are swapped out to be resumed when their relative priority increases (as a function of "ready time"), or when enough main memory is available to accommodate all preceding tasks.

The above scheduling policy is imposed as the partial order on the set P as the relation "≤" on the shared object utilization coefficients u_i corresponding to each $p_i \in P$, where $u_i = \sum_{j=1}^{N} o_{ij} \times count(j)$ characterizes utilization of shared objects *i-th* by the application task. Note, that the poset P includes also the currently executing tasks. Therefore, if a currently executing task is preceded in the poset P by other tasks, that are in the ready state, and its processing time slice exceeded the preestablished limit, it will be swapped out and its state will be changed to "ready". 1

6 CONCLUSION

We have presented an implementation approach to development of the logic query processing capability for a deductive database system. The principal contribution of our work is the proposal of a dedicated virtual storage mechanism that is to support efficient query processing.

Our current research concentrate on development of the cost model, and the corresponding performance model, to study the performance aspects of the virtual memory subsystem. The aim of this study is to confront the proposed solutions with the known transitive closure query processing techniques, in particular with those presented in [12, 23].

References

1 Apt, K., Blair, H., and Walker, A.,Towards a theory of declarative knowledge, *Foundations of Deductive Databases and Logic Programming*, J. Minker (ed.), Morgan Kauffman, Los Altos, CA, 1988, 89-148.

2 Balbin, I., Ramamohanarao, K.,A Generalization of the Differential Approach to Recursive Query Evaluation, *Journal of Logic Programming*, 4, 1987.

3 Bancilhon, F., Naive Evaluation of Recursively Defined Relations, in *On Knowledge Base Management Systems - Integrating Database and AI Systems*, M.L. Brodie and J. Mylopoulos (Eds.), Springer-Verlag.

4 Bancilhon, F., Ramakrishnan, R., An Amateur's Introduction to Recursive Query Processing, *Proc. of the 1986 ACM SIGMOD Conference on Management of Data*, 1986.

5 Beeri, C., Ramakrishnan, R., On the Power of Magic, *Proc. of the 6th ACM SIGMOD-SIGACT Symposium on Principles of Database Systems*, 1987.

6 Belcastro, V., Dutkowski, A., Kaminski, W., Kowalewski, M., Mallamaci, L., Mostardi, T., Scrocco, F.P., Staniszkis, W., and Turco, G., An Overview of the Distributed Query System, *Proc. of the EDBT'88 Conference*, Venice, March 1988, Springer Verlag.

7 Bocca, J., On the Evaluation Strategy of Educe, *Proc. of the 1986 ACM SIGMOD Conference on Management of Data*, 1986.

8 Ceri, S., Gottlob, Wiederhold, G., Interfacing Relational Databases and Prolog Efficiently, *in Expert Database Systems*, L. Kerchberg (ed.), Benjamin/Cummings.

9 Chimenti, D., O'Hare, T., Krishnamurthy, R., Naqvi, S., Tsur, S., West, C., Zaniolo, C., An Overview of the LDL System, *Data Engineering*, 10,4, September 1987.

10 Greco, S., Leone, N., and Staniszkis, W., Supporting a Logic Query Language in the Deductive Database System, *CRAI Research Report*, September, 1989.

11 Hall, P., et al,Relations and Entities, in *Modelling in DBMS*, G.M. Nijssen (Ed.), North-Holland 1976.

11 Henschen, L., and Naqvi, S., On Compiling Queries in Recursive First-Order Data Bases, *JACM*, Vol. 31, January 1984.

12 Ioannidis, Y.E., On the Computation of the Transitive Closure of Relational Operators, *Proc. of the 12th Conf. on Very Large Databases*, Kyoto, Japan, August 1986.

13 Jarke, M., Clifford, J., Vassilou, Y., An Optimizing Prolog Front End to a Relational Query System, *Proc. of the 1984 ACM SIGMOD Conference on Management of Data*, 1984.

14 Kunifji, S., Yokota, H., Prolog and Relational Databases for 5th Geeration Computer Systems, in *Advances in Logic and Databases*, Vol.2, Gallaire, Minker and Nicholas (eds.), Plenum, New York, 1984.

15 Levi, G., Modesti M., Kouloumdjian J., Status and evolution of the Epsilos prototype, *Proc. ESPRIT Technical Week*, Bruxelles, Belgium !987.

16 Morris, K., Naughton, J., Saraiya, Y., Ullman, J., Van Gelder, A.,YAWN! (Yet Another Window on Nail), *Data Engineering*, 10,4, September 1987.

17 Naqvi, S., Tsur, S., *A Logic Language for Data and Knowledge Bases*, Academic Press, New York, 1989.

18 Sacca', D., Zaniolo, C., Implementation of Recursive Queries for a Data Language based on Pure Horn Logic, *Proc. of the Fourth Int. Conference on Logic Programming*, Melbourne, Australia, 1987.

19 Sacca', D., Zaniolo, C., Magic Counting Methods, *Proc. of the 1987 ACM SIGMOD Conference on Management of Data*, 1987.

20 Sacca', D., Dispinzeri, M., Mecchia, A., Pizzuti, C., Del Gracco, C., Naggar, P., The Advanced Database Environment of the KIWI System, *Data Engineering*, 10,4, September 1987.

21 Sacca', D., Zaniolo, C., Differential Fixpoint Methods and Stratification of Logic Programs, *Proc. of the 3rd Int. Conference on Data and Knowledge Bases*, June 1988, Jerusalem, Israel.

22 Shapiro, S., Martins, J., McKay, D., Bi-Directional Inference, *Proc. of the 4th Annual Conference of the Cognitive Science Society*, Ann Arbor, Michigan, 1982.

23 Valduriez, P., Boral, H., Evaluation of Recursive Queries Using Join Indices, *Proc. of the 1st Int. Conf. on Expert Database Systems*, Charleston, South Carolina, April 1986.

24 Vieille, L., Recursive Axioms in Deductive Databases: The Query/Subquery Approach, *Proc. of the First Int. Conference on Expert Database Systems*, Charleston, 1986.

25 Ullman, J.D., Implementation of Logical Query Languages for Databases, ACM TODS, 10,3, 1985.

26 Ullman, J.D., *Principles of Database and Knowledge-Base Management System*, Academic Press, 1988,

28 Zaniolo, C., Design and Implementation of a Logic Based Language for Data Intensive Applications, *unpublished manuscript, MCC*, June 1988.

QUESTIONS

Dr. R. Lucas (Aberdeen University).

RL. Have you any figures for the performance of the system?

Mr. N. Leone.

NL. We are now making the performance models and cost models for the system. At the moment, we don't know. We try to avoid the intensive interaction between the DBMS's and the system because we think in many systems this is the major factor.

RL. Does the deduction system compute a set of results?

NL. It does.

RL. But what if the user only wants one result?

NL. We provide the user with the whole set as specified by the query.

RL. But the user may only require one. He might be developing a query. He may be incrementally trying to get a result so he may only require the first solution to his query to see what such a solution looks like. In which case, the database system is doing an optimisation on all tuples. It's very wasteful of processing time.

NL. In our case, a query specifies a set of tuples meeting logical criteria. Our approach is set-oriented, not tuple-oriented as in PROLOG.

RL. But the user may not be set-orientated, you're saying you're forcing the user to be set-orientated.

NL. But that is realistic. Our system is based on the first order logic. It is to provide the logic query interface to a database, hence the answer is a set.

7 A Database Administration Tool Using a Prolog/ORACLE Coupling

R. J. Lucas and A. Yip

ABSTRACT

Coupling Prolog to a relational database is an attractive proposition for several reasons; perhaps the most significant is that datasets of a commercial scale can be processed by a Prolog rule base, allowing database applications to adopt an Expert System style of programming. This paper briefly discusses a tight coupling between the Quintus Prolog compiler and the Oracle Database Management System and goes on to show how aspects of a system for Database Administration were written in Prolog. The advantages of the Prolog development and the performance of the interface and the Administration system are discussed.

1. Introduction

There is a straightforward mapping between rows in a relational database table and facts in a Prolog system. For example, this relational table described in appendix I can be mapped into the Prolog facts:

```
module(b741,programming1,basic,8).
module(b742,hardware,basic,8).
module(b743,'data proc1',basic,8).
module(b744,programming2,int,11).
```

This mapping can be exploited to enable Prolog to process the information held in external databases exactly as though that information was held in Prolog's internal database. Two of the available options to achieve this are:

(1) download the necessary database tables into Prolog's internal database;

(2) implement an interface that mimics Prolog's search and backtracking over the database tables.

The first method is often called 'loose coupling' and quite obviously has many limitations[3].

The second method is called 'tight coupling' and is the method used by the interface described here. Another example of this strategy is described in[1].

The tight coupling is achieved by using an object code library of general purpose database access routines (This is usually known as a 'call' or 'host language' library or interface);

The Oracle Database System has such a Host Language Interface the use of which has the advantage of ensuring database integrity and security , automatic use of indexes and concurrency. This is because you are using the same database access routines that the rest of the system will be built from. One disadvantage which is often pointed to, is the question of efficiency of what must essentially be a 'tuple by tuple' method of processing. This is dealt with in the section on performance.

Only the main points of the interface are discussed here; for further details the reader is referred to[4] which describes a similar interface with the Mimer database system.

The earlier system was used to prototype several expert systems. Examples of these are for fault processing on a large scale network, the filtering of suspects for burglary, and the batching of cars on a conveyor for robot paint sprayers[5].

1.1. Accessing Table entries.

If the programmer wishes to access an Oracle table as though it were a set of Prolog facts, he must declare the table as external, in the following fashion:

```
?-c_external(module,'MODULE').
```

The table is henceforth referred to as 'module' from Prolog.

Joins across tables may be made as though the tables were present as facts in Prolog's database and select conditions are set simply by the values of in-line constants or variables.

When a goal that corresponds to a table access is activated for the first time, it is processed as follows:

(1) A template is built of the known and unknown values in the record;

(2) column names, types and lengths are obtained from the data dictionary;

(3) a table cursor is opened for this search

(4) the selection conditions are set from the known values in the template;

(5) the values from the table are projected into the 'gaps' in the template;

(6) if there are more matching records the cursor is stacked;

(7) the unresolved variables are matched against the corresponding template entries.

The cursor is the device that lets us continue a search from a position that is not at the start of the table, and it is an indicator to the relevant select conditions and the current search position within the table.

When a goal is activated that corresponds to a database access and that has been activated through backtracking, the processing is as follows:

(1) the cursor is popped;

(2) the values from the table are projected into the 'gaps' in the template;

(3) if there are more matching records the cursor is stacked;

(4) the unresolved variables are matched against the corresponding template entries.

It is the stacking of the cursors on a last in first out basis that mimics the Prolog search strategy.

The Quintus Oracle interface is built in two sections. The first is written in Prolog and builds the template and sends it to the second part which is written in C and manages the Oracle HLI calls for selection and projection. The front-end also deals with processing the completed template and preserving the necessary backtrack points for continued searches.

2. Performance

This benchmark uses the test on Hilbert generated unit ground clauses of the *vertex* type[7].

For this test there is no index and the search is therefore sequential.

Sequential 65536 records		
Test	Prolog-Oracle	Oracle SQL
All args ground	38	33
Set on 1st arg	32	30
Set on 3rd arg	48	38

The above results are in seconds of real elapsed time averaged over three retrievals on a SUN 3/160M running Unix 4.2.

The first test is matching on the 65,536th record.

This shows the interface in a poorer light than is actually the case, because if, with 64K records present, and you are trying to match on a ground term, with Prolog the search will stop AS SOON AS IT REACHES THE MATCH, with SQL you are always committed to a total search.

For example with the same data, looking for a match on the 16,384th record with Prolog-Oracle takes 10 seconds. The equivalent SQL query takes 33 seconds.

When the table holds <= 10,000 records, the difference between the access times for Prolog/Oracle and Oracle SQL are very nearly the same.

When there is an index the time delay in both cases is too small to be measured accurately. The results given here are approximate only.

Indexed 65536 records		
Test	Prolog-Oracle	Oracle SQL
All args ground	1.0	0.5
Set on 1st arg	1.0	0.5

As each table search from Prolog is being performed as a separate call to the Oracle software, there is no optimisation being done by Oracle (or anything else) on joins. So joins where there are no indexes to speed access will be significantly slower from Prolog than SQL. SQL can treat the join as a single operation and can speed it up by, for example, sort-merge techniques. This method of operation does not suit Prolog's methodology which is based on processing a tuple at a time.

However, the full advantage of Oracle's optimization on joins can be obtained from within Prolog by defining the relevant view, and then accessing this view as though it were a table.

For example, a view of a join between the emp and dept tables can be created by this SQL command:

```
create view empo as
    select ename, loc
    from emp,dept
```

```
where emp.deptno = dept.deptno;
```

Which is equivalent to the Prolog:

```
empno(Ename,Loc):-
    emp(Deptno,Ename,_,_,_,_),
    dept(Deptno,_,_,Loc,_).
```

From Prolog a *c_external* can be used to access this view, ie:

```
?-c_external(ejoin,'EMPO').
```

The accessing is then performed in the normal way, ie:

```
?-ejoin(Ename,Loc).
```

These tests show that the interface is not significantly slower than SQL and also allows optimisation to be applied to joins in a very straightforward manner by the definition of appropriate views.

3. Other aspects of the Interface

The interface is not just limited to retrieval of user datasets. A predicate *d_external* parallels *c_external* but allows access to any of the system (data-dictionary) tables. There are predicates defined individually for creation of tables and indexes, removal of these, for turning commitment on and off and many other tasks. There is also a 'catch all' predicate *anysql* which takes as an argument any legal non-retrieval SQL string. This ensures that the user can perform any SQL database operation from the interface.

4. The Oracle Database Administrator

4.1. Duties of a Database Administrator

This section describes the duties of the DBA in some detail. Only two of the facilities of the Prolog DBA Support System are described in later sections, backing up the database and examining tables for third normal form. This is because they represent good examples of the main implementation approaches for the entire system. The DBA's duties are:

(1) Start and stop the database system. Since the database system is independent of the operating system on which it resides, it can be started and stopped. When the database system is shut data cannot be accessed.

(2) Initialise the database, and populate it with data. When the database is set-up for the first time, it is the DBA's responsibility to populate it with data from external sources.

(3) Perform regular backup and recovery procedures. Recovery of the database after a failure may not always be automatic. The DBA must ensure that a copy of the recent database state is available for restoration after a major failure.

(4) Ensure data security and privacy. The DBA is responsible for the security and privacy of the database. This includes access control of the database resources to authorised personnel and software.

(5) Monitor statistics on database system activities. This involves examination of static and dynamic information on the database system. Static information includes the distribution of space in the database files, actual sizes of tables, etc. Dynamic information includes usage activities during runtime, frequency of access on tables and time taken for queries, etc.

(6) Use the above statistical information to achieve performance optimisation. This duty is also termed as tuning the database and involves re-organisation and re-structuring of data. Data is re-organised by re-arranging its physical displacement. For example, copying and dropping tables reclaims fragmented space in the database files. Re-structuring of data involves changes in the conceptual schema. For example, normalisation of tables to third normal form resolves update and retrieval problems.

4.2. Using Oracle's existing DBA facilities from Prolog

Many of these facilities can be supported by an Oracle utility tool. Examples of these are: the IOR utility, for initialising, starting and stopping the database; the ODS (Oracle Display System) for monitoring the usage of the database. A significant problem for an inexpert DBA is that these tools are separate rather than integrated and it can be difficult to know where to start to look for a particular utility. The problem is made worse by many DBA tasks requiring the use of more than one utility tool.

The Support System was designed to automate parts of the general tasks, thus reducing the amount of effort required for their completion.

The best way to demonstrate this aspect of the Support System is to compare the execution of a task using the Support System against not using it.

One of the regular duties of the DBA is to backup an entire database. Below are the procedural steps for a regular backup using the available Oracle tools :

description	utility tool invoked
Find the names of the database files which make up the database.	SQL*plus {Oracle product}
Shut the database system down.	IOR utility tool {Oracle product}
For each database file, create a backup copy.	UNIX tool {e.g. cp}
Re-start the database system for general use.	IOR utility tool {Oracle product}

Using the Support System to perform the same task involves :

user action :	Select the backup facility.
Support System :	1. Retrieve names of the database files.
	2. Shut the database system down.
	3. Ask user for the name of a backup copy for each DB file.
	4. Create the backup files.
	5. Re-start the database system.
	6. Return to user.

It is evident that the Support System simplifies the DBA's tasks, and make his/her job easier. Moreover, the Prolog to integrate these tasks is relatively straightforward and offers few problems for long term maintenance. An example of how Prolog can be used very succinctly is given in the next section. Unfortunately it is not possible to reproduce substantial parts of the Prolog code in such a short paper.

5. The use made of the Oracle tight coupling

The Support System has to access Oracle data frequently. One of the most important design issues is how the Support System should communicate with the database. Without a tight coupling to the database the alternative accessing method would be via a high level language using embedded dynamic SQL.

SQL is a data manipulation language which is employed by Oracle as the data access language. The SQL would need to be embedded in some conventional language and the support system coded in this language, or this language's object code would need to be linked to the Prolog compiler. This method of implementation requires another Oracle product. For example, if the Support System is written in 'C', the Oracle product Pro*C is required to precompile the SQL commands.

To contrast these two different approaches of implementation, an example of how each method retrieves data from Oracle is given. The example uses the Oracle table MODULE(MODNO, MNAME, STATUS, UNITPOINTS) to find the mname and status of the module whose number is b742. (See Appendix I for the contents of the table MODULE.) All comments in the code are enclosed in '{..}'.

The coding involved using 'C' and dynamic SQL :

```
EXEC SQL BEGIN DECLARE SECTION;  {declare all C variables referring to}
VARCHAR mname[20];               {Oracle data.}
VARCHAR status[20];
EXEC SQL END DECLARE SECTION;

EXEC SQL DECLARE C1 CURSOR FOR   {set up a cursor which will point to}
SELECT MNAME, STATUS             {the tuple satisfying the stated }
FROM MODULE                                {conditions.}
WHERE MODNO = 'b742';
EXEC SQL OPEN C1;                {put the column values into the C}
                                 {variables.}
EXEC SQL FETCH C1 INTO :mname, :status;
```

The coding involved using Prolog :

```
c_external( module, 'MODULE'),            {connect DEPT to predicate dept.}
module( b742, Mname, Status, Unitpoints). {instantiate the column values to the }
                                          {variables.}
```

Using the PROLOG/ORACLE interface is the better alternative because the program structure takes on a more direct approach. Moreover, Prolog has a backtracking inference engine and a powerful pattern matching mechanism. These two features are advantageous for database search and construction of data structures. Moreover, being able to use a recursive search, which is not available by using embedded SQL, was a major advantage to the facility described in the next section.

6. Normalisation

The other DBA facilities that were implemented by linking together Oracle utilities with database searches performed via the interface will not be explored further. Rather we will turn our attention to a rather different type of utility which is not provided for by any of the existing Oracle software.

E.F. Codd, in his 1970 landmark paper on the relational model[2] , identified problems on data manipulation which some tables have due to certain relationships that exist between columns. He categorised tables into different normal forms, i.e. first, second and third normal forms.

The definitions of Codd's normal forms on tables are as follows :

(1) First Normal Form - A table is in first normal form if all columns are atomic, i.e. no data aggregates are present. All tables in a relational database are in 1st

NF.

(2) Second normal form - A table is in second normal form if all non-key columns are fully functionally dependent on the key. The key may consist of one or more columns. Another interpretation of second normal form is that the key determines the non-key columns.
The common notation is : X -> Y,
where X is the key and Y is any non-key column.

(3) Third normal form - A table is in third normal form if there is no transitive dependency. That is, there is no functional dependency between non-key columns.

Normalisation is a reversible process. That is to say, any table can be converted from Nth normal form to (N-1)th normal form and vice versa. Conversion of a table from Nth to (N-1)th normal form is achieved by a natural join operation on the group of Nth normal form tables. The result of the join is the table in (N-1)th normal form. For example, tables STATUS3nf and MODULE3nf are the third normal form of table MODULE. A join on the column STATUS of these two tables gives the table MODULE.

6.1. Why is normalisation to third normal form necessary?

J.D. Ullman in his book 'Principles of database systems'[6] describes the types of problems that can arise if a table is not in third normal form. These problems include deletions and insertions of tuples. Using the table MODULE as an example to illustrate these problems :

Insertion.
If a new status 'project work' is introduced which has 5 unit points, a tuple containing this piece of information cannot be inserted because the status does not relate to any particular course module.

Deletion.
If the course module 'programming2' is cancelled, its tuple is deleted. The fact on intermediate status having 11 unit points is lost because the deleted tuple is the only one which has the information.

In addition, updating tuples of a table which is not in third normal form is inefficient. For example, if the unit points for the basic status is increased from 8 to 9, every tuple where STATUS has the value 'basic' is updated.

If the table MODULE is normalised to third normal form, that is, converted to tables STATUS3nf and MODULE3nf, the above insertion and deletion problems are solved, and updates are more efficient.

6.2. Normalisation from second to third normal form

Since the system facility advises how to convert a table from second to third normal form, a summary of the theoretical approach to this normalisation process is explained briefly in this section, and illustrated by an example.

The process has one fundamental rule : remove all transitive dependency that exist in the 2nd NF table by splitting it into two or more tables.

For example, consider the table MODULE, there is transitive dependency between columns STATUS and UNITPOINTS. By removing the column UNITPOINTS from the table, it becomes a third normal form table. Another table consisting of columns

STATUS and UNITPOINTS is created in order to retain all the information from the original MODULE table.

6.3. Practical approach to normalisation

This section explains briefly how the process of normalisation is incorporated into the system facility. The facility does the normalisation in two stages : inspect the table for transitive dependency, and work out how it can be normalised to a set of third normal form tables.

During the inspection stage, non-key columns which have at least twenty percent duplication in their column values are selected. (Why this selection stage is necessary will become clear later on in this section.) Every possible column pair generated from this column set is then examined for subtuple consistency.

Subtuple consistency is defined as : for a column pair, whenever the value of a column is X, the value of the other column is always Y, and vice versa. For example, in table MODULE, all subtuples of the column pair STATUS and UNITPOINTS are consistent.

The following Prolog code checks for this consistency, by repeatedly examining all tuples of column pairs. The *subtuples_mismatch* predicate is satisfied as soon as a counter example for functional dependence between the two columns is found, i.e. if there exist two subtuples such that the column values of one column are the same but the column values of the other are different.

```
examine_all_dependency( Table, [], []) :- !.

  /* no dependency exists for these 2 columns */
examine_all_dependency( Table, [S|R], DependPairs) :-
    write('examining column number pair  '),
    write( S), write('  ..'), nl,
    subtuples_mismatch( Table, S), !,
    examine_all_dependency( Table, R, DependPairs).

  /* dependency exists for these 2 columns */
examine_all_dependency( Table, [S|R], [S|DependPairs]) :-
    examine_all_dependency( Table, R, DependPairs).


subtuples_mismatch( Table, [C1pos, C2pos]) :-
    return_values_from_table( Table, C1pos, C2pos, C1val, C2val),
    subtuples_mismatch(  Table, C1pos, C2pos, C1val, C2val),
    reset_cursors.

subtuples_mismatch( Table, C1pos, C2pos, OldC1val, OldC2val) :-
    return_values_from_table(  Table, C1pos, C2pos, C1val, C2val),
    mismatch_pairs( OldC1val, OldC2val, C1val, C2val),
    reset_cursors.

mismatch_pairs( C1, C2a, C1, C2b) :-
    not( C2a = C2b).
mismatch_pairs( C1a, C2, C1b, C2) :-
    not( C1a = C1b).
```

The values from the table are fetched via the *ext* interface routine. This predicate is used in preference to the *c_external* method described earlier, because it returns the record as a Prolog list. In other respects it behaves as the previous example, back-tracking retrieves the tuples one at a time. The list form for the record is extremely convenient for processing when the size of the record is variable or unknown.

```
return_values_from_table( Table, C1Colno, C2Colno, C1Val, C2Val) :-
    ext( Table, ordinary, Record),
    get_nth_elem( C1Colno, Record, C1Val),
    get_nth_elem( C2Colno, Record, C2Val).
```

The direct nature of the Prolog code in implementing a fairly complex recursive search should be noted. It is the programming style to carry over from Prolog into the database. The programmer is using the same style of programming for his internal and external databases.

It should be noted that establishing this functional dependency by examining the tuple values is not completely reliant as any key field (no repeating values) will have all the other columns as functionally dependent on it!. To ensure a high probability that the columns are functionally dependent we look for twenty percent duplication in the sub-tuples.

Once all the non-key column pairs of the table are examined, the facility can determine how the table could be split into a set of third normal form tables.

As mentioned in an earlier section, transitively dependent column pairs are taken out of the table to form a new table. Relationships between the columns are kept intact by retaining in the old table one of the columns of the new table.

The example below demonstrates how a table in second normal form is normalised to third normal form by this facility.

A table has eight columns, namely Ci where (0 <= i <= 7) , and C0 is the primary key column. It has the following transitively dependent column pairs :

(C1,C2) ; (C2,C3) ; (C1,C3); (C4,C5)

Columns C1, C2 and C3 have the 'same transitive dependency', and therefore form a new table. Columns C4 and C5 also form a new table. The original table can now be modified to have columns C0, C6, C7, Cm and Cn,
where m is (1 <= m <= 3), and n is (4 <= n <= 5).

The resulting three tables, namely :

Table 1 (C1, C2, C3),
Table 2 (C4, C5),
Table 3 (C0, C6, C7, Cm, Cn),

make up the normalised set of third normal form tables.

6.4. Performance of the facility

The system facility works as planned for model tables. The advantage of such a facility is that when users complain to the DBA about data retrieval problems on a certain table, the DBA could use the facility to determine whether the problem is caused by the table being not in 3rd NF. If appropriate, he could rectify the situation by converting the table into third normal form tables.

6.5. Restriction of the facility

The time taken for inspecting the whole table is not a linear function of its size. A test table which has fourteen tuples, seven columns, and four transitively dependent column pairs took five minutes to complete the inspection.

The main overhead is that inspection of subtuples for consistency is exhaustive, i.e. every subtuple in the table is examined, unless an inconsistency is found. Therefore one way to improve the speed of the facility is to reduce the number of subtuples required to be examined. That is, for a column pair, when the number of consistent subtuples found reaches a threshold, it is determined to be transitively dependent.

7. Conclusions

An administration package has been implemented with the following facilities: start and stop the database, initialise the database, perform regular backup and recovery procedures, ensure security and privacy of the database, monitoring of database statistics, and performance optimisation.

This development has fully exploited the interface from Prolog into Oracle. This has allowed the development of concise and elegant code, which completely lack any kind of fudging at the database accessing level due to the transparency of the interface.

It is hoped that this paper demonstrates that Prolog is a powerful database application tool which can be used effectively with a commercial database.

Second Normal Form Tables

MODULE			
MODNO	MNAME	STATUS	UNITPOINTS
b741	programming1	basic	8
b742	hardware	basic	8
b743	data proc1	basic	8
b744	programming2	int	11
b751	adv prog	adv	15
b752	micros	adv	15

Third Normal Form Tables

MODULE3nf		
MODNO	MNAME	STATUS
b741	programming1	basic
b742	hardware	basic
b743	data proc1	basic
b744	programming2	int
b751	adv prog	adv
b752	micros	adv

STATUS3nf	
STATUS	UNITPOINTS
adv	15
basic	8
int	11

1. Bocca, J., *A Marriage of Convenience: Prolog and a Relational DBMS.*, Proc. 1986 SLP Third IEEE Symposium on Logic Programming (September 1986).

2. Codd, E. F., *Relational Model of Data for large Data Banks*, Communications of the Association for Computing Machinery (1970).

3. Jarke, M. and Vassiliou, Y., *Databases and expert systems: opportunities and architectures for integration*, New Applications of Databases. Acedemic Press (1984).

4. Lucas, R.J. and Le Vine, G.A., "A Prolog-relational database interface," in *Prolog and Databases: Implementations and new Directions*, ed. Gray, P.M.D. and Lucas, R.J.,Ellis Horwood. Computer Science series (1988).

5. Lucas, R.J., *Database applications using Prolog*, Ellis Horwood. Computer Science series (1988).

6. Ullman, J.D., *Principles of database systems,* Pitman (1983).

7. Williams, H., Massey, P.A., and Crammond, J.A., ''Benchmarking Prolog for Database Applications,'' in *Prolog and Databases: Implementations and new Directions*, ed. Gray, P.M.D. and Lucas, R.J.,Ellis Horwood. Computer Science series (1988).

QUESTIONS

Dr. R. Moore (Software Sciences).
RM. Do you think you've thrown a lot away by only allowing yourself to get at one table at a time?

Dr. R. Lucas.
RL. One table at a time? I can get at any number of tables at a time.

RM. Yes, but you have to use views to do things like "join".

RL. No, you don't have to. That's an efficiency issue.

RM. I appreciate that. What I'm saying is that you're not able to get as much mileage out of the database interface as the SQL facility grants to you. I suppose you might, if you had a slightly more sophisticated interface. In a sense, you're effectively saying, "Get me some fields out of that particular table." That table may actually really be a view. It seems to me you've lost a bit of the ease of access as you've got to go through two stages in order to get to the database.

RL. No. I don't think so. I think perhaps, maybe, I overstressed it. If you've got a table out there, whatever it's called, you do one command. You do this once only. (Of course, when you embed it in your code, you never do it at all.) You just say c_external, give it whatever ORACLE knows it by, and you're home and dry. From there on, you can call it just as though it were in the internal database. And if you've got selection values in here, that's passed out to ORACLE. So it's an efficient access. I don't know how I created the impression you got, there's no restriction here. If I wanted to join 'emp' to 'dept', I would simply do it as pure PROLOG.

It's a transparent interface. You connect to your tables and that's it. From then on, you can just pretend they're all in internal memory in the PROLOG system. But if at the end of the day you say "I've got these joins here from these database accesses, and I need this application to run faster," then you can define a view and then access the view. That's all I'm saying.

Mr. P. Singleton (University of Keele).
PS. I just want to qualify what you said; "If you have a conjunction, an "and" in the PROLOG, indeed any composite goal, you can put it down in SQL, or in ORACLE, as a view." That is true only if the data is purely atomic, not structured and there are no variables to

be held, and your goal is not recursive, and that very rarely happens. Now your applications meet those criteria, mine don't.

RL. You're coming at it from a different point of view. You're starting from PROLOG and then saying "Perhaps I'd like to use a database." I'm saying, "There's all this data out there in databases and we're providing PROLOG really as a means of accessing that data on the same footing as all the other database tools. And this is as transparent as you're going to get it.

PS. And for non-recursive queries, you can set up views?

RL. Yes.

Q. You talked about giving access to PROLOG recursive queries. Does that mean your in cursor stack, you're also taking into account indications of depth from PROLOG as well?

RL. The cursor stack is done really naively and that's all that needs to be done. Because if you start a search on the table, M, the cursor goes on the stack. Now into another table, cursor goes on the stack. Go back to table M, another cursor goes on the stack. So that you naturally have recursion, just by doing that. It's just stack, last in, first out. That's the whole thing.

Dr. R. Moore (Software Sciences Ltd.).
RM. Do you run into any implementation problem with the number of cursors that you use?

RL. They don't take up a lot of room. They're thirty-two bytes I think.

RM. I was thinking more along the lines of, does ORACLE actually set some finite limit to how many?

RL. A hundred. But you can change it. Never known anyone run out. I think my colleague, Alice, when she was doing horrific, recursive searches, looking for these numbers of matches and things, at one stage ran into trouble because she wasn't resetting the cursors and never ever shutting them. In the middle of her project, she did have problems with that. But it was easily solved. She didn't know she had the facility of telling ORACLE to close down all its cursors and basically start again.

RM. I've had that problem too.

RL. They themselves don't take up much room. But you've got to be a little bit careful. It's very easy to use ORACLE, as it is PROLOG, on a large machine like a SUN or something and not really ever come across the way it's using its memory. It becomes far more vivid when you try to run ORACLE and PROLOG applications on a PC. That's what I've been doing mainly and then you really find out what's going on because the memory is just so much more crucial.

PS. Well, I've still got reservations about doing a join between a very small table and a very large one. In my look-up example, I had a table which was, effectively, just a set with three elements. I wanted to look them up in a binary relation of 20,000 tuples. Now, because there are only three of them, it's more efficient to take them one by one and look them up in the table and do a union on the results, than it is to do a sort merge. I don't think they do that sort of optimisation.

RL. That's quite interesting.

8 Combining Prolog with an RDBMS for Applications in Software Configuration Management

C. D. Farris and P. Singleton

1 Introduction

We describe an experimental combination of Prolog and relational database technology, applied to the management of software libraries and configurations. One particular application employs the transitive closure of a large relation, and we compare a number of algorithms for computing this closure on demand.

2 Prolog as a generalisation of relational algebra

Aside from differences in jargon and concrete syntax, Prolog generalises certain fundamental properties of a typical relational database (RDB) thus:

- *values*: while an RDB's *values* are essentially atomic, Prolog's *terms* are labelled trees of arbitrary size, allowing representations of sequences, sets, maps, relations and graphs (etc.) to be constructed, dismantled and passed around as data items.
- *variables*: while an RDB's values should be non-*null* if queries are to yield logically consistent results, Prolog's terms may be *uninstantiated*: such terms (*variables*) behave as algebraic unknowns. Incompletely specified structures may be passed around as data items, thus allowing abstractions to be represented, compared and specialised.
- *recursion*: while an RDB's *views* must not be (directly or indirectly) recursive, Prolog's *rules* may usefully be so.

In contrast to an RDB's typical breadth-first computation, Prolog proves its goals depth-first. Thus recursive rules may be employed usefully (i.e. without necessarily giving rise to infinite results). A disadvantage is that a *join* may have a quadratic cost (i.e. of the order of the product of the sizes of the joined relations), rather than the "N.logN" cost of an RDB's sort-merge technique. Sort-merge join can however, be implemented in Prolog (using the higher-order "call" predicate), while depth-first search seems infeasible in an RDB, so Prolog can fairly be said to generalise this area too.

Prolog's efficacy as a programming language arises from the combination of variables, recursion and structured data (not to mention its non- and super-logical features such as *cut* and *call*).

3 Limitations of conventional Prolog implementations

The majority of current implementations of Prolog have the following drawbacks:

- *capacity*: the rulebase is copied into main (virtual) memory before use; thus computation performance degrades with increasing rulebase size, due to paging or swapping.
- *persistence*: any changes to this "incore" rulebase are visible only to the process which performed them, and die with it (they cannot be committed).
- *shareability*: goals are proven only against this private copy of the rulebase; changes made by other processes are not perceived.

4 Possible combinations of Prolog and RDBs

There are two broad ways in which we could hope to combine Prolog and relational databases:

- *multiplicatively*: ideally, we would like to combine the maturity of implementation of RDBs with the functionality of Prolog: the result would be a multi-user super-Prolog with transaction management, user-defined indexing, unlimited capacity, etc. This was quite infeasible within the terms of our research (into software configuration management).
- *additively*: more realistically, we could quickly achieve a more modest (and less transparent) coupling between commercially available products, whereby our application data would be stored either in the Prolog rulebase or in the RDB according to characteristics such as its quantity, and the need to index it or to access it with very low latency, etc.

We took the latter approach, and describe it below.

5 Our application area

We set out to employ Prolog to provide smart assistance in the management of substantial software libraries of an informal software development project (our own) [1]. We wanted to facilitate informal, incremental development and rapid prototyping in the traditional *compile/test/edit* cycle, and soon realised the importance of the interdependencies of the source fragments.

The source fragments in our libraries are written exclusively in Prolog, and the very simple structure of this language meant that our cross-reference scheme was also simple:

- no *types* are declared or used;
- there is no distinction between *code* and *data* (a Prolog *procedure* serves both purposes);

although it was slightly complicated by one characteristic of Prolog:

- two distinct Prolog procedures may have the same *name*, as long as they have different *arities* (numbers of arguments).

In order to contain the potential complexity of interdependence among many thousands of procedures, we employ a system of *libraries* (which, incidentally, reflects the corresponding run-time concept of *modules*).

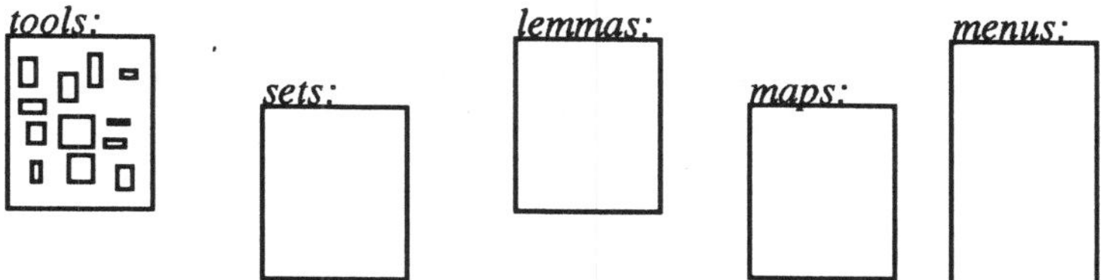

Fig 8.1 *pcm* embraces a number (>200) of libraries

Each library contains the source texts of a number of procedures:

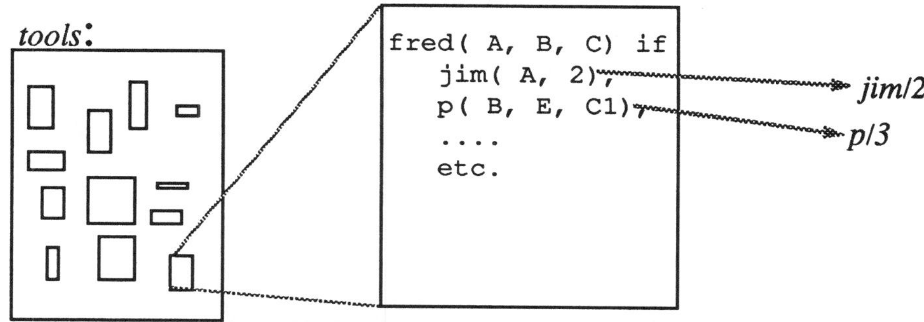

Fig 8.2 Each *library* embraces a number of *procedures*

and by parsing each procedure's source text, **pcm** determines which other procedures may be called. Each library nominates a (small) number of other libraries in which its *needed* procedures may be found (if not within itself), and the final outcome of the *resolution* process is a set of facts of the form:

```
rneeds( L1:N1/A1, L2:N2/A2) :-
        procedure L1:N1/A1
        may directly call procedure L2:N2/A2
```

where a procedure is denoted (unambiguously) by a structure of the name of its library **Li**, its own name **Ni** and its arity **Ai** (e.g. *tools:fred/3*).

These facts constitute the *rneeds* ("resolved needs") relation: this relation and its transitive closure are the subjects of the rest of the paper.

6 Properties of the *rneeds* relation

The *rneeds* relation describes a directed graph, which is typically cyclic (as a result of mutually recursive procedure definitions). Its transitive closure describes this relation:

"*Procedure **P1** may (directly or indirectly) call procedure **P2**.*"

but its value is better suggested by this interpretation:

*"If you are likely to need procedure **P1**,*
*then you are likely to need procedure **P2**."*

So while the mechanically-extracted facts define the *direct* rneeds relation, we are often interested in the *indirect* rneeds - the transitive closure of the direct relation.

The *rneeds* relation presently comprises about 17,000 facts; the numbers of arcs leaving each node are shown histogrammatically in Fig 8.3.

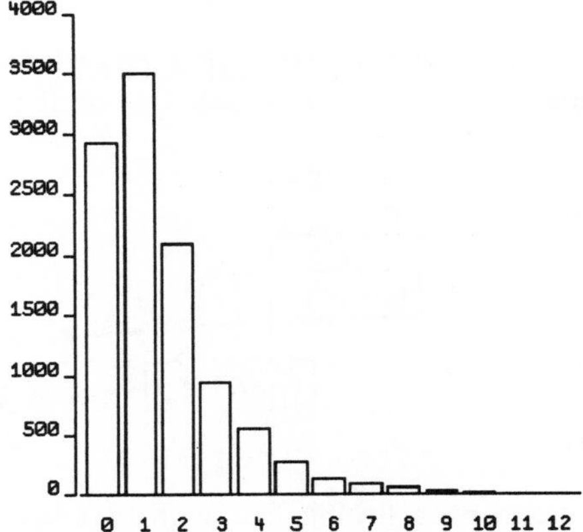

Fig 8.3 Number of procedures against their number of callees

The transitive closure of this graph is almost certainly inconveniently larger than the graph itself, and (more importantly) would be awkward to revise incrementally whenever procedures are modified (the *rneeds* relation is fairly easy to alter), so we compute portions of the closure as and when needed.

7 Some applications of the *rneeds* relation

The *rneeds* relation is central to the *pcm* programming environment, and is in almost constant use. Whenever the *editor* is invoked to modify a library procedure (*pcm* has a crude, update-in-place approach to version management), its new source text is parsed, and *rneeds* is updated accordingly.

The most commonly used tool for inspecting library components is the *browser*, an interactive tool which allows the user to navigate the *rneeds* graph, looking at the source texts at the nodes, or moving (via dynamically-constructed menus) to a direct callee, and so on recursively (so the user can unwind his path).

A more crucial application, however, is the *packager*, whereby the user specifies a set of procedures which are to be copied and packaged for testing or delivery. We use *pcm* for experimental rapid prototyping, we are our only customers, and we work without formal configuration management procedures such as change authorisation. Our main requirement of packages is that they should be complete, and we achieve this by determining (mechanically) all the direct and indirect needs of the specified procedures.

For rapid prototyping and experimentation, an incremental version of the *packager* is used in combination with the *browser* and *editor*, so that the edit/test cycle can proceed without having to rebuild completely after each edit. In both these packaging applications, the transitive closure of the *rneeds* graph is crucial, and it must be cheaply computed as needed.

8 Representations of the *rneeds* relation

Thanks to Prolog's support for structured values, we can represent a procedure by a structure of its *library* name, its own *name* and its *arity* (we call this structure an *lna*).

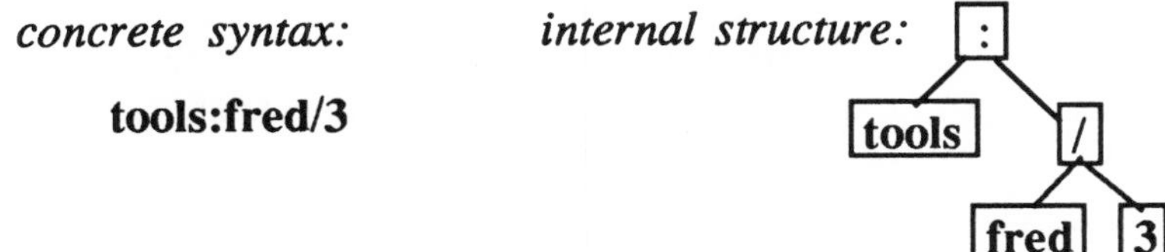

Fig 8.4 Prolog representations of an example *lna*

We can represent each arc of the *rneeds* graph by a Prolog fact with two *lna* arguments:

```
rneeds( tools:fred/3, maps:jim/1)
```

Alternatively, we could represent the graph by relating each node to the set of its direct neighbours:

```
rneeds_graph( tools:fred/3,
        [maps:jim/1,coercions:p/3])
```

where the second argument of *rneeds_graph* is a list of direct neighbour *lna*s. This convention has the advantage of allowing the representation of isolated nodes:

```
rneeds_graph( tools:lonely/4, [])
```

in which case the second argument is an empty list, but although this structure is convenient for navigating "forwards" through the graph it is unsuitable for navigating backwards.

For storage in a relational database, neither of these formats is possible, and we must "explode" the arcs into a relation of six fields:

LIB 1	NAME_1	ARITY_1	LIB 2	NAME_2	ARITY_2
tools	fred	3	maps	jim	1
tools	fred	3	coercions	p	3
....	....	....	....	....	....

Fig 8.5 Relational representation of the *rneeds* graph

9 Storage of the *rneeds* relation

The *pcm* environment is implemented almost entirely in (Quintus) Prolog, but the libraries and their cross-reference data must be shared and persistent in the manner of a typical RDB. Although the *rneeds* relation is derived mechanically from the library components, it is too expensive to do this on demand, and we therefore store and update the relation in the filestore. Although this seems an obvious application for an RDB, we did not initially have any database system with a suitable interface to Prolog, and we therefore developed a simple scheme of *textual relations.*

10 Textual storage of the *rneeds* relation

Our first storage technique partitioned the relation according to its first field (effectively a "GROUP BY"), and stored each resulting five-column relation (one per library) as a tabulated text file.

tools:					
	fred	3	maps	jim	1
	fred	3	coercions	p	3
	....	....	....	....	....
	....	....	....	....	....

Fig 8.6 Each library contains a table of *rneeds* facts derived from its components

We built a tightly-coupled interface between Prolog and such *textual relations* [2], mapping them into Prolog as (virtual) sets of facts. Certain queries of this relation proceed acceptably slowly, others unacceptably so: finding the direct *callees* of a particular procedure involves a linear search of a table of perhaps a few hundred tuples, but finding the *callers* requires (almost unacceptably) that all such tables be searched. The salient characteristics of this scheme are as follows:

- *poorly indexed*: the relation is partitioned on its first field, reducing search costs when this value (the *caller* library) is known: the individual tables, however, are always searched linearly.
- *explicit*: the text files containing the relations are readily manipulated by several general-purpose UNIX utilities; this was valuable while *pcm* was being developed and debugged.
- *non-updateable*: changes to a textual relation are effected by rewriting it, as the UNIX file model does not support insertion or deletion. This is acceptable when libraries are small (as they should be: they are there to reduce complexity).

11 RDB storage of the *rneeds* relation

Recent developments [3] allow Prolog systems to be coupled to RDBs in a similar "tight" manner: that is, by mating the backtracking fact-searching behaviour of Prolog to the lower-level tuple retrieval facilities of the database. Although this is attractively elegant, we shall show that it may not be the most efficient way of combining the distinctive computational abilities of the two systems. Salient features of the RDB scheme are:

- *indexable*: indexing is readily available, and can reduce search costs dramatically, making them independent of database size;
- *updateable*: unlike the textual relations, RDB relations can be altered incrementally (cheaply, and independently of size)
- *arcane*: RDB relations can only be accessed via RDB routines.

12 Computing the transitive closure of the *rneeds* relation

As explained above, the transitive closure is heavily used during the *edit/test* cycle, to ensure that any procedure likely to be called is loaded. The likely costs of storing and updating the closure are unacceptably high: instead, we compute portions of the closure on demand.

Algorithms for computing the reachable nodes of a given node (or, generally, set of nodes) range from the naive to the bizarre, and are described next.

13 Naive closure

The simplest closure algorithm is the classic recursive *ancestor* relation: given some binary relation *dc* (meaning "directly connected"), we can define the transitive closure *idc* (meaning "indirectly or directly connected") thus:

```
idc( A, B) IF
        (     dc( A, B)
        OR    (     dc( A, A2)
              AND   idc( A2, B)
              )
        ).
```

The syntax of this example is an impromptu variation on both Prolog and SQL:

my notation:	*Prolog:*	*SQL:*
`IF`	`:-`	`CREATE VIEW ... AS`
`OR`	`;`	`UNION`
`AND`	`,`	`SELECT ... WHERE`

Although this definition is syntactically expressible as a SQL view, it is prohibited by the typical RDB on the grounds of its recursion ("table or view `idc` does not exist").

In Prolog, this is not only expressible, but executable (depth-first), although it will get stuck in the first cycle encountered, endlessly generating non-novel reachable nodes *B*.

14 Cycle-avoiding closure

Infinite recursion can be eliminated (in a depth-first algorithm) by testing each newly-reached node to see if it is on the path from the starting point: if it is, then no further exploration is made, and the search backtracks to the most recent choice point (for which the "OR" is responsible). A modified definition follows:

```
idc( A, B) IF
        (       empty_set( Seen)
        AND     idc_1( A, Seen, B)
        ).

idc1( A, Seen, B) IF
        (       NOT element( A, Seen)
        AND     (       dc( A, B)
                OR      (       dc( A, A2)
                        AND     add_element( Seen, A, Seen2)
                        AND     idc( A2, Seen2, B)
                        )
                )
        ).
```

This is indigestible to the typical RDB, due to the structured values (the variables `Seen` and `Seen2` stand for sets of "seen" nodes) which are being passed around. It may look like a program, but it also has a relational interpretation. Furthermore, it works in Prolog (given a suitable implementation of *sets*, e.g. as lists), but although it traverses a cyclic graph in a finite time, it may wastefully explore some regions of the graph more than once (i.e. if they can be reached by more than one path). The next variant fixes that.

15 Node-accumulating closure

The next improvement requires the abandonment of backtracking, and the accumulation, not of the nodes on the current path from the starting point, but of all the nodes so far visited:

```
idc( A, Bs) :-
        empty_set( Seen),
        idc_1( A, Seen, Bs).

idc_1( A, Seen, Cs) :-
        IF      element( A, Seen)
        THEN    Cs = Seen
        ELSE    idc_2( A, Bs),
                add_element( Seen, A, Seen2),
                idc_3( Bs, Seen2, Cs)
        FI.
```

```
idc_2( A, Bs) :-
      set_of_all( B, dc(A,B), Bs).

idc_3( [], Cs, Cs).

idc_3( [B|Bs], Seen, Cs) :-
      idc_1( B, Seen, Seen2),
      idc_3( Bs, Seen2, Cs).
```

Features such as "IF-THEN-ELSE-FI" and "set_add_element" may seem procedural, but they also have a relational interpretation (in "IF a THEN b ELSE c FI" the goal "a" should be determinate, in which case the whole expression is equivalent to "(a AND b) OR (NOT a AND c)"). This technique is practicable, and can be used with a direct relation dc which is stored either in the Prolog rulebase or as a table in the RDB (accessed through the tightly-coupled interface described earlier).

16 Optimised node-accumulating closure

The previous algorithm gets reasonable results from the RDB, as long as the direct relation is suitably indexed. In the case of *rneeds*, we employ a secondary index on the first three arguments jointly. The *textual relation* interface fares worse, because indexing is effectively only available on the first of the six arguments, and finding the direct neighbours of a node may cause several hundred superfluous tuples to be fetched serially into Prolog for testing (and rejection).

A major purpose of the *library* concept is to contain complexity, by partitioning the source fragments so as to (approximately) maximise intra-library cross references and minimise inter-library cross references. This suggests a heuristic optimisation. In any closure computation, we would expect a small number of libraries to be searched repeatedly, and having fetched all the *rneeds* tuples pertaining to a particular library, we might cache them within Prolog (if only for the duration of the computation), and hence avoid fetching them again. This optimisation has a dramatic effect with both *textual relation* and RDB interfaces: with the former, overall costs fall to a fifth or less; with the latter, costs are nearly trebled.

17 Heavy-handed SQL breadth-first closure

So far, then, our home-brewed *textual relation* interface is supporting the cheapest closure calculations. In a determined attempt to exploit the legendary economy of the RDB *join*, we turned to the "loosely-coupled" aspects of the Prolog-RDB interface. These allow SQL commands to be sent from Prolog, and we therefore devised and implemented on-demand transitive closure in SQL.

U *is the set of unexplored nodes*	$\mathbf{U} \subset \mathbf{N}$
X *is the set of explored nodes*	$\mathbf{X} \subset \mathbf{N}$
r *is the graph, regarded as a function*	$\mathbf{r{:}N \rightarrow N}$

initially: $\mathbf{U} \leftarrow$ *<the start nodes>*
$\mathbf{X} \leftarrow$ *<the empty set>*

iteratively: $\mathbf{U'} \leftarrow r(\mathbf{U}) - \mathbf{X}$
$\mathbf{X'} \leftarrow \mathbf{X} \cup \mathbf{U}$

until: $\mathbf{U} =$ *<the empty set>*

whereupon: $\mathbf{X} =$ *<the set of direct-or-indirect neighbours>*

Fig 8.7 Breadth-first transitive closure (set algebraic notation)

18 Optimised "to-and-fro" SQL breadth-first closure

Much of the computational cost of the obvious implementation of the algorithm above is incurred in *create table*, *drop table* and *rename* commands. The implementation below works "to-and-fro" between two tables `U1` and `U2`, avoids all *create*, *drop* and *rename* commands, and is substantially cheaper.

initially:

```
    delete from U1;
    insert into U1 values( a);

    delete from X;
```

tail-recursively:

```
    if  select count (*) from U1 == 0
    then  select * from X          /* i.e. finished */
    else  insert into U2
                select distinct a2
                from U1, R
                where U1.a = R.a1
          minus select a
                from X;
          do the inverse, i.e. from U2 to U1
    fi
```

Fig 8.8 "to-and-fro" closure in SQL (plus control structures)

The algorithm is driven by Prolog, which sends the SQL commands (typewriter-face in Fig 3.8) to the RDB, and tests the result of "`select count (*) from U1`".

19 Comparisons of costs (experimental)

This table presents a crude comparison of the costs of the various closure algorithms when interfaced to our textual relations (*textrels*) and to the RDB. The times noted are seconds of *real* time on a Sun 3/50 running Quintus Prolog 2.4.2 and Oracle 5.1.22: the test query was a modest closure yielding a total of 65 directly-or-indirectly reachable nodes.

Table 8.1 Time taken by the six algorithms for a test closure

version	*algorithm*	*textrels*	*RDB*
v1	backtracking (naive)	∞	∞
v2	backtracking (cautious)	270	115
v3	gathering	130	60
v4	v3 optimised for textual relations	15	150
v5	breadth-first (heavy-handed)	n/a	90
v6	breadth-first (to-and-fro)	n/a	15

20 Observations on the costs

Separate experiments showed that the retrieval "bandwidth" of our interface to textual relations was about 300 tuples per second, while the corresponding measure for the interface to the RDB was about 30 tuples per second. Thus the cost advantage of the latter's superior indexing does not inevitably make it the best choice.

The *textrels* interface performed worse in *v2* and *v3* because it retrieved more tuples (due to its inadequate indexing) to test and (mostly) reject them within Prolog, while the RDB interface retrieved only exact hits (we set up RDB indexes to serve the algorithms as well as possible).

The optimised (for textrels) gathering algorithm (*v4*) cached and re-used the extraneous tuples read in over the textrels interface to great advantage, while applying this trick to the RDB interface evidently causes a net overall increase in tuple traffic.

Our first attempt (*v5*) at a breadth-first closure spent most of its time in *create, drop* and *rename* operations on RDB tables, which are evidently expensive.

Furthermore, the "branchiness" of the graph (see Fig. 3) was low, and the breadth-first strategy took 15 cycles (compared to 65 iterations for depth-first). Defining a "direct-or-one-step-removed" view may speed this up.

Our second attempt (*v6*) was only as good as the best *textrels* algorithm, although we expect to tune it further. In particular, we wonder whether the RDB join is inefficient in the case when a very small relation (<10 tuples in this case) is joined to a large one (20,000 tuples in this case).

21 Conclusions

- Prolog's essential functionality usefully subsumes that of a typical RDB.
- Prolog's typical implementation is inferior to an RDB in at least these areas: size, persistence, shareability of the database; transaction processing and auditing.
- Recursive queries do arise in real-life applications.
- Tightly coupling an RDB to Prolog allowed large relations to be shared and updated, but gave disappointing performance (due partly to a low tuple retrieval bandwidth from the RDB).
- For an efficient combination, it may be necessary to perform some of the computation within the RDB. This generally requires recursion and structured data, which SQL does not provide.
- With some modest (?) generalisations of their data and execution models, RDBs could be used in conjunction with Prolog to provide efficient support for many knowledge-based applications.

22 References

1. P. Singleton, Software Configuration Management: Rationale and Realisation, in *Software Engineering Environments: Research and Practice*, K.H. Bennett (Ed.), pp. 203-216, Ellis Horwood (1989).

2. R.J. Lucas and G.A. Le Vine, A Prolog-relational database interface, in *Prolog and databases: implementations and new directions*, P.M.D. Gray and R.J. Lucas (Ed.), pp. 67-80, Ellis Horwood (1988).

3. P. Singleton and C. D. Farris, Software Configuration Management using Prolog, in *Prolog and databases: implementations and new directions*, P.M.D. Gray and R.J. Lucas (Ed.), pp. 340-356, Ellis Horwood (1988).

4. P.M.D. Gray, *Logic Algebra and Databases*, Ellis Horwood (1984).

9 Integration of Database Systems at the Navigational Level by Using Prolog

M. Takizawa and M. Katsumata

ABSTRACT

In the distributed database system, views independent of heterogeneity and distribution of database systems have to be provided. We adopt a Prolog-like system as the common interface on the database systems. Although many researchers have tried to integrate multiple database systems at the higher level like the relational model, we try to integrate them at the lower, navigational level. Because every database system provides the navigational interface, no additional overhead is added to the database systems. In this paper, we discuss how to get an efficient access program from the non-procedural Prolog-like query on the navigational database systems like conventional network database systems, Unix file systems, and even relational database systems. Conventional optimization methods aim at decreasing the number of access units, i.e. pages, records. However, our method aims at reducing not only the number of access units but also the number of redundant answers. Also, the access program is tried to be executed in parallel.

1. INTRODUCTION

Current information systems include various database systems interconnected by communication networks. Database systems provide different types of data models, i.e. relational model[5], network model[4], and file system. In order for users to access easily the database systems, a common interface system has to be provided, through which users can manipulate the database systems as if they were of the same type. Most of distributed database systems[12,14,19] have adopted higher level models like the relational model as the common model. The internationally standardized data language SQL[7] is used as the common language. In order to provide such higher level interfaces on the existing lower level database systems, additional interface modules have to be installed on them. The interfaces give additional overhead to the existing database systems. On the other hand, every database system provides navigational level interface, e.g. record-at-a-time level. If we integrate multiple database systems at the navigational level, no additional overhead is posed on the existing database systems. So, existing database systems are integrated at the navigational level in our system.

In our system, Prolog[11,13] is adopted as the common model, since it can define application programs and data structure uniformly and recursively. The uniformity is one of the most important points for users. So far, the logical relationships among the relational model and Prolog have been discussed by a lot of researchers[1,9,10,18,20]. However, the relationships among the network model and the Prolog have been discussed by a few papers[15,17].

In this paper, we try to provide a common Prolog interface through which users can access more than one navigational database system. Navigational database systems are not only the conventional network database systems but also the file systems like UNIX file system. First, users can view the distributed navigational database systems as a set of navigational objects. The navigational objects are abstraction of navigational level of conventional database systems at the navigational level. Users do not need to distinguish them, e.g. record types and set types in the network database systems or files in the file systems. Users write application programs on the navigational objects. We try to get all the non-redundant answers without using intermediate files. Next, the programs have to be efficiently executed. In this paper, we discuss two methods, i.e. navigational and parallel ones. Since it is important not to give any additional overhead to existing database systems in our system, we try to get all the answers without using any intermediate files. This method is navigational. In the parallel method, we present how to execute them in parallel on the distributed navigational database system.

In section 2, we define the navigational objects. In section 3, the translation of simple queries to navigational programs is discussed. In section 4, we discuss a case that there are multiple input rules. In section 5, we discuss the parallel execution.

2. DISTRIBUTED NAVIGATIONAL DATABASE SYSTEM

In our system, navigational level interfaces of database systems are abstracted to a common framework named navigational objects.

2.1 Navigational Objects

The navigational database D is a set of navigational objects. The navigational object O is composed of a totally ordered set OD_O of instances and a collection P_O of operations on OD_O. Instances in O are composed of attributes $@O, a_1, \ldots, a_m$, i.e. $O(@O, a_1, \ldots, a_m)$ ($m \geq 0$). $@O$ is a special attribute named an object identifier. Each instance has unique value of $@O$ in the database D. OD_O is a sequence of instances, $\langle t_0, t_1, \ldots, t_{n-1} \rangle$. For every instance t_j, let $next(t_j)$ denote t_{j+1} and $prior(t_{j+1})$ denote t_j (for $j=0,1,\ldots,n-1$). Also, let $first(OD_O)$ and $last(OD_O)$ denote t_0 and t_{n-1}, respectively.

The object O has a register CUR_O which denotes an instance most recently accessed in OD_O. The most recently accessed instance is denoted by CUR_O. Initially, CUR_O denote $NULL$. There are the following operations on OD_O. Let $*CUR_O$ mean an instance denoted by CUR_O.

[Navigational Operations] The following operations change CUR_O and then return an instance denoted by CUR_O, i.e. $*CUR_O$.

(1) *First(O)*; CUR_O is let to denote *first*(OD_O).

(2) *Last(O)*; CUR_O is let to denote *last*(OD_O).

(3) *Next(O)*; CUR_O is let to denote *next*($*CUR_O$).

(4) *Prior(O)*; CUR_O is let to denote *prior*($*CUR_O$).□

Also, the navigational object provides direct access methods.

[Direct Access Operations]

(1) *Locate(O, id)*; CUR_O is let to denote an instance whose object identifier is *id*.

(2) *Access*(O, a_j, *val*); CUR_O is let to denote an instance whose a_j value is *val*.□

Access operation cannot always be applied to every attribute in the object. It can be applied to attributes which provide special direct access facilities like the conventional indexing and hashing mechanisms. If any instance satisfying the semantics of the operations does not exist, the operation returns *NULL*. For example, if $*CUR_O$ = *last*(OD_O), then *Next(O)* is *NULL*. The operations can correspond to the record-at-a-time operations in the conventional DML[4] operations and file operations. Also, they correspond to the tuple-at-a-time operations based on the cursors[7] in the relational model.

The objects are hierarchically composed of objects. The first object type is a database object type which has operations, open and close the database. The second type is a navigational object type. The instance of the navigational object type *O* is created by issuing an operation *creatOBJ(O)*. The navigational operations of the type *O* are inherited to the instance.

A distributed navigational database system is composed of more than one navigational database system. Users view them to be a collection of navigational objects. For example, a navigational database system is composed of three navigational database systems DB_1, DB_2, and DB_3. Each navigational database system includes the following navigational object instances.

DB_1: *s*(<u>@*s*</u>, *sname*) DB_2: *p*(<u>@*p*</u>, *pname*)
DB_3: *sp*(<u>@*sp*</u>,@*p*,@*s*), *pb*(<u>@*pb*</u>,@*b*,@*p*), *bp*(<u>@*bp*</u>,@*b*,@*p*), *b*(<u>@*b*</u>, *role*)

Fig. 1 Distributed navigational database

DB_1 has a navigational object *s* which has information on suppliers of parts. DB_2 has an object *p* which represents the parts. DB_3 has objects *sp* which represents a functional relationship from *p* to *s*, and *b*, *pb*, and *bp* which represent the parts-subparts relationship among *p*. The instances in *s* are sequenced in an ascending order of @*s*. The instances in *sp* are sequenced in an ascending order of major @*s* and minor @*p*. @*s* provides the direct access method to *sp*. We suppose that attributes @*p*, @*s*, and @*p* in the objects *pb*, *sp*, and *bp* provides direct access facilities, respectively.

2.2 Queries

A view (or rule) on the distributed navigational databases as shown in figure 1 is defined as follows. The view *ssp* means that a supplier *SNAM* supplies parts *PNAM*.

ssp(SNAM,PNAM) :- s(S,SNAM), sp(P,S), p(P,PNAM).

Users write queries in a following form.

$query(X) \text{ :- } B_1, \ldots, B_m .$

Here, B_j is an atom of a form $O_j\ (t_{j1}, \ldots, t_{jk})$ where O_j is an object name and t_{jh} is a variable or constant ($h=1,\ldots,k$, $j=1,\ldots,m$). X is a list of variables named target variables. For example, a query "find parts supplied by a supplier *a*" is written as

query(PN) :- ssp("a", PN).

Here, *PN* is a target variable and "*a*" is a constant. In this paper, we consider only non-recursive queries.

A substitution[11,13] θ is a set of bindings $\{X_1/T_1, \ldots, X_h/T_h\}$ where X_j is a variable and T_j is a term composed of variables and constants ($j=1,\ldots,h$). If θ is empty, it is an identity substitution ε. For an expression E, $E\theta$ is one obtained by replacing variables X_j occurred in E with T_j simultaneously. Let A be an atom $O(t_1, \ldots, t_k)$. A is said to be satisfied by an instance t in OD_A iff there exists a substitution θ such that $A\theta = t$. Also, A is said to be satisfied by the database. Let T be a set of atoms. For every atom A in T, if there exists a substitution θ and an instance t in OD_A such that $A\theta = t$, θ is said to be an answer of T.

3. NAVIGATIONAL PROGRAM

Now, we try to obtain a set of answer substitutions for a query by accessing the distributed databases navigationally, i.e. without creating any intermediate files. In this paper, in addition to reducing the number of instances accessed, the number of the same answers is tried to be reduced.

3.1 Navigational Tree

We introduce a navigational tree for a query $Q = query(X)\text{:-}B_1, \ldots, B_n$. Now, the query Q is written in a set $\{B_1, \ldots, B_n\}$.

[Definition] A navigational tree $T = (V, B)$ for a query $Q = \{B_1, \ldots, B_n\}$ is defined as follows.

(1) V is a set of nodes. For each atom B in Q, there exists a node $N_B = \langle B, \theta_B, \sigma_B \rangle$, where θ_B and σ_B are substitutions.

(2) B is a set of branches. In each branch from a parent node $N_P = \langle P,\theta_P,\sigma_P \rangle$ to a child node $N_C = \langle C, \theta_C, \sigma_C \rangle$, $\theta_C = \sigma_P$ and σ_C is a substitution which instantiates $C\theta_C$.□

Now, for a given query Q, let us consider how to get a navigational tree T. Here, let *vinst(A)* be a function which gives an unused constant for each uninstantiated variable in an atom A. $cost(A)$[15,17] gives an estimated cost to get all instances which satisfy A from the object. For a query Q, an ordered tree named a navigational tree T is constructed by the following procedure SP.

[Simple Procedure (SP) for a query Q]

(1) Select an atom A whose $cost(A\theta_A)$ is the minimum in Q. $\theta_A := \varepsilon$ (identity substitution). Let σ_A be $vinst(A)$. Create a node $N_A = <A,\theta_A,\sigma_A>$, where N_A is a root of T. $P := A$ and $N_P := N_A$. Remove A from Q. $\theta := \sigma_A$.

(2) Select an atom A whose $cost(A\theta_P)$ is the minimum among a subset $\{B_1,..., B_m\}$ in Q, where each $B_j\theta_P\sigma_P$ and $P\theta_P\sigma_P$ share uninstantiated variables (for $j=1,...,m$).

(3) [A is found] Let σ_A be $vinst(A\theta_A\sigma_P)$. $\theta_A:=\sigma_p\theta_p$. Create a node $N_A = <A,\theta_A,\sigma_A>$ as the rightmost child of N_P. Remove A from Q. $P := A$. $\theta:=\theta\sigma_A$. Go to (2).

(4) [A is not found]
4-1) If Q is empty, terminate. Here, a projection of θ on the target variable is an answer substitution.
4-2) If N_P is not the root, then $N_P := N_P$'s parent and go to (2).
4-3) Otherwise, select an atom A whose $cost(A\theta_P\sigma_P)$ is the minimum in Q and go to (2).□

Let T be a navigational tree obtained by applying the SP to the query Q. Here, let $root(T)$ denote a root of T, and for a node A, let $parent(A)$ be A's parent in T and $child(A)$ be a set of A's children. A's ancestors and descendants are defined as usual. Let $<_T$ be a depth-first ordering on nodes in T. For nodes N and M, if $N <_T M$, M is said to be higher than N. $N <<_T M$ iff $N <_T M$ and no node L such that $N <_T L <_T M$.

Let $N_A = <A,\theta_A,\sigma_A>$ be a node in a navigational tree T. If $A\theta_A$ includes some target variable X, N_A is said to be a target node of X.

Let $Sub(N)$ be a subtree whose root is N in T, and $tail(N)$ be a highest leaf in $Sub(N)$. Let $tail(T)$ denote $tail(root(T))$ and $tlast(T)$ a highest target node in T. The following notations are introduced.

$ltarg(N)$ = a highest target node M such that $M <_T N$.
$rtarg(N)$ = a lowest target node M such that $N <_T M$.
$join(N,M)$ = a least common ancestors of N and M.
$njoin(N,M)$ = an A's ancestor L such that $join(N,M)$ is $parent(L)$.
$rjoin(N) = njoin(rtarg(N), N)$.
$ljoin(N) = njoin(N, ltarg(N))$.

We consider a following query Q on the database as shown in figure 1.

Q: query(Y, PP) :- p(P,Y), pb(B,P), p(PP,X), b(B), bp(B,PP).

A tree in figure 2 is an example of a navigational tree obtained by applying the SP to Q. In figure 2, nodes (3) and (4) are target nodes of variables Y and PP, respectively, and $join((3), (4))$ = (1), $njoin((3), (4))$ = (3), $rjoin((2))$ = (3), $ljoin((5))$ = (4), $rtarg((3))$ = (4), $tlast(T)$ = (4), and (2) $<_T$ (5) and (1) $<<_T$ (2) $<<_T$ (3) $<<_T$ (4) $<<_T$ (5). $tail((2))$ = (3) and $tail((1))$ = (5).

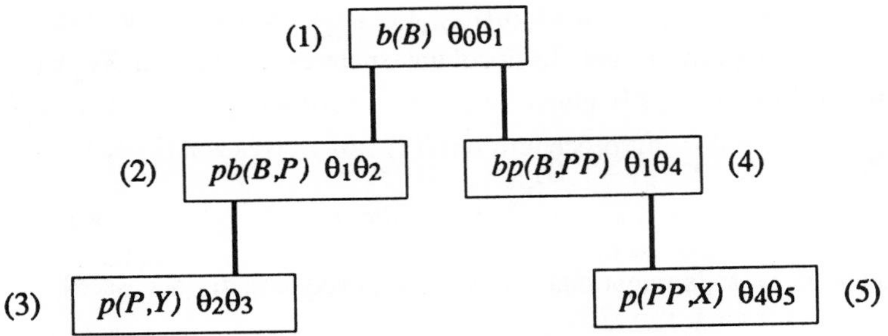

$\theta_0 = \varepsilon$, $\theta_1 = \theta_0\{B/c_B\}$, $\theta_2 = \theta_1\{P/c_P\}$, $\theta_3 = \theta_2\{Y/c_Y\}$,
$\theta_4 = \theta_1\{PP/c_{PP}\}$, $\theta_5 = \theta_4\{X/c_X\}$

Fig. 2 Navigational tree

Suppose that a node $N_A = \langle A, \theta_A, \sigma_A \rangle$ in the navigational tree T has $child(A) = \{N_{A_1}, \ldots, N_{A_m}\}$ where $N_{A_j} <_T N_{A_k}$ iff $j < k$. Let T_A and T_{A_j} denote subtrees $Sub(N_A)$ and $Sub(N_{A_j})(j=1,\ldots,m)$, respectively. Let ST_A be a set $\{T_{A_1}, \ldots, T_{A_m}\}$. The subtrees have the following properties according to the definition of the *SP*.

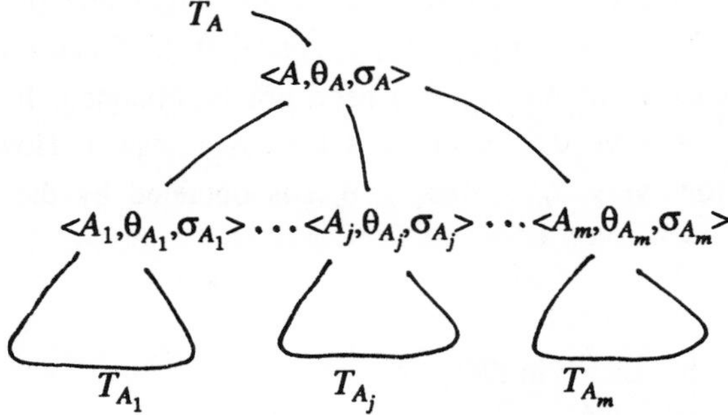

Fig. 3 Subtree T_A

[Property 1] Let N_A be a node $\langle A, \theta_A, \sigma_A \rangle$. For every two different subtrees T_{A_j} and T_{A_k} of N_A, $T_{A_j}\theta_{A_j}$ $(=\sigma_A)$ and $T_{A_k}\theta_{A_k}$ $(=\sigma_A)$ have no common variables.□

[Property 2] If some different nodes $N_A = \langle A, \theta_A, \sigma_A \rangle$ and $N_B = \langle B, \theta_B, \sigma_B \rangle$ have some common variable X, some common ancestor of N_A and N_B includes X.□

In figure 2, $pb(B,P)\theta_1$ and $bp(B,PP)\theta_1$ have no common variable, and a common ancestor $b(B)$ of $pb(B,P)$ and $bp(B,PP)$ includes a common variable B.

3.2 Reduction of Redundant Answers

Let X_{A_j} be a set of variables in $T_{A_j}\theta_{A_j}$ for every θ_A in figure 3. Let $Ans(T_{A_j}\theta_{A_j})$ be a collection of substitutions θ_{A_j} of X_{A_j} where $T_{A_j}\theta_{A_j}\ \theta_{A_j}$ is satisfied by the database.

Let $Targ(T_{A_j}\theta_{A_j})$ be a projection of $Ans(T_{A_j}\theta_{A_j})$ on the target variables in $T_{A_j}\theta_{A_j}$. According to the property 1 and 2, since the subtrees $T_{A_1}\theta_{A_1},..., T_{A_m}\theta_{A_m}$ have no common variable, $Ans(T_A\sigma_A)$ is given by taking a cartesian product $Ans(T_{A_1}\theta_{A_1}) \times ... \times Ans(T_{A_m}\theta_{A_m})$. The following procedure $ans1(T_A, \theta_P)$ gives $Ans(T_A\theta_P)$.

```
ans1 (T_A ,θ_P)
    { ANS := φ; [navigational object O_O is sequentially accessed]
        for each t in OD_A
        if t satisfies Aθ_P, then
            { θ_A := θ_P σ such that Aθ_P σ= t;
              for each T_Aj in ST_A (j=1,...,m)
                  { ANS_j := ans1(T_Aj , θ_A);
                    if ANS_j is empty, return(φ); }
            ANS := ANS ∪ {θ_A } × ANS_1 ×...× ANS_m;} return(ANS);}
```

Next, let S_A be a subset of the subtrees $\{S_{A_1},..., S_{A_p}\} \subseteq ST_A$ where each S_{A_j} includes target variables, and let N_A be $\{N_{A_1},..., N_{A_q}\} \subseteq ST_A$ where each N_{A_j} includes no target. S_{A_j} is a target subtree $(j=1,...,p)$ and N_{A_l} a non-target one $(l=1,...,q)$. Also, $Targ(T_A\theta_A) = Targ(S_{A_1}\theta_A) \times ... \times Targ(S_{A_p}\theta_A) \subseteq Ans(T_A\theta_A)$. Since our purpose is to get $Targ\ (T_A\theta_A)$, all answers in $Ans(N_{A_j}\theta_A)$ need not be obtained. It is sufficient to find that for every N_{A_j}, $Ans(N_{A_j}\theta_A)$ includes at least one answer. However, we have to obtain $Ans(S_{A_j}\theta_A)$ for every S_{A_j}. $Ans(T_A\ \theta_P)$ is obtained by the following procedure *ans2*.

```
ans2 (T_A ,θ_P)
    { ANS := φ; for each t in OD_A , {
    if t satisfies Aθ_P, then
        { θ_A := θ_P σ such that Aθ_P σ= t;
            for each N_Ah in N_A, if exist(N_Ah , θ_A) = F, return(φ);
            for each S_Aj in S_A (j=1,...,p),
                { ANS_j := ans1(S_Aj ,θ_A); if ANS_j =φ, return(φ); }
            ANS := ANS ∪ {θ_A } × ANS_1 ×...× ANS_p;}
     return(ANS); }

exist(T_A ,θ)
    {for each t in OD_A ,
        { if t satisfies θ, then
        if ST_A =φ, return(T); else
        { θ_A :=θ_P σ such that Aθσ= t;
        for each T_Aj in ST_A , if exist(T_Aj , θ_A) = F, return(F);
        return(T); }}
    return(F);} }
```

Let *C1* and *C2* be the numbers of refutations obtained by the procedures *ans1* and *ans2*. Here, $C1 = |Ans(T_A\theta)| = |Ans(T_{A_1})| \times ... \times |Ans(T_{A_m})|$, and $C2 = |Ans(T_A\theta)| =$

$|Ans(S_{A_1})| \times ... \times |Ans(S_{A_p})|$. Since $S_A \subseteq ST_A$, $C2 \leq C1$. That is, a set of answers $Targ(T_A \theta)$ can be obtained by accessing less instances by *ans2* than *ans1*.

3.3 Navigational Access Without Using Intermediates

Let us consider how to get all the answers for $T_A \theta_A$ without using intermediate files.

[Definition] A navigational program is a sequence of object operations, which accesses navigationally the database without using intermediate files.□

As stated before, for every non-target subtree N_{A_j}, it is sufficient to get only one answer in $Ans(N_{A_j} \theta_A)$. For every target subtree S_{A_j}, all answers in $Ans(N_{A_j} \theta_A)$ have to be obtained. Here, assume that there exists a buffer for each node N_A in T, which can store one instance in the object denoted by the atom A. "for each" is realized by *First* and *Next* operations.

First, let us consider a navigational program for *ans1*. Let T be a navigational tree where $N_{A_1} \ll_T ... \ll_T NA_n$. The recursive program *ans1* can be represented by a navigational program *nans1*. Note that *nans1* is similar to the Prolog refutation procedure[11].

```
nans1 (T) {
for each instance t1 in ODA1,
if t1 satisfies A1ε, {let θ1 be one such that A1θ1 =t1;
      for each t2 in ODA2,
       if t2 satisfies A2θ1, { let θ2 be one such that A2θ1θ2 =t2;
            ...
            for each tn in ODAn ,
            if tn satisfies Anθn-1 ,
                  { construct θn such that Anθ1...θn-1θn =tn; project θn on the
                  target variables in T and output it}...}} }
```

Next, we try to translate *ans2* to a navigational program in order to reduce the number of instances accessed and the number of redundant answers. Suppose that a subtree S_{A_j} in T_A includes a target node O and one answer θ_{A_j} for S_{A_j} is obtained already. We try to get all the substitutions for the target variables in O by reducing the number of instances accessed. Here, for θ and a subtree S in a tree T, let $\theta[S]$ denote a projection of θ on the variables in S. Also, let $T - S$ be a tree obtained by removing S from T. Since θ_{A_j} is already obtained, we try to get only another substitutions θ_O^1 for $T_O \theta'$ while $\theta' = \theta_{A_j}[S_{A_j} - T_O]$ remains unchanged. After one answer θ_{A_j} is obtained, if another answers $\theta_O^1, \theta_O^2, ...$ of $T_O \theta'$ are derived, the answers $\theta'\theta_O^1$, $\theta'\theta_O^2, ...$ are obtained. After all the answers for $T_O \theta'$ are obtained, another answer θ_P^1, $\theta_P^2, ...$ for a parent P of O and $\theta'' = \theta[T - T_P]$ is tried to be derived. By that, the answers $\theta''\theta_P^1$, $\theta''\theta_P^2, ...$ are obtained. $Ans(S_{A_j} \theta_A)$ is a set of substitutions obtained by this procedure. It includes all the substitutions for the target variables in S_{A_j}.

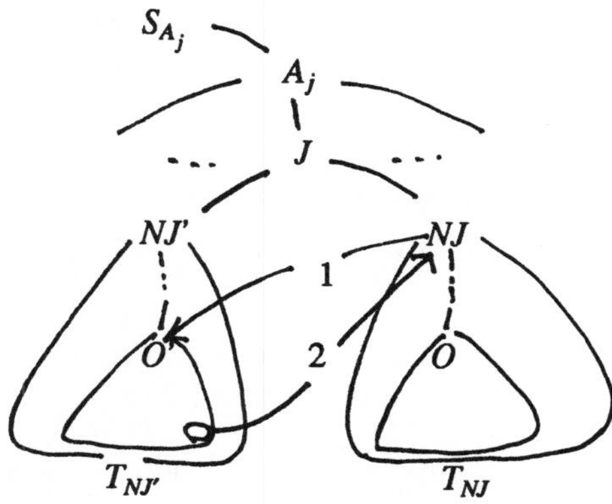

Fig. 4 Subtree S_{A_j}

Next, suppose that S_{A_j} includes two target nodes O and O' where $O' <_T O$. Let J, NJ, and NJ' be *join(O,O')*, *njoin(O,O')*, and *njoin(O',O)* [figure 4], respectively. Suppose that one answer θ_{A_j} is already obtained. As stated in the previous paragraph, $Ans(T_O\ \theta[S_{A_j} - T_O])$, $Ans(T_{parent(O)}\ \theta[S_{A_j} - T_{parent(O)}])$, $Ans(T_{parent(parent(O))}\ \theta[S_{A_j} - T_{parent(parent(O))}])$,... are obtained. Now, suppose that $Ans(T_{NJ})\ \theta[S_{A_j} - T_{NJ}])$ is just obtained. If we get $Ans(T_J\ \theta\ [S_{A_j} - T_J])$ since $J = parent(NJ)$, the substitutions $\theta_{O'}$ for variables included in a path from A_j to O' may be changed although $Ans(T_{O'})\theta[S_{A_j} - T_{O'}])$ is not derived yet. Hence, instead of getting $Ans(T_J)\theta[S_{A_j} - T_J])$, $Ans(T_{O'})\theta[S_{A_j} - T_{O'}])$ is tried to be obtained [1 in figure 4]. Each time one answer $\theta^h_{O'}$ in $Ans(T_{O'})\theta[S_{A_j} - T_{O'}]$ is obtained, all the answers θ^1_{NJ} in $Ans(T_{NJ}\ \theta[S_{A_j} - T_{NJ}])$ are derived [2 in figure 4]. Here, let θ' be $\theta[S_{A_j} - T_{O'} - T_{NJ}]$. That is, for each $\theta^h_{O'}$, the answers $\theta''\theta^h_{O'}\theta^1_{NJ}$, $\theta''\theta^h_{O'}\theta^2_{NJ}$, $\theta''\theta^h_{O'}\theta^3_{NJ}$,... for S_{A_j} are derived.

3.4 Navigational Program

Since it is difficult to represent this procedure in a non-recursive fashion like *ans1*, we represent the navigational program in a network of objects where the objects are nodes in T and two special objects *ST* and *OUT*. The edges represent relationships among nodes as follows.

[Edges of Navigational Program]

(1) For every node N which is not a root of T, create a first failure (*FL*) edge N ++> *parent(N)*. For a root node N of T, N ++> *ST*.

(2) For every node N and M where $N <<_T M$, create a first success (*SC*) edge N --> M. For a root node of T, *ST* --> N.

(3) For every leaf node N, if there exists some node L such that N is in $T_{rjoin(L)}$ and a target node M such that $M = rtarg(N)$, then create a next success (*NSC*) edge N ==> M, otherwise N ==> *OUT*.

(4) For every node N and target node M, if $N = rjoin(M)$, create a next fail (NFL) edge N **> M.

(5) For a target node N such that $N = ltarg(T)$, create an NFL edge OUT **> N.□

Here, if N ==> M and N **> L, M and L are named an NSC and NFL nodes of N, respectively. For example, figure 5 shows an navigational program for Q.

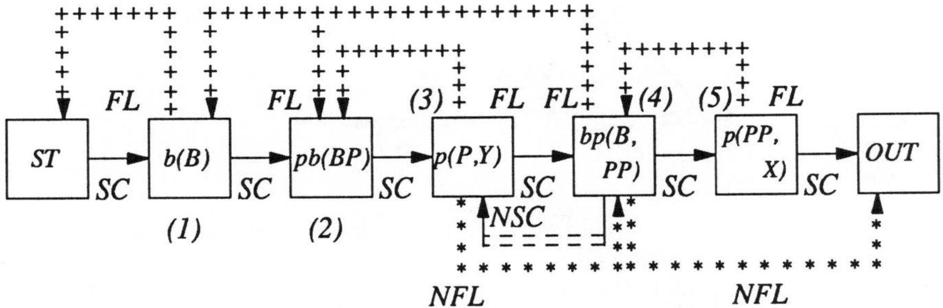

Fig. 5 Navigational program

Each node in the navigational program is a passive object, i.e. on receipt of some message at some income edge, it does the corresponding action and sends a message to one outcome edge. First, a message <F, $root(T)$, $tail(T)$, ε> is sent to $root(T)$ from the ST node, where ε is an identity substitution. Each node N_A behaves as follows.

[Behavior of a Node N_A] On receipt of a message <I, B, E, θ> at the edge SC or FL,

(1) If I = "N", then if $B = E = \_$ or $N_A <_T B$, then $B := N_A$ and $E := tail(N_A)$.

(2) OD_A is accessed sequentially by using the navigational operations $First(N_A)$ and $Next(N_A)$ if the message is received at the SC edge, else by using $Next(N_A)$. If an instance t in OD_A such that $A\theta\sigma = t$ is found,
2-1) if I = "N" and $E = N_A$, then <"N",_,_,θσ> is sent at the NSC edge ==>,
2-2) if I = "F" or $B \le_T N_A <_T E$, <I, B, E, θσ> is sent at the SC edge -->.

(3) If no satisfiable instance is obtained,
3-1) if I = "F" or $B <_T N_A \le_T E$, then <I, B, E, θ> is sent at the FL edge ++>,
3-2) if I = "N" and N_A = B and N_A has an income NFL edge, then <"N",_,_,θ> is sent at the NFL edge **>,
3-3) otherwise, <"N",_,_,θ> is sent at the FL edge ++>.□

Two special nodes ST and OUT behave as follows.

[Behavior of ST node] First, the ST sends <"F", $root(T)$, $tail(T)$, ε> to $root(T)$ at the SC edge. On receipt of a message, it forces all nodes terminate.
[Behavior of OUT node] On receipt of <...,θ>, an answer substitution from θ is output and <"N",_,_, θ> is sent at the NFL edge **>.□

It is clear that the following proposition holds.

[Proposition] For a given navigational tree T, less instances are accessed and less redundant answers are obtained by the navigational program than the *nans1*.□

That is, if the Prolog computation rule selects the atoms in the same order as our navigational program *T*, the Prolog program accesses more instances and gets more redundant instances as the target set.

4. NAVIGATIONAL PROGRAM FOR MULTIPLE INPUT RULES

First, let us consider the following query as an example.

query(T,U) :- A(X,Y), B(X,T), C(T), V(Y,U).
V(P,Q) :- D(P,Q,Z), E(Z).
V(P,Q) :- F(P,V,Z), G(V,Q), H(Z).

The views in the query are replaced by the right hand side of the views. For example, the following queries are obtained.

query1(T,U) :- A(X,Y), B(X,T), C(T), D(Y,U,Z), E(Z).
query2(T,U) :- A(X,Y), B(X,T), C(T), F(Y,V,Z), G(V,U), H(Z).

Figure 6 and 7 show the navigational trees of *query1* and *query2*, respectively. Here, underlined atoms are target nodes.

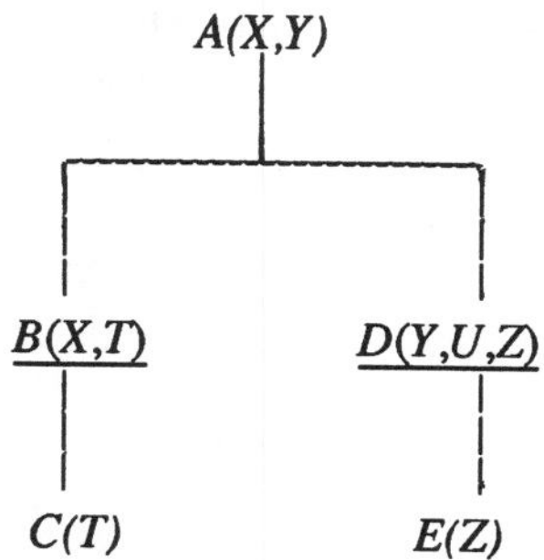

Fig. 6 Navigational tree of *query1*

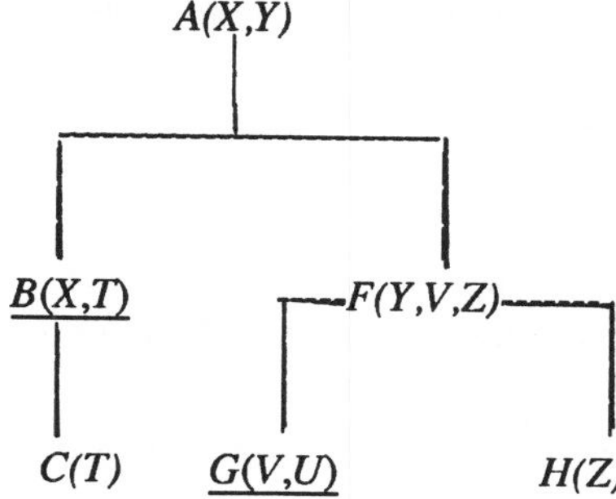

Fig. 7 Navigational tree of *query2*

Figure 6 and 7 are merged to one tree as shown in figure 8 by introducing a new *BR* (branch) node *O*.

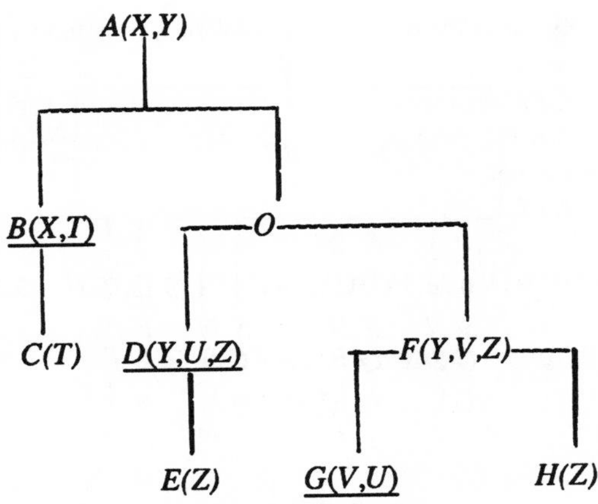

Fig. 8 Navigational tree with *BR* node *O*

The navigational tree with the *BR* object is constructed by the following procedure *GTP*.

[General Tree construction Procedure (*GTP*)]

(1) When constructing a tree for a given query *Q* by the *SP*, if a rule atom *A* is selected for a parent node N_P, a *BR* node O^A is created as a child of N_P.

(2) Then, a view R :- $B_1,\dots, B_k$ is selected where there exists a substitution θ such that $R\theta = A\theta$. *R* is removed from *Q*, and $\{B_1,\dots, B_k\}\theta$ is added to *Q*. For N_P, an atom *A* is selected by the *SP*, a node N_A is created as a child of N_P.

(3) When *Q* is empty, by going back to the *BR* node O^A, another view for *A* is selected and go to (2).□

The *BR* node *O* is connected to the navigational tree *T* by the following procedure.

[Edge to the *BR* node *O*] Let *O* be an *BR* node and $N_{B_1},\dots, N_{B_m}$ be its children, where N_{B_j} is a root of subtree T_j (j=1,...,m). Let N_A be a node such that $N_A \ll_T O$. The following directed edges are added to the navigational program.

(1) an *SC* edge N_A --> *O*,

(2) an *FL* edge *O* ++> *parent*(*O*),

(3) *SC* edges *O* --> N_{B_j} and *FL* edges N_{B_j} ++>*O* for j=1,...,n,

(4) Let *C* be a node *rtarg*(T_j) and N_{B_j} be *rjoin*(*C*, T_j). If N_{B_j} is in T_j, *NSC* edges *O*==>N_{B_j} and *tail*(*C*)==>*O*, and *NFL* edges N_{B_j} **>*O* and *O***>*C*.□

[Property 3] For every subtrees T_j of every *BR* node *O*, an *NSC* node of T_j is the same.

[Proof] It is clear that the view atom is selected at the last in the GTP.□

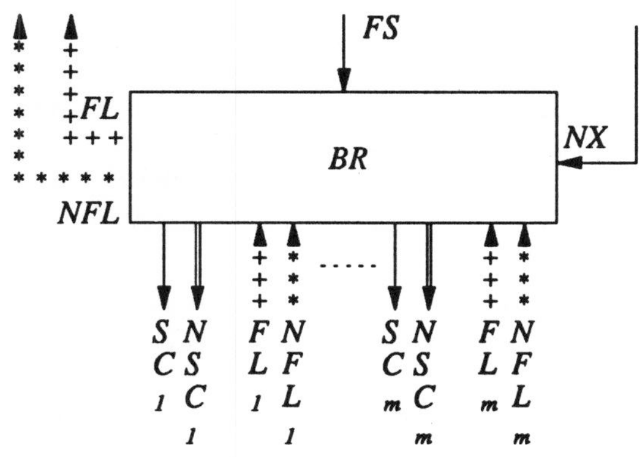

Fig. 9 *BR* node

We present the behavior of the *BR* node *O*.

[Behavior of *BR* node *O*] Here, suppose that *O* has *m* children in *T*.

(1) On receipt of a message <"*F*", *B*, *E*, θ> at the *FS* edge, $j := 1$, θ'=θ, and *state* := *F*.

(2) For a subtree T_j, <"*F*", *B*, *E*, θ> where *E* := *tail(B)* in T_j is sent from the SC_j edge.

(3) On receipt of <*T*, *B*, *E*, θ> at the *NX* edge from T_j, if *T* = "*N*", *state* := *S*. $j := j + 1$. If $j > m$, then if *state* = *S*, <"*N*", *B*, *E*, θ> is sent from the *NFL* edge, else <"*F*", *B*, *E*, θ> is sent from the *FL* edge. If $j \le m$, go to (2).□

5. PARALLEL NAVIGATIONAL PROGRAM

In the navigational program, only one object is activated at a time, since there exists only one message. Next, we try to execute a query in parallel[6].

5.1 OR Nodes

First, we try to execute concurrently a program for a navigational tree *T* as shown in figure 8. One method to get the answers of the query is to execute two subtrees of the *BR* node *O* in parallel and take the union of two results obtained by them. In order to realize the parallel execution, a new *OR* node is introduced.

There are two kinds of *OR* nodes, i.e. all-wait and one-wait *OR* nodes. Suppose that the subtrees of an *OR* node *O* in *T* do not include any target node. If one of the subtree of *O* succeeds, we do not have to wait for the completion of all the other subtrees at the *OR* node *O*. This type of *OR* node is named a one-wait *OR (OWO)* node. On the other hand, if the subtrees of *O* include some target node, even if all the answer substitutions for one subtree are obtained, we cannot stop waiting for the completion of the other subtrees. Only when all the deductions for all the subtrees are obtained, we can backtrack to the ancestor node of O. This type of the *OR* node is named an all-wait *OR (AWO)* node. Also, according to the property 1 and 2, it is clear that if one subtree includes target nodes, the other subtrees include targets. The *BR* node in figure 8 is replaced with an *AWO* node, since the subtrees include a target variable Y. The behavior of the *OWO* and *AWA* nodes is shown as follows.

[Behavior of *OWO* node O]

(1) On receipt of a message <"F", B, E, θ> at the *FS* edge, for each subtree T_j, in T_j and <"F", B, E, θ> where E := *tail(B)* is sent at the SC_j edge (for j=1,...,n).

(2) On receipt of <"N", B, E, θ> at some NX_k edge, <"N", B, E, θ> is sent at the *FL* to the parent of O, and <*STOP*> is sent at every SC_j edge (for j=1 ,...,n , $k \neq j$).

(3) If <"F",...> is received at the *FL* edge from every subtree, <"F",...> is sent at the *FL* edge. □

[Behavior of *AWO* node O]

(1) On receipt of <"F", B, E, θ> at the *FS* edge, for each subtree T_j, <"F", B, E, θ> where E := *tail(B)* in T_j is sent at the SC_j edge (for j = 1,...,n).

(2) If <"F",...> is received at the *SC* edge from every subtree, <"F",...> is sent at the *FL* edge to the parent of O.

(3) If some <"N",...> is received at the *SC* edge and messages are received at the *FL* edges from all the subtrees, <"N",...> is sent at the *NFL* edge (if exists) or the *FL* edge.

(4) If <"N", B, E, θ> is received at the *SC* edge, for each subtree T_j, <"N", B, E, θ> where E := *tail(B)* in T_j is sent at every NSC_j edge (if exists) or SC_j edge where <"N",...> has been received.□

(4) represents a case that after answer substitutions are obtained, another answer substitutions are obtained without redundancy.

5.2 AND Node

Let us consider how to get $Targ(T_A \theta_A)$ for every θ_A. From the property 1, after θ_A is obtained, queries for the target subtrees $S_{A_j} \theta_A$ (j=1 ,...,p) can be executed in parallel independently of each other, i.e. without communicating with each other. If every subtree $T_{A_j} \theta_A$ has at least one answer, $T_{A_j} \theta_A$ is said to be satisfied. If some subtree has no answer, $T_A \theta_A$ is not satisfied. Hence, if it is found that some subtree is not satisfied, parallel executions of queries are terminated successfully. For every non-target subtree $N_{A_j} \theta_A$, if one answer is obtained, it is terminated without obtaining all the answers. For every target subtree $S_{A_j} \theta_A$, $Targ(T_{A_j} \theta_A)$ is tried to be obtained. If all the non-target subtrees are satisfied and all the answers for all the target subtrees are obtained, a cartesian product $Ans(T_A \theta_A) = Ans(S_{A_1} \theta_A) \times ... \times Ans(S_{A_p} \theta_A)$ is taken. From the considerations, we introduce an object named *AND*.

[Tree Construction]

(1) When constructing a tree for a given query Q by the *SP*, suppose m nodes N_{A_1},..., N_{A_m} are selected as the children of a node N_P . Here, an *AND* node O is created as a child of N_P and as the parent of N_{A_1},..., N_{A_m} .

(2) If N_A is a tail node of some target node, an *OUT* node is created as the child of N_A .□

By introducing the *AND* node, a navigational tree shown in figure 8 is modified into figure 10.

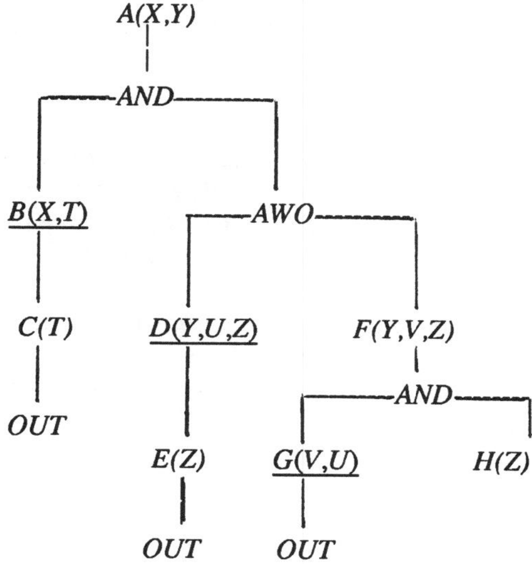

Fig. 10 Navigational tree

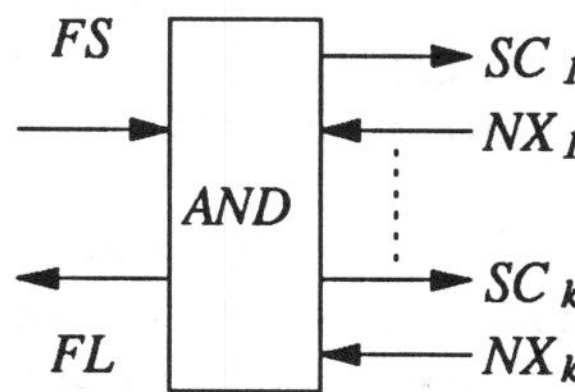

Fig. 11 *AND* node

Now, we present the behavior of the *AND* node.

[Behavior of *AND* node]

(1) On receipt of a message <...> at the *FS* edge, for each subtree T_j, <...> is sent at the SC_j edge (for $j=1,...,n$).

(2) On receipt of <"*F*", *B*, *E*, θ> at *NX* from some subtree T_k , <*STOP*> is sent at every SC_j (for $j=1,...,n$, $k \neq j$), and <"*F*", *B*, *E*, θ> is sent at the *FL* edge.

(3) On receipt of <"N", B, E, θ> at NX from some T_k, AND node waits for token <"N", B, E, θ> at every NX_j (for $j=1,...,n$, $k \neq j$). It receives a message from every NX_j (for $j=1,...,n$, $k \neq j$), <"N", B, E, θ> is sent at the FL.

(4) On receipt of <$STOP$> at the FS, <$STOP$> is sent to every SC_j and terminate (for $j=1,...,n$).□

In the parallel execution, intermediate files are required. In order to store and manipulate the intermediates, each AND, OR, and OUT node O has a file $BUFF_O$. Here, let A be a node and $B_1,..., B_m$ be its children. Let T_j be a subtree of T whose root is B_j (for $j=1,...,m$). $BUFF_A$ is defined inductively, i.e. (1) if A is either an OUT, AND, or OR node O, then $BUFF_A$ is $BUFF_O$, and (2) if a subtree T_A includes one OUT node O, $BUFF_A$ is $BUFF_O$.

Here, for a node A, let T_j be a subtree of A ($j=1,...,n$), and $BUFF_j$ be a buffer of T_j. In the AND node A, an intersection of $BUFF_1,..., BUFF_m$ is taken and stored to $BUFF_A$. In the OR node A, a union of $BUFF_1,..., BUFF_m$ is taken and stored to $BUFF_A$. After that, all the buffers $BUFF_1,..., BUFF_m$ are cleared.

One problem is where to create AND and OR nodes. In our system, each node is created in the site where major of the neighboring nodes exist in order to decrease the intersite communication. The OUT nodes are created in a site where the query issued in order to give the answer to the users.

6. CONCLUDING REMARKS

In this paper, we have presented a Prolog-like query language interface on the multiple various navigational database systems like the conventional network database systems and Unix file systems. In our distributed database system, database systems are integrated at the navigational level, in order not pose additional overhead on the database systems. This system has been implemented by using Sun workstations, a minicomputer A400(Facom), and a big mainframe M380(Facom).

In our system, the derivations of the redundant answers are prevented by accessing navigationally the database without making intermediate files. Our method can not only apply to the navigational database systems but also the relational database systems. As a matter of fact, our system includes relational database systems managed by UNIFY and INGRES. The relational database system provides tuple-at-a-time interface like cursor in addition to the non-procedural SQL interface. In another method, intermediate results are created. We think that it is difficult to efficiently access the intermediate files because they does not provide efficient access path other than sequential access method. We have shown the method to realize the parallelism so as to decrease the redundant answer substitutions. At present, we have evaluated our system to compare the performance with another distributed database system[14] where the database systems are integrated by using the higher level relational model.

REFERENCES

1 Chang, C. L., On Evaluation of Queries Containing Derived Relations in a Relational Data Base, *Logics and Database*, Plenum Press (1981).

2 Chen, P. P. S., The Entity-Relationship Model - Toward a Unified View of Data, *ACM TODS*, Vol.1, No.1 (1976), pp.9-36.

3 Clocksin, W. F. and Mellish, C. S., Programming in Prolog, *Springer-Verlag* (1984).

4 CODASYL DDL Committee, CODASYL Data Description Language, *Journal of Development* (1973), (1978).

5 Codd, E. F., A Relational Model of Data for Large Shared Data Bank, *CACM*, Vol.13, No.6 (1970), pp.337-387.

6 Conery, J. F., Parallel Execution of Logic Programs, *Kluwer Academic Publishers* (1987).

7 Date, C. J., A Guide to The SQL Standard, *Addison-wesley* (1987).

8 Enderton, H., Mathematical Introduction to Logic, *Academic Press* (1972).

9 Gallaire, H., Minker, J., and Nicolas, J. M., Logic and Database: A Deductive Approach, *ACM Computing Survey*, Vol.16, No.2 (1984), pp.153-185.

10 Henschen, L. J. and Naqvi, S. A., On Compiling Queries in Recursive First-order Databases, *JACM*, Vol.31 (1984), pp.47-107.

11 Kowalski, R., Logic for Problem Solving, *Research Studies Press* (1979).

12 Landers, T. and Rosenberg, R. L., An Overview of MULTIBASE, *Distributed Databases* (Schneider, H.J. ed.), North-holland (1982).

13 Lloyd, D., Foundation of Logic Programming, *Springer-verlag* (1985).

14 Takizawa, M., Distributed Database System-JDDBS, *JARECT*, Ohm-sha and North-holland, Vol.7 (1983), pp.262-283.

15 Takizawa, M., et al., Logic Interface System on Navigational Database System, *Lecture Notes in Computer Science*, Springer-Verlag, No.264 (1987), pp.70-80.

16 Takizawa, M. and Miyajima, K., Concurrent Execution of Prolog Transaction, *Lecture Notes in Computer Science*, No.315, Springer-Verlag (1988), pp.313-327.

17 Takizawa, M. and Katsumata, M., Access Procedure to Minimize Redundant Refutations on the Network Database System, *Lecture Notes in Artificial Intelligence*, No.383, Springer-Verlag (1989), pp.156-171.

18 Warren, D. H. D., Efficient Processing of Interactive Relational Database Queries Expressed in Logic, *Proc. of the VLDB* (1981), pp.272-281.

19 Wilmes, P. F. et al., I wish I were Over There: Distributed Execution Protocols for Data Definition in R^*, *Proc. of the ACM SIGMOD* (1983), pp.238-242.

20 Ullman, J. D., Implementation of Logical Query Languages for Databases, *ACM TODS*, Vol.10, No.3 (1985), pp.289-321.

QUESTIONS

Prof. S. M. Deen (University of Keele).

SMD.Since you are talking about distributed systems, why do you go for a navigational approach rather than use higher level queries?

Prof. M. Takizawa.

MT. We think that many database applications are based on navigational access to a database. Since many database systems provide navigational access interfaces, we can integrate database systems without introducing too much additional overhead.

If we try to use higher level queries, we have to provide the networked databases with appropriate interfaces for those higher level queries.

SMD.Which is the bigger overhead; a higher level system, or the excess communication which you have in the navigational model?

MT. This is a problem. There is a trade-off between the communication overhead implied by navigational access and the overhead of the higher level interface. In my opinion, the overhead incurred by the use of a higher level interface is larger than the communication overhead.

Dr. R. Lucas (Aberdeen University).

RL. I can't really see what you're getting by calling these sets of tuples 'objects'. It seems to me you have sets of tuples and various mechanisms for searching. Why call them objects? What is it gaining you? There's not a large amount of inheritance, there's not a large amount of partitioning.

MT. We abstract each element of the system into some core framework. The core framework is a navigational object. Each piece of information you get is called an object.

SMD..Do you do data duplication?

MT. Yes

SMD.You mention you don't use intermediate storage, but intermediate evaluations sometimes increase efficiency and allow parallelism.

MT. We have to introduce intermediate parts. But what we can do is work out answers without using any intermediates.

SMD.Do you really gain in performance by changing things into PROLOG-like clauses rather than using a more standard canonical high-level interface? Have you measured any gain?

MT. Not yet. This is my future work. Since we have already developed the distributed database system JDDBS which uses a higher level similar to SQL, we will measure our system by comparing it to JDDBS.

10 Integrating Expert Systems and Relational Databases: Results of an Initial Case Study Using a User/Task-oriented Design Framework [1]

M. Brayshaw [2], D. S. Brée, K. Burgwal [3],
M. Hoevenaars [4], B. C. Papegaaij [3], J. F. Schreinemakers,
J. J. Sirks, R. A. Smit

ABSTRACT

The paper describes a proposed design methodology for integrated relational databases and knowledge based techniques. The approach aims to tackle the issue from the users perspective and make the user's problem itself the focus of the interaction with the machine. Other components, e.g. knowledge-bases or relational databases, while acknowledged as important, are considered to be low-level components subordinate to the higher level tasks involved in solving a problem. The solution presented here is to provide an intelligent interface that allows the user to solve a problem at a level that maps more closely onto how the user thinks about and conceives the problem, and to de-emphasise the role of various tools for accomplishing sub-parts of the task. The rationale for the localisation of domain dependent information in a separate knowledge base, as opposed to in an extended database, is discussed. A detailed account of a frame based interface between database and knowledge-base is outlined as a method of enabling reasoning about the contents of the database. Finally, a system is proposed, based upon an investigation of the problem solving methods employed by domain experts, which attempts to apply these notions to off-shore engineering. An intelligent interface employs graphical techniques to allow the user to navigate through large amounts of data and select items of interest. Domain specific knowledge is used in the production of models based on selected data and in the evaluation of simulations. Iterative refinement of the models is subsequently done until a successful candidate is identified. The paper presents a methodology and demonstrates its practicality in detail based on the currently conceived system. Lastly a detailed end-user interaction scenario is presented.

1 The authors thank the following institutions for their active support of this project: the Foundation for Knowledge-Based Systems, NMB Bank, BSO Artificial Intelligence and The Royal Dutch Shell Group. In particular we would like to thank Lena Decunha and Chris Shaw of Shell who provided the domain expertise. Peter Krijnen analysed the protocols and provided much practical assistance.

2 On secondment from the Human Cognition Research Laboratory, The Open University, England.

3 On secondment from BSO Artificial Intelligence, The Netherlands.

4 On secondment from the NMB Bank, The Netherlands.

1 Introduction

Fourth generation software systems have seen the growth of a variety of very large databases containing all manner of information. In many cases the compilation of all this data was a large undertaking in the first place and the usefulness of such systems as repositories of valuable information is guaranteed well into the future. While all this was going on, the new technology in knowledge-based systems that could provide practical solutions to real world problems was emerging (e.g. Buchanan and Shortliffe, 1984; McDermott, 1984). As Brachman and Levesque (1986) have pointed out, both of these types of system are knowledge-bearing systems, and thus fundamentally connected.

For designers of databases, Artificial Intelligence (AI) techniques provided a means for accessing the data, while, from an AI perspective, a relational database was seen as a massive and as yet untapped source of knowledge for use in knowledge-based systems. Possibly as a result of these two views, emerging as they do from the opposing camps in the argument, two general approaches to integrating database and expert system technologies have emerged. The first is to expand databases to contain extra knowledge-based information and meta-knowledge about the database's contents. In support of this approach is the claim that, as the knowledge-based information gets huge (currently a typical large AI application might contain only a few hundred rules), database techniques will be required to manipulate it, so the information should profitably be placed in the database in the first place. However it is not clear how large a knowledge-base is going to grow and, for single applications, its size may not be great. From the AI perspective researchers have proposed using databases as repositories of information which can be added on to AI systems. The AI community has strong reasons for wishing to represent large scale information in a given architecture (e.g. Lenat and Feigenbaum, 1987), and indeed AI/Cognitive Science may have strong a priori reasons requiring information to be represented in certain manners (e.g. ACT*, Anderson, 1983; SOAR, Rosenbloom, Laird, and Newell, 1987). In sympathy with this approach there has been considerable effort to try to interface databases with logic programming and the popular AI programming language Prolog in particular (e.g. Brodie and Jarke, 1986; Dahl, 1986; Zaniolo, 1986).

In both approaches the tightness of the bonding between the AI system and the database has become an issue. A weakly bonded link might contain only an interface from the AI system to the database query language itself, whereas a strongly bonded system would argue for the complete integration of the knowledge-base and database into one unifying environment. For example, as Chang and Walker (1986) have pointed out, Prolog might be extended to have the functionality of a full database management system, but the cost of doing so would be expensive. If it is not known in advance what type of queries are going to be asked of the system, the full power of a database management query system must be included within the interface.

In this study, we will explore an approach based on the user's task requirements. A distinct advantage of this essentially top-down approach is that it is possible for the system to know what types of query and answer will be required in advance, and thus it can precisely be specified what type of interface and what extra information will be required between the two systems. The approach taken here is influenced by and hereby acknowledges the pioneering work in user-centred design systems of Norman and Draper (1986 and papers contained therein). We are strongly inclined to the view of placing the user's needs and requirements at the centre of the design task. Consequently, it stresses the particular task involved and the user's perspectives of that task as suitable starting points to guide the design of the system. In this report the route, outlined in Norman and Draper, of keeping the perspective end-users involved in all the aspects of the design phase is followed.

Research here is focussed on databases that are used in the process of performing a particular task, where the database itself is only a tool encountered on the solution path and not the focus of the task in its own right. Concentrating not on the tools involved, but instead on what the user is trying to achieve by using these systems, offers an alternative view of the problem. The task for the system designer now becomes one of helping users solve problems as well as they can. Now in an ideal world a user could invoke an intelligent assistant to help solve the problem in the most desirable way, oblivious to the low-level practical details. In such a scenario, when information was needed, it would simply be asked for. Users would not care whether the information was the result of an immensely complicated and skillfully derived SQL query, or derived by knowledge-based heuristics.

The approach advocated here aims to move closer to this idealised intelligent assistant by raising the level of dialogue with the system away from that of simply using tools (e.g. relational databases) and to focus instead on the goals and intentions users have when they are performing a given task. The motivation for this is threefold:

a To allow a user to solve a particular problem in a manner that more closely follows his line of natural reasoning,

b To provide for the user those tools that would most directly aid the problem-solving task and

c To remove from the problem solving cycle steps or concepts that are the result of a particular low-level solution, but do not contribute directly to solving the problem.

The result, as far as the user is concerned, is a unified system in the sense that the user can't see the joins; it is a system that hides away from users issues they need not be concerned with. It is an important point to realise that taking the user and the task as the central points to motivate the design may have important things to say about the final architecture of the system. Thus moving to this principled top-down approach to system design may lead to the placing of important constraints on how the knowledge-base is structured and interacts with the database. It is one of the research goals to see how this approach impacts on the system architecture.

In addition this work also focuses on the design of graphical interfaces to database. This is an area of emerging interest in its own right. In a recent report on the future directions of database management systems, the participants (The Languna Beach Participants, 1988) noted that there were "virtually no researchers investigating better end-user interfaces to data bases or better data base application development tools" and that "there was universal consensus that this was an extremely important area, and that it received more support from the participants than any other area." The work here aims to redress this imbalance by applying modern interfacing techniques to databases. This differs from the approach taken by G.Rohr, IBM Germany, by concentrating on domain specific solutions rather than searching for general metaphors. The rationale for this is that the degrees of freedom in the design and implementation of a database are so large that we do not believe that widely applicable metaphors are easily identified and used. Indeed if widely usable metaphors are located they are likely to be lower down in the system, maybe reflecting implementation issues. As such one could well imagine a graphical SQL. This is likely to be a useful tool for the application developer but not for the end user. It is at too low a level for the goals we aim to address.

The system described here has a basic three tier architecture. The top level is the interface with the user. It is designed specifically for the domain in question. The system interacts with the database by means of a Query and Answer Generator (QAG). This is a frame-based system that interrogates the database and hands information back to the system. Between those two layers is the concept translator (CT) which is responsible for taking the requests and/or requirements of the user and handing these back to the interface. This is done by a series of rules which interact with the systems knowledge-base and the database via the QAG. Each of these three levels will be described in turn. Figure 1 gives an overview of the system.

The remainder of this paper will be structured as follows. First it presents a brief overview of the task-centred approach to the problem that is proposed. A description will follow of each of the three main components in the system. The next part gives a detailed case study of this approach and finally the issue of generality is tackled.

2 A Case Study

2.1 Designing systems from the user perspective

Let us first distinguish between two types of database systems in terms of their usage. In the first type fall those databases that are consulted for a single piece of information. For such tasks current systems are very adequate. In the second type fall those databases that are used in some larger task, where the user will make repeated use of the database in order to gain necessary information for that task. If one wishes to make the process of solving that task easier for the user, techniques from AI may be included to make the tools at hand more powerful. However there is an important consideration to note. More powerful tools, if they are harder to learn and use, may actually make the task of solving a problem more complex, not less. If a new tool is more complicated to use than its predecessor the result may be that not all of its functionality will be explored or used, with a resulting decrease in the power of the tool itself. It is a danger which should be noted in integrating AI knowledge-based tools and relational databases. If the integration is done in an unprincipled fashion one may get carried away with the functionality and size of the knowledge resources available. The result could be the creation of a very powerful system which, for all its mouse options and menus, has a very limited potential audience. Hence the process of designing an interface for the appropriate set of users is central to the whole process. Failing to realise this is to invite the types of problems described above. The methodology explored here aims to capture the functionality without sacrificing the usability.

Let us step back for a moment and consider what the consequences are of integrating databases with knowledge-based systems. The overall concern is to help a user do two types of things:

a more easily and effectively access information (regardless of how it is stored) and

b perform a task with this information.

The approach taken here is as follows. Initially a given problem area is identified. Then users are studied solving the tasks both using existing tools and in abstract terms. A model is then derived of the users actual problem solving.

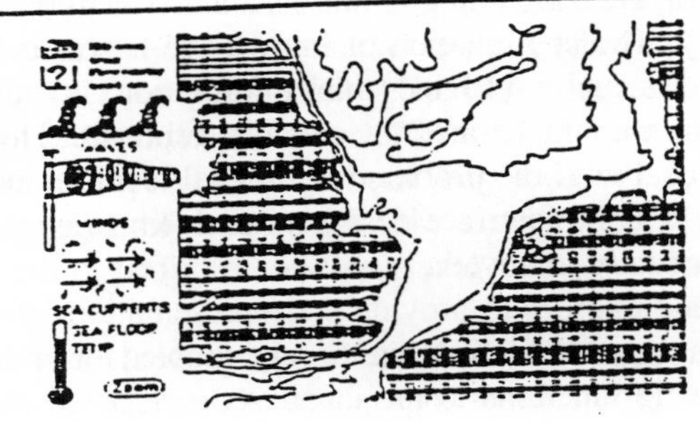

Graphical Interface

Domain Specific Interface with the databasee

Concept Translator

(p rule1
variable
the likes of joe is jane
-->
(make <happy>)

integrated frame engine

OPS5 based rule-engine

Takes information from the user, hands the questions to the QAG and then returns the information to the user

Query Answer Generator

LOCATION_LONGITUDE RANGE: (AND (>=2) (<=4))
EXTRACTION: none
DESCRIPTION:(FIELD location.longitude)

LOCATION_LATITUDE RANGE: (AND (>=52) (<=54))
EXTRACTION: none
DESCRIPTION:(FIELD location.latitude)

Interfaces with the database itself via a set of frames. Queries initiated by the CT are answered here

Fig 1 Overview of the knowledge-based interface

This model is used as the basis of an easy to use and intelligent interface. The interface should make it easy to find and locate information. In large databases this is going to become an ever more difficult problem as the database grows. By providing intelligent search and navigation aids and graphical browsing facilities, massive amounts of information can be searched more easily. The combination of knowledge-based and relational database techniques required to actually provide this information is not apparent to the user when these low lying techniques are not actually relevant. The intelligent interface thus allows the user to deal with the problem at the goal level rather than worrying about underlying machinery. It is the interface designers problem to work out how particular goals and sub-goals are actually achieved.

As a consequence of the goals above, and in order to provide the representations for AI reasoning techniques, the approach of having at the low end a loosely coupled system, with a separate knowledge-base and accessing functions to the database, is adopted. A further motivation for this approach was to see what was possible by taking an existing commercially used database and the design rationale described above, and to derive a first pass framework for combining the two. As the database will not be modified, any extra information the intelligent interface requires must be present in the knowledge base. The knowledge-base chosen for the purpose is one developed by Shell[5] called Metocean-2, which is described below.

Employing this type of design methodology may result in a set of architectural constraints that the system will need to follow. These constraints will effect the interfacing (or combining) of database and knowledge-based sources of information. Thus, following this design rationale may effect all levels of the system and how they are designed and work. Being aware of attempts to produce more intelligent databases (e.g. NAIL) this project instead has much more practical concerns. There are a huge number of existing commercial databases. Even if intelligent databases were already satisfactorily achieved, in reality the number of such databases that would actually be re-written using this new technology is expected to be very small. A very large number would remain in use. The methodology proposed is thus highly pragmatic in that it seeks to apply the gains from Artificial Intelligence to current databases. The methodological aim is to demonstrate a technique of problem analysis, modelling and system specification that can be applied in general to such systems. The technology used, however, explicitly aims to take systems *off the shelf* and to incorporate them into a new intelligent system.

The process of analysing the expert here is comparable to knowledge-elicitation in normal expert system design. The aim is to understand the experts and provide intelligent support for them. It was a central notion of this approach to provide an enhanced environment for existing experts and not to replace them. As such the approach could be viewed as a partial model of the expert, realised in an intelligent interface. The approach would also be entirely upwardly compatible with an attempt to produce an expert system to do the whole task. The crucial differences are that:

a The important issue of the actual criteria that the user has for selecting a piece of information and subsequently choosing different pieces of information is not addressed. For this the system would require a so-called deep knowledge-based model of what constituted a good answer to the problem of predicting the conditions at a particular location.

---

5 Shell International Petroleum Maatschappij B.V., Exploration and Production Division, The Netherlands

b The final model evaluation is left to the user. Again this could conceivably be mechanised in the system.

The extensions to provide *a* and *b* are non-trivial. Although we believe that this existing approach is at least part way along this route, pragmatic considerations and the belief that intelligent interfaces in their own right are most valuable, means that we here aim to facilitate existing expertise rather than replace it.

2.2 A case study using Metocean-2

2.2.1 Understanding the Problem

Metocean-2 is a database being built by Shell that contains large amounts of information about particular sites at sea. It is intended to be used for locating or predicting the conditions that would prevail at a particular point in the ocean. The forecast provides the design criteria for engineers engaged in two different areas, namely structure engineers, who design off-shore structures, and pipeline engineers, who build pipelines. Metocean-2 is used by an expert to locate information, choosing from a series of possible sets of data to produce a *data set*. A model is fitted to the *data set* and used to predict the conditions at a new location. Then the user determines whether or not this prediction gives a good picture for that point in the ocean. If not, subsequent refinement of the data is done until a model is found that better predicts that particular location.

Our first task was to take protocols of the experts who use the database. The protocols included, in addition to a standard thinking aloud protocol of experts solving typical problems, protocols of the experts solving the problem in the abstract, without reference to any tools that they might have available. A protocol was also obtained of an expert solving a problem before the database came into common use and without its supporting facilities. Lastly concept sorting techniques were used to get a grasp of the type of conceptual organisation the user had of the domain. As a result of the above a model was derived of the general problems solving mechanisms used in the domain as shown in figure 2.

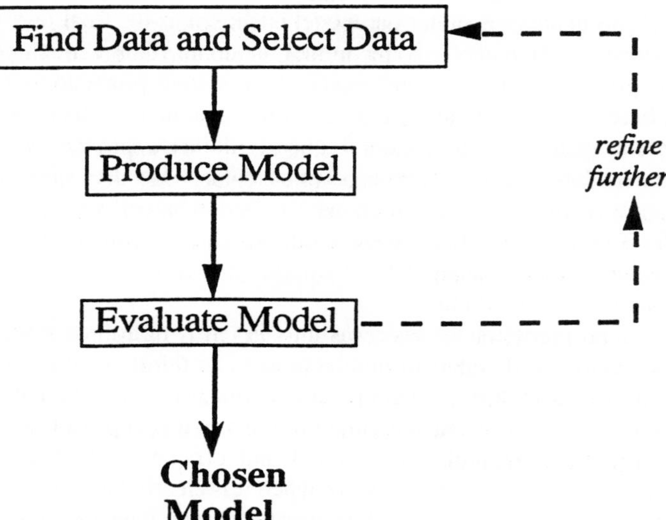

Fig 2 Model of the basic strategy in model generation

The initial problem was finding what was appropriate data to be included. For certain sites this was easy because the required data was already at hand. In other cases extrapolation was necessary in order to determine what data to include in the *data set*. It was apparent from the protocols that just finding the information in the first place was a major task and one that could easily benefit from knowledge-based aids in both navigating through all this data and in selectively filtering the data. Further, the type of data required varied depending upon the task and it is thus possible to know in advance which is appropriate data to show the user and at which points. In order to find out about selecting appropriate types of data for different types of task, concept sorting techniques were used in order to define those attributes of data that were appropriate to given concepts involved in particular tasks. The result was a clear model of how (but not why) the expert selected data, how they themselves classified the data, what was considered to be good data and what was considered to be substandard, and what types of information were considered relevant and when. This was considered at the knowledge level (Newell, 1982) in terms of the overall problem solving behaviour observed. A conscious attempt was made to build this model at a level above that of the database used, and eliminate any practical considerations about how to obtain this desired information. The idea was to ascertain how the user ideally would like to go about this task and not how the users might modify their behaviour if they were presented with a powerful tool like a database. The notion of a database-like tool was deliberately de-emphasised and at frequent points in the protocol the experts were asked what, in a *perfect world*, they would like to be able to do at various points during the problem solving task. The second stage of the expert's task was to produce a model from the given chosen data set. One possible route for this to take is to use mathematical modelling techniques. However additionally it was apparent from the protocols that the experts could also produce their own evaluation of a data set and select among models produced by data sets as they considered alternative data sets. This was noted as an area where we believed that qualitative simulations based on existing AI techniques could be usefully employed, as we shall discuss later.

The next stage identified in the protocol analysis was model *evaluation*. A model is evaluated against other models and against other selection criteria e.g the age or the quality of the data used in the model, and also the presence of confounding factors. As a result of this evaluation either the model is chosen as the final one, or (as is more likely) a subsequent refinement of the model is done. This refinement typically involves choosing other sets of data and seeing the resulting predictions that would result from using these. The experts also made two other comments which were noted and featured in the final system design. It was frequently the case that they would produce different possible models and then choose between them. Also they often wished to experiment and supply made up or modified data to see what effect this had on the prediction models. Both these two features were not possible with the current database system they were using, but arose when they were prompted at various points to explain the type of functionality they would like.

The final model of the task was thus in terms of a three stage model. First find the data. Secondly use that data to build a model and thirdly evaluate the resulting model. If the model is satisfactory then the process is finished; if not the data must be modified by going back to stage one. An important proviso of this approach is that the way the expert wishes to solve the problem is sound and efficient, which in this case it is. This methodology will however only work when it is clearly the case that the user is just using a database in a particular task. If however the system they are using is already guiding the user and allowing them to solve the problem in a more efficient manner (i.e. the system is already an intelligent interface) then the effectiveness of the outlined approach will depend upon how good the existing intelligent interface is. If these existing tools can be incorporated into a large system (e.g. the ways the model simulation system is incorporated into the current approach) then this also is a possible route to take. It is assumed in the proposals outlined here that there exists an efficient solution path which the expert can identify and that an intelligent interface can be designed to support.

2.2.2 An intelligent interface for predicting the extreme values at locations in the world's oceans.

Using this task model as a basis, a first-pass attempt at an intelligent interface for this type of engineering task was designed. Once this was done the task model was presented to the experts and they were asked for their feedback. Their reaction to the task model indicated further areas for subsequent protocol studies. Suggestions by the experts were filtered back into the design of the system. We attempted to produce a model of how the user would solve the problem in an idealised setting. The attempt was to build an interface that would support readily the users in their tasks and also provide those types of facilities that would maximise the users' efficiency in solving the problem. To this end the experts were asked to draw-up a hypothetical wish list of what functionality they would require, when and why.

From the protocols it was clear that the initial and most basic problem was finding and choosing the data to use in the first place. A second problem was that certain types of information were represented in the database in ways that made it hard for the user to use effectively. For example positional data of various locations were represented in terms of their longitude and latitude which made it harder for users to get a good model of the topography of the data sites in a particular area. The most obvious solution to this problem, and the one adopted here is to use a map style interface. However using a map presents its own problems. There may be a very large amount of information present, so there needs to be a means of navigation through all this information in a sensible manner. Brayshaw and Eisenstadt (1988) have pointed out that scale alone cannot solve all the problems in dealing with large amounts of data and that the solution to this problem lies in different levels of granularity of representation appropriate to different levels of detail in the task.

In the current domain, the experts indicated that there were four basic sorts of data that they typically worked with (sea currents, wind speeds, waves and sea bottom temperatures), and that for each type of data, there were typically three ways of deriving it (by observations, by surveys, and as a result of mathematical simulations). These indices give us a convenient way of sorting the data. As a result of these considerations a graphical interface was designed based upon the notion of a spinning globe. The user first inputs the location of the site they are interested in or alternatively zooms into it using the globe on the screen. Figure 3 indicates a typical outcome of this process. In this case the selected area is the southern part of the North Sea, with land indicated by the grey shaded areas.

On the left of figure 3 you will notice four icons. These indicate the four typical types of data that the expert looks for. Their meanings are described in figure 4. The icons allow the user an easy way of selecting the data he wishes to see. The four way division of the data is a direct result of the experts classification schema. So if all types of data are of interest then all the icons should be selected. If the user were only interested in wind and waves then only those items need be chosen. Selected items are always distinctively indicated so that users always know what they are looking at.

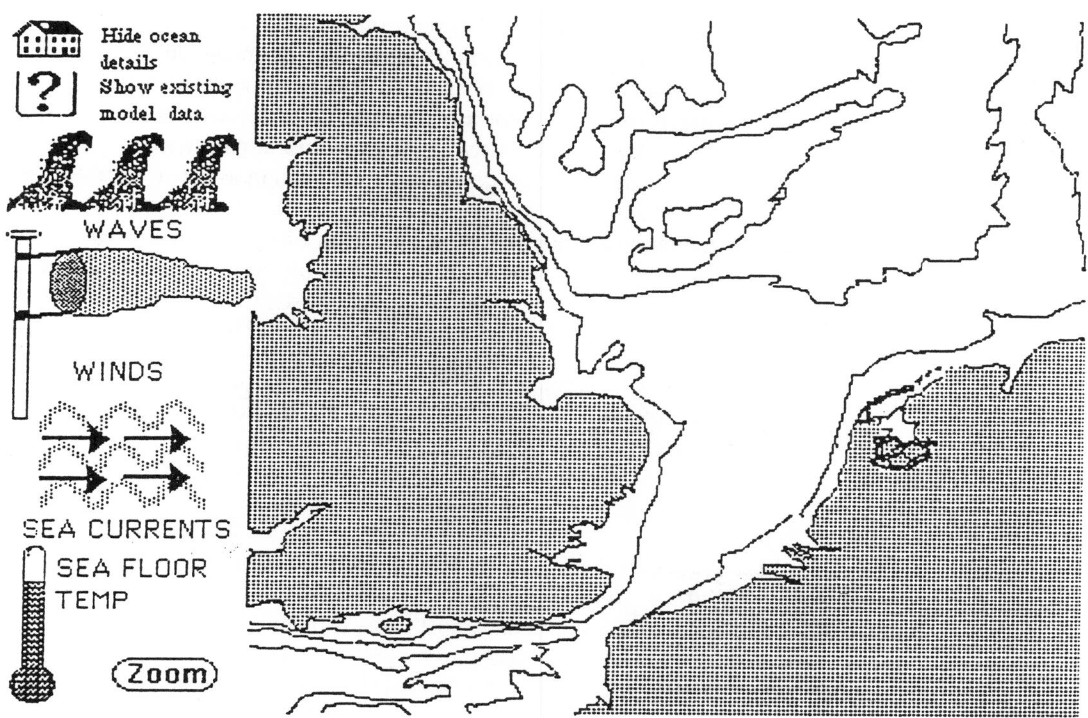

Fig 3 Example screen snapshot from Hypercard interface demonstrator

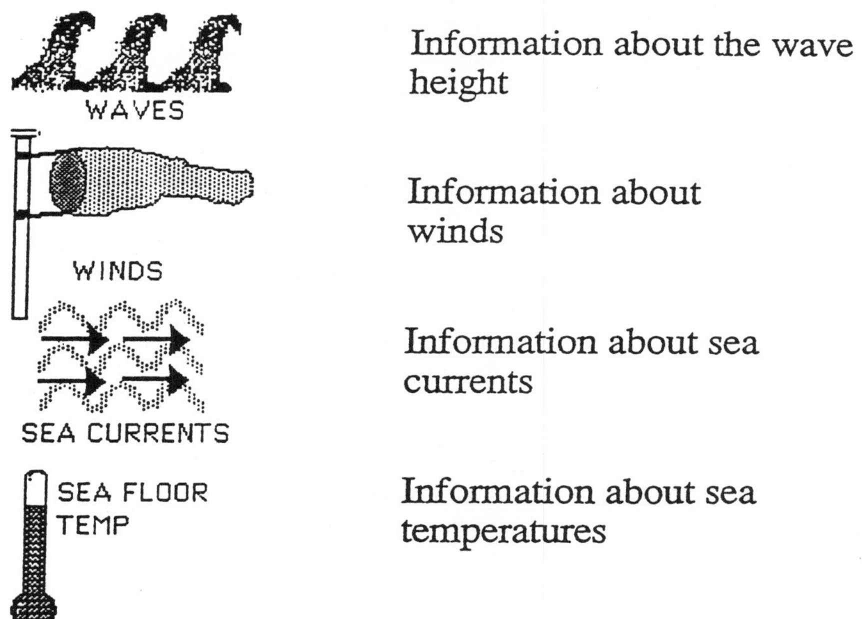

Fig 4 The meaning of the icons

A button at the top of the map switches between showing the prevailing conditions and surface elevation information for the area in view and showing sites for which models have already been derived, as tiny pin spots. As the protocols revealed, this is useful because if there already is a model for a point geographically close to the current area of interest, this model can often be used as it stands or at least as a basis for generating a new model. Typically this precise data is not available for a suitable site except in very well charted areas.

Clearly the area on the map is a very large one, covering a large amount of data. The proposed system allows users to narrow the focus of interest further by selecting an area they wish to look at in finer detail. This maps onto the first phase of data selection observed in the experts, namely narrowing down the task to an initial geographic area of interest. It is proposed that to make such a choice, the user clicks the mouse at the top-right-hand corner of where he wishes the marked area to be and then drags the mouse down to produce a mark that indicates the desired range of interest. Sites that are located in the selected area are shown in the finer detailed view, see figure 5.

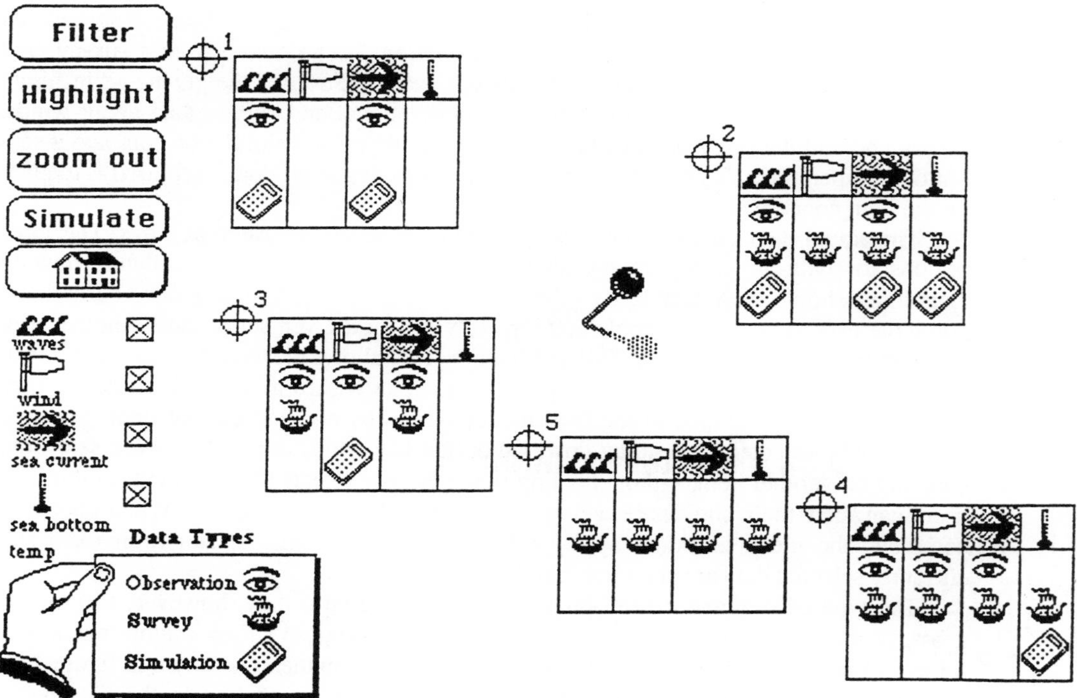

Fig 5 Close-up view of a selected area of the North Sea showing five selected sites of interest

The selected area is shown with a pin indicating the target, and the numbered sites indicate those places for which data exists. Small menus appear next to each of the sites. A closer look at these types of menus is shown in figure 6.

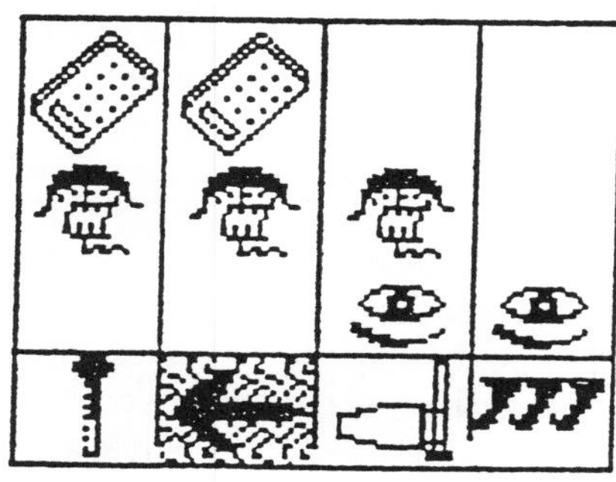

Fig 6 A detailed view of the menus found in the close-up view

In figure 6 information is shown on currents, winds, waves and sea-bottom temperatures. For any given type of data the protocol shows three ways of deriving that data, as a result of observations (e.g. books or logs), or of a survey, or of a mathematical simulation. To indicate this visually the icon of an eye is used to indicate observational data, the icon of a ship to indicate something that has been derived from a survey, and that of an abacus to indicate mathematically derived data. So, for the given site in figure 6, their is observational data about waves, observational and survey data about winds, survey and simulation data about sea currents, and survey and simulation data about sea-bottom temperatures. To see any of this data in more detail, all that is required is to click on the item concerned.

The actual data can be viewed in any one of a variety of different ways. The three options for data are as a straight table, as a graph, or as a bar chart. Other viewing techniques should be available for other types of data. Pre-specified options beforehand allow the user to customise the default type of view for a given set of data. Another user initiated feature is the add-data-by-hand feature. This allows the expert to do exactly that. If it is selected then he can simply type in the data he wishes to see. Otherwise the user selects data to be included in the final model simply by clicking on that item. Multiple items may be selected by holding down an option key whilst doing the mouse selection. Clicking on another item without holding down the key selects the new item. In this way users can alter their choices. Existing choices are always highlighted. When choice is complete, the menu is exited by the *OK* button. If the menu is later re-invoked any currently selected data are shown as highlighted.

The type of summarised information we see if figure 6 may, however, still be too gross for the particular situation. To overcome this we propose a filter option that allows for even finer discrimination of data. A typical filter pop-up menu is shown in figure 7.

The filter menu shows types of constraints that can be applied to the data being selected. Data may be limited to a particular time period, to a particular method of data gathering, or to a particular contractor/firm/institution/survey, that gathered the data in the first place. The menu shown allows the user to filter information, i.e. select items for display, or to reject it, i.e. to remove information from further consideration.

As the user selectively builds up these constraints on the data, a diagram is drawn in the left half of the menu showing the constraints being built up. It is possible to combine filters and rejection signs as is shown graphically on the left of the menu. For instance, in order to filter the information to data from within a given time period collected by a particular source, but also to remove any data of a particular type, the following is done.

We first select the time icon. A pop-up menu will appear and we can now select the time period we wish to consider. A funnel containing a watch will appear on the left of the menu once this has been selected.

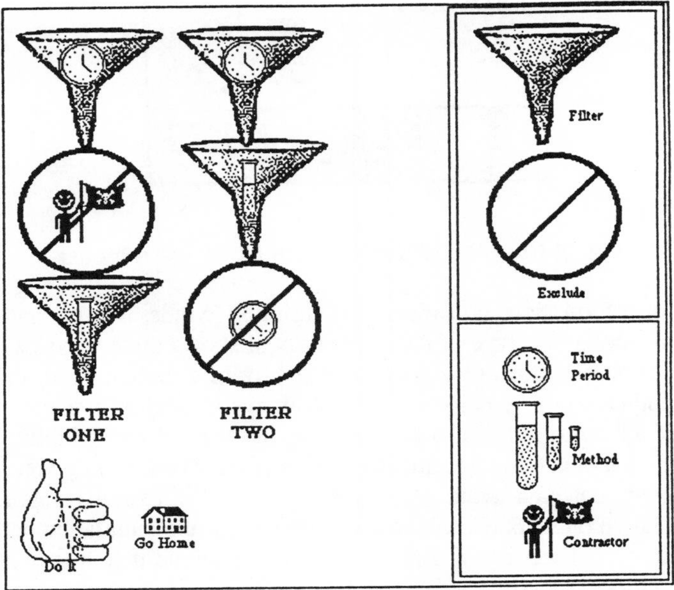

Fig 7 The filter menu

If we wish to further specialise this information, say for contractor, we simply drag the required items across from the menus on the left to the menu at the required place. Once we have chosen both a filter type and method of filtering a pop-up-menu results, and we can choose from a menu list of known contractors those whom we wish to consider. Multiple choices may be made by multiple mouse selection from the menu. The result of such a choice is again reflected in the left of the menu by a second filter, this time marked with the contractor icon, appearing at the bottom of the graphics area. It is drawn below the previous time filter to indicate the subsequent filter effect that it has. If we wish to throw out all types of information of a particular sort at this point we can define a rejection box in an analogous way.

Clicking on any of the graphics drawn as a result of specifying a constraint brings the relevant pop-up menu for that constraint back onto the screen allowing easy editing (or even deletion) of the filter. Multiple sets of filter combinations can be defined.

Once a set of data is chosen the next task is to model this data. A program which currently exists carries out a manipulation of this data. The results of this program are displayed in a graphical form, see figure 8 below.

The various extreme value conditions for the site are shown. The icons used are the same as in figure 5. Talking to the expert revealed the need to test for various other possibilities. Notice in the diagram we have a 100 year extreme wave height of 24m, if we wish to see the possibility of a 20m wave height in the same time span, we can (in the proposed system) mouse click on the waves icon. We are prompted to supply a value.

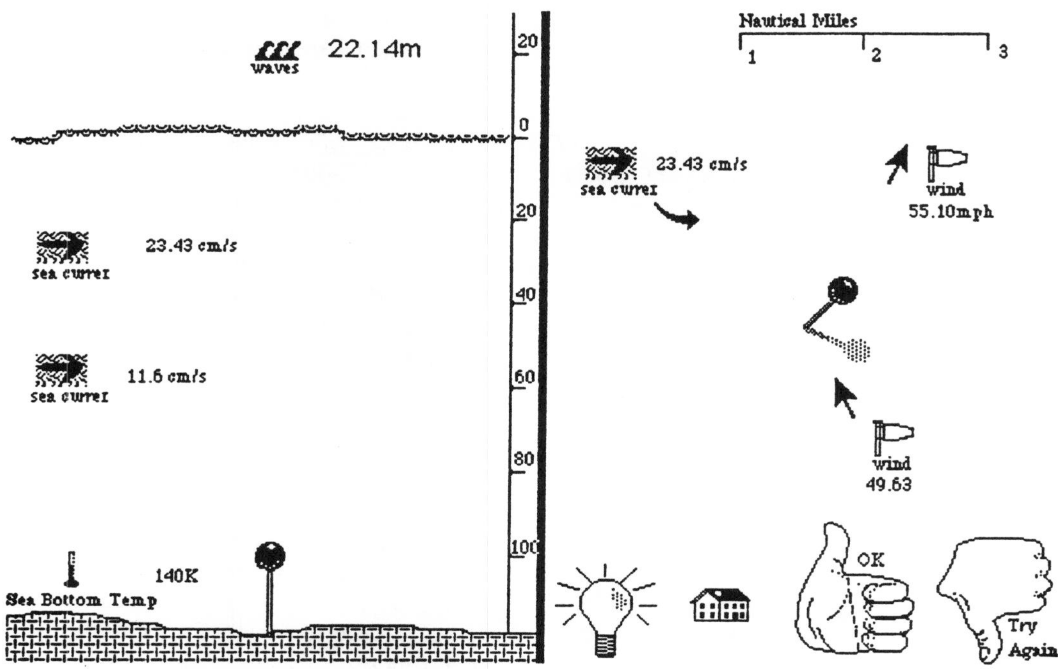

Fig 8 View of model of current selected data

In such a way the user is able to display the results of the model simulation. The above is an attempt to summarise the collected data. At present various statistical techniques are being used to present the information in the database. We are currently investigating methods of integrating these techniques into the current system. The current thinking aims to present the summary of the findings of these other techniques in the manner displayed above. If the user subsequently wants to see the rest of this information, he mouse clicks on the item in the above figure and goes straight to the required place.

3 The concept translator

As shown in figure 1, the system has three major components. The second of these is the concept translator. This is the part that translates requests made at the interface level to the queries at the database level. From there it is the job of the Query and Answer Generator (QAG) to worry about the practicality of these queries. The concept translator (CT) translates the concepts which the user is dealing in, to those that are specific enough for the (QAG) to develop SQL (or whatever relevant language) code. It relates the concepts used in the interface to the information stored in the database. That is, for all the actions in the interface, e.g. requesting information or specifying filters or constraints, it is able to translate this into a query, or series of queries and pass these down to the QAG.

This is done by a set of rules, each designed to be appropriate for the task. The concept translator contains the procedural knowledge on what information is needed and the mapping of concepts onto system functions or protocol vocabularies. As such the language with which users refer to the database is not limited to that of the database itself but may include their own pre-defined terms. It is the job of the CT to allow for this mapping. Secondly the CT is able to initiate the update of the interface as a result of these actions. It does all this by a series of production rules with an integrated frame engine. The frame engine consists of two parts. The knowledge-base which is local to the particular system, and the interface with the QAG. Thus as far as the CT is concerned knowledge is stored in a series of frames. From the translators point of view, it doesn't matter where the information is stored. It will first try to look this up to see if the information is in the local knowledge-base, if it fails to find it there it then passes the query on to the QAG. Results of the QAG are placed in the local frame memory thereby stopping repeated use of the QAG for the same piece of information. CT rules look like the following.

```
(rule <name> <left-hand-side> --> <right-hand-side>)
```

For the rule to fire the left-hand side (LHS) of the rule must be satisfied. That is, in our scheme, all the elements of the LHS must be contained in either frame memory (either locally or via a query to the database) or in working memory. If there is more than one rule with a satisfied LHS then the set of rules are placed in a conflict set and a set of strategies used to decide which rule to fire. These strategies are recency, refractoriness, and specificity and are variously described elsewhere (Forgy, 1981; Brownston, 1985; Cooper and Wogrin, 1988; Kahney et al., 1989). Below are an example rules.

```
(rule  locate-data-type-close-up-view
          (data-of-interest ^data)
          (the constraints of ^data is ^constraints)
          (the location of site_of_interest is ^site)
   -->
          (add-to-wm (constraints ^constraints ^data))
          (add-to-wm (sitename ^site))
          (add-to-wm (data-type ^data)))

(rule time-&-contractor-filter-for-data-type
          (data-type ^Type)
          (constraint (time ^time-filter)
               (contractor ^contractor-filter) ^Type)
          (sitename ^site)
          (the types-of-data ^Type for ^site
               with time-constraint ^time-filter and
                    contractor-filter ^contractor-filter

               is ^data-types)
   -->
          (show ^data-types for ^Type at-site ^site))
```

```
(rule time-&-method-filter-for-data-type
        (data-type ^Type)
        (constraint (time ^time-filter)
                    (method ^method-filter) ^Type)
        (sitename ^site)
        (the types-of-data ^Type for ^site
             with time-constraint ^time-filter and
                  contractor-filter ^contractor-filter

             is ^data-types)
  -->
        (show ^data-types for ^Type at-site ^site))
```

This example illustrates how a rule can be triggered to show what type of information is available for winds at a set of sites in the close-up view of the site (e.g. see figure 6). In local frame memory is always located information about the user's currently chosen environment, e.g. about selected filters. Suppose we wish to see the type of information that is available for waves. To do this we first seed the database with the following working memory fact **(data-of-interest waves)** and invoke the interpreter with the command **run.** The rule **locate-data-type-close-up-view** first fires. Notice that it will be placed in the conflict set a series of times, with different instantiations of the variable **^site.** Due to exhaustive search eventually all of these different rule instantiations will fire allowing all sites to be updated. Conflict resolution ensures that at no time do rules with the same set of instantiations fire a second time, thus removing the possibility of a loop. Next, the rule **time-&-contractor-filter-for-data-type** is fired. There are two things to note here. First notice the left-hand-side element that is shown in italics (for the readers benefit only, it is transparent to the system). This is a query to hand to the QAG. First however, local frame memory is checked to see if the answer to the query is located there, which it will be if the question has already been answered by the system during the current user session. If it is not then the system hands the query down to the QAG. The concepts used in the query are those that are agreed in the protocol between the two components. In the rule **time-&-contractor-filter-for-data-type** we can see on the right-hand-side of the rule the directive **show.** This is the command to go and update the interface. The command predicates a pre-defined LISP function that takes the information and updates accordingly.

The basic rule syntax is as follows:

```
(rule <name>    (precondition-1)
                (precondition-2)
                ....
                -->
                (action-1)
                (action-2)
                .....
                )
```

OR and NOT can be added as follows:

```
(rule A-or-B
                    (not out-of-work)
                    or
                    (not have-cold)
                    -->
                    (write "then I'm a happy man"))
```

The rule checks to see if not **out-of-work** or not **have-cold** is true. If this is the case it uses another right-hand-side directive, **write** to print out the message *then I'm a happy man* Other right-hand-side directives include **add-to-wm** (see rules above), **show** (also above), **halt** (halt the interpreter at this point), and **add-to-fm** which adds the specified item into local frame memory. A final option is **deduce** which invokes a backward-chaining rule-interpreter; it is envisaged that this will be used to do more sophisticated (i.e. diagnostic) reasoning about the domain at a latter date. Frames are always addressed in the following manner:

the Attr of Obj is Value

Working memory patterns can be arbitrary lists.

The system works not only in translating the actions of the user into interactions with the database. It also contains information about what subsequent behaviours are required. The approach allows portability, flexibility and easy programming style and thus we prefer it to the possibility of hard-wiring SQL onto the back of our graphical front-end. It is intended to allow expert users the option of direct access to the database. To do this a CT, employing a semantic network is planned. This will allow expert users a much more flexible vocabulary because the system will attempt to recognize their input and translate it into the standard CT one. Additionally the user can edit and browse the hierarchy. This will allow the user first to identify and understand the concepts used in the domain. Secondly users can introduce their own concepts and define them in terms of the system definitions. This will allow much greater user flexibility in how the user can approach the database. For example suppose that a given task requires the concept **velocity-of-particles-perpendicular-to-a-pipeline** and the user would like to talk to the database about this concept. To do so all he has to do is to define the meaning of this concept in terms of the existing library of concepts. In this way commonly occurring concepts can be built up and referred to directly. The CT will handle a tricky bit of input, turning it into something the QAG (and from there, the database) can understand.

As we have mentioned before, our task here is to build an intelligent interface with the user, not to mechanise the task. However we believe that by having a full-fledged inference engine at this level of the system, the possibility to mechanise trivial, repetitive, or boring tasks is realised; and a second phase development, to model more of the expertise of the expert, is naturally incorporated.

4 A frame-based Query/Answer Generator (QAG)

The preceding section has concentrated on describing the system from the perspective of the user. We have not however described the lower level components of the system. The most important of these is the query/answer generator. The query/answer generator is responsible for the actual retrieval of the information. It generates the database query and returns the information in the form of a frame. This information is manipulated and acted upon by the CT, which takes input directly from the intelligent interface and translates this information into concepts which will be understood by the QAG. The CT derives from the user input a series of unconnected queries about the single concepts. These concepts are stored in a *concept hierarchy*. The QAG and the CT communicate with each other by this concept exchange. The top-down design of the system allows the pre-definition of a dictionary of concepts that allow this communication to proceed. The top-down design also ensures that the number of concepts employed is limited to just those that are strictly necessary. Many existing databases use so called data-dictionaries. It may be the case that we can employ these data dictionaries, plus the constraints we now generate, to guide the construction of the concept hierarchies we require. If this is the case this would greatly facilitate the generalisation of this approach to other SQL application areas or in principle to any other database.

The QAG is first invoked when the CT produces a *query frame*. This is an instance of one of the available concepts, with its slots filled in. The values in the slots together form the conditions each instance of the concept must meet to be retrieved. Using this the QAG proceeds to interrogate the database. Having a single data-structure as the only means of communication keeps interfaces between modules narrow. It does mean, on the other hand, that the actual data structures used must be flexible enough to provide all necessary communication functions. In choosing frames we were mindful of two things. Firstly that their structure naturally mirrored that of the database itself; and secondly that frames provide a powerful and flexible structure for reasoning about knowledge in an AI setting.

Each concept is represented as a frame. The concepts (and hence the frames) are arranged according to a pre-defined concept hierarchy. In each slot property values may be placed. Additionally there are special slots, dubbed *communication slots*, which contain extra information controlling the information exchange between the QAG and the CT, typically in one of two forms. The first is requests for a particular operation the CT wishes the QAG to perform. The second type are comments the QAG hands back to the translator. These comments, e.g. error messages, are derived from a restricted vocabulary making them understandable by both modules.

In addition to the above each slot may have a further 3 fields associated with it, as follows.

- Restrictions: here the CT specifies the (range of) values each retrieved instance may have for this slot.
- Extractions: the CT can instruct the QAG whether or not the values should be returned in the answer, or whether the function specified in the *operation slot* should be applied to this particular one. Each slot inherits certain default values through the concept hierarchy. For instance, slots that function as unique identifiers of instances of a concept will be shown in an SQL LIST operation unless the CT specifies differently.
- Value: this is the place where the QAG will put the value(s) it retrieves from the database. Appropriate error messages may also be placed here when necessary.

On receipt of the query frame, with restrictions and extraction information filled in, the QAG will receive this frame and use it as the basis of the database query. After that, it will return the frame to the CT with either the requested slots filled in, or one or more error messages explaining why the query was unsuccessful.

Inside the QAG, invisible to the CT, each concept is linked to a detailed description, which tells the QAG how to process each of the slots in the concept. The description contains

a The boundaries within which the values of a particular slot must lie. From these boundaries the QAG can deduce whether or not a database query is likely to result in an answer.
b The data-retrieval information which indicates to the QAG what is the relation between the slots and the information stored in the database. In many cases there will be a simple one-to-one mapping between a slot in a concept frame and a field in a database table. Things can be more complicated, however, in several ways:

    i The value to be put in the slot is not the value to be retrieved from the database, but something derived from the database value by means of a procedure. For example, if we had a frame representing a particular person, which has a slot for birth-date but not for age, and this frame is queried from age, it is clearly possible to derive this value from the birth-date of the person without having the age explicitly stored. In order to do this we can store a description of where to find a basic value, and a procedure which tells the QAG how to derive the desired result.
    ii The value to be put in the slot is a combination of several values to be retrieved from the database. A company's mail address, for example, is a string composed of the P.O.Box number, the postal code, and city, all three of which can be retrieved from the database. The system stores information on how to retrieve each individual piece of information, and a procedural description on how to combine them into a single value.

In order to place the above in context, let's now consider an example. It is based on the METOCEAN database. Its purpose is to show how the actual query to the database is created and how the CT receives an answer.

4.1 Query Generation

The query generation globally decomposes into three phases:

1 In the first phase the CT query is copied and matched against the concept hierarchy: information about the default extractions are included, restrictions are checked and the attributes are linked to entries in the data dictionary. If needed the CT query can be divided into several queries, each processed in parallel. All the queries that do not pass on to the second phase are put aside with a relevant message.
2 In the second phase all tables (or files) needed to perform the individual query are looked up, together with information about how they are linked together (*join-conditions*). The query at this phase is represented in an intermediate form avoiding prior commitment to the final form of the SQL query or to any other language. This phase merely consists of a search problem. The actual implementation depends on the type of data dictionary used.
3 In the third phase the actual query is generated and performed. In our example we go as far as the generation of SQL. The implementation of this phase greatly depends on the tools used and on the type of database queried.

For the purpose of this example lets consider the following type of query which could be generated by the CT e.g. as a result of a highlight request.

```
List the time, contractor and maximum speed, of all
measurements taken between 01/01/1988 and 31/01/1988 in
the region delimited by longitudes 2 and 4 and latitudes
52 and 54
```

Within the QAG all the concepts it *knows* about are stored in a *concept hierarchy.* For example the concept **measurement** has been divided into the sub-concepts **meteorological-measurement, surface-elevation-measurement, wind-measurement, wave-measurement** and **current-measurement**. With such a scenario the query will be dealt with as follows.

The system in this instance requires the time, contractor and maximum speed. Since time and maximum speed are not defined within the measurement concept, the query cannot be solved at the measurement-level. So we have to look at all the different types of measurement and possibly generate a query for each one of them.

Time is a valid slot for every type of measurement. However, the maximum speed has only been defined for two of these, namely the measurements for winds and for currents. So only the latter two measurements can appear in the answer. However, looking at the range for the maximum current speed, it is noted that the absolute maximum for this speed is 30 m/s. This leaves the query about wind measurements. After looking up the field descriptions and the tables needed, the query results in:

```
SELECT MEASUREMENT_TIME, CONTRACTOR_NAME, MAXIMUM_WIND_SPEED
FROM  WIND_MEASUREMENT,  WIND_PROCESS,  DEPLOYMENT,  SITE,
   LOCATION, SURVEY, CONTRACTOR
WHERE MEASUREMENT_TIME >= 01/01/88
.AND. MEASUREMENT_TIME <= 31/12/88
.AND. LONGITUDE >= 2 .AND. LONGITUDE <= 4
.AND. LATITUDE >= 52 .AND. LATITUDE <= 54
.AND. MAXIMUM_WIND_SPEED >= 50
.AND. WIND_MEASUREMENT.PROCESSING_ID =
            WIND_PROCESS.PROCESSING_ID
.AND. WIND_PROCESS.DEPLOYMENT_ID = DEPLOYMENT.DEPLOYMENT_ID
.AND. DEPLOYMENT.SITE_ID = SITE.SITE_ID
.AND. LOCATION.SITE_ID = SITE.SITE_ID
.AND. DEPLOYMENT.SURVEY_ID = SURVEY.SURVEY_ID
.AND. SURVEY.CONTRACTOR_ID = CONTRACTOR.CONTRACTOR_ID
```

After all this information is gathered from a successful query (or series of queries) it is handed back to the CT. If the query was one that the QAG couldn't deal with, then an appropriate error is generated and returned in a like manner.

5 Generalising this approach to other domains

Although the system we have proposed is clearly highly domain dependent, the method by which the system was produced was not. There is a difficult trade-off in AI systems between power and generality. In order to get powerful systems that are of real benefit to the user, they must take into consideration the task and domain. The result of this is a loss of generality to other task and domains. In the approach we advocate here, we directly tune the system to the users and their problems and allow these constraints to propagate down the layers of the system to influence lower level details. We believe that this produces a better system in the long term, and often it makes the integration of the various sub-parts (e.g. database and knowledge-base) easier because we know in advance what is the range of functionality we require and thus exactly how powerful our interface needs to be. The down-side to all this is loss of modularity in the sense that these low level solutions tie the various parts to the particular application and it is not clear whether they could be used elsewhere. The solution to this problem however is that the method by which we came up with the proposed solution is portable to other approaches as are the central design tenants we have chosen to follow. Specifically the notion of designing the interface from the perspective of the user and their task, allows access to information without recourse to things like databases.

6 Conclusions

We conclude:

- That it is desirable to view the task from the perspective of the user and their problem solving.
- That these top-down considerations have important implications for the architecture of the system low-down.
- That these considerations influence the interfacing of the knowledge-base and database into a unified system.
- That there is more to this interface than just linking two things together or combining one set of data in terms of another set of data.
- That the top-down approach seeks a unified system from the point of view of the user and that this is the correct level to approach the task. If the notions of a knowledge-base or a database are not a useful ones for the user when they are solving a problem, then they should be dispensed with. Thus, although knowledge resource areas are present in the system, their exact location and physical make-up (e.g. an Oracle database), are not important so long as the users can get what they want from them.

References

1 Anderson, J.R. *The architecture of cognition*. Harvard Press, 1983.

2 Brachman, R.J. and Levesque, H.J. Tales from the far side of KRYPTON: lessons for expert database Systems from knowledge representation. In Kerschberg (1986) pp. 3-43.

3 Brayshaw, M. and Eisenstadt, M. Adding data and procedure abstraction to the transparent Prolog machine. In R.A. Kowalski and K.A. Bowen (eds.), *Logic Programming*. Volume 1. MIT Press, 1988, pp. 532-547.

4 Brodie M. and Jarke, M. On integrating logic programming and databases. In Kerschberg (1986) pp. 191-208.

5 Brownston, L. *Programming expert systems in OPS5*. Addison-Wesley, 1985.

6 Buchanan, B.G. and Shortliffe, E.H. *Rule-based expert systems: the MYCIN experiments of the Heuristic Programming Project*. Addison-Wesley, 1983.

7 Chang, C.L. and Walker, A. PROSQL: A Prolog programming interface with SQL. In Kerschberg (1986), pp. 233-246.

8 Cooper, T. and Wogrin, N., *Rule-based programming with OPS5*. Morgan-Kaufmann, Los Altos, 1988.

9 Dahl, V. Logic programming for constructive expert database systems. In Kerschberg (1986), pp. 209-218.

10 Forgy, C.L. *OPS5 user's manual*. Department of Computer Science Technical Report, CMU-CS-81-135, Carnegie-Mellon University, Pittsburgh, Pennsylvania 156213.

11 Kahney, J.H. ed. *Knowledge Engineering*. Open University Press, Milton Keynes, 1988.

12 Kerschberg, L. (Ed.) *Proceedings from the First International Workshop on Expert Database Systems*. Benjamin/Cummings, 1986.

13 Languna Beach Participants[6], Future Directions in DBMS Research.

14 Laird, J., Rosenbloom, P. and Newell, A. *Universal subgoaling and chunking*. Kluwer, 1987.

15 Lenat, D.B. and Feigenbaum, E.A. On the thresholds of knowledge. In *Proceeding of the tenth International Conference on AI (IJCAI-87)*. Morgan Kaufmann, Los Altos, 1987, pp. 1173-1182,.

16 Newell, A. The knowledge level. *Artificial Intelligence*, 1982, **18**, pp. 87-127.

17 Norman, D.A. and Draper, S.W., eds, *User centered system design: new perspectives on human-computer interaction*. Lawrence Erlbaum, 1986.

18 McDermott, J. R1 revisited: four years in the trenches. *AI Magazine*, 1984, pp. 21-32.

19 Zaniolo, C, Prolog: A database query language for all seasons. In Kerschberg (1986), pp. 219-232.

---

6 The Languna Beach Participants were Philip A. Bernstein, Umeshwar Dayal, David De Witt, Dieter Gawlick, Jim Gray, Matthias Jarke, Bruce G. Lindsay, Peter C. Lockermann, David Maier, Erich J. Neuhold, Andreas Reuter, Lawrence A. Rowe, Hans J. Schek, Joachim W. Smidt, Michael Schriel, and Michael Stonebraker.

QUESTIONS

Dr. S. Bennett (Sheffield University).

SB. If I understand correctly, what you're saying is that in the knowledge base you actually create a model on the basis of the queries that the user is putting into the system, and that then extracts data from the database. Is there any means whereby, if the user then finds that some of the data is inconsistent that that can be put back into the system?

Dr. B. Papegaaij.

BP. First of all, the interaction with the user is all done within this knowledge base. Indeed, this knowledge base constructs a model of what the user has been doing so far. If that user finds that certain data is inconsistent or unreliable, it will not be updated in the database itself, the database is shielded off in this respect. It's a corporate database that we cannot tamper with. But it will be updated in the knowledge base, and it will be recorded there, so that when the same user starts using the same, the knowledge base will know that that particular user has found the data to be inconsistent or unreliable there, and it will take that into account. So, as far as the user is concerned, what he puts in as being inconsistent or unreliable will be remembered by the system. But we cannot tamper with the database, that's a severe restriction. We are not allowed to do that because so many more departments use that database as it is.

Ms. J. Kennedy (Napier Polytechnic).

JK. I was quite interested in the iconic interface side of the system and I see how you use it in creating the system. But when it comes to actually displaying data from the database, how do you display this in a concise and meaningful way to the user? Do you still use some sort of iconic representation, or do you actually give them the data straight out of the database.

BP. We almost never give raw data. What the user is interested in is this model, this evaluation model. This evaluation model has a great deal of parameters and this sort of standard form which the user recognizes. That is the way the data is returned. Raw data is almost never displayed. In certain rare cases the raw data will be shown, for example, when the user, sees that the evaluation model is absolutely rubbish and demands to see what data was used as the basis for it. At that time we put tables up on the screen. We don't like to do that, but sometimes there is no choice.

Dr. T. Barsalou (Stanford University).

TB. You mentioned generalizing your work to apply to another domain. What does that really involve? Is it just changing the knowledge component?

BP. The generalization of what we've done so far is the main concern for next year and as far as I can see, it involves only the knowledge component and a bit of interfacing.

Changing the knowledge component may be quite a large task, we do not underestimate. We've put a lot of knowledge engineering into it. As I said, six months of intensive knowledge engineering has been put into this knowledge base. Changing it to another domain will probably mean another six months. We have tried to define a method to speed up the process, but we're not sure what we're going to do. But I've already got some ideas from this conference.

TB. What kind of tools are you using for the interface?

BP. We're using a graphical interface on SUN stations. We're using KEE as well. We use ORACLE database. We do not use any programming languages other than LISP and KEE.

11 A Knowledge Assistant for the Design of Information Systems

S. Ip and T. Holden

ABSTRACT

Information Systems Design (ISD) is a relatively new and diversified discipline and a number of IS "methodologies", with different emphases, have been offered in the last decade. It is observed that most researches that attempt to apply results in AI to ISD have inevitably concentrated on the use of AI techniques. This paper represents the first stage of an ongoing project which attempts to go beyond the "technique level" and to investigate into the "knowledge/information level". It consists of three major parts. Firstly, a unified framework of Knowledge and Information Systems is outlined as the theoretical foundation of the work. Secondly, a new approach to ISD, known as the Knowledge Assistant approach, is proposed. The key note is to recognise the multi-meta-level and multi-dimensional nature of the knowledge involved in ISD. Finally, the architecture of a knowledge-based system called KADIS (a Knowledge Assistant for the Design of Information Systems) is discussed. It is argued that a multi-level viewpoint structure can be used to represent IS domain dependent knowledge in the design process. Other IS domain independent knowledge support is also listed.

Keywords: AI, knowledge-based system, information systems design, unified framework, meta-knowledge level, multi-level viewpoint structure

1. Introduction

Perhaps one of the most important conclusions of research in AI is that "intelligence requires knowledge". Lots of high quality knowledge. Yet most work that attempts to apply AI to ISD has a tendency to concentrate on the use of AI techniques, for example, natural language processing (Kersten, 1987; Cauvet et al., 1988). The fundamental belief of this work is that the marriage at this *technique level* is not enough. The problem under investigation is how to support the "knowledge" involved in the design of some systems purporting to deal with "information". Hence the required integration must start from the *knowledge/information level.* The next section of this paper attempts this integration by outlining a unified framework for the discussion of Knowledge System (KS) and Information System (IS). Based on this framework, section three briefly examines the structure of the knowledge involved in IS design and associated problems. Section four then presents a new approach to support IS design, namely, the *Knowledge Assistant* approach. The main theme of the approach is the *recognition of the multi-meta-level and the multi-dimensional nature of the knowledge involved in ISD*. The overall architecture of KADIS is also presented. A multi-level viewpoint structure is proposed for the dynamic representation of IS domain dependent knowledge. Four other IS domain independent knowledge support modules are also discussed briefly.

2. A Unified Framework for Knowledge and Information Systems

2.1 Objectives and Motivations

This section outlines a unified framework for KS/IS and related activities.[1] The objectives of such a framework include a better understanding of the structure of the knowledge involved in the design of IS, a firm basis for comparison of different KS/IS and a departure point for construction of further theories. It is hoped that this framework can provide the theoretical foundation for the development of a knowledge assistant of IS design.

The framework is motivated by ideas from a variety of sources. Its fundamental outlook is determined by theories in systems thinking and semiotics.[2] Systems thinking's emphasis on hierarchy and emergence forms the motivation for the meta-knowledge structure of our framework while semiotics' (ie. the study of signs) impression on our work is apparent. Furthermore, our work also utilizes ideas freely from IS and KBS research communities including: object systems and their contexts (Lyytinen, 1987), Weltanschuaang (Checkland, 1981), semantic approach to IS (Stamper, 1987), meta-knowledge (Lenat et al., 1983), the three element view of knowledge and the three cognitive modes for acting (Williams et al., 1988).[3] Discussions on the integration of data and knowledge bases have helped to shape part of

[1]The author is currently working on a more detailed and formalised version of the framework.

[2]Examples are the work of Lange (1962), Klir (1985), Orchard et al. (1988), and Nowakowska (1980).

[3]It must be acknowledged that Auramaki et al.'s (1988) "universal" framework for information activities lays an important foundation for our work. Our framework can be considered a natural extension of theirs.

our framework. "Semantic" data models[4] provide some basic ingredients of our work and Brachman et al.'s (1986) suggestion that the integration of data and knowledge bases should be at the "knowledge" instead of the "symbol" level is basically followed here.

2.2 Basic Constructs and the Information Representation Triangle

Let us consider the idea of an object. An *object* is a "thing" or "entity" which can be distinctly identified,[1] that is, readily distinguishable from other things (Chen, 1976). An object can have some *attributes* which will assume different, and possibly time-varying, *values*. A *relationship* is an association among entities. Attributes, values and relationships are also objects themselves.

Any representation of an object is called a *sign* (Nowakowska, 1980). Signs may take graphical, verbal, and many other forms; in fact, sometimes it is not possible to pinpoint the exact form of a sign. A collection of signs can also be known as a piece of *data*.

A set of objects may be "perceived" to be significant for a particular topic and form the *object system* concerned. All the other objects will by definition form the *environment* of the object system. The boundary between an object system and its environment is sometimes arbitrary and ill-defined.[2] Any data (ie. collection of signs) relevant to the object system is known as *information*.

The Information Representation Triangle (IRT)[3]

The concept of a IRT is the fundamental building block of our framework and is illustrated in fig.1. A IRT has three basic components on its base-line. *Actor* is a special class of objects which can act on other objects. These "actions" may include creation, modification, and application of other objects and are carried out through a set of *processes*. The set of objects being acted upon (which may include some actors) is known as the *object base* (OB).

[4]Such as extensions of relational models (Codd, 1979), object-oriented databases (Dittrich, 1987) and Chen's (1976) Entity Relationship Model.

[1]Stamper (1987) severely criticised this requirement of individuality and identity of an object. The examples he gives indeed pose some technical difficulties on the concept but they can be overcome to some extent by putting any object in the context of our meta-level structure. An object may be transformed into another totally different object(s) but some representations of the objects (which are themselves objects at other meta-levels, see next subsection) must persist.

[2]Auramaki (1987/8) and Lyytinen (1987) discuss the idea of object systems.

[3]The basic idea of IRT is very similar to Auramaki et al.'s (1987/8) IST (information system triangle) but with an extended scope.

At the vertex of a IRT is the *information base* (IB). It consists of the information (which, by definition, is a collection of signs) that describes and/or prescribes the connections among the various components at the base-line. It can be divided into two components: a *structural* IB which deals with the relationships and the attributes of the OB and a *functional* IB which deals with the interactions between the actors and the OB through the processes.

2.3 A Hierarchical Meta-Level Structure of KS/IS

In order to construct a hierarchy of IBs, we have to consider the principle behind linguistic (or semiotic) abstraction. Basically, it states that a meta-language can always be used to describe/prescribe the syntax, the semantics, and the pragmatics of another language (Lyons, 1977). Expressed more simply in terms of our basic constructs, we have

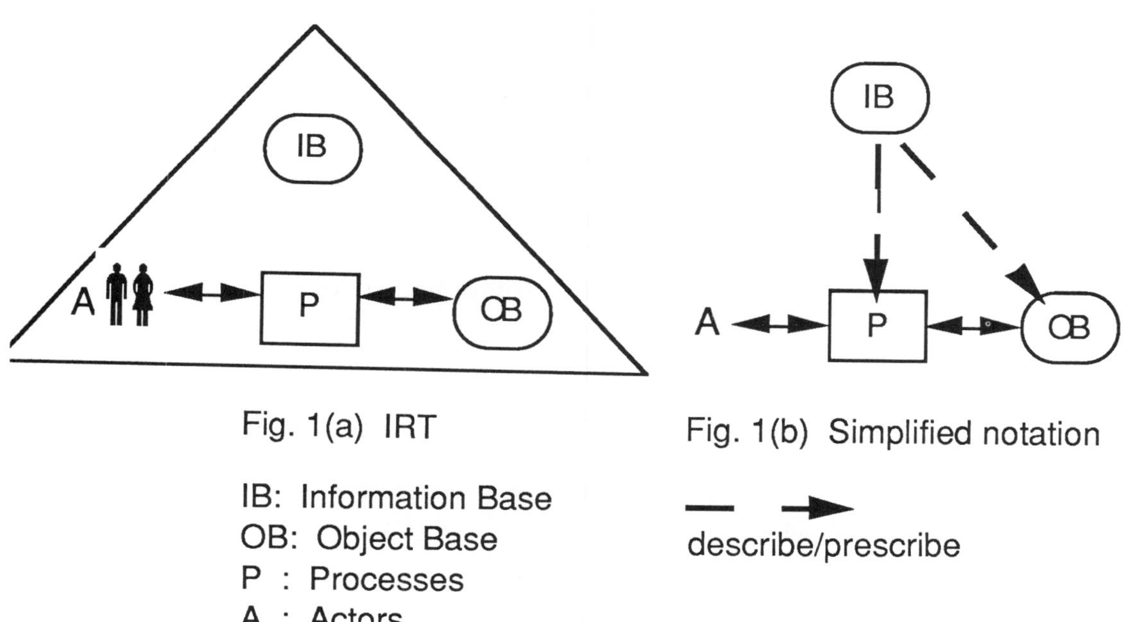

Fig. 1(a) IRT

IB: Information Base
OB: Object Base
P : Processes
A : Actors

Fig. 1(b) Simplified notation

— → describe/prescribe

Axiom 1 *A sign is itself an object.*

Hence the IB of any IRT can form the OB of another IRT. The IB of the latter IRT is then a meta-IB[1] because it contains information about another IB. This process of "meta-abstraction" can be repeated for an arbitrary number of times to form a hierarchy of meta-levels of IBs, given by the formula

[1]By definition, a meta-X is a X of/about X.

$$IB_i = OB_{i+1}, \quad i=0,1,2,... \qquad (1)$$

where i is the meta-level of the IRT *relative to the IB at its vertex* and OB_0 is defined to be the set of real (ie. non-sign) objects. The structure is illustrated in fig.2.

So far, the notion of "knowledge" have not been discussed. Let us consider the transformation of a set of signs from one form to another (eg. from verbal to graphical) in order to give more "useful" information to the actors involved. To facilitate such an improvement, one needs to "know" the syntax of both forms and what the actors would recognise as more useful. This informal concept of "knowing" can be generalised in terms of our basic constructs as

Axiom 2 *Knowledge is meta-information (ie. information about information)*

Hence a KB is a meta-IB and we have a special case of IRT, where the OB contains objects which are signs, known as the *knowledge-information representation triangle* (KIRT), represented in fig.3. For our purpose, we will seldom need to discuss directly about the real OB, and the meta-level hierarchy is redefined by the formula

$$KB_i = IB_{i+1}, \quad i=0,1,2,.... \qquad (2)$$

where i is now the meta-level of the KIRT *relative to the KB at its vertex*. The structure is illustrated in fig.4. Note that the indexing of IBs is the same as in fig.2 but all the indices of actors and processes are decreased by one.[1] It is now possible to give a definition of a KS/IS:

> A *KS/IS* is a collection (loosely or tightly coupled) of KB/IBs at various meta-levels. Such a decomposition of the KS/IS is known as the *knowledge (or information) structure* of the system.

Some final comments on actors must be made. The general nature of actors in the IRT involving real objects is probably quite complex. But for a KIRT (whose OB must consist of signs only), it is postulated that the actors involved must either be people or computers. Moreover, any one particular person (or machine) can play the actor role in a number of KB/IBs, possibly at different meta-levels.

2.4 A Taxonomy of KBs

This section attempts to give a rough classification of KBs along a few important *dimensions*.

The meta-level dimension is the most fundamental dimension in our framework and is discussed in detail above. This dimension can be compared to some other proposed knowledge (or data) architectures. In

[1]It is noted that in fig.3-2 the object system is equal to the sum of all the IBs and OBs since IBs contains signs which are also objects. The *Universe of Discourse* (UoD) is now defined as the object system excluding real objects (ie. OB_0). In fig.3-4, UoD is the sum of all KBs and IB_0.

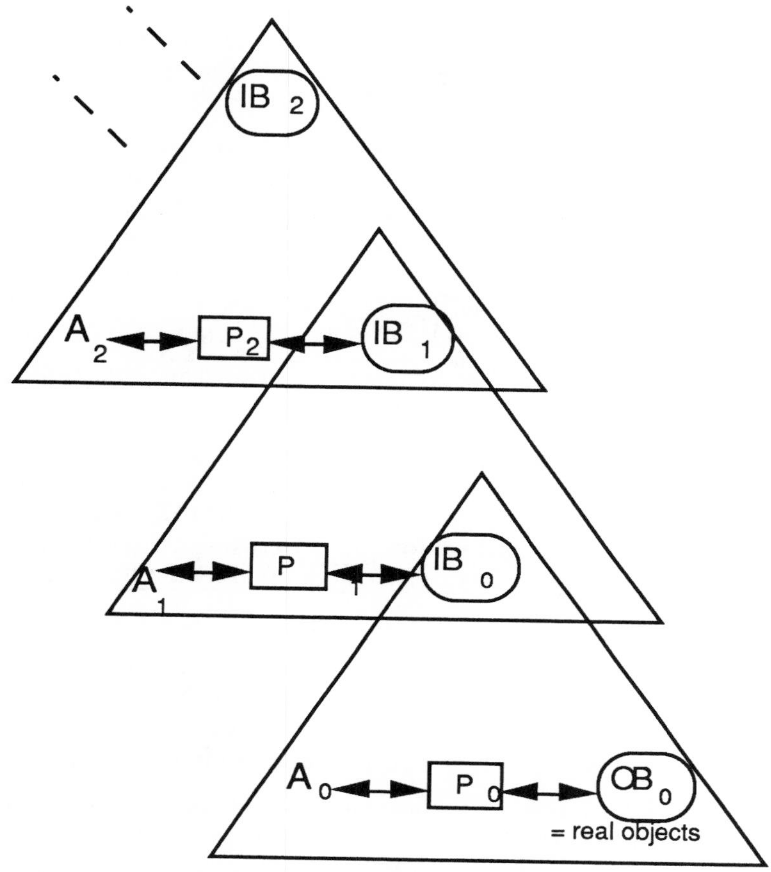

Fig. 2 A meta-level hierarchy of IB/OBs

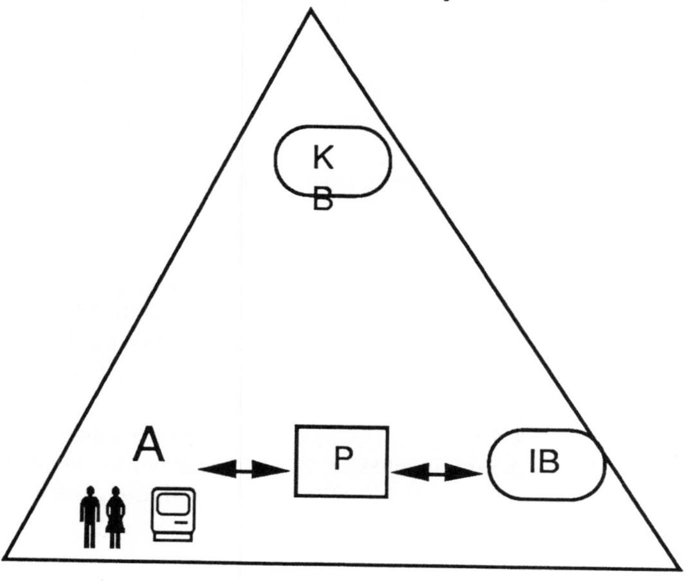

Fig. 3 KIRT

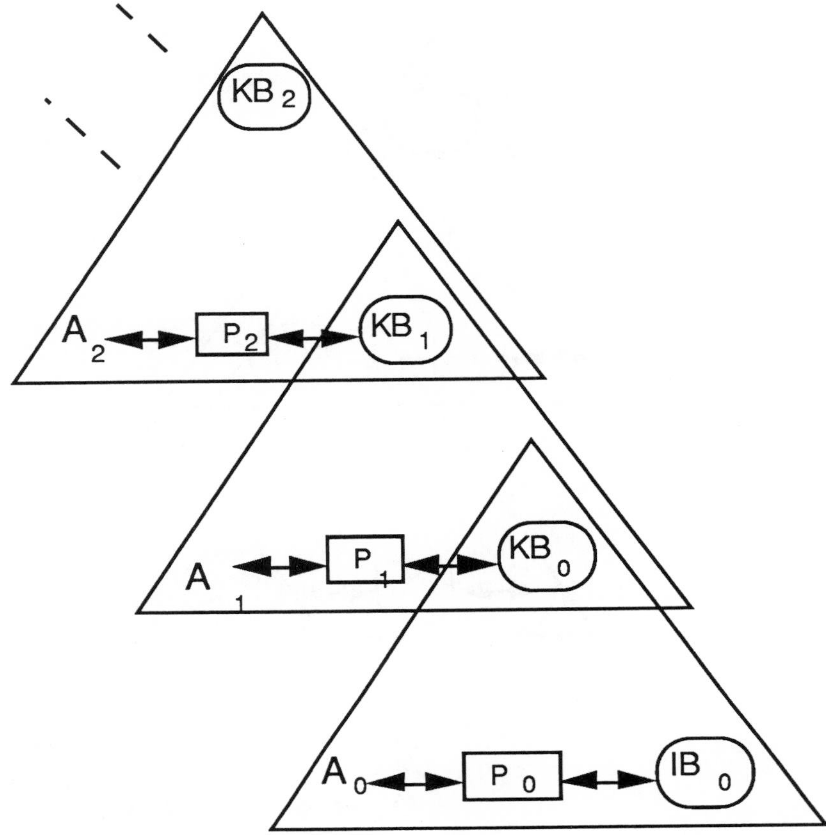

Fig.4 A meta-level hierarchy of KB/IB

typical database terminology, any KB is the intention of its lower meta-level KB and the extension of its higher meta-level KB.[1]

The structural/functional dimension is already discussed in section 2.2. A structural KB (at met-level i) can be further partitioned along the *syntactical/semantical dimension*; the former deals rather narrowly with the relationships among the objects (signs) within KB_{i-1} while the latter deals with KB_{i-1}'s "meaning" which includes its relationship with all KB/IBs (and their associated actors and processes) at meta-levels lower than i-1.

A *descriptive* KB is about what the interactions or relationships among the various components at the base line of its KIRT *actually are* while a *prescriptive* one is about what they *should be*. This dimension seems to

[1]Williams et al.'s (1988) three elements of knowledge- namely, generic concepts, specific concepts, and data- bears similarity to the KB_0, IB_0 and OB_0 respectively in our framework while Coeiho et al.'s (1985) three level architecture for management environments (meta KB, specifications KB, and the ground KB) correspond to our KB_1, KB_0, and IB_0.

have rather complex connections with the structural/functional dimension and needs further investigation.

A *formal* KB is one which can be encapsulated in some form of computational model. In this sense, all real knowledge is *informal* because of the interconnected relationships among them. But information encapsulation is a matter of degree (Williams et al., 1988) and useful formal representation can usually be captured. The formality of a KB refers to its potential encapsulation in a machine but one must still distinguish whether a KB is actually *human or machine captured.*

All the above dimensions (except the meta-level one) aim at partitioning a KB into a few *compatible* KBs. But different *incompatible* KBs can exist at any meta-level and there are different ways of classifying them according to the source of the incompatibility or the different dependence dimensions of a KB.

The *domain* of a KB at meta-level i is the part of the object system at meta-levels lower than or equal to i-2 (ie. the sum of OB_0, IB_0, KB_0, KB_1,...KB_{i-2}) and the associated processes and actors. Incompatible and unrelated KBs can exist at the same meta-level because of the different domain they describe/prescribe. A KB which remain unchanged for all domains under consideration is *domain-independent.*

Different KBs about the same domain can exist if they have different meta-KBs. This phenomenon is called *meta-knowledge-dependence.* Just as a different syntax would always give a different language, completely different meta-KBs always give different KBs, ie. all KBs are meta-KB-dependent. Yet we can talk about a relatively meta-KB-independent KB if only part of the meta-KB is changed.

Given the same meta-KB and domain, there can still be a few incompatible KBs because the actors who can interact with these KBs may have different *Weltanschauugen* (world-view; abbrev. W). The sources of such difference may indeed be different "meta-KBs" in the form of different histories and social and political cultures. But these elements are usually too remote and ill-defined in scope to be included in the UoD of the KS/IS. They can better be considered as part of the environment to the problem. If certain part of a KB can be agreed upon by all the actors interacting with it, it becomes *W-independent.*

Let us consider a few different KBs about the same domain. If the IBs described/prescribed by them are all subsets of a larger IB (ie. all of them are compatible), the KBs are said to be *information-independent* of each other. This dimension is exactly the same as the requirement of *data-independence* in data base terminology (Date, 1986).

3. The Knowledge for IS Design

3.1 The Structure of the Knowledge for ISD

The knowledge structure of IS Design involves at least four meta-levels (fig.5). The bottom level is the *enterprise DB* (a meta-level 0 IB). The model for this DB and IS end-users' interaction with it is described/prescribed by a set of *IS models*. These models (meta-level 0 KBs) are the actual objects that are being "designed". The IS designers create, update, and transform these models through IS design processes. A number of *IS design KBs* (at meta-level 1) describe/prescribe the various dimensions of the IS models and the design process behind them. In fact, the complexity and diversity of these design KBs implies that their correct application requires coordination. Such coordination, control, and planning are done by the ISD coordinator. Finally, a meta-level 2 KB describes the coordination process and the interrelationships among the

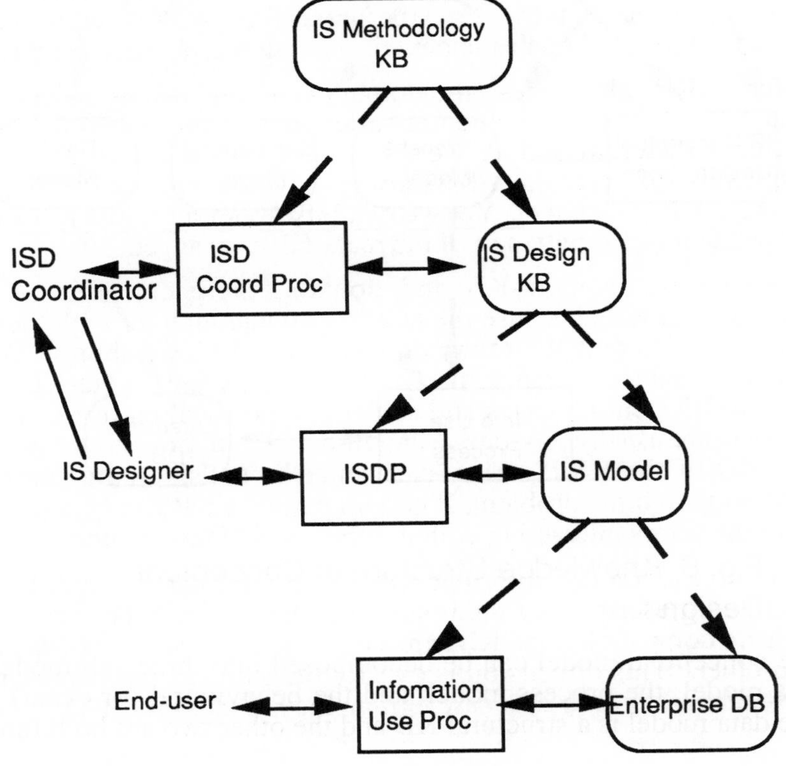

Fig. 5 Structure of Knowledge for ISD

various design KBs. This highest meta-level KB is known as the *IS methodology KB*[1].

Two classes of IS models exist: *conceptual/logical* models and *physical/implementational* models. (The implementational model, together with the enterprise DB, actually form the operational IS of the enterprise.) Such a distinction enables the designer to abstract from implementational details and limitations during the conceptual design phase and increases the flexibility and portability of the design. Relatively "intelligent" IS design KBs can be machine-captured to automatize the transformation from conceptual to physical IS models (Briand et al., 1985). Our work will , however, concentrate on providing support for the design of conceptual models (fig.6).

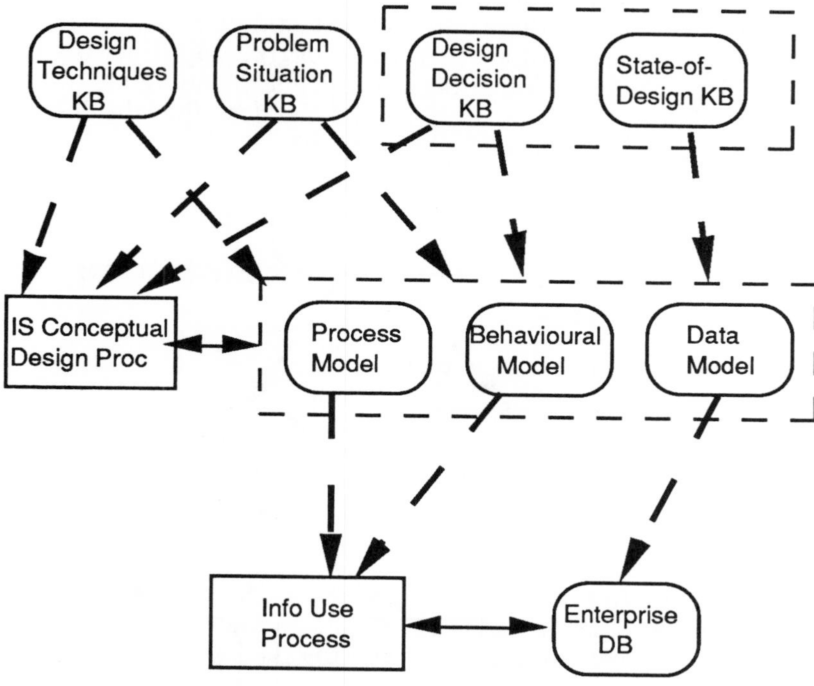

Fig. 6 Knowledge Structure of Conceptual Design

The conceptual model can be decomposed into three sub-models: the data model, the process model, and the behavioural (or event) model. The data model is a structural KB and the other two are both functional

[1]Note that the term "methodology" is used in a rather restricted sense here. It refers to the knowledge about the coordination and planning of other design knowledges. Normally some of these design KBs (such as the techniques of ERM, DFDs, etc.) are included in a "methodology".

ones. Four major design KBs (at meta-level 1) describes/prescribes these models and the design processes behind them:

- *the design techniques KB* describes the syntax and semantics of the various techniques used (eg. ERM, DFDs) and how they are used in the design process. It is both structural and functional.
- *the problem situation KB* contains knowledge about the needs and problems of the situation. It also includes knowledge traditionally described as IS requirements or specifications. Checkland's "root definitions" also belongs to this KB. It both describes what the current model is and prescribes what the target model should be.
- *the state-of-design KB* contains knowledge about the different "versions" of conceptual models (et. their completeness and usefulness) and the relationships among them.
- *the design decision KB* helps the designer to assess the relative merits of the various models. It contains a set of design criteria (eg. coherence, completeness, degree of coupling) and a description of how to evaluate a model using these criteria. This KB is closely related to the state-of-design KB.

3.2 Problems in ISD: Complexity and Uncertainty

The problems in any design can be classified into two groups: complexity and uncertainty (Williams et al., 1988). The problem of complexity arises when too much knowledge (or information) is presented to the designer. Uncertainty refers to the inability to choose among a number of alternatives due to lack of knowledge. These problems in ISD are now examined in the light of its knowledge structure.

There are four main types of complexities in ISD: 1) *size complexity* The size of some KBs in ISD (eg. a data model of several hundred entities) often overwhelms a human designer and leads to inconsistencies and incompleteness; 2) *process complexity* the problem is not simply a large KB but a lot of different "versions" of the same KB especially due to the iterative nature of IS design; 3) *multi-dimensional complexity* different dimensional components of a KB (eg. structural/functional) can interact combinatorially to generate another type of complexity and 4) *multi-meta-level complexity* the KBs for ISD are at a few different meta-levels and this further increases the burden of analysis and comprehension on the designer.

On the other hand, there are three types of uncertainties: 1) *problem uncertainty* (the difficulty in formulating the problem and finding finite number of alternatives); 2) *end uncertainty* (the difficulty in finding the right end-product to meet users' requirements) and 3) *means uncertainty* (the difficulty in deciding what techniques to use at each point and in what manners).

As commented above, the ultimate cause of any uncertainty is the lack of knowledge. In ISD the problem is further highlighted by the dual nature of the source of knowledge. Two parties are involved in ISD: the client/end-user and the expert designer; and each of them has part of the knowledge required. Typically the end-user has some knowledge in the problem situation KB and some in the IS conceptual models (but usually in the wrong form!) while the designers have the design technique KB and the IS methodology KB. The former's KBs are essential for overcoming problem and end uncertainties and the latter for means uncertainty. Except in the special case of the end-user being an expert designer himself, lack of certain KBs becomes inevitable.

4. A Knowledge Assistant for the Design of IS (KADIS)

4.1 The Knowledge Assistant Approach

The nature of a KBS can be classified in a number of ways. Perhaps the most popular distinction is the one between the "toolkit" approach (where a set of CAD tools are made available for designers to use creatively) and the "automatic" approach (where the designer is guided through a sequence of specific steps).[1] All such distinctions are both valid and useful but simply too narrow in scope. It fails to recognise that KBs at different meta-levels and of different dimensions can have different degrees of "intelligence" or "automation".

We hereby propose a new approach to support IS design. The approach, known as the *Knowledge Assistant* (KA) approach, can however be generalised for other purposes. The essence of the approach is to *recognise the multi-meta-level and multi-dimensional nature of the knowledge involved in ISD*. It is firmly based on the unified framework discussed in section two. The human designer is the principal actor and the computer system the KA in the actor roles of different KIRTs in ISD.

The KA supports the knowledge in IS design in four primary ways:

- to allow designers/users to reduce the complexity by *decomposing* the problem in a variety of ways. A flat unstructured knowledge representation can provide only one degree of decomposition. To overcome various complexities, the designer must be allowed to decompose the knowledge into different meta-levels, different dimensions, and different versions.

[1]Most of the ISD workbenches, eg. IEW, DDEW(Reiner et al., 1987), ICASE/SSADM(Walker et al., 1988), follow the toolkit approach while natural language strategies, eg. ACME(Kersten et al., 1987), OICSI(Cauvet et al., 1988), and Mannino et al. (1987), adapt the automatic one.

- to capture any KB completely into formal computational forms whenever it is possible. This usually requires a formal and robust KB (which often means domain and W-independence) .Such KBs can evolve from relatively passive "toolkit" to more active "automatic" modes at possibly different speed.
- to store, to retrieve, and to manipulate more informal and unstable KBs. Substantial parts of these KBs still need to be human captured, but some useful abstractions can be stored in the machine.
- to provide a dynamic knowledge representation mechanism to facilitate the propagation of the effect of the change in any KBs to other meta-levels.

Such an approach allows a very dynamic development of the KBs and a more realistic and flexible support for the actual design.

4.2 The Overall Architecture of KADIS

In order to understand the overall architecture of KADIS, it is important to distinguish two different types of "domains". The first one is the domain for which the IS is designed. It can be called the IS domain. But the ISD processes and related KBs themselves form a domain for higher meta-level KBs such as inferencing mechanisms and general representation formalisms such as frames. This class of domains can be called general domains.

The overall architecture of KADIS is illustrated in fig.7. It distinguishes between three different classes of KBs:

- general domain-independent KBs (eg. inference engine, inheritance mechanisms for frames)
- IS domain independent KBs (eg. design technique KBs, design decision KBs, and IS methodology KBs).
- IS domain dependent KBs (eg. problem-situation KBs, state-of-design KBs).

General domain independent KBs are very robust and seldom needs any changes. They are therefore the basic building block of the KADIS and can form the immediate meta-KBs for other KBs. For example, frames can be used to represent KBs at different meta-levels and of different dimensions.

The IS domain dependent KBs are very unstable and have a great varieties of specific meta-levels and dimensions. A highly dynamic inter-connected knowledge representation is therefore necessary. The knowledge is organised into a multi-level viewpoint structure and will be discussed in details in the next sub-section.

IS domain independent KBs' characteristics lie somewhere between the above two. A KB belonging to this class does interact with different

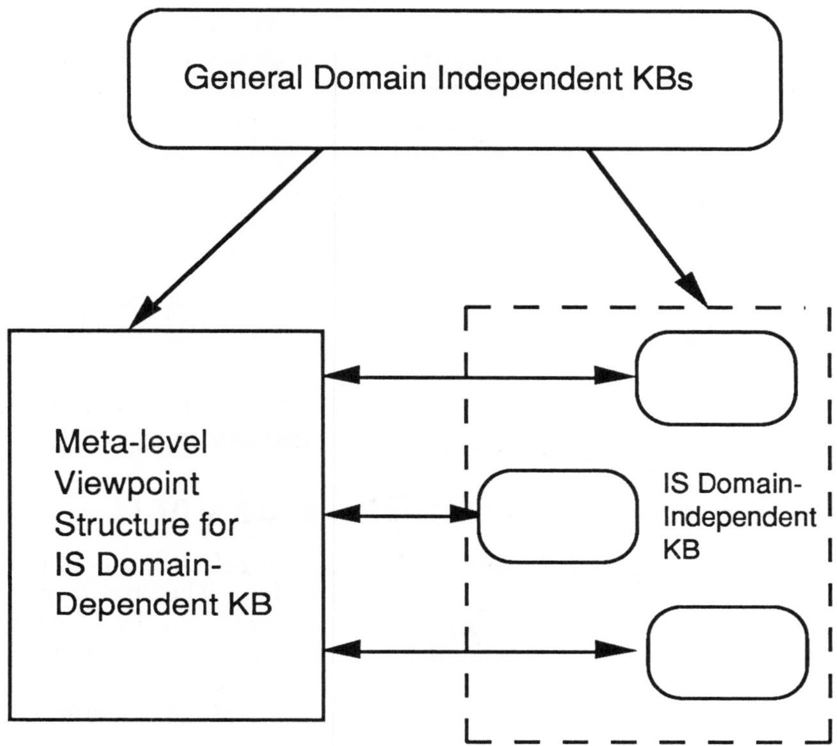

Fig. 7 Overall Architecture of KADIS

viewpoint levels of IS domain dependent KBs. But they are relatively independent of each other and only evolve slowly over time. Hence a simple modular structure seems to be the best architecture for this class[1].

4.3 A Multi-Level Viewpoint Structure for IS Domain Dependent Knowledge

Terms like "view" and "context" are becoming more popular in KS/IS literature. This subsection attempts to define the generic elements behind

[1]Further details in section 5.

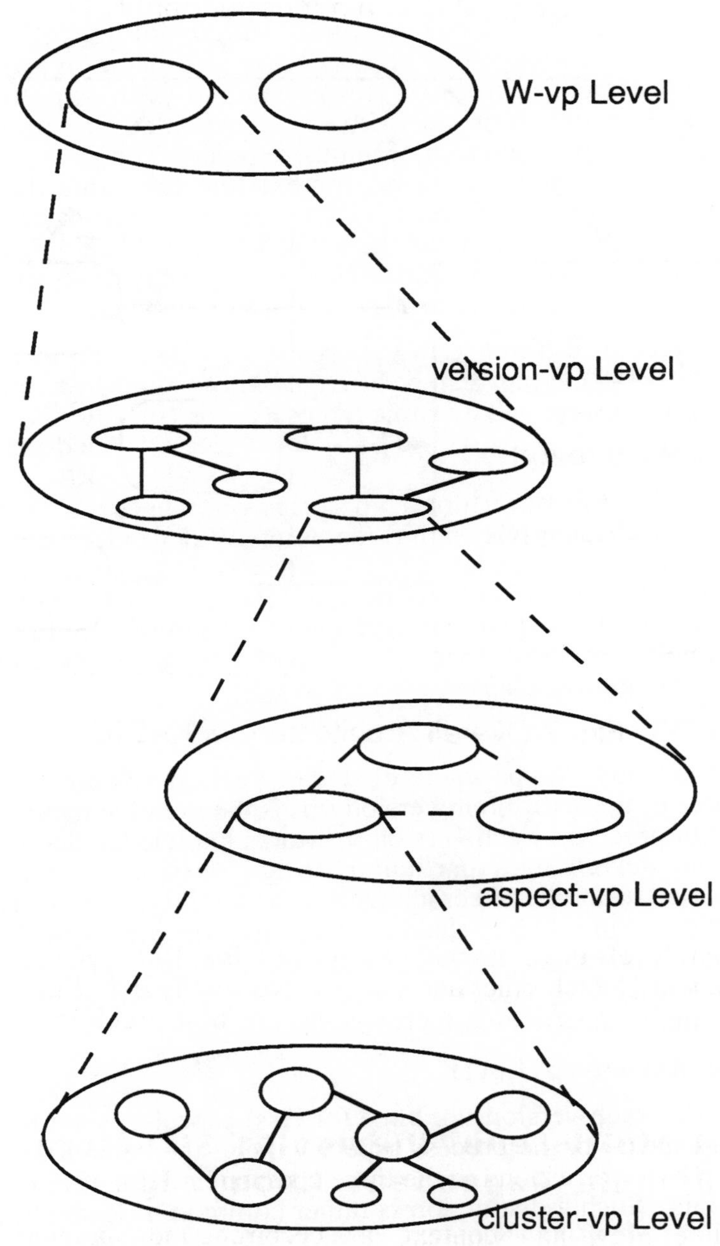

Fig. 8 A Four Level Viewpoint Structure
of IS Domain Dependent KB

different usage of views and construct a multi-level viewpoint (vp) structure to represent IS domain dependent knowledge in ISD.[1]

A *viewpoint* is defined to be the *scope of validity* for a set of KB(s), that is, a piece of knowledge in a vp may cease to be valid in another. We can have different sources of viewpoints and form a multi-level vp structure. A *context* is then defined as a viewpoint (of a certain source) looking from a particular vp of another source. For example, we can discuss a building in the same context (eg. the same direction of viewing) but from different viewpoints (eg. different times of discussion). It can be seen that the whole vp level concerning directions is "contained within" a vp of time. Hence a hierarchy of vp levels can be constructed with one level "inside" or "outside" another.

Four sources of difference in viewpoints are identified in IS domain dependent KBs and they can be arranged into a multi-level structure to allow a very flexible and dynamic representation (fig.8).

- **The W-vp Level**

  This is the outermost vp (viewpoint) level. A W-vp (Weltanschauung-viewpoint) represents W-dependent knowledge in a problem-situation KB (fig.6). Such knowledge is usually very informal and difficult to be machine captured. Some useful representations do exist and can be captured in the KADIS. Examples are SSM's root definitions of relevant systems and Eden's (1988) cognitive maps.

- **The Version-vp Level**

  "Inside" any W-vp, whole chains of version-vps are found. The source of these different version-vps is the iterative nature of the IS design process. Each version-vp stores knowledge about the state of the design in a particular design version. This includes knowledge about the completeness, the validity, and the usefulness of the version. The "chains" of version-vps are formed by some kind of inheritance structure[2] and together represent a simple state-of-design KB (fig.6). More comprehensive representation structures can also be used (Chang et al., 1989).

- **The Aspect-vp Level**

  "Inside" each version-vp, three (or less) aspect-vps are found: the data aspect-vp, the process aspect-vp, and the behavioural aspect-vp. These correspond to the three component KBs of IS conceptual models. Such a distinction is rather common in IS methodologies (Olle et al., 1988; Nicholas, 1986). The data aspect-vp contains

[1]The idea of "views" comes primarily from ART(Clayton, 1988) and Habermann et al. (1988) but with an extended scope.

[2]In ART (Clayton, 1988) the viewpoints of any level are represented by an inheritance tree.

knowledge about the data model of an enterprise and may employ representations such as ERM or relational models. The knowledge in the process aspect-vp is represented in DFDs or process dependency diagrams. The behavioural aspect-vp looks at "events" which have impact on certain data. SSADM and IE use entity life cycle (or history) diagrams to represent this aspect. The KBs in both the process and the behavioural aspect-vp are functional and sometimes complementary in nature.

- **The Cluster-vp Level**

  A Cluster-vp is the innermost vp in the whole structure. It stores a subset of the KB in any one of the three aspect-vps plus a small amount of (optional) knowledge about the "reason" for choosing such a subset. For example, Feldman et al. (1986) proposes that the data aspect-vp should be partitioned into cluster-vps according to different "logical horizons". Other reasons for forming cluster-vps inside a data aspect-vp include different user needs or process needs (Carswell et al., 1987). As for a process aspect-vp, different DFDs at possibly different levels can already be seen as different cluster-vps inside it.

The W-vp level is chosen to be the outermost level because, by the nature of W-dependence, the differences in W-vps are due to factors outside the UoD of the problem. Furthermore, the aspect-vp level should be inside both the W-vp and the version-vp levels because the KBs represented in the last two vp levels are meta-KBs of the three aspects of IS design models. The vp structure is only a manifestation of the meta-KB-dependence phenomenon. Finally, it is simply natural to put the cluster-vps inside the aspect-vp because the KB in the former is by- and-large a subset of the KB in the latter.

It is important to realise that the vp levels are fundamentally different in terms of the compatibility among different vps in the same level. Different vps in the W-vp and the version-vp levels are *incompatible by nature* [1]while those in the aspect-vp and the cluster-vp levels are *incompatible by accident*. In other words, incompatibilities are inherent in the two outer up-levels but in the inner ones they are only temporary and must be eliminated eventually.

Any two vps at the same level can be "merged" together to form a new vp. This means that knowledge valid in either of the original vps would also be valid in the new one. When two vps are merged, the whole vp-level(s) inside them must also be merged. There are two possible strategies to deal with incompatibilities during merging. In the case of incompatibility by nature, *vp-resolution* is carried out to make sure that the new vp is self-consistent but the original vps are left intact. On the other hand, if the two original vps are incompatible by accident, *vp-*

[1]Different version-vps inside the same W-vp can still be incompatible by nature.

integration is performed after the inconsistencies are eliminated from the original vps.

Three types of knowledge support must be provided for the four level vp structure: 1) a highly interactive *diagram editor* which allows the designer to enter knowledge into the structure diagrammatically; 2) a *knowledge browser* which lets the designer browse the knowledge stored in any vps, the connections among various vps in one level, and the overall structure across different vp levels and 3) a knowledge validator which maintains the consistencies both within and across vp levels. The latter is done during both vp-resolutions and vp-integrations.

4.4 IS Domain Independent Knowledge Support in KADIS

The multi-level vp structure represents a highly dynamic and flexible environment for storing and manipulating IS domain dependent knowledge. It therefore allows different IS domain independent knowledge support to be provided in an evolutionary and highly modular fashion. Each module is effectively a small KA on its own. Four such possible KAs are now briefly examined. Firstly, a *Design Decision KA* can be constructed.[1] It can help the designer to evaluate any design version in terms of a set of design criteria, to create, store, retrieve and manipulate different W-dependent knowledge, and to conduct "what-if" analysis on the effect of different design actions. Secondly, an *Enterprise Modelling KA* can be built to facilitate the construction of first estimates of a IS design.[2] Knowledge about any IS domain can be stored a priori in the KA, with some core vps and a number of optional ones. Given any enterprise, vps from appropriate domain(s) can be combined to form a first estimate of the design. Inconsistencies and incompleteness arise during such integration can be dealt with interactively by the designer. Thirdly, an *Advisory Design Methodology and Techniques KA* can be built to give advice and explanations on any concepts in IS design methodology and technique. It can be represented by a hierarchical conceptual thesaurus, not unlike the one used by Williams et al. (1988) to represent knowledge about Control Systems Design. Finally, a *Design Planning KA* can be used to coordinate the *process* of ISD.[3] A number of ISD operators can be implemented as goal-driven sequence of ISD actions which transforms the state-of-design. Plans can then be generated as (possibly hierarchical) partial order of operators to achieve a certain goal.

[1]See Sprague (1980), Keen(1980), and Belew(1985) for detailed discussions on decision support.

[2]The idea presented bears certain similarity to the Programmer Apprentice's concept of programming by inspection (Rich, 1988).

[3]The same AI paradigm has been used in software development (Huff, 1988).

5. Conclusions

The vision of a new approach, known as the Knowledge Assistant approach, to IS design is presented in this paper. Its main objective is to fully recognise and support the multi-meta-level and multi-dimensional knowledge involved in IS design. We are beginning to develop a prototype of KADIS on a Symbolics machine. Initial investigations have been conducted on the suitability of various knowledge-based system environments and Inference ART seems a plausible candidate. Certain aspects of IS design (eg. database design) will be taken as the starting point for implementation. However, it is believed that the KA approach can be a fruitful one for many possible applications, for example, software design and CAD.

Acknowledgement

The authors would like to thank Dr Andy Galloway whose professional experience in IS design has helped us understand some of the fundamental issues involved in this work.

References

[1] AURAMAKI, E., LEPPANEN, M. and SAVOLAINEN, V. "Universal Framework for Information Activities". *Data Base,* pp. 11–20, Fall/Winter 1987/88.

[2] BADER, J., EDWARDS, J., HARRIS-JONES, C. and HANNAFORD, D. "Practical Engineering of Knowledge-based Systems". *Information and Software Technology,* **30**(5) pp. 266–277, Jun 1988.

[3] BELEW, R. K. "Evolutionary Decision Support System: An Architecture Based on Information Structure". In L. B. Methlie and R. H. Sprague, (eds.), *Knowledge Representation for Decision Support System, Proc. IFIP WG 8-3 Working Conference,* pp. 147–160, North-Holland, 1985.

[4] BRACHMAN, R. J. and LEVESQUE, H. J. "What Makes a Knowledge Base Knowledgeable? A View of Databases from the Knowledge Level". In L. Kerschberg, (ed.), *Expert Database Systems, Proc. First Int'l Workshop,* pp. 67–78, 1986.

[5] CARSWELL, J. L., JR., and NAVATHE, S. B. "SA-ER: A Methodology That Links Structured Analysis and Entity-Relationship Modeling for Database Design". In S. Spaccapietra, (ed.), *Entity-Relationship Approach, Proc. Fifth Int'l Conf. on EntityRelationship Approach, France, 1986,* pp. 381–397, North-Holland, 1987.

[6] CAUVET, C., PROIX, C. and ROLLAND, C. "Information Systems Design: An Expert System Approach". In *EDBT'88 Proc. Advances in Database Technology Lecture Notes inComputer Science, No. 303,* pp. 113–133, Springer-Verlag, 1988.

[7] CHANG, E. E., GEDYE, D. and KATZ, R. H. "The Design and Implementation of a Version Server for Computer-Aided Design Data". *Software: Practice and Experience,* **19**(3) pp. 199–222, Mar 1989.

[8] CHECKLAND, P. *Systems Thinking, Systems Practice.* Chichester: John Wiley, 1981.

[9] CHEN, P. P. "The Entity-Relationship Model: Toward a Unified View of Data". *ACM Transactions on Database Systems,* **1**(1) pp. 9–36, Mar 1976.

[10] CLAYTON, P. *ART Tutorial.* vol. 1-4, Inference Corporation, 1988.

[11] CODD, E. F. "Extending the Database Relational Model to Capture More Meaning". *ACM-TODS,* **4**(4) pp. 397–434, Dec 1979.

[12] COELHO, H. and RODRIGUES, A. J. "Knowledge Architecture for Management Environments". In L. B. Methlie and R. H. Sprague, (eds.), *Knowledge Representation for Decision Support System, Proc. IFIP WG 8-3 Working Conference,* pp. 167–175, North-Holland, 1985.

[13] DITTRICH, K. R. "Object-Oriented Database System: A Workshop Report". In S. Spaccapietra, (ed.), *Entity-Relationship Approach, Proc. Fifth Int'l Conf. on EntityRelationship Approach, France, 1986,* pp. 51–66, North-Holland, 1987.

[14] EDEN, C. "Cognitive mapping". *European Journal of Operational Research,* **36** pp. 1–13, 1988.

[15] Feldman, J., Fanty, M. A., Goddard, N. H. and Lynne, K. J. "Computing witl Structured Connectionist Networks". *CACM*, **31**(2) pp. 170–187, 1988.

[16] Habermann, A. N., Krueger, C., Pierce, B., Staudt, B. and Wenn, J. *Programmin; with Views.* vol. 29, Carnegie-Mellon Technical Report, Jan 1988.

[17] Huff, K. E. and Lesser, V. R. "A Plan-Based Intelligent Assistant that Supports th Software Development Process". *P. ACM SIGSOFT/SIGPLAN SES*, **24**(2) pp. 97–106, 1989

[18] Keen, P. G. W. "Decision Support Systems: A Research Perspective". In G. Fick anc R. H. Sprague, (eds.), *Decision Support Systems: Issues and Challenges*, pp. 23–44, Pergamor Press, 1980.

[19] Kersten, M. L. "A Conceptual Modelling Expert System". In S. Spaccapietra, (ed.), *Entity Relationship Approach, Proc. Fifth Int'l Conf. on EntityRelationship Approach, France, 1986* pp. 35–48, North-Holland, 1987.

[20] Klir, G. J. *Architecture of Systems Problem Solving.* NY: Plenum Press, 1985.

[21] Lange, O. *Wholes and Parts.* London: Pergamon Press, 1962.

[22] Lenat, D. B., Davis, R., Doyle, J., Genesereth, I., M. andGoldstein an(Schrobe, H. "Reasoning about Reasoning". In F. Hayes-Roth, D. A. Waterman an(D. B. Lenat, (eds.), *Building Expert Systems*, pp. 219–240, Addison-Wesley, 1983.

[23] Lyons, J. *Semantics.* Cambridge: CUP, 1977.

[24] Lyytinen, K. "A Taxonomic Perspective of Information Systems Development: Theoretica Constructs and Recommendations". In R. J. Boland, Jr. and R. A. Hirschheim, (eds.), *Critica Issues in Information Systems Research*, pp. 3–41, John Wiley and Sons, 1987.

[25] Mannino, M. V., Choobineh, J. and Hwang, J. J. "Acquisition and Use of Con textual Knowledge in a Form-DrivenDatabase Design Methodology". In S. Spaccapietra (ed.), *Entity-Relationship Approach, Proc. Fifth Int'l Conf. on EntityRelationship Approach France, 1986*, pp. 361–337, North-Holland, 1987.

[26] Miles, R. K. "Combining 'Soft' and 'Hard' Systems Practice: Grafting or Embedding?". J *Applied Systems Analysis*, **15** pp. 55–, 1988.

[27] Nicholas, D. *Introducing SSADM: The NCC Guide.* NCC, 1987.

[28] Nowakowska, M. "Semiotic Systems and Knowledge Representation". *Int'l J. Man-Machin Studies*, **13** pp. 223–257, 1980.

[29] Olle, T. W., Hagelstein, J., Macdonald, I. G., Rolland, C., Sol., , G., H. Van Assche, F. J. M. and Verrijn-Stuart, A. A. *Information Systems Methodolc gies: A Framework for Understanding.* Addison-Wesley, 1988.

[30] Orchard, R. A. and Tausner, M. R. "General Systems: A Basis for Knowledge Engi neering". *Systems Practice*, **1**(1) pp. 165–179, 1988.

[31] Reiner, D., Brown, G., Friedell, M., Lehman, J., McKee, R., Rheingans, P. an Rosenthal, A. "A Database Designer's Workbench". In S. Spaccapietra, (ed.), *Entity Relationship Approach, Proc. Fifth Int'l Conf. on EntityRelationship Approach, France, 198(* pp. 347–359, North-Holland, 1987.

[32] RICH, C. and WATERS, R. C. "The Programmer's Apprentice: A Research Overview". *Computer*, pp. 10–25, Nov 1988.

[33] SPRAGUE, R. H. and JR., . "A Framework for Research on Decision Support Systems". In G. Fick and R. H. Sprague, (eds.), *Decision Support Systems: Issues and Challenges*, pp. 5–22, Pergamon Press, 1980.

[34] STAMPER, R. "Semantics". In R. J. Boland, Jr. and R. A. Hirschheim, (eds.), *Critical Issues in Information Systems Research*, pp. 43–78, John Wiley and Sons, 1987.

[35] WALKER, S. and MCGOWAN, S. *I-CASE/SSADM - An Overview*. Alvey: FORTUNE, Nov 1988.

[36] WILLIAMS, D. O., BOYLE, J. and MACFARLANE, A. G. J. *Developing Knowledge-Based Support Systems*. Report No. CUED/F-INFENG/TR.28, 1988.

QUESTIONS

Prof. S. M. Deen (University of Keele).

SMD. Did you try this model on a real application to see to what extent these conceptual ideas of yours are relevant?

Mr. S. Ip.

SI. No, we haven't tried it on a real application.

SMD. When you try it, you might find that it's slightly different. I'm not saying you'll necessarily find it is, but you may.

A second question in this. You have defined knowledge at a kind of meta-level. Where do 'rules' go? Are they data or knowledge, or both? Where does 'constraint' go? And where does 'access control' go? Where does the definition of data structure go? Could they go in both, depending on the situation?

SI. In a sense, anything is a piece of data. But not everything is knowledge. This table is a real-life object. And a piece of data on this object may be for example, 'This is a table'. This sentence is a piece of information about it. And the syntax of English in that context is knowledge, because it's meta-information.

So, in a sense, all knowledge is data at that meta-level according to our framework. And, in a sense, data structure is a piece of meta-information. In fact, my partner in research is quite interested in the software engineering side of it. He's just presented a paper in Japan and he has applied a similar framework to this, (not this one exactly, that's why I say it's not yet been applied to a real application), to compiler design. He discussed the various different levels and he said that their structure is definite knowledge. The extent of knowledge in the framework at a meta-level one or zero depends on how you look at it.

12 Knowledge-based Applications = Knowledge Base + Mappings + Applications

P. K. C. Pun and H. J. Kahn

Abstract

While the current proliferation of research work carried out in knowledge-based systems sheds much light upon issues of knowledge representation and knowledge acquisition, the issue of how this knowledge, once captured and stored in a knowledge base, can be incorporated into and reused in different application programs has not received enough attention. The main difficulty of having application programs which are independent of a knowledge base, (while knowledge stored in the knowledge base can still be incorporated into these application programs), is the inherent differences between modelling concepts manifested by the objects described in the knowledge base and those manifested by the data structures manipulated within the application programs. The aim of this paper is to investigate this issue in a more formal way and try to propose a systematic approach in which the mappings between these two different modelling concepts can be deduced.

In order to study the problem systematically, a formal framework for deducing the modelling concepts from the relationships among objects inside a knowledge-based system and from that among application data structures is presented. Using this formal framework, a data functionalization process is defined which provides an abstraction in which different modelling concepts can be expressed both in terms of sets of data entities and in terms of data functions. Two types of mappings, the data entity mapping and the data function mapping, are then deduced so that a particular object or relationship in the knowledge base can be associated with the appropriate data structures in the application programs.

Keywords: Knowledge Base, Data Model, Data Model Mapping

1. Introduction

Knowledge-based systems represent the first step in integrating AI technology with conventional database systems. Although expert knowledge rather than atomic data is supposed to be stored in a knowledge base, both a knowledge base and a database serve as central pools which allow information to be shared and reused in different situations as appropriate. Research carried out in the AI area in recent years has concentrated mainly on knowledge acquisition and knowledge representation. However, the problem of how this knowledge, once captured and stored in a knowledge base, can be incorporated into different application programs has typically been ignored.

Research work in the area of knowledge-based systems developed so far is application oriented rather than generally applicable. Different knowledge bases with different representation schemes are built for different applications. These applications are, in turn, written in a way highly influenced by the corresponding knowledge representation schema. Application programs using a knowledge base are usually required to be written in a specific language, e.g. EMYCIN [1], in which the constructs are structurally similar to the representation schema used in representing different objects described in the knowledge base. In some more extreme cases, programmers are even forced to use a built-in application language provided by the knowledge base, e.g. OPS [2], to avoid interfacing problems between the knowledge base and the applications. Such a tightly-coupled relationship between a knowledge base and its application programs undoubtedly mitigates knowledge reusability and restricts the boundary of its area of application.

Most knowledge-based applications are built in such a restrictive fashion because of the inherent difficulty of establishing mappings between objects described in a knowledge base and the physical data structures manipulated within the application programs. The problem of establishing such mappings can be eliminated by using a language which has similar constructs to the schema in which the knowledge is represented. Such a strategy is not, however, appropriate when really complex applications are considered. Recent efforts aimed at solving the problems of communicating between different languages has resulted in the development of better interfaces as a result of which declarative languages can invoke procedural codes written in procedural languages or vice versa [3, 4]. These interfaces only establish mappings of different data structures between languages, e.g. how a Pascal record is represented by a list in Prolog. However, these mappings are still too primitive to serve the purpose of bridging between knowledge-based objects and application program data structures.

If knowledge-based applications are to become part of major software systems, then the need to write applications independent of the internal constructs of the knowledge base while maintaining the ability to exploit information in the knowledge base must be recognized. Complex systems often do not fit into a single language, but instead will need a variety of representations. There must therefore be a properly engineered way of allowing knowledge based applications, whose implementations are mainly oriented towards efficiency and standard hardware, to exploit knowledge stored in the knowledge base, whose constructs are mainly influenced by the declarative nature of its internal operations.

1.1. Knowledge Bases Versus DataBases

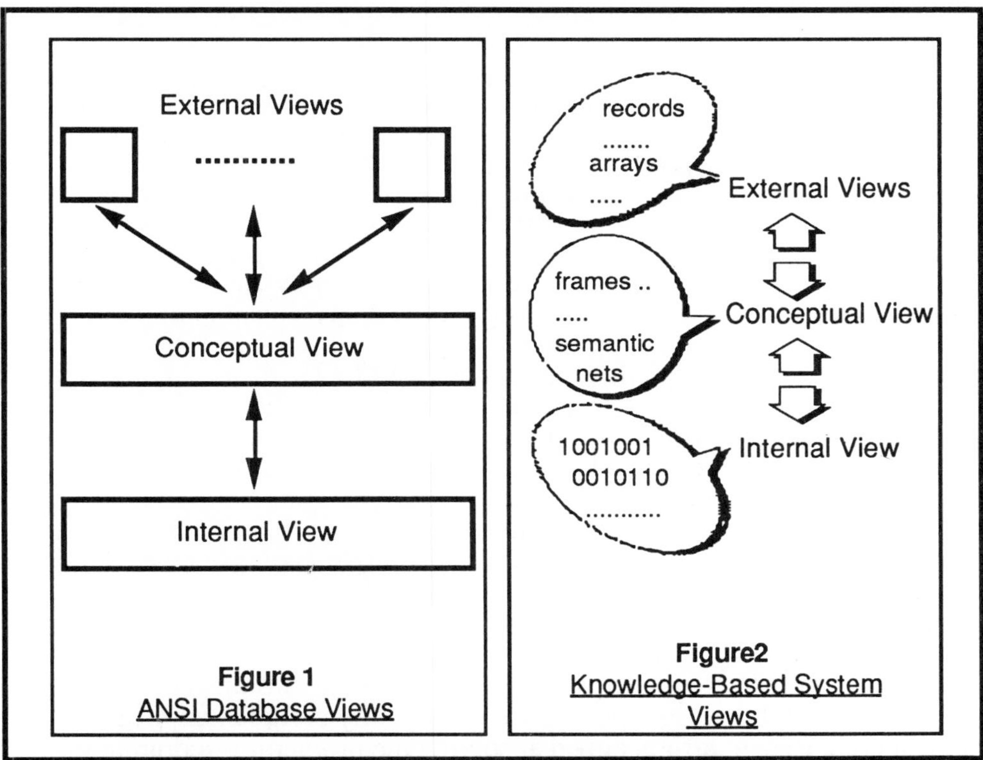

Figure 1
ANSI Database Views

Figure2
Knowledge-Based System Views

In the discussion above, it is emphasized that a loosely-coupled relationship should be maintained between application programs and the relevant knowledge base so that knowledge stored in the knowledge base can be reused in different situations as appropriate. Although much research material has been presented to clarify the major differences between a knowledge-based system and a database system [5, 6, 7], it seems that they all overlook an important fact: a similar loosely-coupled relationship between a *database* and its *applications* has long been motivated by the ANSI report [8]. It is recommended in the report that three database description views (figure 1) — the internal view, the conceptual view and the external view — should be provided by any database system. It is through the establishment of a mapping between the external view of the database imposed by an application program and the conceptual view implicit in that particular database, that different application programs can reuse data stored in the database with a view appropriate to their specific needs and desired data models.

In a similar way to a database, a knowledge-based system can be divided into three logical views (figure 2). The internal view represents types of physical data structures, devices and access methods. It is the internal view which determines how knowledge in a knowledge base is physically stored. The conceptual view represents the various objects and their associated relationships modelled in the knowledge base. The conceptual view determines what kind of knowledge is going to be conveyed by a particular knowledge base; in other words, it defines the knowledge domain of the knowledge base. Finally, the external views allow knowledge-based applications to specify the different views they require of the objects and relationships held in the knowledge base and they are, in reality, different ways of looking at the same set of objects and relationships that are modelled in that particular knowledge-based system. Within different application programs, these external views are usually manifested as different physical data structures.

The conceptual view of a knowledge base and the knowledge representation schema employed by it are two different notions. Two popular knowledge representation schemes, frames [9] and semantic nets [10], whilst they both encompass the conceptual view of the underlying knowledge base, are at the same time conveying operational mechanisms. The frame representation provides active slot values and if-then rules while the semantic net representation offers inheritance hierarchies and cancellations [11]. Different knowledge representation schemes may carry the same conceptual view if they are used to represent the same sets of objects and relationships modelled in a knowledge base. The different operational mechanisms of different knowledge representation schemes are relevant to the various internal operations of the knowledge base, e.g. internal consistency maintenance and internal knowledge inference, and they are considered to be outside the scope of the discussion of this paper.

1.2. Mappings Between a Knowledge Base and its Application Programs

The architecture proposed above requires several mapping functions, from the conceptual view to the internal view and from the conceptual view to each external view. The mapping function between the conceptual view and the internal view is responsible for internal storage, the maintenance of internal consistency and correctness of the knowledge base. The mapping functions between the conceptual view and the various external views imposed by different application programs make it possible for the knowledge stored in the knowledge base to be reusable in different applications. For example, a certain engineering application program may want to make use of some rules stored inside a particular engineering knowledge base to check against an engineering design represented by a set of data structures. Before these particular rules can be executed, the appropriate mapping function between the conceptual view of the knowledge base and the external view imposed by that particular set of application data structures must be established. Objects and their relationships described in a particular rule can then be associated with the correct information conveyed by the relevant set of data structures. If different mapping functions can be deduced for different application programs which have different data structures and if these different sets of data structures are compatible with the knowledge base, the process of rule execution can then be carried out within different contexts (figure 3). In other words, knowledge stored in this knowledge base can be reused in different applications which have their own external views of the objects and relationships modelled within the knowledge base.

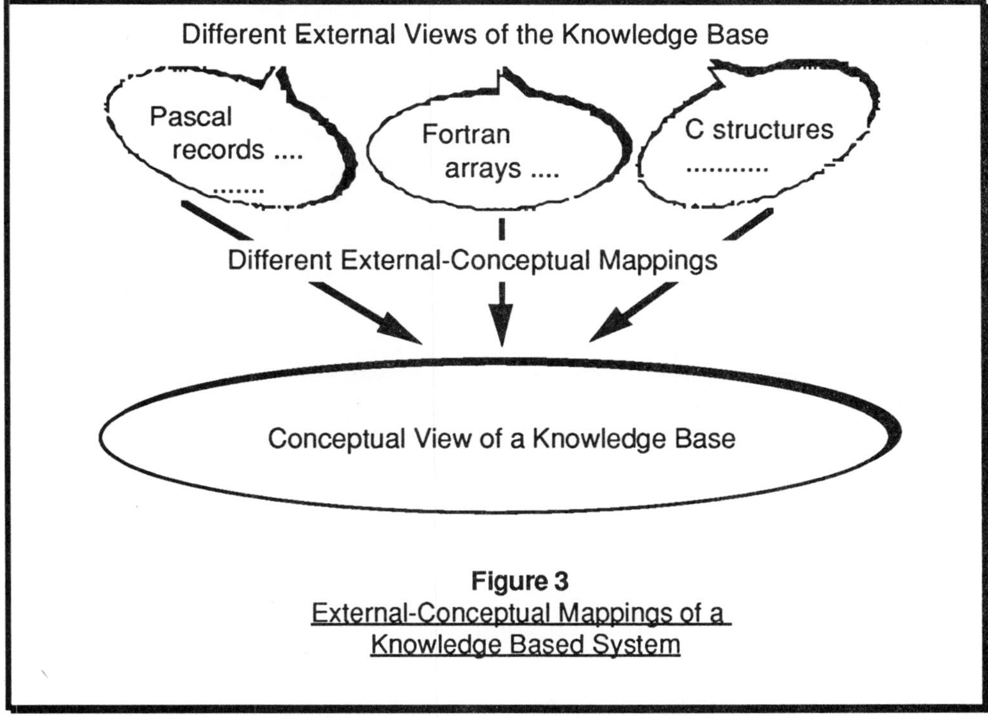

Figure 3
External-Conceptual Mappings of a Knowledge Based System

2. From Unbounded to Bounded Universes

Some questions can be raised in the light of the preceding discussion:

- How does one describe the conceptual view of a knowledge base?
- How does one describe the external view imposed by a set of data structures on a knowledge base?

- How does one know if a particular set of data structures is compatible with the conceptual view of a knowledge base?
- How does one deduce the mapping between the conceptual view and the external view of a knowledge base?

In order to answer these questions, one first needs clear definitions of the various concepts under discussion. These formal definitions will not only shape the mapping problem in a more structured manner, but are also tools for reasoning and so help to connect various ideas together. In this section, formal definitions of the terms 'knowledge-based system', 'knowledge base' and 'knowledge-based application' are presented. Using this framework, the first three questions will be answered and a more specific version of the last question will be stated.

2.1 A Formal Framework of Knowledge-Based System

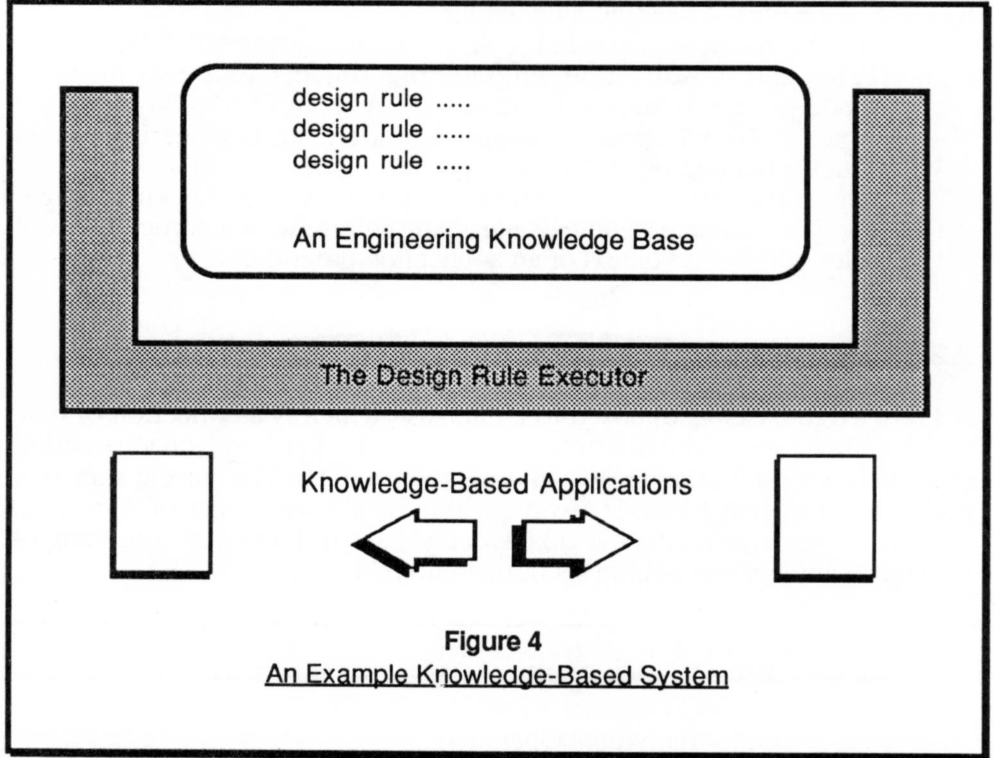

Figure 4
An Example Knowledge-Based System

A knowledge-based system is a programming environment in which application programs can be developed which embody some aspects of human knowledge and expertise to perform tasks ordinarily done by human experts. In a knowledge-based system, human knowledge and expertise are stored in a knowledge base external to the application programs. The reason for having a separate knowledge base is that rather than mixing the knowledge inside the application programs, this expert knowledge will retain its meaning outside the scope of a particular application program and can be reused in different situations. In order to support knowledge retrieval and knowledge usage in different application programs, a knowledge-application interface will serve as a communication medium between the knowledge base and its application programs. In this way, a knowledge-based system is then defined as consisting of a knowledge base, a knowledge-application interface and a (finite or infinite) set of knowledge-based applications.

> KBS = (KB, KAI, {KBA_1, KBA_2, ...})
> where KBS = Knowledge-Based System
> KB = Knowledge Base
> KAI = Knowledge-Application Interface
> KBA_i = Individual Knowledge-Based Application

Consider as an example the engineering knowledge-based system shown in figure 4. This particular system consists of:

- An engineering knowledge base which stores rules about the behaviour of different engineering objects and relationships modelled in this knowledge base.
- A set of knowledge-based application, e.g. an engineering design checker, an intelligent layout tool.
- An engineering rule executor which provides the knowledge-application interface to execute a particular rule or a particular set of rules within the context of an application program.

2.2. A Formal Framework for A Knowledge Base

A knowledge base, as opposed to a database which is a collection of data representing facts, contains information at a higher level of abstraction representing expert knowledge. In order to ensure that the current state of a particular knowledge base is always within its allowable sets of states, i.e. to ensure internal consistency, a knowledge base is defined as consisting of a conceptual view and a finite set of operations.

> KB = (CV, {OP_1, OP_2, ..., OP_n})
> where KB = Knowledge Base
> CV = Conceptual View
> OP_i = Individual Operation

The conceptual view of a knowledge base defines the domain of the knowledge which is going to be stored in that particular knowledge base. It is the conceptual view which specifies what kinds of objects and relationships can be described as knowledge fragments stored in the knowledge base. In this way, a conceptual view is then defined as consisting of a finite set of objects and a finite set of inter-object relationships.

$$CV = (\{O_1, O_2, ..., O_n\}, \{Inter_1, Inter_2, ..., Inter_n\})$$

where O_i = Individual objects

$Inter_i$ = Individual Inter-Object Relationships

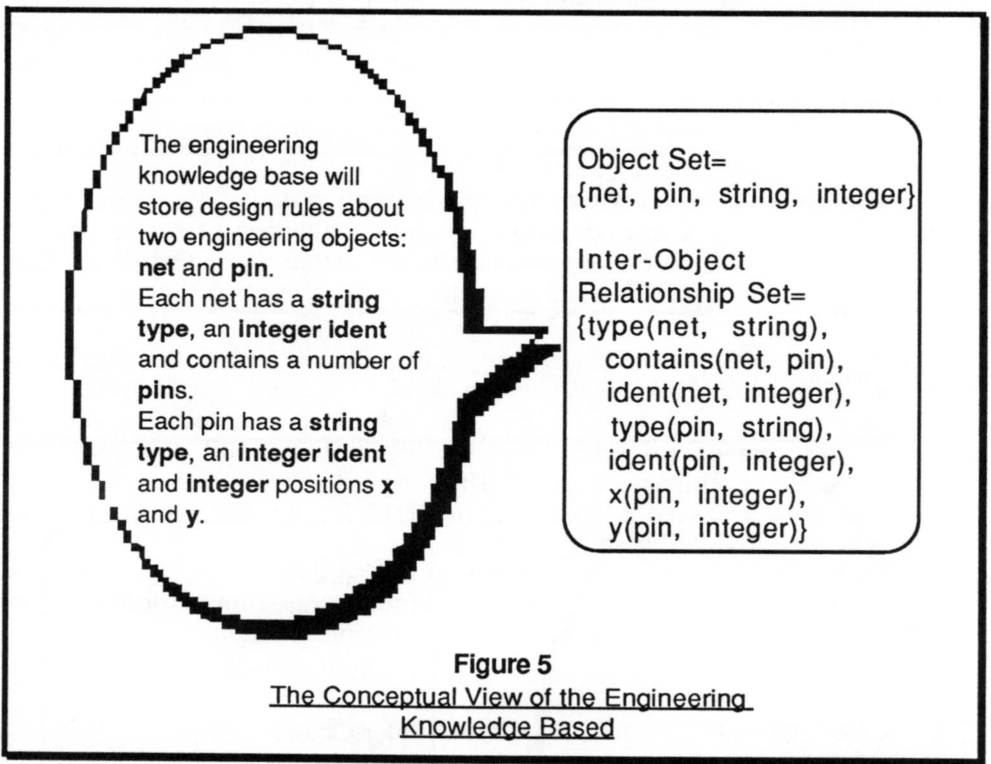

The engineering knowledge base will store design rules about two engineering objects: **net** and **pin**.
Each net has a **string type**, an **integer ident** and contains a number of **pins**.
Each pin has a **string type**, an **integer ident** and **integer** positions **x** and **y**.
Object Set=
{net, pin, string, integer}
Inter-Object Relationship Set=
{type(net, string),
contains(net, pin),
ident(net, integer),
type(pin, string),
ident(pin, integer),
x(pin, integer),
y(pin, integer)}

Figure 5

The Conceptual View of the Engineering Knowledge Based

The finite set of objects in the conceptual view specifies the allowable objects which can be used to compose a fragment of knowledge to be stored in the knowledge base. The inter-object relationships set specifies the relationships between different objects. Figure 5 gives an example of a conceptual view of the hypothetical engineering knowledge base. This conceptual view states that knowledge about two engineering objects, 'pin' and 'net', is going to be stored in the knowledge base. The inter-object relationships specify the different kinds of relationships one can describe in the knowledge base. An example of such a knowledge rule will be:

for every net with type = "power" there is not a pin with type = "output"

In the rule above, two engineering objects 'pin' and 'net' are described. Two inter-object relationships are described in the rule, i.e. 'type_of_net(net, string)' and 'type_of_pin(pin, string)' which specify some internal values for the corresponding objects. The inter-object relationship 'pin_of_net(net, pin)' serves as a connection between the two objects described in the rule.

Finally, the set of operations,OP_i, in the definition of a knowledge base, are a set of functions which map each possible knowledge base state into another knowledge base state.

$$OP_i : \text{Knowledge Base State} \rightarrow \text{Knowledge Base State}$$

These operations are concerned with the internal status of the knowledge base, e.g. addition of a rule, deletion of a rule, deduction of a rule. Since these kinds of operation are not relevant to this paper, their further details are not discussed here.

2.3. A Formal Framework for A Knowledge-Based Application

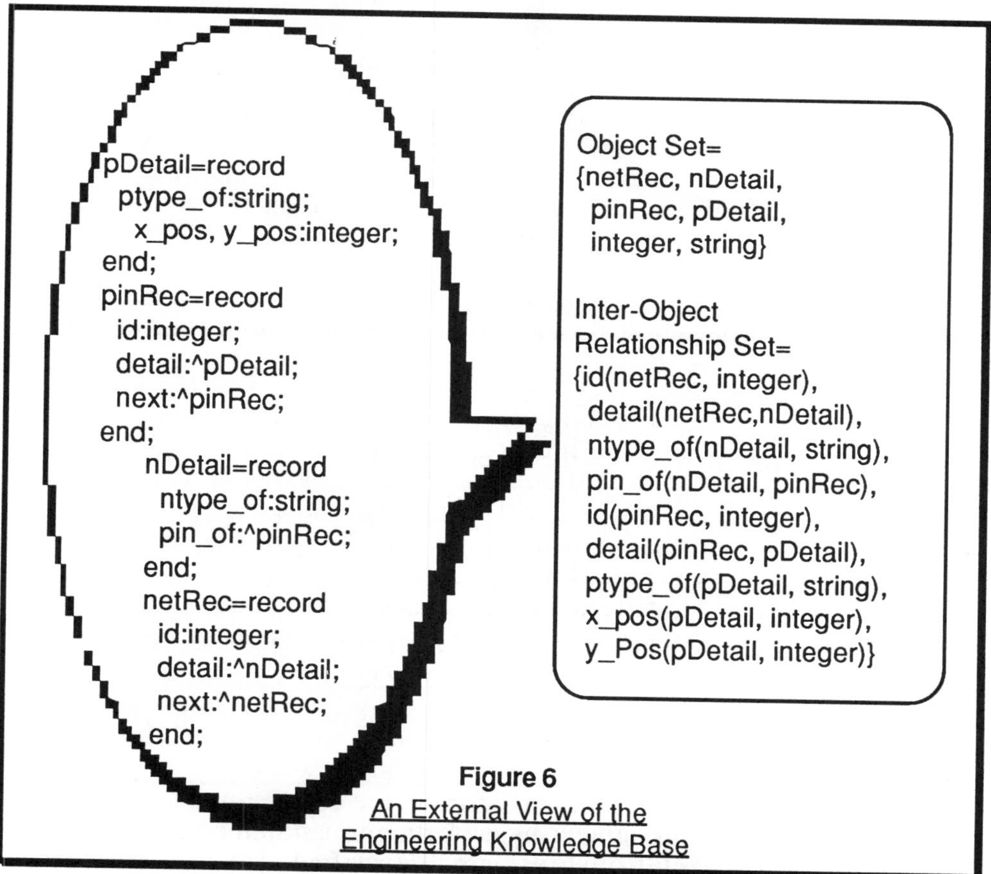

pDetail=record
ptype_of:string;
x_pos, y_pos:integer;
end;
pinRec=record
id:integer;
detail:^pDetail;
next:^pinRec;
end;
nDetail=record
ntype_of:string;
pin_of:^pinRec;
end;
netRec=record
id:integer;
detail:^nDetail;
next:^netRec;
end;
Object Set=
{netRec, nDetail,
pinRec, pDetail,
integer, string}
Inter-Object
Relationship Set=
{id(netRec, integer),
detail(netRec,nDetail),
ntype_of(nDetail, string),
pin_of(nDetail, pinRec),
id(pinRec, integer),
detail(pinRec, pDetail),
ptype_of(pDetail, string),
x_pos(pDetail, integer),
y_Pos(pDetail, integer)}

Figure 6
An External View of the Engineering Knowledge Base

A knowledge-based application corresponds to the usual notion of application programs written in any programming language. The only difference here is the way of looking at the data structures manipulated inside a knowledge-based application. This set of data structures is interpreted as the external view imposed by that particular application on the objects and relationships modelled in the knowledge base. In this way, a knowledge-based application is defined as consisting of an external view of the knowledge base and a sequence of internal functions which transform the application from its initial state to its target state.

$$KBA = (EV, (F_1, F_2, ..., F_n))$$
where EV = External View
F_i = Individual Internal Function

In a similar way to the conceptual view, the external view can also be defined as consisting of a finite set of objects and a finite set of inter-object relationships.

$$EV = (\{O_1, O_2, ..., O_n\}, \{Inter_1, Inter_2, ..., Inter_n\})$$
where O_i = Individual objects
$Inter_i$ = Individual Inter-Object Relationships

Figure 6 shows the external view deduced from a set of data structures taken from a hypothetical knowledge-based application. In this external view, most of the structural information of the data structures is filtered away. In the example, each data type is considered as an object in the object set, each field in a record is considered as a relationship in the inter-object relationship set.

The conceptual view of a knowledge base will be exactly **equivalent** to the external view if and only if the object sets and the relationship sets in the two views are exactly equal to each other. However, this constraint on writing knowledge-based application is too restrictive because it requires different applications to be written with a fixed set of data structures so that both the conceptual view and the external view share the same definition. Nijssen [12] points out that the chosen data model provides a 'mental model' and a 'mental model has a close analogy with religion, which is hopefully selected in freedom'. In this way, it should be justifiable to allow knowledge-based applications to choose their own data structures freely on the condition that the external view conveyed by this set of data structures is compatible with the conceptual view of the knowledge base. An external view is said to be **compatible** with the conceptual view of a knowledge base when it conveys a superset definition with respect to that of the conceptual view. A more formal definition of this compatibility will be given in terms of data entities and data functions in section 3.

Finally, the sequence of internal functions in the definition of a knowledge-based application is just a sequence of program statements, function or procedure calls which drive the program towards its target state. Since they are not relevant in this paper, no detailed analysis will be given here.

2.4. Why Mappings?

The term 'knowledge-application interface' has been used in defining a knowledge-based system without any further explanation. The specific form of the knowledge-application interface depends on how the knowledge stored in the knowledge base is going to be used in the application programs. In our example of the hypothetical engineering knowledge-based system, the knowledge-application interface takes the form of a piece of program, the rule executor, which checks the engineering design provided by an application against certain behavioural requirements encoded in the form of rules stored in the knowledge base. This rule executor must be able to associate the objects and relationships described in a rule with the appropriate data structures before rule execution can be started.

If the conceptual view and the external view of a knowledge base share the same definition this association will be no problem at all, since both the rule executor and the application program are then sharing the same set of data structures. As mentioned before, it is not, however, reasonable to restrict application programs to use a fixed set of data structures. Application programs should be able to choose data structures for their own needs as long as these data structures are conveying an external view which is compatible with the conceptual view of the knowledge base. This relaxation leads to two complications in implementing the rule executor. Firstly, these data structures may contain more than the necessary information needed for rule execution and this extra information may be used by other parts of the application program. Secondly, the objects and associated relationships modelled in the knowledge base may be manifested in different ways by different data structures manipulated in different application programs. These two complications imply that either different rule executors for different applications should be developed or a single rule executor which is able to adapt to different data structure contexts should be built. Obviously, the first solution is too expensive to be considered. The question then is how this data structure independent rule executor can be implemented.

Definitions of the external view and conceptual view have been given. Provided a certain external view is compatible with the corresponding conceptual view, a set of mappings can be deduced through which a particular object in the conceptual view definition can be expressed in terms of objects in the external view. The same reasoning applies in the inter-object relationship sets. This set of mappings between the two views is the association required to associate objects and relationships modelled in the knowledge base with the appropriate data structures in the application programs. From the operational point of view, these mappings will correspond to the definitions of a set of function calls, one for every object and relationship defined in the conceptual view of the knowledge base. The data independent rule executor can then be implemented by calling appropriate functions in this fixed set according to what kinds of objects and relationships are described in a particular rule. The exact definitions of these functions will be determined by the mappings between the external view and the conceptual view of the knowledge base; those mappings are deduced from the different data structures manipulated by different application programs. In this way, the problem of deducing the mappings between the conceptual view and the external view can be rephrased more specifically as the problem of deducing a set of function definitions in which the objects and relationships modelled in the knowledge base can be expressed in terms of the objects and relationships modelled by the appropriate set of data structures.

3. Data Functionalization Process

From the above discussion, both the conceptual view and the external view of a knowledge base have been defined in terms of a set of objects and a set of inter-object relationships. The problem of deducing the mappings between a knowledge base and its application programs is rephrased as the problem of how objects and their associated relationships, in the conceptual view, can be expressed in terms of those in the external view. In practical terms, we would hope that these mappings can be expressed as a set of algorithms rather than an explicit enumeration of equivalent relationships. It is this set of algorithms which would actually allow the implementation of an application independent knowledge-application interface so that knowledge stored in the knowledge base can be reused under different scopes of application.
The data functionalization process provides an operational framework in which both the conceptual view and the external view are expressed as sets of data entities and data functions. Each object in the conceptual view and the external view definitions will correspond to a data entity. Data entities themselves are non-information bearing, i.e. there is no specification of what these data entities are, what values they have, or how they relate to any other data entities. Instead, all information about a data entity is embodied in its associated data functions. A data function is a mapping from one data entity into another. Each data function has a fanin entity which is the domain data entity and a fanout entity which is the range data entity. The set of available data functions for a data entity represents the behaviour of the data entity.
The data functionalization process is defined as consisting of two functions. These functions will operate on object and relationship sets and produce the corresponding sets of data entities and data functions.

DFP = (O2E, R2F) where DFP = Data Functionalization Process

Figure 7a and figure 7b show the entity-function diagram produced after the data functionalization process has been applied on the conceptual view and the external view given in figure 5 and figure 6 respectively. In these two figures, each node denotes a data entity while each edge between nodes is the data function.

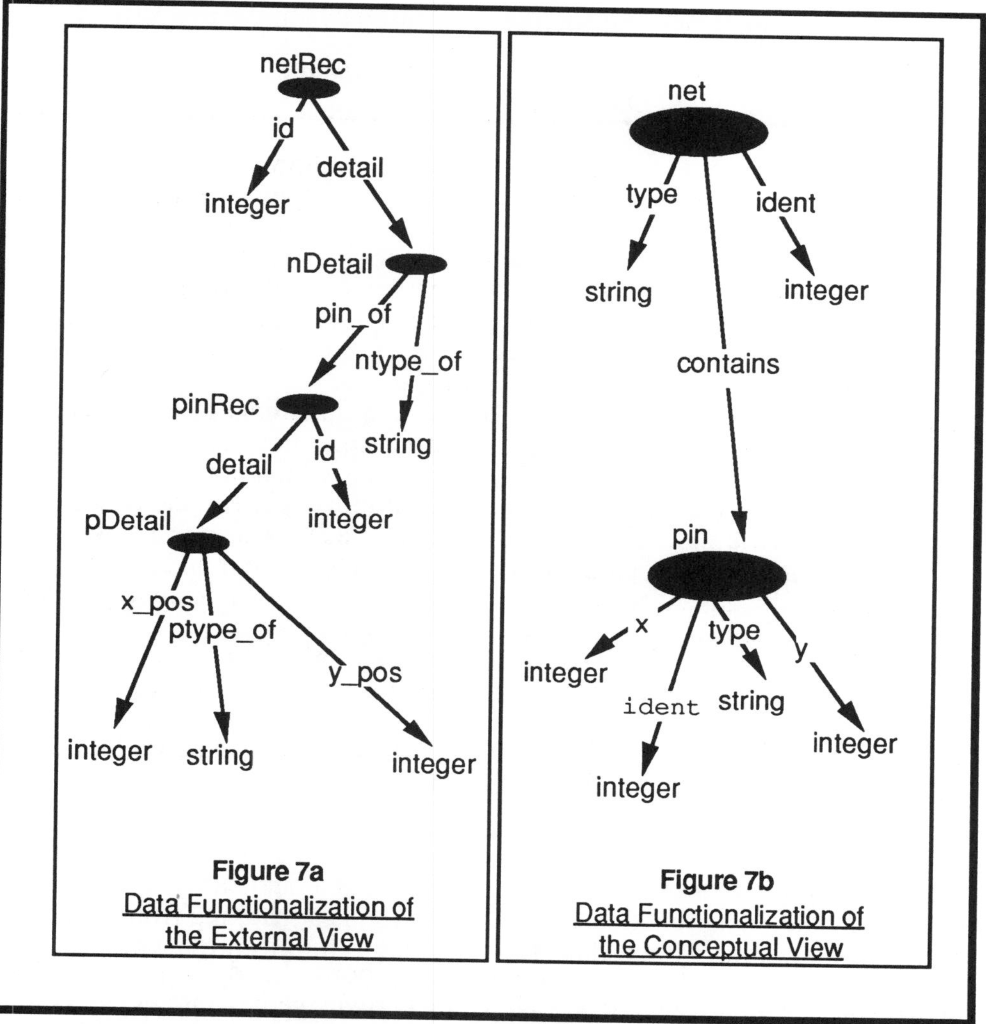

Figure 7a
Data Functionalization of the External View

Figure 7b
Data Functionalization of the Conceptual View

O2E is an onto function which maps each object to its corresponding unique data entity.

O2E : O $\rightarrow$ E where O = Set of Objects E = Set of Data Entities

For example, in figure 7a and figure 7b, each data entity comes from a unique object defined in the conceptual view and the external view respectively.

R2F is function which maps each inter-object relationship to its corresponding data function.

R2F : Inter → F
where Inter = Set of Inter-Object Relationships
F = Set of Data Functions

The mapping is carried out under the following conditions:

- The fanin data entity of the data function mapped is equal to the data entity of the source object in a particular relationship.
- The fanout data entity of the data function mapped is equal to the data entity of the target object in a particular relationship.

For example, in figure 7a and figure 7b, each data function will come from and go into data entities which represent the source object and target object respectively, of the corresponding relationship.

One of the attractive features offered by the data functionalization process is the power to combine various functions together using functional compositions. It is these functional compositions which provide the way to express the operational meaning of the compatibility between the conceptual view and the external view of a knowledge base. An external view is compatible with the conceptual view of a knowledge base if and only if:

- For each data entity in the conceptual view, a semantically equivalent data entity can be found in the external view.
- For each data function in the conceptual view, a semantically equivalent data function or data function composition can be found in the external view.

The definitions of semantically equivalent data entities and data functions will be discussed in detail in the next section.

4. Mappings

By the process of data functionalization, both the definitions of the conceptual view and the external view of a knowledge base are expressed in terms of a set of data entities and a set of data functions. The problem of deducing the mappings between these two views can be reconstructed more operationally into two steps:

- The problem of deducing the data entity mappings, i.e. how to express a data entity in the conceptual view with its semantically equivalent counterpart in the external view.
- The problem of deducing the data function mappings, i.e. how to express a data function in the conceptual view with its semantically equivalent counterpart in the external view.

4.1. Data Function Mappings

In this subsection, it is assumed that somehow the data entity mappings have already been deduced between the conceptual view and the external view of a knowledge base. With this assumption, the data function mappings will be deduced. In the next subsection, detailed discussion will show how these data entity mappings can be deduced in the first place. First of all, what is the definition of semantically equivalent data functions? Each data function has its own signature which signifies its characteristics. Since every data function must come from a particular data entity and go into another one, the characteristics of a data function will be its fanin and fanout entities. The same reasoning applies when considering functional compositions as well. No matter how many functions are involved in a functional composition, there will only be one unique entry point and one unique exit point. Based on this discussion, the definition of semantically equivalent data functions is:

> A data function is semantically equivalent to another data function or data function composition if they both share semantically equivalent fanin and fanout entities.

Assume that somehow it is deduced that the data entity 'netRec' in figure 7a is semantically equivalent to the data entity 'net' in figure 7b. The same assumption applies to the data entity 'pinRec' in figure 7a and the data entity 'pin' in figure 7b. Using the definition of semantically equivalent data functions given above, let us see how one can deduce the data function mapping of a data function, say 'type' with fanout entity 'pin' and fanout entity 'string'. By definition, a semantically equivalent function of the data function 'type' should have a fanout entity which is semantically equivalent to 'pin' and a fanout entity which is semantically equivalent to 'string'. Obviously, the only candidate which satisfies this condition is the functional composition of two functions 'detail' and 'ptype_of' in figure 7a.

> type(pin) = ptype_of(detail(pinRec))

In cases where there is more than one candidate satisfying the semantically equivalent condition, the definition given above does not define how to choose among them. There is, in fact, no definite answer to this ambiguity. One sensible operation to perform here is to order these alternative candidates according to the strengths of their naming similarities with respect to their corresponding data functions. Alternative candidates are then presented to the user in this particular order and confirmation from the user is used to solve the ambiguity. Naming comparisons seem to be a reasonable way of detecting semantic similarities because the name of a particular data function can convey much information about what it means.

4.2. Data Entity Mappings

In the subsection above, the term 'semantically equivalent data functions' is defined in terms of semantically equivalent data entities. The term 'semantically equivalent data entities' is defined in this subsection. First of all, a certain group of data entities is classed as atomic data entities. Atomic data entities are those elementary entities which exist independently of the conceptual view and the external view of the knowledge base. These entities include integers, real numbers, strings and booleans. With this classification, the definition of semantically equivalent data entities is two-fold:

> An atomic data entity can only be semantically equivalent to itself.

> A non-atomic data entity E_1 is semantically equivalent to another non-atomic data entity E_2 if for every data function f_i in E_1 there is a data function or data function composition g_i in E_2 such that both f_i and g_i have semantically equivalent fanout data entities.

Using these two definitions and referring to figure 7a and figure 7b, it is not difficult to deduce the previous assumption that data entity 'pin' is semantically equivalent to the data entity 'pinRec' and the data entity 'net' is semantically equivalent to the data entity 'netRec'. In cases where more than one candidate satisfies the data entity equivalent definitions, the same strategy of naming comparison is employed to choose among ambiguities.

5. Conclusions

Finally, what does it mean if no sensible mappings can be deduced using the definitions given above? According to the definition of compatibility in section 3, the only sensible conclusion which can be drawn in this case is that the external view imposed by that particular set of data structures on the knowledge base is incompatible with respect to the conceptual view of the knowledge base. Obviously an application with incompatible data structures will not be able to use knowledge in the knowledge base until suitable modifications are made.

From the two general strategies presented in subsection 4.1 and 4.2, it is possible to deduce a set of functional mappings so that each data entity and data function in the conceptual view of the knowledge base can be expressed in terms of those in the external view. Provided enough structural information is recorded during the data functionalization of the data structures, these functional mapping should be sufficient to generate codings which will interpret objects and relationships modelled in a knowledge base in terms of appropriate data structures in different application programs. In this way, the data structure independent knowledge-application interface discussed in subsection 2.4 can adapt itself and operate correctly under different contexts. Hence knowledge-based applications can realistically be considered as knowledge base + mappings + applications.

6. Acknowledgements

One of the authors, Paul K. C. Pun would like to thank the Croucher Foundation for the financial support given during the period of this research.

7. References

[1] W. van Melle, E. H. Shortliffe and B. G. Buchanan, EMYCIN: *"A Domain-Independent system that aids in constructing Knowledge-based Consultation Programs"*, in Machine Intelligence, Infotech State of the Art Report 9, No. 3, 1981.

[2] C. Forgy and J. McDermott, *"OPS: A Domain-Independent Production System Language"*, in Proc. IJCAI, 1977.

[3] N. P. Filer, *"The Use of Knowledge Based Techniques for Electronic Computer Aided Design"*, PhD. Thesis, Department of Computer Science, University of Manchester, January 1988.

[4] Quintus Prolog User's Guide and Reference Manual, Version 2.3, Quintus Computer Systems, 1988.

[5] U. Reimer and U. Hahn, *"A Formal Approach to the Semantics of a Frame Data Model"*, in Proc. IJCAI, 1983.

[6] G. Wiederhold, *"Knowledge and Database Management"*, in IEEE Software, Vol. 1, No. 1, January 1984.

[7] M. Brodie and J. Mylopoulos, *"Knowledge Bases Versus Databases"*, in On Knowledge Base Management Systems, M. Brodie and J. Mylopoulos (eds.), Springer-Verlag, New York, 1986.

[8] ANSI/X3/SPARC Study Group on Data Base Management Systems, Interim Report, in FDT, Vol. 7, No. 2, 1975.

[9] M. Minsky, *"A Framework for Representing Knowledge"*, in Psychology of Computer Vision, P. Winston (ed.), McGraw-Hill, 1975.

[10] M. R. Quillian, *"Semantic Memory"*, in Semantic Information Processing, M. Minsky (ed.), MIT Press, 1968.

[11] H. Levesque, *"A View of Knowledge Representation"*, in On Knowledge Base Management Systems, M. Brodie and J. Mylopoulos (eds.), Springer-Verlag, New York, 1986.

[12] Nijssen, G. M., *"A Gross Architecture for the next generation Database Management Systems"*, in Modelling in Data Base Management Systems, Nijssen, G. M. (ed.), North-Holland Publishing Company, New York, 1976.

QUESTIONS

Prof. S. M. Deen (university of Keele).
SMD.

You have defined semantical inferencing. How do you use this semantical treatment?

Mr. P. Pun.

PP. We are talking about the length between a knowledge object and an application data and most of the time they are variable. When people are building expert systems, they have an application in mind so they can construct particular objects that can actually look into the data structures to extract information, to actually execute that particular knowledge to get information. But in the generalized system we are talking about, we have an intermediate knowledge base, but we are supporting deeper applications communicating with the knowledge base itself. In that sense, we are giving the programmes the freedom to choose their own data representation or data model, so they may have an interpretation of the reality which is totally different to our thoughts of it when constructing the knowledge base.

But anyway, no matter how many rules you are going to take for a knowledge base system, you must have a domain scheme; what kind of objects you are talking about, what kind of relationships you are talking about in the knowledge, etc.

*SMD.*In the context of that, can you look, anyway at all, at any special issues of contradiction there are in mapping expert systems and databases? Are there any conceptual problems in mapping expert systems and databases?

PP. Because, in my own view, I consider expert systems themselves as knowledge-based systems of some kind, and databases actually a piece of application which will use the knowledge in our knowledge base, I will consider database as an application. So if you want to use database as an example, what happens in my generalized knowledge based system is that you now have a knowledge base, and you have different heterogeneous databases using the knowledge, so the same problems come out, different kinds of schema representing in different database. So first of all we need to sort it out. We don't want to have an individual basis attached to each database. I can't see why we can't make a generalized interface because provided we don't build in any interpretation of how data is represented externally, the interface should be universal and the complications should be sorted out in the particular applications.

Note that I'm saying that database will be in the role of application. I'm not saying that database is itself an application, but when you are talking about putting database into a large data system, then database will become the application.

13 A Graphical Knowledge Base for Large Industrial Domains

J. W. Butler, J. W. Shepherdson, W. N. Stein, J. Bigham

ABSTRACT

This paper describes a tool to represent switch design knowledge. This includes generic information, where there is a need to represent greater richness, hence knowledge representation; and instance information, where a large number of details need to be listed as in a data base. The tool called GKR (Graphical Knowledge Representation), forms the foundation of a Knowledge Based System development aimed at supporting operations and maintenance. It provides a means for naive users to build knowledge based structures interactively via graphical interfaces; allows the reuse of generic structures which provide efficiency of representation and eases knowledge acquisition for actual installations. It has features originating from specific telecommunication domain requirements, but is equally applicable to other industrial applications, where a generic structure is specialised differently for several physical realisations. A GKR knowledge base is being used to investigate the integration of high level heuristics with detailed design knowledge and also to aid the development of a fault information correlation tool.

1 Introduction

A complete, consistent and up to date store of knowledge is central to the correct functioning of a Knowledge Based System in large industrial domains. In addition, support for the subsequent evolution of the domain is required. Although this is difficult to achieve, help can be provided by the use of specialised knowledge acquisition and representation tools.

A knowledge representation tool, GKR (Graphical Knowledge Representation), was developed to try to represent a telecommunications switch adequately. It is thought that the facilities within GKR are relevant to a class of problems in industrial applications. GKR has been developed for domains where there is a need to represent, manipulate and maintain large amounts of design knowledge; and where there are many variations of a system type. Operational installations can vary considerably in size and configuration, but are still specific instances of a generic type. It is this generic and specific information that we wish to define within a representation tool in a flexible, economical way. The generic knowledge also has intrinsic value as it can provide useful general information where details are too onerous to represent or are not available.

2 Background

Digital exchanges are made from specified building blocks, which can be interconnected in particular ways. The configuration chosen for an installation depends on factors such as required security and traffic handling capacity. So, whilst all exchanges of the same type are built from similar generic units, each one varies in its actual arrangement. When equipment is first deployed, no detailed heuristics exist for its operation and maintenance. Procedures and actions can only be developed by considering design information and manuals. A similar approach needs to be followed for a Knowledge Based System to support such equipment [Williamson]. That is, the Knowledge Based System must reason from the exchange design information [Chandrasekaran], hence there is a need to acquire and represent this design information. The acquisition and application of heuristics are de-emphasised in the applications for which GKR has been developed. This is also reflected in the work of [Genesereth].

Heuristic associations often use design information and can lead to representation of redundant information. Since most industrial systems are continually updated, previously valid heuristics can become inconsistent with the new structure and function. The identification of invalid heuristics is a potentially difficult task. Updates are more easily carried out through changes to design knowledge, since this is the language of the domain expert. The inference mechanisms used in maintenance systems being developed use design knowledge and hence require no modifications when design changes are made.

A feature of our knowledge representation tool, GKR, is the ability to represent both generic and specific information in a distinct and manageable fashion. It is being used to represent generic information about a particular type of digital telephone exchange and detailed information is being added about a specific exchange. This knowledge base forms the foundation for research into reasoning from design information; it is being used to support the development of a tool for fault information correlation [Bigham] and also investigations into the integration of high level heuristics with detailed system information for fault diagnosis. Further details on the value and role of Knowledge Based Systems to telecommunications can be found in [Fox].

GKR was built using an object-oriented approach. This provides the ability to associate code with data, and the use of inheritance [Stroustrup]. Inheritance allows more efficient information representation through the use of data decomposition. For a discussion of object-oriented issues see [Stefik]. Differences between knowledge bases and data bases tend to be along the axes of connectivity; data persistence and stability; and the number of classes and entries for each class. Knowledge bases tend to have rich connectivity, undergo many changes and have relatively large numbers of classes with small numbers of entries in each class; whereas data bases have more limited connectivity, greater data stability and a smaller number of classes with very large numbers of entries per class. This work involves the integration of knowledge and data base ideas. The approach to the work has been from the knowledge base direction, although conventional data base facilities are also relevant and will be required to a greater extent in the development of a final product.

The knowledge representation used at the generic level is frame based [Fikes] with many of the features available in well known systems such as KEE or CRL. By concentrating tool features on specific domain requirements, greater support has been provided for knowledge acquisition from manuals and design documents by domain experts rather than knowledge engineers. The objectives of GKR differ from software aided knowledge acquisition systems such as DETEKTR (Development Environment for Tektronix Troubleshooting) [Freiling] or KRITON [Diederich]. In DETEKTR a complete methodology for developing expert systems incrementally is given. KRITON is a hybrid system integrating three types of knowledge with three associated acquisition methods (interviews, protocol analysis and incremental content analysis). GKR primarily supports the acquisition and representation of design knowledge.

An area of knowledge acquisition which has not been tackled and where some of the ideas in the tools above could be of value is the acquisition of control knowledge. In the MUM system [Gruber] Gruber and Cohen gave three design principles, which were used to construct control rules. The rules were declarative, expressed in task level terms, and did not generalise beyond situations with which the expert was familiar. The Knowledge Description Language and Intelligent Graphical Interface System of the knowledge acquisition tool KEATS [Eisenstadt] have similarities to GKR. KEATS is designed to support the acquisition of heuristics by knowledge engineers. The advantages of a graphical knowledge representation approach include easier inspection and information access. Further, this can be used for explanation and justification of knowledge based reasoning [Dodson].

3 GKR - Graphical Knowledge Representation Tool

The tools described above concentrate on representing information about particular systems. GKR tries to generalise this and represent a type of system and then the various physical realisations of it in an economical way. This follows naturally from the generic exchange designs from which actual installations are formed. This approach acts as an aid to detailed knowledge acquisition. GKR is WIMPS (windows, icons, menus and pointers) driven and therefore requires no previous experience of either a programming language or object-oriented programming in general. It provides a developer with three interfaces that together allow complex interrelationships to be constructed graphically between objects and a fourth interface for data browsing.

The structure of the knowledge base is created through the manipulation of iconic representations of the relevant objects. Relationships between objects are also treated as objects in their own right and are represented by connector icons. Relationships are created simply by connecting relevant objects together using the connector icons on the screen. When saving the knowledge base, GKR automatically generates code to capture the structure and data, which it logically partitions into separate files.

The system is flexible enough to allow the capture of data relevant to small or very large domains. It offers many useful features, which can be used as the requirements of the knowledge representation problem demand. GKR allows a distinction between generic and specific objects to be made at many different levels. This approach enables a developer to build a generic application, which can be specialised as often as required, without the need to modify the existing generic structure. These various specialisations can then be accessed as required.

GKR was developed on a Symbolics Lisp workstation and makes extensive use of the Flavors programming environment.

3.1 Applications, Views and Diagrams in GKR

A problem area is referred to as an Application, an example is a particular type of digital telephone exchange. Each Application can contain any number of Views, where each View is a means of looking at part of the knowledge. This subdivision of an Application into Views has the distinct advantage of allowing the problem under consideration to be presented in manageable portions, avoiding the risk of swamping the user with vast amounts of complex data. For example in the exchange Application, Views would include those giving dependency information, like powering and timing distribution; functional block relationships; physical layout of racks, shelves, cables etc.; and functional connectivity.

Large numbers of attributes are required to represent complex domain objects. Often these attributes can be divided in sensible ways. GKR allows these smaller groupings to be arranged so that they appear in different Views. Since it is useful to take advantage of inheritance for these groups of attributes, the Knowledge Editor allows the graphical design of the required inheritance path for the attributes of objects in each View. GKR also provides for a different icon design for an object in each View it appears in. This provides easy visual distinction between Views by giving an appropriate iconic representation for each object. An example of this would be to split an Application into physical layout and functional dependency Views and to draw icons for each object that indicate physical and functional properties.

Applications are, in effect, conceptual frameworks that delineate the boundaries between different domains. Views are used to describe various relationships within a particular subdivision of the information of a domain. Diagrams are subdivisions of Views and consist of iconic representations of a number of objects used in a View and any logical connections between them. It is the Diagrams that contain the information. A user navigates the knowledge base by moving from one Diagram to another. Whether a route taken is within a single View or moves across many, depends upon whether a user chooses to examine a single relationship between objects in detail or to look at one object and its place in each of the Views.

There are two drawing modes in GKR (straight lines or horizontal and vertical lines), which help to ensure that diagrams appear like those found in engineering documentation. By using a number of Views, a user can represent different attributes of components in a natural way. The system therefore brings together the usually disparate engineering information into one knowledge base. For example, a physical layout View can show the actual physical layout, whilst an electrical View can show the usual wiring diagram. Then tracing an electrically connected component can be carried out in the electrical View and switching to the physical layout View can indicate the physical location.

Different levels of information (detail/abstraction) are represented by Diagrams within a View being arranged in hierarchies. Once established, hierarchies can be traversed to provide more detail or increased abstraction. GKR aids the building of Diagram hierarchies. It allows the creation of an object to represent an entire Diagram, whose icon can then be placed in a Diagram that is superior to the one it represents. Another way involves selection of an object that is to have a diagram directly below it and creating a new diagram to hold the required detail. In each case, the process can be repeated to create further levels.

Division of information into Views and Diagrams provides for logical partitioning into files, enabling GKR to load only those Diagrams required in a particular session. Information is primarily divided by Application, View and Diagram, with a number of files per Diagram. It is conceivable that a multi-user version of GKR could be produced that uses this in-built partitioning to provide a form of concurrency control.

4 GKR Interfaces

GKR has four distinct interfaces, three are designed for data input and manipulation purposes, the fourth solely for information browsing. The three development interfaces are referred to as the Drawing, Icon and Knowledge Editors. The other is the User Editor. A developer creates an Application and associated Views by selecting appropriate menu options and then typing suitable names to given prompts. The four interfaces can be used in virtually any order. This allows great flexibility as changes or additions can be made when required.

4.1 GKR Interfaces - The Icon Editor

The Icon Editor (figure 1) can be used first to create (and/or kill) generic objects within an Application. As each generic object is created, it is assigned the default icon and may be incorporated into Diagrams using the Diagram Editor. First, however, it is sensible to distinguish between the various generic objects in the different Views by editing the icons. The Icon Editor provides a detailed drawing area and options with which distinctive icons for each object in each View can be designed. Changes made to existing icons are immediately reflected in those Diagrams in which the icons appear.

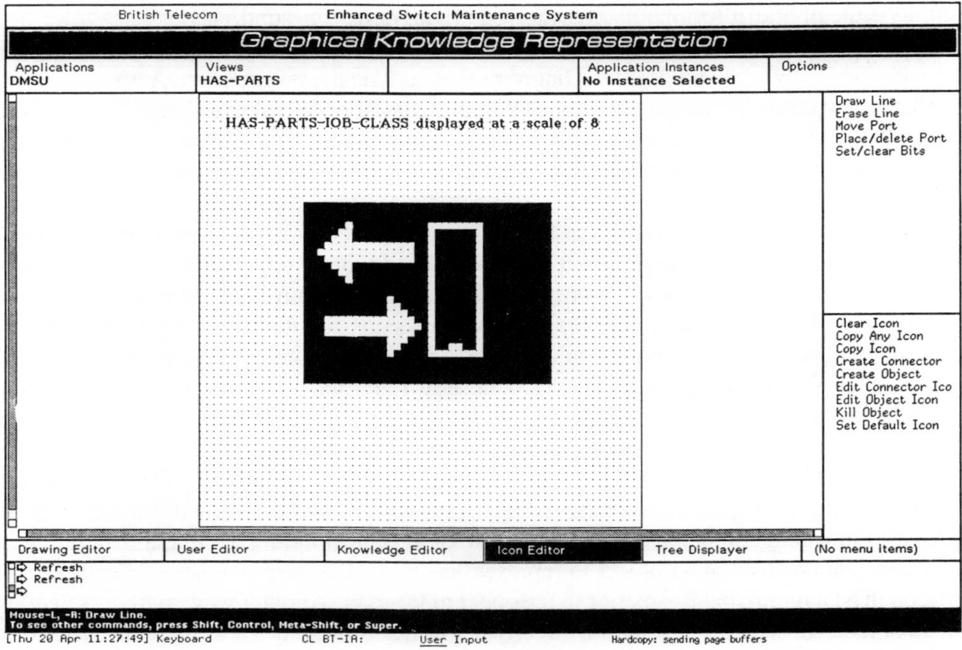

Figure 1 The Icon Editor

4.2 GKR Interfaces - The Knowledge Editor

The Knowledge Editor (figure 2) allows a developer to specify the data fields, and associated default values, for every generic object in each View. Each generic object can only be placed - and therefore defined - once in each View.

Base or intermediate groupings of data fields (mixins) required for inheritance are created using menu commands. The number, names and default values of data fields are entered via pop-up menus. Mixins appear as icons on the screen and inheritance is arranged via menu options. Inheritance paths are displayed as lines between the relevant icons. The use of inheritance aids knowledge base modification since it reduces the need to specify information in a redundant fashion. The task of developing the right structure for an Application is very important and difficult and the Knowledge Editor allows changes to be made at any time. If, at a later stage, data fields are added, changed or removed from either a mixin or an individual generic object, changes can be immediately propagated.

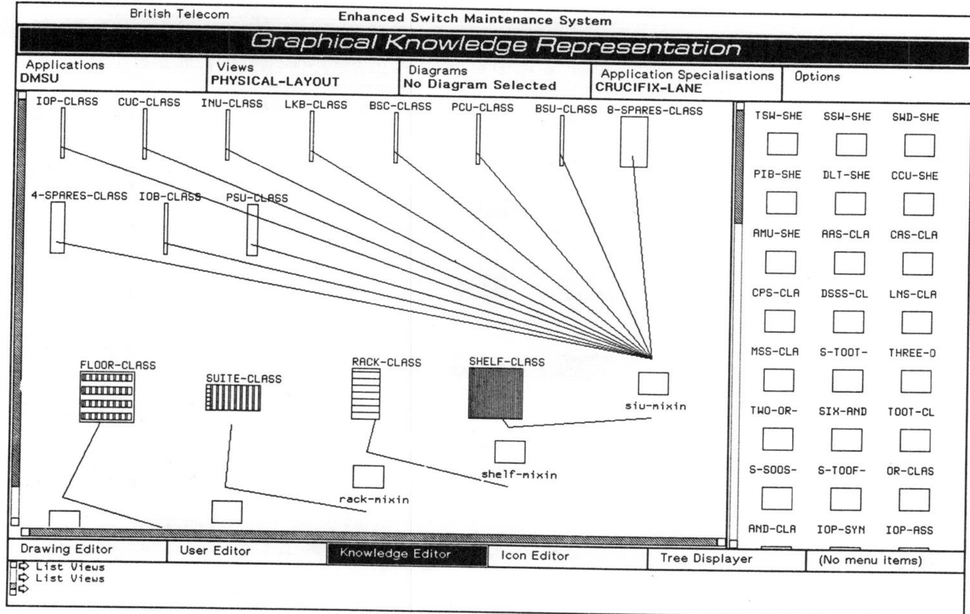

Figure 2 The Knowledge Editor

As well as arranging the inheritance network for each View, a developer is also able to assign View independent data to generic objects. This means a generic object can have a unique set of data fields and values associated with it for each of the Views that it appears in (View dependent data) and another set, which is available in all the Views (View independent data). For clarity, it is sensible to keep the number of View independent data fields to a minimum. An example of a View independent data field is a name field, whereas resistance would be View dependent data associated with the electrical View.

4.3 GKR Interfaces - The Drawing Editor

The Drawing Editor is used for the design of Diagrams within a selected View (figure 3). All the generic objects appear on a menu pane, represented by the user assigned icon for the View selected. A generic object can be selected for display in a Diagram and a copy placed as required. In fact a user has the option to place a new copy or to add to an existing one placed in another View. This feature allows the user to build descriptions of complex generic objects, which appear in several different Views.

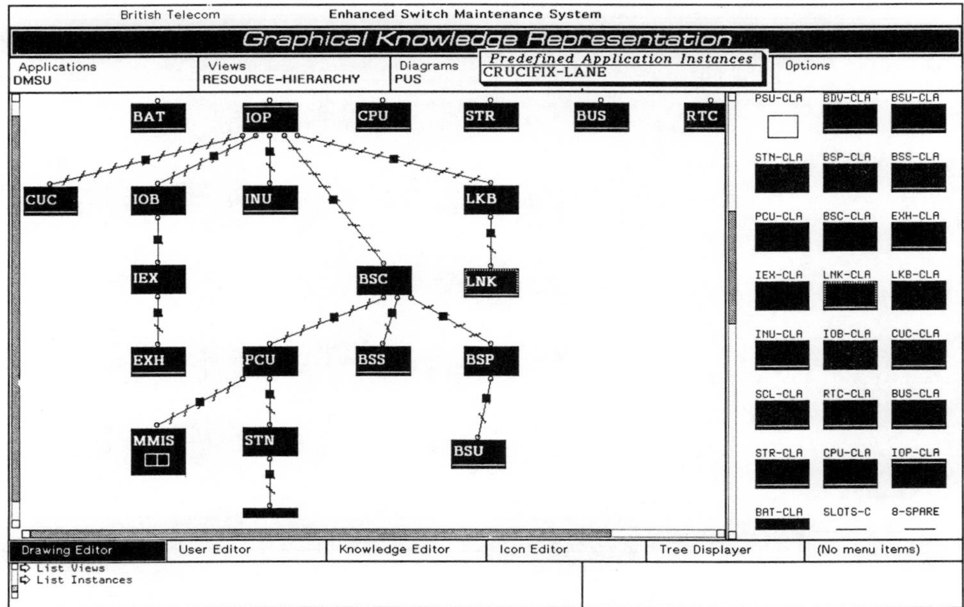

Figure 3 The Drawing Editor

The Drawing Editor incorporates features that are generally available in graphics system to allow easy movement, alignment and removal of objects once they have been placed in a Diagram. It is also possible to modify the contents of any inherited data fields for an object, if the assigned defaults are unsuitable for a particular situation.

4.4 GKR Interfaces - The User Editor

The User Editor is the interface that is designed for browsing the data (figure 4) . The user is able to select any Application (and Application Specialisation), then access all the Views and Diagrams that were created using the Drawing Editor, follow any links that exist between them or individual objects and examine the contents of the data fields for any of the objects, created in the Knowledge Editor.

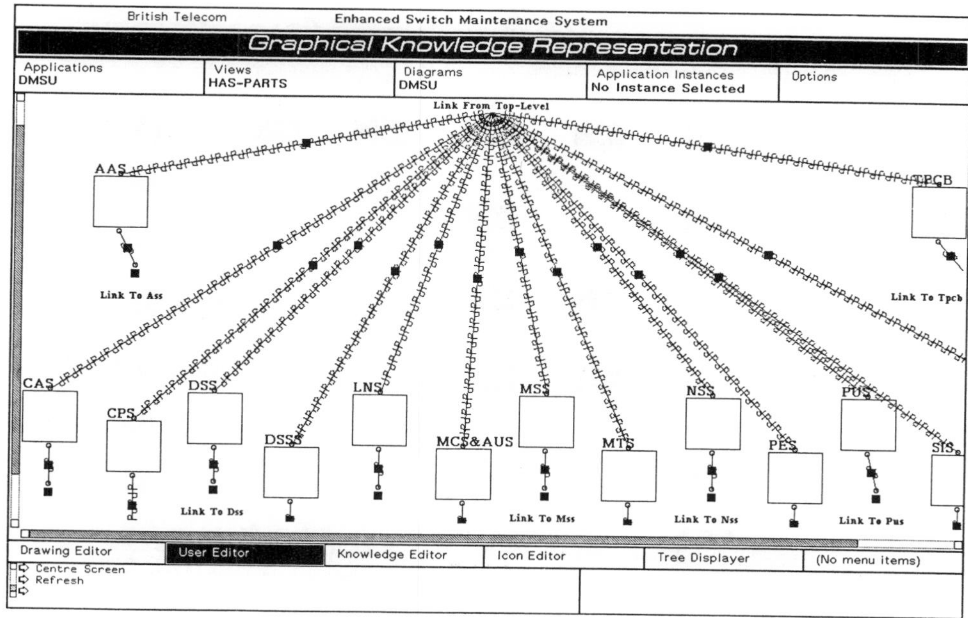

Figure 4 The User Editor

5 Application Specialisation in GKR

When the construction of the generic knowledge base is completed, it can then be specialised. In the digital exchange Application, the generic knowledge base would contain general exchange information. Specialisation would provide details about particular exchange installations. Specialisation is carried out by adding the instance details to each of the objects in the Diagrams in turn, where each generic object can have many instances. Specialised information can be saved and loaded by menu options. Each generic Application can have many sets of specialisations - these are referred to as Application Specialisations. So an Application, once its attribute fields and diagrammatic layout has been completed and saved, can be thought of as a reusable resource. This reusability derives from the existence of Application Specialisation data, each set of which encapsulates an entire specialisation of the Application. It is possible to switch easily between specific and generic information and to alternative specialisations.

Generic objects in GKR are built automatically from Flavors when using the Knowledge Editor. Generic diagram are built from instances of Flavors in the Drawing Editor. Specialisation data is stored using an alternative mechanism.

For an example of the use of generic and instance Diagrams see figures 5 and 6. Figure 5 shows specific instance data loaded, but displayed as thermometers showing proportion of actual resources in and out of service. Figure 6 shows the same Diagram, but with some instance data about resource status explicitly displayed.

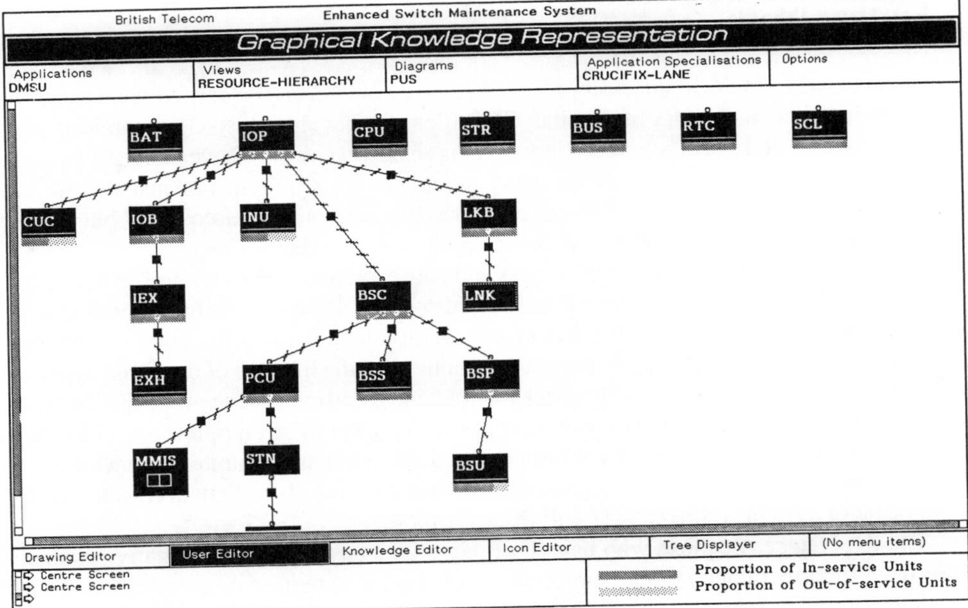

Figure 5 Generic Diagram

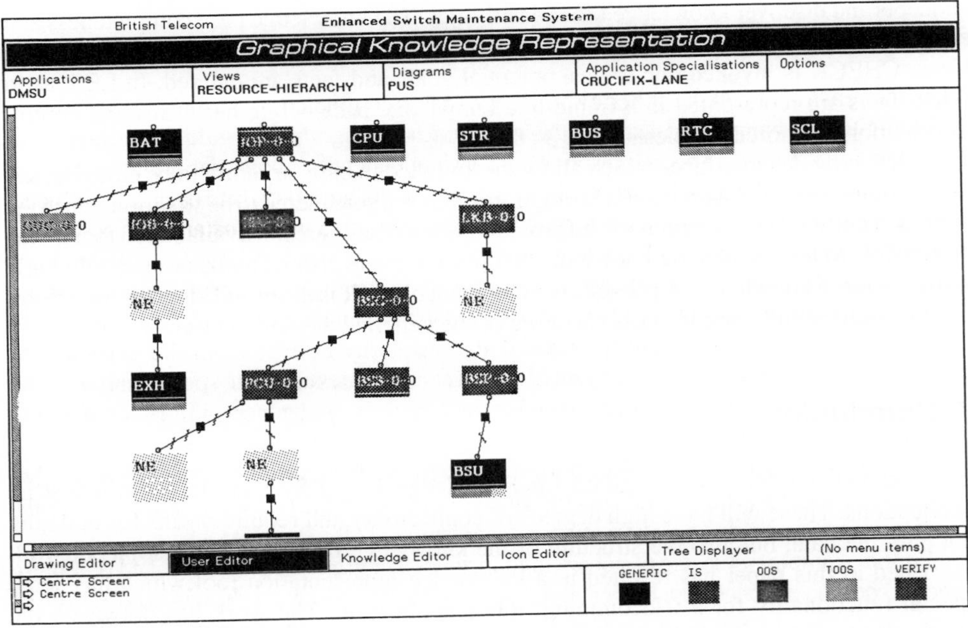

Figure 6 Instance Diagram

6 Further Work

Using the current graphical interface, entry and editing of data can be carried out easily, but provision for direct bulk entry of data into GKR files is applicable. Also GKR supports one-to-one mappings of objects between Views, that is an object can only have one realisation in each View. In some situations one-to-many mappings are required. For instance, in the exchange example an object could be considered as one icon in a resource View, but consist of several parts in a physical View - requiring a number of icons.

Attaining knowledge base completeness and consistency is a difficult problem. It is felt that working directly from engineering design information, some knowledge inconsistencies can be avoided. Also graphical displays of information help the identification of potential problems. Since knowledge acquisition can continue over the lifetime of deployed systems, additional computer aided support to check completeness and consistency is desirable. It has to be remembered however that knowledge bases can appear to be complete and consistent even though important concepts have been omitted. No amount of automatic checking will discover omissions. Only well designed and executed knowledge elicitation followed by monitoring of systems on live cases will discover these.

The experiences of those who have built large data bases shows that many problems arise from incorrect contextual assumptions made by the expert or user consulted. These problems can be reduced if the knowledge base carries extra data on its sources, which help in the automatic resolution of inconsistencies in later tests and checks. Automatic test case generation, as for example in the TIMM system [TIMM], is useful. These can generate test cases which are quite different from previous cases and therefore more likely to elicit new concepts and discover knowledge base sensitivities. The knowledge base completeness and consistency program CHECK, in the LES expert system [Ngyen], contains many useful ideas. CHECK is invoked once rules, potential goals and facts are entered. In LES, as in GKR, facts are represented in a frame-like knowledge base, while heuristics and control information are stored as rules.

GKR provides interfaces which allow the knowledge base structure to be edited at any time. Completeness of Application Specialisations is not considered to be so serious since the approach outlined provides generic information when details are not available. In fact it may be possible to use the generic knowledge to question the exchange and automatically build up the instance knowledge. A possible development of GKR is the provision of more support for consistency and completeness checking of the generic knowledge base.

7 Conclusion

Large knowledge bases are required for Knowledge Based Systems in some industrial applications. These will have high degrees of connectivity and require means for updating not only the data, but also the structure of the knowledge base itself. Development work described in this paper has resulted in a knowledge representation tool which has some special functionality for a telecommunications application. The work has drawn on the approach of object-oriented knowledge representation and like [Andrews] tries to bring together some conventional data base techniques and AI knowledge representation ideas. A distinction between generic and specialised information is made and supported. Diagrammatic representation and display of information with the ability to switch rapidly between Diagrams is provided. Easy and rapid access to object data in different Views is provided, along with automatic partitioning of the knowledge base into manageable files.

GKR underpins a software system which includes an inferencing mechanism and a Truth Maintenance System. The use of an object-oriented programming language has eased the development and integration of these modules. Some integration is achieved by certain reserved attribute names provided in GKR, which have associated special functionality. For example, the addition of an inferencing data field to an object in GKR can provide automatic access to default information, when explicit information is not available. This allows an inferencing mechanism to arrive at a general result when detailed information is not available.

The primary reason for developing and subsequently using GKR is to develop a Knowledge Based System which will work from design knowledge. Whilst doing this the value of the representation has been shown by its use to graphically indicate the status of exchange resources (using colour). Further, the knowledge base is also being used to support an enhanced exchange interface. This uses information from various data fields of the exchange Application to provide help for engineers entering exchange commands. For example, the range and validity of commands and associated parameters is provided for the engineer with respect to either generic or specific exchange information.

Acknowledgements

Early coding was carried out by Intelligent Applications Ltd (Dr Robert Milne, Chris Nelson and Craig Strachan).

Thanks to Dave Saunders (Queen Mary College) for helpful discussions on completeness and consistency in large knowledge bases.

Acknowledgement is made to the Research and Technology Board of British Telecom for permission to publish this paper

References

Andrews
Combining Language and Database Advances in an Object-Oriented Development Environment
Timothy Andrews & Craig Harris
OOPSLA 1987 Proceedings

Bigham
Logical Assumption Based Truth Maintenance System
Dr John Bigham (Queen Mary College, London)
Technical Paper, Department of Electrical & Electronic Engineering, Queen Mary College, London

Chandrasekaran
"Deep" Models and Their Relation to Diagnosis
B Chandrasekaran, J Smith & J Sticklen

The Ohio State University - Technical Report 87-BC-Japan

Diederich
KRITON: a knowledge acquisition tool for expert systems
J Deiderich, I Ruhman & M May
International Journal of Machine Studies, 1987

Dodson
Interaction with Knowledge Systems Though Connection Diagrams: Please Adjust Your Diagrams
David C Dodson
Proceedings of the Expert Systems Conference, December 1988

Eisenstadt
Support for knowledge Acquisition in the Knowledge Engineer's Assistant (KEATS)
Marc Eisenstadt, Kent Pitman & Malcolm West
Expert Systems, February 1988, Volume 5, No 1.

Fikes
The Role of Frame-Based Representation in Reasoning
Richard Fikes & Tom Kehler
Communications of the ACM, Volume 28, No 9, September 1985

Fox
The Role of Expert Systems in Switch Maintenance Operations and the Generation of Switch Analysis Requirements
Jane R Fox & Gary M Slawsky
IEEE Journal on Selected Areas in Communications, Volume 6, No 4, May 1988

Freiling
Starting a knowledge engineering project: a step by step approach DETEKTR (Development Environment for Tektronix Troubleshooting)
M Freiling, J Alexander, S Messick, S Rehfuss & S Shulman
The AI Magazine, 1985

Genesereth
The Use of Design Knowledge in Automated Diagnosis
Michael R Genesereth
Artificial Intelligence No 24, 1984

Gruber
Design for acquisition: principles of knowledge-system design to facilitate knowledge acquisition
T Gruber & P R Cohen
Int. Journal of Man-Machine Studies, No 26, pp143-159, 1987

Ngyen
Knowledge Base Verification
T A Ngyen, W A Perkins, T J Laffey & D Pecora
The AI Magazine, Volume 8, No 2, Summer 1987

Stefik
Object-Oriented Programming: Themes and Variations
Mark Stefik & Daniel G Bobrow
The AI Magazine, Volume 6 No 4, Winter 1986

Stroustrup
What is Object-Oriented Programming?
Bjarne Stroustrup
IEEE Software May 1988

TIMM
TIMM Users Manual
General Research Corporation, Santa Barbara, California, 1985

Williamson
Using KBS in Telecoms II
George I Williamson, John W Butler, Simon King (BT - RT3422, London) & Dr John Bigham (Queen Mary College, London)
ESPRIT Technical Proceedings 1987

QUESTIONS

Dr. S. Bennett (Sheffield University).

SB. Could you say a bit more about how you segment the knowledge base? You say you only have a small part of it loaded at any one time. On what sort of principles does it do the segmentation?

Mr. W. Stein.

WS. As I said, we split things up into applications, views and diagrams. When you first load up an application, you load up one file. And as and when you want to access information, you load up other files. At any time you'll have a certain number of data files loaded relevant to all the things that you have been looking at recently. Now on what basis you throw files away, i.e. remove them from working memory, there are a number of possible algorithms you can use. The one that we currently use is simply keep whatever dozen diagram files, (that is files associated with diagrams), most recently used. Obviously some sort of study of what would be the best way of deciding which bits of data should be taken out of working memory and put back into storage would bear investigation.

SB. Do you then maintain the generic components in memory all the time?

WS. It is not necessary to have the complete generic structure loaded all of the time. Instead, components are loaded and accessed as and when they are required. When I say a number of diagrams are loaded at any time, I'm talking about the data files associated with generic components within diagrams. When you want to look at the information in particular exchanges (currently we're only working to one exchange, but there's no reason why you couldn't be working on a large number), it's on a diagram basis, so for a generic diagram which has one data file, there will also be a datafile for that diagram describing a particular exchange.

SB. When an engineer constructs a diagram, is there any checking that the connection rules for the components have been followed?

WS. Yes. However, the maintenance engineer would not construct the diagrams. The construction of the diagrams at a generic level would be done by somebody familiar with the system and that each of the different exchanges would be just overlay information onto that structure. So it would be dangerous to allow the engineers to actually construct their own diagrams. What they might be allowed to do is to have their own version of icons. They could decide that they wanted an icon to have a different representation on their diagrams from the ones we had decided. But the idea is that, in advance, we would build up the diagrams representing the generic exchange and they would be fairly static compared to actual exchange changes, in size and so forth. Also components would vary. That is the sort of information that will change whereas the generic structure won't change. So it's conceivable that people like ourselves will tend to construct the generic exchange representation.

Dr. R. Moore (Software Sciences Ltd.).

RM. You were saying that the data was held in several files. If you make changes, is the change incrementally propagated to hidden files, or do you actually, for each individual piece of information, only have one representation of it, so you only actually update one thing?

WS. If you make changes within the knowledge editor, which is where you can add new fields or delete fields, there is the possibility to make those changes immediately reflected within the associated diagrams.

RM. It's more a matter of if you have a number of different representations of the same thing, different views where the same object appears, if you change it in one of those contexts, is it propagated to the others automatically?

WS. Yes. I make a distinction between the dependent and the independent slots. The independent slots are those that appear in every view. Make a change to an independent slot and that change appears in every view immediately. A dependent slot only appears in one view. So you can change it and there's no worry about changes in other views.

Perhaps, I haven't got the message across completely, that what we're talking about is that engineers will not be modifying the diagrams or modifying the data. The fact is that, unlike a lot of things that have been discussed in the last couple of days, where it is necessary for users to update things, we're talking about an exchange where we can get the information in advance, put that information in, and that information shouldn't need to be updated. The actual engineers using the system will not be able to update this for themselves because there's no need for them to.

Mr. C. Church (Hitachi Europe Ltd.).

CC. How well do you think your work would translate into other domains? For instance, you can take a telephone exchange as being something of a computer these days. Could your system be used for a major hardware manufacturer to build his computers? Is this translatable? Is it translatable to domains like, perhaps, retailing units or military formations? What is the strength you have in the control of the domain? In particular, you seem to be highlighting the hardware aspects of the domain. Is there the possibility that what you've done in the BT environment, could translate over into looking at software applications?

WS. We believe that GKR is a very flexible tool. We have a number of other applications we can use to demonstrate to people who aren't familiar with telephone exchanges. For example, we have an application of a car, looking at that in a number of different views. Basically, I think that the problem is that, whilst it is a dynamic knowledge base, it's dynamic in the sense of changes that come along periodically rather than necessarily being used when you're going to want to update data all the time. That sort of domain where you're going to want a user to be able to update data themselves, is perhaps not directly suited to GKR as it currently stands. But there are a large number of industrial domains where the sort of changes that you're going to need to make, whilst being relatively frequent, (for example, a new release of software in the case of an exchange), can be installed without the actual end user having to make the updates. You then can write mechanisms to carry out the updates rather than allowing the end user to carry them out.

Q. How did you implement it?

WS. I neglected to say that we didn't use any sort of expert system shell. It is written on a SYMBOLICS, so we are using the LISP Flavours environment. Extensions to that were necessary because of certain limitations within the environment. For example, to update existing instances to flavours automatically, we had to write utilities to allow that. Obviously you get a lot of facilities in a SYMBOLICS work station, but we started from scratch on that machine.

Q. You brought up the issue of attaching rules to slot values?

WS. It's part of our future work. There's no reason why rules shouldn't be stored as slots. For example, there's no reason why you can't inherit default rules, if rules for a particular object don't exist. It's an area which we want to pursue in the future.

14 The Generis Knowledge Base Management System: an Exploratory Review

J. B. Kennedy and M. A. Crerar

ABSTRACT

This paper explores the fusion of techniques from database technology and expert systems work, in the emerging area of knowledge base management systems, (KBMSs). Some of the shortcomings of relational database systems are reviewed, and the general properties of KBMSs introduced. The specific features of a new KBMS product, Generis [+] , are outlined, and the authors address problems of data modelling using Generis, for the implementation of an academic bibliographic retrieval system. The extent to which Generis fulfils KBMS criteria is discussed and issues are raised concerning the adequacy of existing data modelling techniques for representing knowledge base applications.

1. INTRODUCTION

The emerging field of knowledge base management systems, (KBMSs), also called expert database systems, arises from the convergence of two formerly separate areas of computing, namely database management systems (DBMSs) and expert systems or knowledge base systems (KBSs).

DBMSs evolved to address the problems of data inconsistency which resulted from the redundancy inherent in discrete file systems, to serve the information sharing needs of large, distributed organisations and to satisfy growing demand for on-line query facilities and ad hoc report generation. The need for reliable multi-user systems capable of handling efficiently large volumes of data, called for the development of methods to provide security, integrity, user-friendly interfaces, and binding the whole together, a theoretical foundation grounded in mathematics, by means of which the operations performed on data could be both specified and proven. The latter requirement has been best satisfied by the relational database model, which is based on set theoretic principles and has superceded both hierarchical and network approaches on account of its formal basis and the intuitive appeal of its conceptually tabular data structures. In addition, supporting data analysis techniques have been

+ Generis is marketed by Deductive Systems Ltd.

developed to facilitate modelling the application area and producing an appropriate set of normalized relations. The database community thus brings to KBMS research a well established discipline, combining theoretical rigour with the empirical experience of building large systems for commercial customers.

KBSs are of more recent origin, and are the most practical outcome so far, of Artificial Intelligence's (AI) general aim to encapsulate in artifacts, human level performance in diverse areas of intelligent behaviour. Early aspirations to build general purpose systems [1], were soon abandoned in favour of the more realistic aim of producing expert systems in limited and well circumscribed domains of expertise. The achievements of expert systems such as R1 [2] and MYCIN [3] are now legendary. Much as ease of implementation and maintenance led database designers to advocate data and program independence, so knowledge engineers realised that by separating the knowledge base from the inference engine and user interface, they could create a general purpose expert system shell suitable for use with a variety of knowledge bases. KBSs draw on many general AI techniques for knowledge representation, search strategies, probabilistic reasoning and programming approaches [4]. The nondeterministic nature of many AI problems has dictated an experimental programming approach which appears to contrast poorly with the increasingly formal direction of mainstream software engineering. However, a degree of formality has been achieved in KBS by the use of first order logic, both to express facts and rules, and as a programming vehicle [5]. On the whole, KBSs have been designed in research environments, as single user systems, with far less attention to issues of efficiency and security than DBMSs require.

KBSs and DBMSs are complementary in that they both seek to model a domain or application area of interest; the DBMS offers multi-user access to large volumes of explicit factual data, while the KBS generally includes less in the way of housekeeping functions but provides, through the inclusion of rules, the powerful facility to perform deductive reasoning on the knowledge base, and thus infer facts which are not explicitly stored. This, coupled with the ability to justify conclusions and explain questions when the system is eliciting knowledge, are features which represent a significant advance over the conventional DBMS. Clearly, there is much to be gained from a marriage of the two fields, in particular, the incorporation of intelligence in relational database systems such that users no longer need to know the table, entity and attribute names in advance in order to query systems, is essential if knowledge sources are to be interconnected and more widely useful. This goal may be approached by adding metaknowledge, or self-referential information, in the form of rules, about the contents of a knowledge base. The use of rules would also enrich the scope of database systems by allowing quantification, that is the specification of information relating to not just a single entity, but to a whole set, for example,

all managers are graduates.

The ability to state properties of sets obviates the need to duplicate common information. Further, the combined use of rules and inference allows entities to inherit the properties of their supersets, for example, from all grey parts are metal

part 123 is grey

we can infer that part 123 is a metal part. The power of this hierarchical inheritance is well known in AI, particularly for modelling taxonomies, but has not previously been available in database systems. Advanced research topics in KBS and DBS demonstrate considerable intersection, notably in areas such as the modelling of time varying data, the preservation of integrity in non-monotonic systems, the handling of fuzzy or incomplete data and the development of intelligent user interfaces.

1.1 Shortcomings of existing DBMSs

Frost summarises the limitations of existing DBMSs under the following headings[6]

- *Data independence is not supported.* This means that even in relational systems, the columns in a relation are not independent and inserting a new column can cause problems.
- *The co-existence of external schemas is not supported.* This point concerns the difficulty of providing multiple views of database content, for instance allowing some users to see an hierarchical subschema where files consist of a set of records containing repeating groups, while offering others a relational model.
- *Semantic integrity checking is not automatic.* The deficiency here is that information from conceptual schemas is not used to provide automatic checking that the database conforms to known constraints in the world being modelled.
- *Deductive retrieval is not supported.* As mentioned above, deductive retrieval means being able to infer from known facts and rules, information which is not explicitly stored.
- *The end-user interfaces are not very friendly.* This relates both to the difficulty of use of database query languages and the need for users of relational systems to know in advance the structure and content of the tables held, and details of how to obtain subsets of information using appropriate relational operators.
- *Most DBMSs are based on inappropriate hardware.* At present very few DBMSs are supported by special purpose hardware. This causes two performance related problems for large relational systems, one is the number of disc accesses required to accomplish complex retrievals across many relations and the second is the fact that backing storage is generally not content-addressable.

The aim of the next generation of Expert Database Systems is to overcome these problems and perhaps also to tackle some of the other goals we have touched upon, such as handling incomplete, fuzzy and time-varying data.

2. GENERIS

Deductive Systems Limited (DSL) describe Generis as *the World's only Intelligent Knowledgebase Management System* and claim, among other things, the following features:

- Extended relational database facilities
- Knowledge representation capability of an expert system
- Interpretive, deductive reasoning and general knowledge capabilities of AI systems
- Multi -media information/document management system within knowledgebase
- Automatic handling of all data entry, update and validation
- Easy report generation and enquiry facilities
- User friendly interface via intelligent query language
- Program interfaces and data gateway to other systems

Generis is the result of many years of research originating from work on the Fact database system [8]. The Fact database comprises a data structure consisting of non-decomposable quadruples - *Facts*, and a conceptual machine which can manipulate them. The model uses the terms *Entity, Fact, Fact number, Relation and Object.* An entity is any distinct thing or concept (concrete or abstract) to be represented in the system. A fact is a unit, which is a named, directed association between two entities, (the subject and object); the association linking them, the relation is also an entity. Each fact is represented by a unique symbol - the Fact number.

Table 1 Complex Facts

Factno	Subject	Relation	Object
F1	X	Y	Z
F2	Z	Y	Q
F3	F2	R	F1

From the specimen table above, it will be apparent that complex facts can be built. Facts are classed as either deductive or non-deductive, deductive facts being those which implicitly incorporate a universal quantifier on the subject. The advantage of deductive facts is that the property indicated by the object, is *inherited* by all members of the powerset of the subject. The effect is as though the data were stored explicitly with each member of the powerset. Non-deductive facts are used by the system as *Semantic Rules* to check the integrity of new data being entered. The Fact machine has at its heart an associative store which has a quadruple structure corresponding to that of the Facts. Efficient extraction of information is achieved through this content addressable device.

Continuing work on the FACT project has resulted in Generis. Generis utilises an entity relationship approach to data representation, based on the *Generic Relational Data Model* (GRDM), an *incomplete relational model*[9]. In the relational model (complete) all information is stored explicitly, whereas the incomplete relational model also permits the implicit storage of information. The latter is realised through the adoption of Smith and Smith's principles for data abstraction[10]. This provides for generalisation, whereby information true of classes need be stored only at the class level, thus information about a particular class member can be deduced from the generic information stored with the class(es) to which the member belongs. The GRDM thus provides a useful inference mechanism founded on a *type lattice* or *Multiple Inheritance Network* which supports a generalised taxonomy where entities may belong to more than one set. Queries are processed by the expansion of implicit sets and tuples into an explicit form.

2.1 The Generis System

Generis is presented to the user as a menu driven system, see Figure 1

Fig 1 Generis Menu System

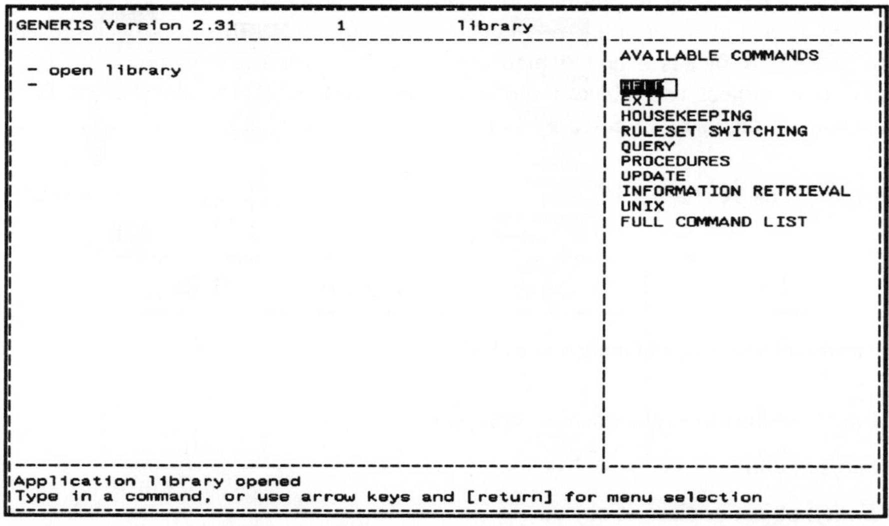

The user may type commands into the left hand system window or select from the options listed in the menu window. Figure 2 shows part of the menu hierarchy for Generis.

Fig 2 Generis Menu Hierarchy

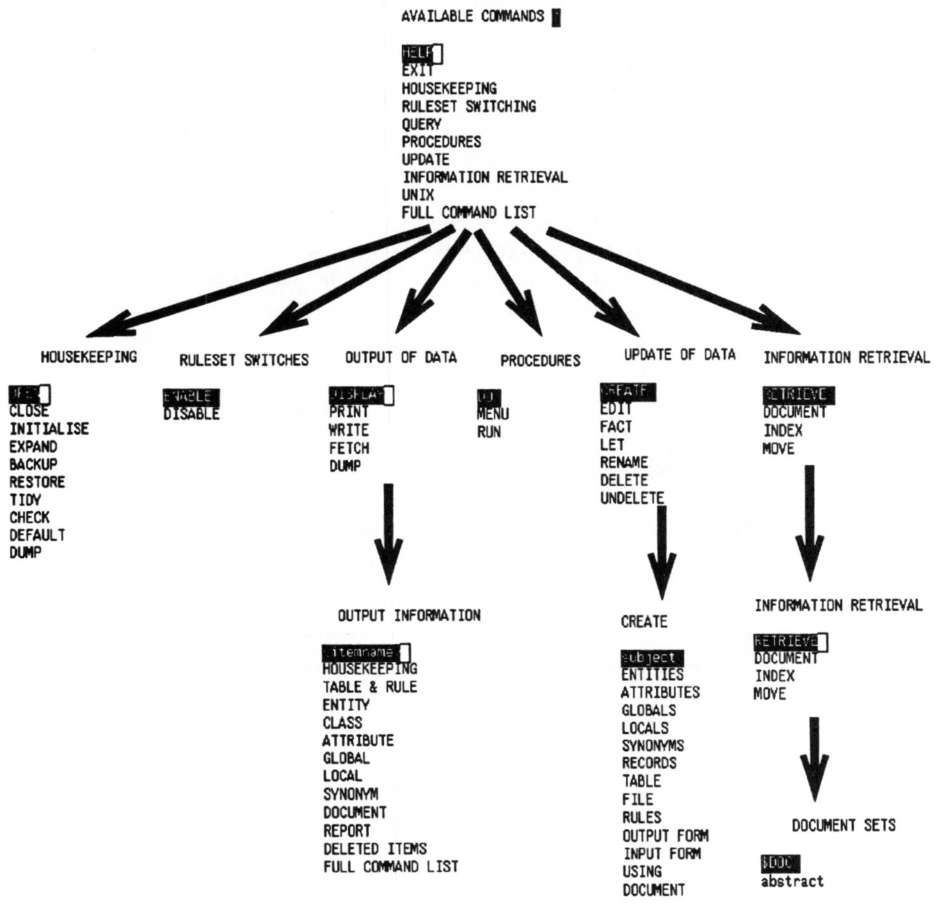

The terminology used in Generis is as follows:

- *Fact* : <subject> <relationship> <property>
- *Subject*: entity
- *Entity*: object or class of objects
- *Property*: entity or an attribute
- *Relationship* : named relationship between the subject and the property

Entities have only names whereas attributes have a name, a type and a value. Generis provides five types of attribute : integer, decimal, date, time and text.

Generic association is represented in Generis by ***is a*** relationships, e.g. book ***is a*** reference. Using the **is a** relationship, one entity is declared to be a member of another, i.e. the latter becomes a class or set containing the former. In general, the upper levels of the class membership structure are specified when the application is designed, while the detailed class memberships are created by the user during data entry.

- *Tables*: store information about named relationships. The relationship can be single-valued or multi-valued. If single valued, the subject may only have one value for each property and this integrity constraint is maintained by the system. Multi-valued tables allow multiple entries for properties of the subject. Entry of information about entities and their relationships is achieved interactively via customised or system default screen forms, on a table or subject basis. Figure 3 shows a system default screen form for the subject book.

Fig 3 Generis Frame for Subject Book

```
Creating records for book
book
book55
has isbn                                           has edition
234-567                                            7
written in       has abstract
1989             abs1

Multi valued records for book
edited by


Multi valued records for book
written by
Kennedy
```

When the user enters data into this frame, Generis defines book55 as both an entity and a member of the class book. Likewise Kennedy is inserted as an entity and a member of the class author. In addition book55 is assigned the given isbn and edition attributes.

Information can also be entered by using the **let** command to assign columns, or via the **fact** command. The fact command requires that any entities used in it are already known to the system, for example,

fact book55 written by Kennedy

would require the prior entry of the following facts

fact book55 is a book

fact kennedy is an author

There is also a range of facilities for data entry from file.

- *Inference rule*: <fact> if <condition>
- *Condition*: any combination of facts, e.g. book is popular if sales >50000

- *Action rule*: similar to inference rule except that the condition can be an external event(s), e.g. specified time, change in data value, use of a particular command. Action rules can be used to effect changes to the knowledgebase or to initiate an external process.
- *Rulesets*: a group of rules
- *Document*: a system file which can be indexed.

The foregoing was a brief overview of Generis' terminology and interface, we now proceed to explore its facilities further through the implementation of an academic bibliographic system.

3. APPLICATION

The identification of an application which calls for all of Generis' features is not an easy undertaking. The authors devoted a considerable amount of time to assessing a variety of candidate areas and concluded that there was no obvious uncontrived application which would exercise all the facilities they wished to explore. This being the case, they opted to create a bibliographic retrieval system which would provide a useful research tool, as well as offering a test environment for Generis, both in terms of assessing the compliance of the product with its advertised capabilities and also its success in meeting the criteria for KBMS as outlined in the literature.[6,7]

The features of Generis the application was specifically intended to address were:

- document management
- class hierarchy
- interface to other systems
- query language
- data entry (forms)

Unfortunately rules proved unnecessary for the application.

In essence, the academic bibliographic retrieval system is an automated version of the academic's card index system, designed to hold not only the usual bibliographic details required for identification/citation, but also personal information such as where the reference was consulted, whether the researcher has a personal copy and if so its identification in his system, a set of keywords and associated with the reference, the text of an abstract or personal notes on the particular bibliographic item. By using Generis' document management facilities to index and search abstracts/personal notes, it was hoped to create an efficient method of organising large amounts of bibliographic material. In order to explore interfacing to other systems, the authors wished to store a variety of citation styles and pipe the output from a Generis search through a standard Unix text formatting utility such as nroff to produce bibliographic output in a predetermined format. The bibliographic system outlined offers a natural hierarchical structure which seems ideal for implementation using inheritance properties.

The primary entity in the system is the item ***reference***, each reference has an associated abstract and keyword list. References can be of different types, for example:

- book
- paper from a book
- paper from proceedings
- paper from a journal
- internal report
- thesis
- unpublished paper, etc

Each of these reference types has a different attribute set. For example, consider the following references which are typical of citations for some of the types listed.

Date, C. J., "An Introduction to Database Systems Volume I", 4th Edition, Addison Wesley, 1986.

Bowers, D. S. "From Data to Database", Van Nostrand Reinhold, 1988.

Atkinson, M.P. & Kulkarni, K.G., "Experimenting with the Functional Data Model", in Databases - Role and Structure, Cambridge University Press, 1984

Bancilhon, F., "Object-Oriented Database Systems", Rapport Technique Altair 16-88, 1988.

Codd, E. F., "Extending the Database Relational Model to Capture more Meaning", ACM TODS, 4, 4, 397-434 , 1979.

Kulkarni, K. G., "Evaluation of Functional Data Models for Database Design and Use", Ph.D., University of Edinburgh, 1983.

From the examples given, it is apparent that all reference types have some common attributes and some extra, specific attributes. For example, they all have a title, abstract and a year in which they were written. However, a book has an attribute publisher, a journal has attributes volume, number and pages, theses have attributes qualification and institution and internal reports have report numbers and institutions. Thus the application is naturally described in terms of entity subtypes; it was therefore expected that the class hierarchy of Generis would model this structure effectively.

4. DATA MODELLING

An entity-relationship approach to modelling the data was adopted, as Generis is based on this method. The original entity-relationship notation proposed by Chen[10] provided facilities for modelling entities, weak entities, attributes, relationships, and existence dependencies, however, it offered no satisfactory way of representing the notion of subtypes (generalisation/specialisation of entities). In particular it is not possible to show that papers, books etc are all references. The standard approach to database design is to produce an entity-relationship diagram for the application domain with all the entities expressed in third normal form. This can then be mapped onto the chosen logical database structure. Although the application seemed to be very straightforward, it proved extremely difficult to find a clear way of representing the structure of the data using the conventional approach, see Figure 4.

Fig 4 Conventional Entity-Relationship Diagram (Chen's notation)

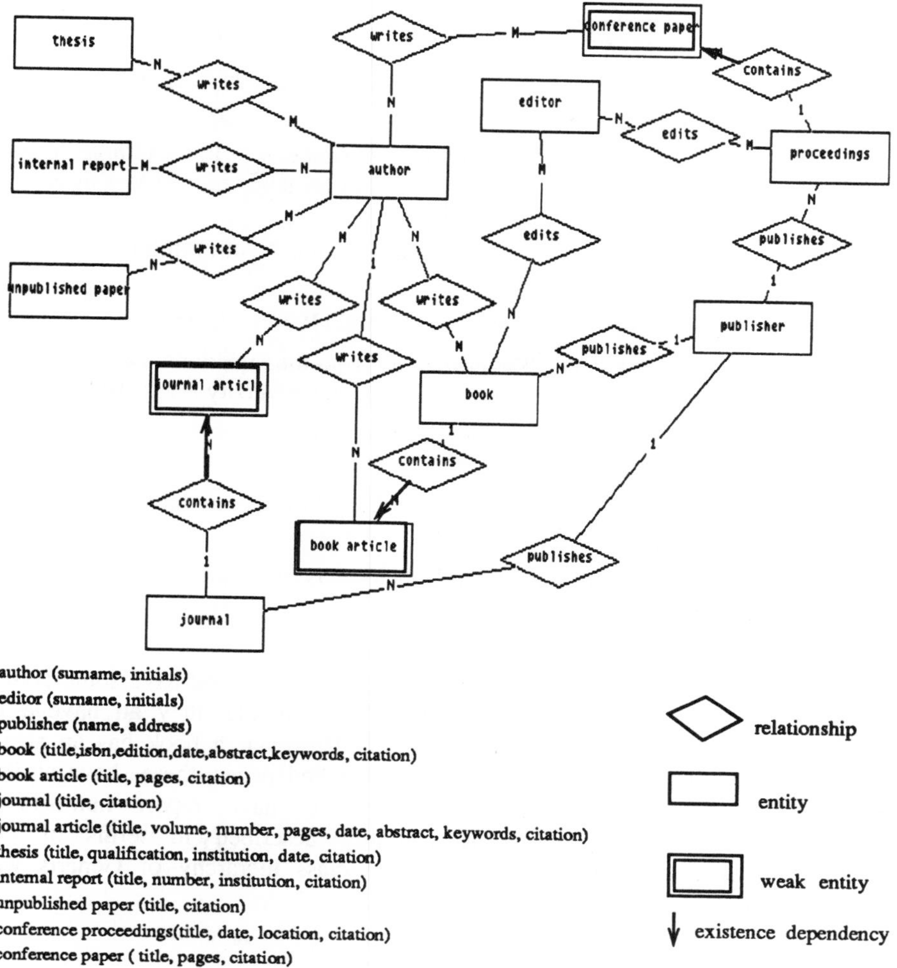

author (surname, initials)
editor (surname, initials)
publisher (name, address)
book (title,isbn,edition,date,abstract,keywords, citation)
book article (title, pages, citation)
journal (title, citation)
journal article (title, volume, number, pages, date, abstract, keywords, citation)
thesis (title, qualification, institution, date, citation)
internal report (title, number, institution, citation)
unpublished paper (title, citation)
conference proceedings(title, date, location, citation)
conference paper (title, pages, citation)

Despite numerous revisions, Figure 4 remains visually chaotic, and fails to convey adequately the inherent structure of the data, due to the lack of specific subtype representation.

Since Chen's original definition of the Entity-Relationship model, a variety of enhancements have been proposed [11,12]. Generis does not insist on entities being normalised and also supports subtyping, it therefore seems inappropriate to adhere to the normalisation process and not to depict subtypes. Figure 5 represents the same information as Figure 4 using conventions adopted by Miller [11], which provide additional notation including that for representing subtypes.

Fig 5 Conceptual Entity-Relationship Model

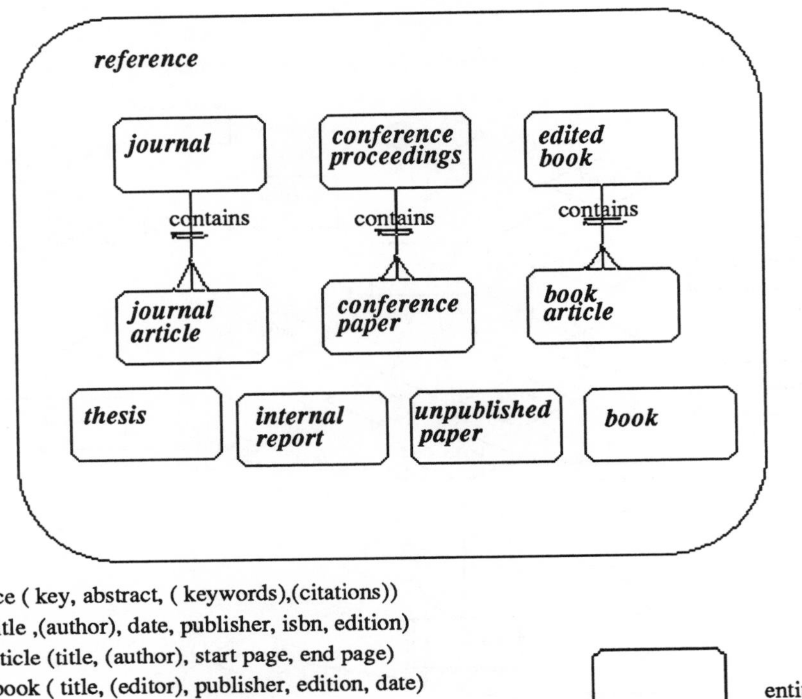

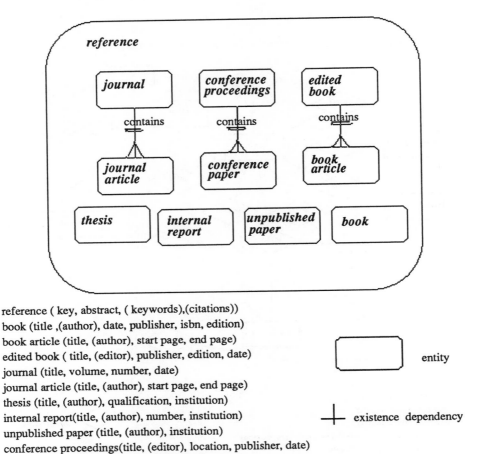

reference (key, abstract, (keywords),(citations))
book (title ,(author), date, publisher, isbn, edition)
book article (title, (author), start page, end page)
edited book (title, (editor), publisher, edition, date)
journal (title, volume, number, date)
journal article (title, (author), start page, end page)
thesis (title, (author), qualification, institution)
internal report(title, (author), number, institution)
unpublished paper (title, (author), institution)
conference proceedings(title, (editor), location, publisher, date)
conference paper (title, (author), start page, end page)

entity

existence dependency

many relationship

This diagram is considerably less cluttered and succeeds in capturing the specialisation of the major entity **reference**. It also has a reduction in the number of entities as we can now consider **author, editor** and **publisher** as attributes of the different types of **reference.** This is how the authors conceptually visualise the entities which are to be held in the knowledgebase. From the list of attributes associated with Figure 5, it can be seen that there are many common between entities. This suggests that there should be further subtyping of the entities to completely remove commonality. Figure 6 shows the result of this process.

Although Figure 6 better captures the hierarchical nature of the entity structures, the same information could be represented in other diagrammatic forms and there is no ready means of determining whether a representation is complete, semantically correct or preferable to semantically equivalent alternatives.

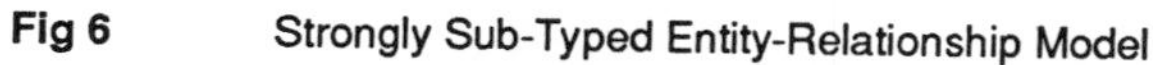

Fig 6 Strongly Sub-Typed Entity-Relationship Model

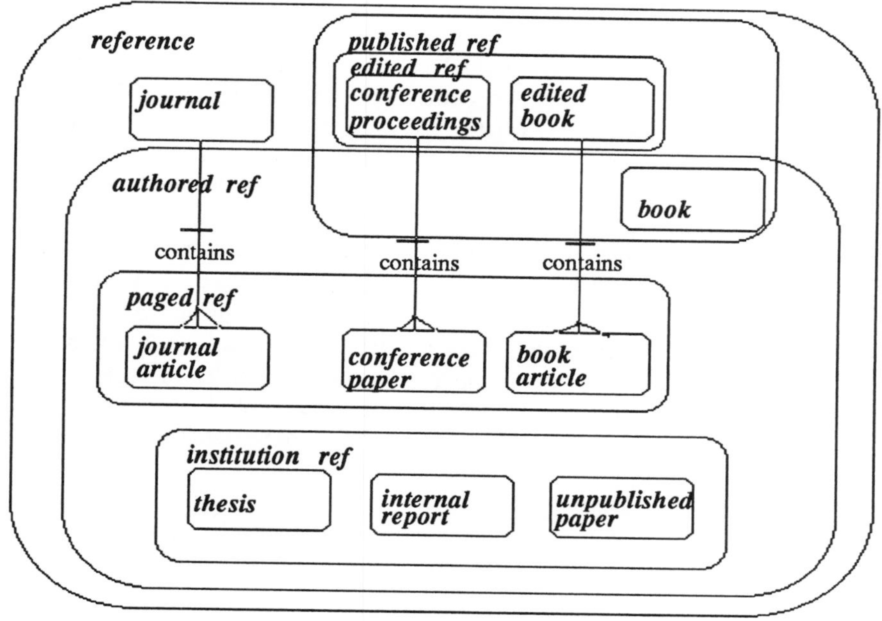

reference (key, title, date, abstract, (keywords), (citations))
published ref (publisher)
edited ref ((editor))
authored ref ((author))
paged ref (papertitle, start page, end page)
institution ref (institution)
book (isbn, edition)
book article ()
edited book ()
journal (volume, number))
journal article ()
thesis (qualification)
internal report (number)
unpublished paper ()
conference proceedings (location)
conference paper ()

The representation of inheritance necessarily involves the creation of abstract entities, such as **authored ref**, which have no real existence in the application domain - the choice of such entities is not obvious. Differentiating between entities and attributes and how best to incorporate inheritance is deceptively problematic even in an application area as well understood as this one. These difficulties are confounded not only by Generis' lack of a suitable design methodology but also by its unorthodox and occasionally inconsistent terminology which causes unnecessary confusion. We refer to this problem in the discussion section which follows.

5. IMPLEMENTATION USING GENERIS

The first step in implementing the application was to map the entity-relationship model on to Generis' structures. This was done by creating tables for entities and grouping in them associated attributes as properties. Tables were also used to represent the relationships between entities, 1:1 and 1:N relationships being modelled by single-valued tables and M:N relationships by multi-valued tables. Single-valued tables represent at least first normal form relations whereas multi-valued tables represent non-first normal form relations. Existence dependency was represented by setting the *restriction* on the property to **<> UNKNOWN**. The generic information inherent in Figure 6 was captured using the ***is a*** facility. Generis includes an information retrieval facility in the form of a datatype **document.** Documents are external text files which can be associated with an entity by declaring a property to be of type document. This allows automatic indexing and was considered to be suitable for the implementation of the property **abstract** of **reference.**

Figure 7 shows the entities, attributes and tables which were defined in the knowledgebase, and Figure 8 overpage gives the structure of the tables.

Fig 7 Knowledgebase Description

ENTITY	CLASS
reference	
published ref	reference
authored ref	reference
journal	reference
book	published ref authored ref
edited ref	published ref
paged ref	authored ref
institution ref	authored ref
conference proceedings	edited ref
edited book	edited ref
conference paper	paged ref
journal article	paged ref
thesis	institution ref
internal report	institution ref
editor	
author	
publisher	
unpublished paper	Institution ref
book article	paged ref

ATTRIBUTE	TYPE
integer	INTEGER
decimal	DECIMAL
text	TEXT
date	DATE
time	TIME
qualification	TEXT
report number	INTEGER
volume	INTEGER
number	INTEGER
title	TEXT
year	INTEGER
isbn	TEXT
edition	INTEGER
start page	INTEGER
end page	INTEGER
institution	TEXT
location	TEXT

Fig 8 Table Structures

Table	Entity	Type	Attribute	Attribute	Attribute
[thesis]	thesis	[SV]	for the degree of qualification (text)		
[internal report]	internal report	[SV]	has report number report number (int)		
[conference paper]	conference paper	[SV]	is in conference proceedings (ent)		
[journal article]	journal article	[SV]	is in journal (ent)		
[reference]	reference	[SV]	has title title (text)	written in year (int)	has abstract abstract (doc)
[book]	book	[SV]	has isbn isbn (text)	has edition edition (int)	
[published ref]	published ref	[SV]	is published by publisher (ent)		
[book article]	book article	[SV]	is in book (ent)		
[edited book]	edited book	[SV]	has isbn isbn (text)		
[paged ref]	paged ref	[SV]	has start page start page (int)	has end page end page (int)	
[keywords]	reference	[MV]	has keyword keyword (ent)		
[conference proceedings]	conference proceedings	[SV]	was located in location (text)		
[institution ref]	institution ref	[SV]	is from institution (text)		
[edited ref]	edited ref	[MV]	is edited by editor (ent)		
[authored ref]	authored ref	[MV]	is written by author (ent)		
[journal]	journal	[SV]	has volume volume (int)	has number number (int)	
[author]	author	[MV]	writes authored ref (ent)		
[editor]	editor	[MV]	edits edited ref (ent)		
[keywordrefs]	keyword	[MV]	is about reference (ent)		
[citation]	refererence	[MV]	is cited in citation (ent)		
[citationrefs]	citation	[MV]	cites reference (ent)		

Defining entities using Generis was very straightforward as the user is only asked for an entity name and a class, if any, to which that entity belongs. Creating tables required further analysis of the kind of relations being modelled. A relation is expressed as a fact in the form,

subject relationship property

where the subject and/or property may be compound. A compound subject is made up of a first subject and secondary subjects. There is a named relationship between the first subject and any secondary subjects and between the compound subject and each property, for example,

supplied by costs

part

supplier cost

models the situation where the cost of a part depends on who supplied it. The questions Generis asked to elicit this information were confusing, for example, initially it was thought that **first subject class name** referred to the entity name, but in fact what was required was an attribute of the entity, preferably the identifier. Many of the subjects in this application were members of the class **reference**, but subjects are of type entity, which is restricted to 32 characters. For this reason, it was not possible to use the full title of a reference as the identifier although it was the preferred candidate, being an attribute common to all references. Instead the authors adopted a unique key system based on the author and date of the reference, e.g. Ken89a.

Having supplied a first subject class name, the user is then prompted for the entities, which with the subject, help identify each record in the table, i.e. any secondary subjects. Again, what the system requires here are what the authors would normally call attributes of the entity (subject). In Generis, attributes (properties) may be of type entity and secondary subjects must be of type entity. The user does not have to supply any, but is then asked if 'these ***fields*** are sufficient to identify each record uniquely'. If the user responds **n,** he/she is informed that a sequence number is being added to the key to uniquely identify the record. If the response is **y** the user is then asked if duplicate subject values are permitted. If they are allowed, the system again supplies a sequence number to identify individual records.

The conceptual difference between a multi-valued table and a single-valued table with multiple records is not immediately apparent. The main difference is the use made of the class hierarchy at query evaluation time. Multiple records for the same subject have the property values combined into one value in single-valued tables with multiple records. For example, if a subject, animal, has a single-valued, multiple record property, colour, and on execution of a query, the resulting colours are *muddy* and *dull*, the system would seek a common member of the classes *muddy* and *dull*, say *brown*, and respond with the answer *brown* as the animal's colour. If on the other hand the result of the query was *brown* and *grey*, where the classes *brown* and *grey* had no common member, then the query would result in a conflict because the system could not resolve the two colours into a single value. Another difference is that when creating a subject which has a multi-valued table(s) associated with it, the frame created by Generis prompts the user for multiple values of the properties in the multi-valued table(s), whereas it prompts for only one value for single-valued properties with duplicate records allowed. It is however possible to enter equivalent data in either format.

The user is next requested to input the property names, their datatype, status and relationship to the subject and any restrictions on that subject. The status of a property may be mandatory, optional or computed. If the property is mandatory the user is not compelled to supply a value for that property, rather optional/mandatory affects subsequent queries on the knowledgebase. If a mandatory property is not supplied when details are entered, the value for that property is set to UNKNOWN, whereas the value of an absent optional property would remain blank. The result of this distinction on subsequent queries involving mandatory properties is that the set of records satisfying the query will be those which match the query condition plus those for which the property value is UNKNOWN e.g. "display for book article is in book1" will retrieve book articles in book1 and book articles for which the value of book is unknown.

To insist on a value being entered for a mandatory property, the restriction facility can be used, for example, specifying **is in book <> UNKNOWN**. Restrictions can also be used to insist that, for example, the book in which a book article is found already exists in the knowledgebase. This is done by setting the restriction on **is in book to exists**. A problem with the restriction facility is that it is not possible to constrain the first subject class name, which as this is the key (or part of the key) presents an integrity risk. Secondary subject class names may however have restrictions placed on them.

It is worth noting that **author**, **editor**, **publisher**, **key** and **citation** although identified as attributes in Figure 6, were implemented as entities in Generis to allow the formulation of inverse rules such as 'author writes authored ref if authored ref is written by author'. These were found necessary to enable queries such as "which references were written by Codd?", because the result of the expansion of inference rules must be compatible with an existing table structure. It is unsatisfactory to have to create tables of the correct structure before queries can be executed, the display of temporary data should not necessitate the prior creation of tables. Inverse relationships must be explicitly defined in Generis and presently this is most easily done by defining inverse rules, however DSL are evaluating more concise methods of specifying this information.

The implementation thus far seemed promising but on starting to use the system some unexpected problems emerged. Entering data for a particular entity worked reasonably well, see Figure 9 for an example of entering a **book article**.

Fig 9 Entering Book Article

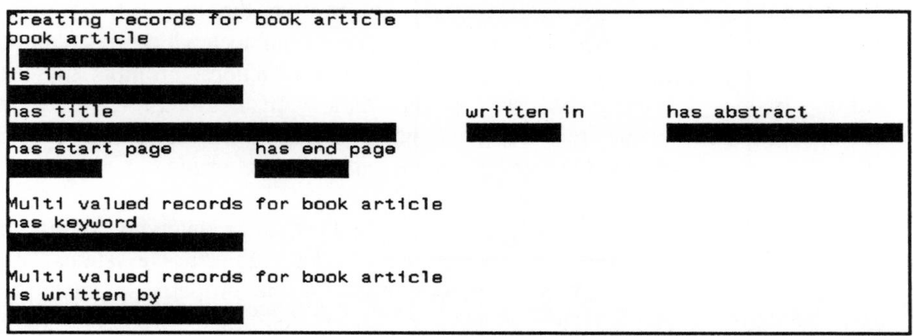
Creating records for book article
book article

is in

has title
written in
has abstract
has start page
has end page
Multi valued records for book article
has keyword
Multi valued records for book article
is written by

When creating a book article the default input frame presented by Generis not only prompts for data directly associated with the subject **book article**, but also properties of entities of which **book article** is a subtype, e.g. **written in** and **has abstract** are properties of **reference**. This proved very satisfactory. One drawback with data entry was that the **is in book** property only required the identifier of the book entity, whereas the user would normally expect to give the full details of the book in which the article appeared, when citing such a reference. The user would therefore have to create a book record for that book. This is tedious. Originally the subjects of tables author and editor were their surnames, and the secondary subject, initials, was required in both cases to provide unique identification. However, there were two problems with this approach. The first was that, for example, on entry of book details, the input frame omitted the initials field for author thereby making it impossible to associate a unique author with a particular book. To circumvent this, it was necessary for the table for book to have a property initials declared. The second difficulty was that on attempting to enter 'Date' as an author's name, the system rejected the input because 'Date' is a reserved datatype!. For both these reasons, it was decided to incorporate initials as part of the subject, the format used is shown in Figure 10 below. DSL are currently addressing the second problem.

Sample data was inserted into the knowledgebase and a selection of typical queries was executed including: display all references for a given keyword - this can be expressed in different ways depending on the desired results, for example,

display reference for database

results in Figure 10.

Fig 10 Query - display reference for database

KEY	is about REFERENCE of key
database	Dat88 Ken78 Loc80 Zan81 Mcl82 Ked80 Kum87 Cod70 Ken89

whereas *display title, 'is written by' author, year, reference for database* results in Figure 11.

Fig 11 Query - display title, 'is written by' author, year, reference for database

KEY	is about REFERENCE of key	has title TITLE of reference	is written by AUTHOR of reference	written in YEAR of reference
database	Dat88	A Guide to DB2	Date, C.J.	1988
	Ken78	Data and Reality	Kent, W.	1978
	Ked80	Non-Two Phase Locking Protocols with Shared and Exclusive Locks	Kedem, Z.	1980
			Silberschatz, A.	
	Kum87	Semantics Based Transaction Management Techniques for Replicated Data	Kumar, A.	1987
			Stonebraker, M.	
	Cod70	A Relational Model for Large Shared Data Banks	Codd, E.	1970
	Ken89	The Generis Knowledgebase Management System, An Exploratory Review	Kennedy, J.B.	1989
			Crerar, M.A.	

In the second form of the query, specific properties about references are requested, and in addition, a relationship **'is written by'** is given. If the relationship is not specified, the system presents a selection of ambiguous paths. These occur when the system detects an intersection(s) in the class hierarchy. For example, in the present case some **authors** are also **editors,** therefore the user must specify which of the two paths is to be taken. The result of queries like this could be better - if the user has specified that the author is desired, the system should take this into consideration when formulating the result. Generis treats the whole knowledgebase as content addressable and does not use column names to choose between valid paths. However, relationship names and the **of** phrase can be used to specify unambiguous queries.

Having defined the generic type **reference** the system successfully provided complete information on a reference irrespective of its specific type, for example book article or book, which have different attributes. The query necessary to request any reference for a specific key is as follows:

display for reference of 'key' or title or author 'is written by' of authored ref or editor 'is edited by ' of edited ref or title of journal or volume or number or start page or end page or qualification or isbn or publisher or report number or location

This was a difficult query to formulate and cumbersome to enter as all the possible attributes of a reference had to be specified in a disjunctive list, nevertheless it produced the desired result. Generis offers no facilities to store such commands as macros, but they can be executed from command files or incorporated in menus.

The following queries are of a similar style, and can be specified in a similar format:

display all references for a given author

display all references cited in a particular paper

The document facility proved useful in that it was possible to query the knowledgebase on keywords indexed automatically by the system, to produce the attributes of the reference which had those keywords in its abstract, for example:

display for (reference or title or author 'is written by' of authored ref) and !!database

This query displays the reference key, title and author for any reference with the keyword 'database' indexed in its abstract and thereby obviates the need for the attribute key of reference which was unnecessarily introduced in an attempt to achieve the same result. It was also possible, using the reporting facility of Generis to generate reports on references which displayed the contents of any abstract for the reference held in the system. Figure 12 shows the result of a user defined report requesting the reference key, title, author and contents of the abstract. Both the abstract and the keywords used for indexing were stored in external files.

Fig 12 Report on Reference showing Abstract Content

```
Cod70

                    A Relational Model for Large Shared Data Banks

Codd, E.

Future users of large data banks must be protected from having
to know how the data is organized in the machine.
A prompting service which supplies such information
is not a satisfactory solution. Activities of users at
terminals and most application programmers should remain
unaffected when the internal representation of data
is changed and even when some aspects of the external
representation are changed. Changes in data representation
will often be needed as a result of changes in query, update,
and report traffic and natural growth in the
types of stored information.

Existing noninferential, formatted data systems provide
users with tree-structured files or slightly more
```

We can summarise the performance of Generis' query facility by noting that queries which specified the properties to be displayed produced expected results, whereas those which relied on the system to determine the properties, often produced unanticipated results.

6. DISCUSSION

At the close of this exploratory review a working implementation of the bibliographic knowledgebase has been achieved which, providing queries are carefully framed, provides most of the retrieval facilities required. However, our intention of interfacing to Unix-based text formatting facilities has not been met in time for this report.

As highlighted in the data modelling section above, the lack of a suitable design methodology for working with Generis made modelling a rather uncertain process. Two related problems were experienced, one was the modelling of the domain in terms of general KBMS concepts, including inheritance, the second was the refinement of that more abstract model through the process of mapping onto Generis' specific features. Lacking guidelines for both activities inevitably resulted in an experimental approach which was hard to evaluate other than pragmatically. The lack of a suitable design method is an impediment to Generis being more widely useful. This lack of accessibility is exacerbated by the user interface, which is poor both in screen presentation and ability to reflect the status of the knowledgebase. DSL are aware of these problems and are currently consulting with the authors in both areas.

The implementation section mentioned the potential confusion between subjects and identifiers arising from the treatment of the subject not only as a type but as an identifier for that type. This is manifest at the design stage where the implementer , on creation of a subject, for example, **person**, must be aware that the identifier for person will also bear the subject name. This is unfortunate as it would be better to allow the declaration of a more meaningful identifier, in this case perhaps name or national insurance number. This confusion arises again at the data entry stage where the user may be prompted for a data value, **person,** having no idea what this designates.

Apart from setting out to explore as many of Generis' novel features as possible through the implementation of a small application, we also wished to discover whether the product succeeded in addressing the perceived shortcomings of existing database systems outlined on page 3. The findings here were mixed. Generis provided no significant advance in support of multiple schemas, user interface or handling of incomplete, fuzzy and time varying data. As mentioned above, Generis does permit a mandatory field to have a value UNKNOWN, but this is only of limited usefulness - one would like to be able to insert what is known, for example, age > 60 and have such information evaluated on interrogation. Generis' data definition facility allows the addition of columns to tables without the need to delete and recreate the tables, however, changing the type of a property is more difficult and necessitates the deletion of the property followed by creation of the new type. With regard to semantic integrity checking, Generis offers some scope through the use of rules and restrictions, but its main advantage over existing DBMSs is the capacity for deductive inference. This worked well, but as mentioned above, the need to formulate inverse rules to effect satisfactory responses was an unwelcome complication. Finally, on the question of hardware, Generis was designed around the notion of a generic associative memory as described above, but the special purpose hardware is not yet available for testing, performance will no doubt improve when the supporting hardware appears.

The authors should stress that Generis provides significant features which were not examined by this application, action rules are chief among these, and it is hoped to include an assessment of these in a future report.

As a result of this study a summary of bugs found, confusions experienced and suggested improvements have been lodged with DSL and several of the problems have already been eliminated.

Despite its shortcomings, Generis does integrate knowledgebase and database approaches. The authors intend to use Generis as the main software support for an honours year module in KBMS in the forthcoming academic session.

ACKNOWLEDGMENT

The authors would like to thank Deductive Systems Ltd., for the cooperative spirit in which they have collaborated during the beta testing of Generis, and in particular, Charlie Nicols for his telephone 'helpline' and perceptive review of an earlier draft of this paper.

BIBLIOGRAPHY

1 Newell A and Simon H A GPS, A Program that Simulates Human Thought, In *Computers and Thought*, E A Feigenbaum and J Feldman (Eds), McGraw Hill, New York, USA, (1963)

2 McDermott J, R1 : A Rule-based Configurer of Computer Systems, *Artificial Intelligence*,vol 19 (1982) pp 39-88

3 Buchanan, B G and Shortliffe, E H *The MYCIN Experiments of the Stanford Heuristic Programming Project*, Addison-Wesley, Reading, MA, USA, (1984)

4 Hayes-Roth, F *Building Expert Systems*, Addison-Wesley, Reading, MA, USA, (1982)

5 Bratko, I *Prolog Programming for Artificial Intelligence*, Addison-Wesley, Reading, MA, USA, (1986)

6 Frost, R A Introduction to Knowledge Base Systems, Collins, London, (1986)

7 Nijssen G M From Databases to Knowledge Bases : A Technical Comparison, In *Databases : State of the Art Report*, P J H King (Ed), Pergamon Press, London, (1984)

8 McGregor D R and Malone J R, The Fact Database An Entity-Based System using Inference, In *Entity-Relationship Approach to Information Modelling and Analysis*, P P Chen (Ed), Elsevier Science Publishers B V., (1983)

9 McGregor D R, McInnes S and Henning M, An Architecture for Associative Processing of Large Knowledge Bases (LKBs), *The Computer Journal*, 30:5, 1987

10 Chen P P, The Entity Relationship Model : Towards a Unified View of Data, *ACM Transactions on Database Systems*, 1, 1, 9-36, (1976).

11 Miller D R, Strategic data Analysis, In S R Holloway (Ed) *Data Analysis in Practice*, The British Computer society's Database Specialist Group, (1985).

12 Chen P P, *Entity-Relationship Approach to Information Modeling and Analysis*, Elsevier Science Publishers B V, (1983).

QUESTIONS

Mr. W. Stein (British Telecom).
WS. You produced these models of the structure you wanted; is there any way of displaying these models to a user?

Ms. J. Kennedy.
JK. From Generis?

W.S. Yes.

JK. Not really. Generis has some facilities to display the class structure; so you can say DISPLAY CLASS, and it will show you how the class hierarchy is designed. And you can also ask for things like DISPLAY ENTITIES and it will tell you all the entities in the system. But there's no pictorial representation. I think there should be, I like to see pictures, they mean more to me. I'd like to see a nice pictorial representation of this sort of information.

WS. The other thing you were saying was, that it went through a number of cycles of building up the structure you wanted. Was that because every time you wanted to make a change you had to throw out how it was before, or because you'd just decided that the whole structure was wrong?

JK. Because the whole overall structure was wrong. I think because we had never used anything like Generis that could incorporate rules etc. It was really due to unfamiliarity with Generis. So we tried modelling one way, then tried it other ways, until we found a way that actually suited Generis best and which we understood.

WS. So it's not the sort of system, (and there are ones like that), where you have to know exactly the structure you want before you actually start building? You can, sort of, incrementally construct your data structure?

JK. Yes, you can incrementally construct it, but I'm not sure to what level. If you're doing major reconstruction, it might become a problem. But, yes, you can change it.

Mr. R. Williams (Warwick University).
RW. Have you evaluated the performance of the system with large volumes of data?

JK. No. We've really been looking at modelling and designing and implemention, how to make use of the facilities?

RW. Well I suspect that if you're storing the text of the abstracts in there, the amount of data on a real system would be very large indeed.

JK. The text and the abstracts aren't actually stored in the knowledge base; they are stored in external file stores. It's only the class hierarchy that's stored by Generis.

WS. You seem to be creating a lot of artificial entities. Can you hide these from the end users?

JK. You can. As you saw, I say, "Right, I want to create BOOK ARTICLE." Generis will pop up the data entry form, which has all the attributes of a book article which it has inherited from all these different artificial entities. So from that point of view, it can. The only unfortunate thing is that it doesn't seem to do that at query time. At query time, what it does, basically, is list all the attributes about a reference but not all the attributes of every different type of reference, unless you specifically request it to do so, which is a shame. Because Generis can inherit attributes at entry time, we feel that it should be able to do so at output time as well in order to improve querying.

15 Quantitative Evaluation Method for Intelligent Interface to a Document Database

S. Kinoshita, Y. Kanou, T. Takahashi, Y. Kobayashi

Abstract

A quantitative evaluation method for an intelligent interface to a document database which can understand ambiguous queries is discussed. In addition, understanding methods for ambiguous queries are proposed, and the understanding methods are validated by the evaluation method.

To retrieve documents according to an ambiguous query requires two phases. Phase 1 clarifies its requirement, and phase 2 achieves the retrieval. Keyword efficiency is used to evaluate the intermediate stage (phase 1), and retrieval efficiency is used to evaluate the final stages (phase 2) of document retrieval.

Two methods of understanding, understanding through dialogue and understanding by analogy, are proposed, and are validated by the evaluation method. Both introduce user models. The evaluation experiment shows that high keyword efficiency is obtained for both methods. At the same time, some problems are revealed.

The major problem is that retrieval efficiency is not high in spite of high Keyword efficiency. By analyzing the evaluation results, approaches to solving the problem are derived. That is, understanding queries from retrieval results (feedback) is shown to be hopeful and useful. The approach also suggests the integration of the two methods of understanding.

1 Introduction

Using traditional natural language interfaces[1] for information retrieval presupposes that users can completely specify their requirements in a natural language[5][6]. In document retrieval, users want to retrieve what they don't know. Therefore, document database users are forced to clearly express their incomplete or ambiguous requirements. Moreover, there are several levels of question formation, from vague to definite[4]. Natural language queries are regarded as being on a rather vague level.

The incompleteness or ambiguity of the natural language queries to document databases is assumed to be inherent, and can be critical in document retrieval. Natural language interfaces to document databases are required to allow incomplete or ambiguous queries.

This paper proposes an evaluation method for a natural language interface to a document database which can understand ambiguous queries using keyword efficiency and retrieval efficiency. Document retrieval systems were evaluated by means of retrieval efficiency (precision/recall). This is sufficient when users can completely specify their requirements. However, it is not sufficient when the users' queries are ambiguous or incomplete. Thus, it is impossible to evaluate whether or not the users' requirements are extracted by means of retrieval efficiency. An index parameter of the degree of extracting the users' requirements is sufficient for evaluating a natural language interface which allows ambiguous queries. In this paper, understanding of the users' requirements is regarded as extracting a keyword set which satisfies the users' requirements. Keyword efficiency is used to evaluate the extracted keyword set.

This paper also proposes ambiguous natural language query understanding methods. Browsing approaches[2][3] are also investigated to clarify achieving adequate document retrieval from vague requirements. They graphically show the document classification schema and help to search adequate documents. On the other hand, our methods clarify the user's ambiguous requirement by natural language understanding strategy. Natural language is preferable for casual users who are not familiar with computers. The evaluating method using keyword and retrieval efficiency is validated by showing that these understanding methods can be well evaluated.

2 Document Retrieval Model and its Evaluation

2.1 A Document Retrieval Model

Ambiguous natural language queries which are approached in this paper are categorized as follows:

(1) Users' own words or idiosyncratic usage.
A user may use his own jargon or terms with a special or uncommon meaning.

(2) Lack of restriction.
A user may not express the terms which restrict his needs.

(3) Over-restriction.
A user may use excessive or over-restrictive terms,such as examples, to express his needs.

In this paper, users' queries which contain the above ambiguities are understood to achieve adequate document retrieval.

In our approach, the document database is regarded as traditional, that is, keyword indexed. Figure 1 shows our model of a document retrieval system. A user's requirement is expressed by a query in a natural language. In this stage, the ambiguity shown before may be contained in the query.

A user's query is processed in two phases:

(phase 1) Synthesizing a meaning representation
The ambiguity contained in the query is recovered and the user's requirement is clarified. The result is represented by keywords and their relationships (meaning representation).

(phase 2) Retrieving a document database
The document database is retrieved according to the meaning representation. Keywords and their relationships contained in the meaning representation are used for the retrieval.

2.2 An Evaluation of a Document Retrieval

To evaluate retrieval based on an ambiguous query, it is desirable to evaluate the two phases both separately and together. Keyword efficiency is used as an index parameter for phase 1, and retrieval efficiency is used for phase 2. Many document retrieval systems were evaluated by means of retrieval efficiency. This means that

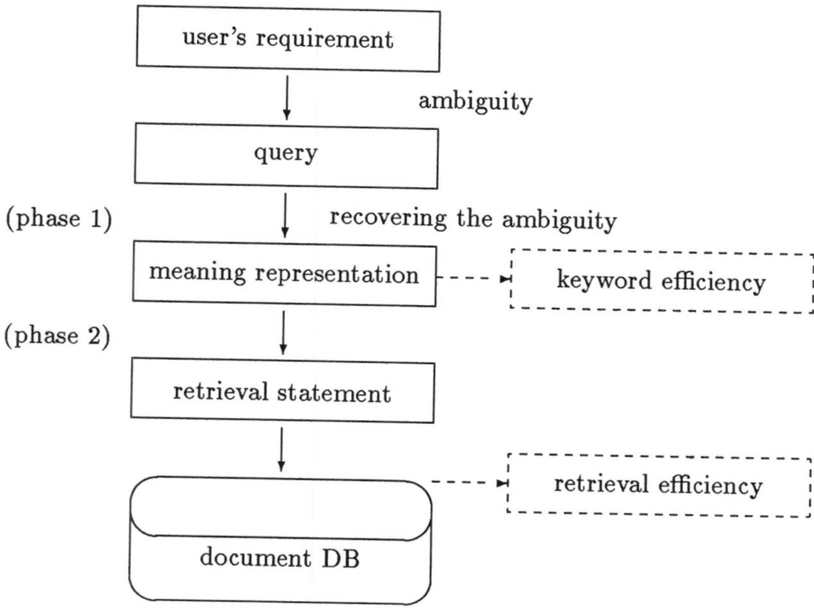

Figure 1: Document Retrieval Model

they were evaluated only in phase 2. No systems were evaluated in the intermediate stages (phase 1) or co-relationships between phase 1 and phase 2 as described here.

keyword efficiency

Meaning representation of a query is constructed in phase 1. Keyword efficiency (keyword precision factor, Kp_q, and keyword recall factor, Kr_q) are defined using the extracted keywords from the meaning representation.

$$Kp_q = \frac{|\ Eq'\ |}{|\ Eq\ |}$$

$$Kr_q = \frac{|\ Eq'\ |}{|\ Pq'\ |}$$

where, $|\ Pq'\ |$: number of keywords suitable for the user's request
$|\ Eq\ |$: number of keywords extracted
$|\ Eq'\ |$: number of keywords suitable for the user's request within the extracted keywords

retrieval efficiency

Retrieval efficiency is defined by the retrieval precision factor (Rp_q) and retrieval recall factor (Rr_q) which are calculated similar to keyword efficiency by replacing "keywords" with "documents". Retrieval efficiency is represented by the "precision/recall curve" in ordered output[9].

3 Query Understanding Methods

3.1 Basic Ideas

Proposed methods for phase 1 are described. These methods map a user's query to the domain knowledge of the retrieved document. The mapped part of the domain knowledge is regarded as the meaning representation. The domain knowledge is, in a sense, the thesaurus of the document database. Basic ideas are as follows:

(a) Introducing user models
The domain knowledge is prepared for each user to understand his own words. Moreover, hidden requirements are inferred using expressed words and the user model.

(b) Understanding by two methods
The first resolves the ambiguity (for example, unknown words) by querying the user (understanding through dialogue). User models are constructed through dialogues. The other is a rough mapping without dialogues using words and relationships between words which are contained in a query (understanding by analogy).

3.2 Representation of Query and User Model

Users' queries to document databases and the domain knowledge can be represented in the same notation because the queries express what the users want to retrieve, and the domain knowledge expresses what is retrieved. In the query, a user expresses the concepts and relationships between concepts of his requirement. Concepts are instantiated by nouns, and the relationships between concepts are instantiated by relationships between nouns.

Table 1 shows the relationships between nouns recognized in example queries. Approximately 250 sample queries ware analyzed to categorize the relationships. Occurrences shown in Table 1 are derived from 136 examples out of 250. The sum of occurrences is not 136 because there are multiple relationships in a query.

Japanese is a nonconfigurational language. That is, word position doesn't control the meaning. Rather, noun attached words (connecting words) control the meaning. The attached words represent the relationships between nouns in the queries.

The "miscellaneous" relationship in Table 1 contains bibliographic items such as authors, publication dates, references, etc. "Miscellaneous" and "place" relation-

Table 1: A classification of relationships between terms in queries

relationship type	relationship	occurrences	connecting words
single		19	
parallel	coexistence	40	*to, oyobi, ya, matawa, aruiwa*
hierarchical	restriction	106	*no, deno, heno, niokeru, nitaisuru*
	exemplification	5	*wofukumu, nadono, tositeno, tokuni, tatoeba*
lateral	means	24	*niyoru, womotiita, wotukatta*
	purpose	5	*notameno, nimotiiru womokutekitosuru womokutekitosita*
	cause and effect	9	*niyoru*
	place	7	*deno niokeru no*
miscellaneous		7	

ships are not implied in our experiment because they do not directly express the contents of requirement.

(a) Representation of Query

The query is represented according to the relationships shown in Table 1. The query is parsed using the connecting words, and the extracted relationships are represented into a case frame-like expression which represents the relationship name and related two nouns.

The representation of the parsed query is shown in an example below.

(natural language query)

Imi-nettowāku <u>*niyoru*</u> *taishou-sekai-moderu* <u>*no*</u> *hyougen nituite sirabetai.* (in Japanese)

(I want papers about the representation of domain models in semantic networks.)

Underlined words are connecting words.

(parsed query)

(means (restriction representation domain-models) semantic-network)

where representation ⇔ *hyougen*

domain-models ⇔ *taishou-sekai moderu*

semantic-network ⇔ *imi-nettowāku*

(⇔ shows English and Japanese correspondence)

(b) Representation of User Model

A user model is a user's individual thesaurus which contains his own classification schema or words. A user model is represented in a semantic network which consists of concept nodes corresponding to nouns and links corresponding to the

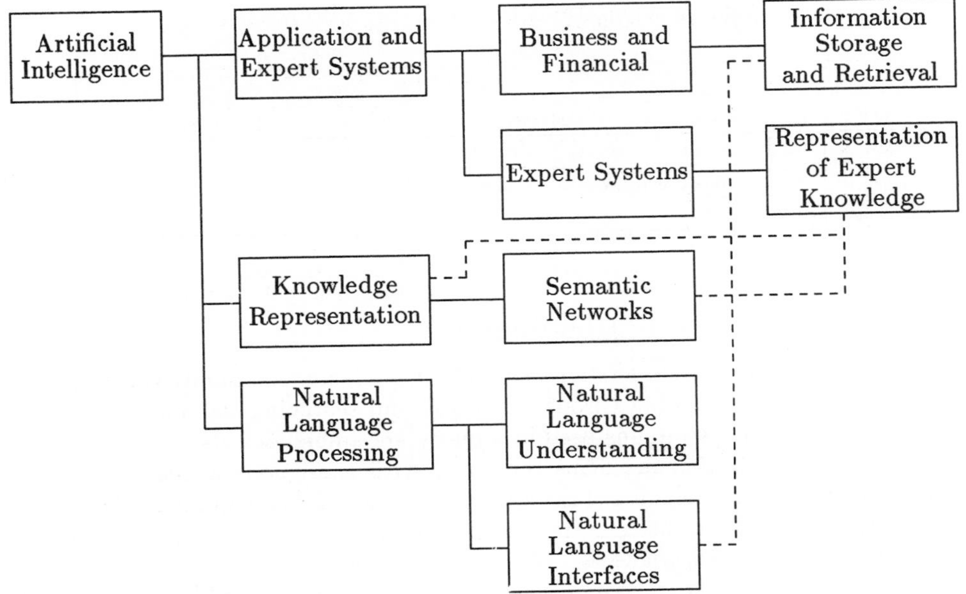

Figure 2: Example of the user model

relationships between nouns. The meaning of a query can be represented within the context of the query. On the other hand, a user model must be represented within the context of all documents or all queries. A hierarchical relationship which holds on every context is most universal. Therefore, a user model is represented in the hierarchical classification schema based on the relationships shown in Table 1.

Figure 2 is an example of the user model. Concept nodes consist of keyword nodes which correspond to indices of documents, and user's word nodes. Links consist of four types of relationships as shown below:

- hierarchy: ancestor-descendant relationship such as "is_a"
- synonym: two nouns represent the same concept
- qualification: one is qualified by the other such as:
  - restriction
  - means
  - purpose
  - cause and effect
- association: other relationships

Hierarchy relationships are shown in solid lines, and the other relationships are shown in dashed lines in Figure 2.

Each link has a level which represents the degree of relationship, that is, "conscious", "not conscious", "initial". The level of a link is used to infer hidden requirements from expressed words. The user model can initially be defined as a typical one, each user model is copied from the typical one, and is modified and added to through dialogues with the user.

Table 2: Operations for modifying user models

	operation
OP1	modify the level of hierarchy, association, or qualification link
OP2	add new user's word node and link to it
OP3	add new link between existing nodes
OP4	delete link

3.3 Mapping through Dialogue

The first method to understand a user's query is understanding through dialogue. It consists of mapping through dialogue and searching the hidden requirement. It assumes that all nouns used in a query are ambiguous.

Mapping through dialogue maps the query with ambiguous nouns to the user model by clarifying the meaning of the ambiguous nouns through questions/answers. That is, the system asks the user the real requirement of the ambiguous nouns, or the meaning of unknown nouns.

The ambiguous nouns are assumed that they should be replaced by more specific or detailed nouns to describe the user's requirement. Therefore, detailed nouns or related nouns of the ambiguous nouns are inquired to the user to clarify his/her requirement. As a result, the ambiguous nouns are mapped to detailed nouns or related nouns which are specified by the user. The unknown nouns are assumed that they should be replaced by known nouns. Therefore, the user is required to explain the unknown nouns by known nouns. As a result, the unknown nouns are mapped to known nouns.

Mapping results are acquired by the user model. These correspond to OP1 and OP2 of Table 2, respectively. Moreover, if the user refers to a new relationship or denies an existing relationship in his/her query or answer, this is also acquired (OP3, OP4).

After mapping the query to the user model, hidden requirements which are not expressed in words are searched. This is described below.

3.4 Mapping by Analogy

The second method to understand a user's query is understanding by analogy. It also consists of mapping by analogy and searching the hidden requirement.

Mapping by analogy maps the query to the user model using the similarity of nouns and relationships between nouns in the query, and nodes and links in the user model. This is done without a dialogue with the user even if the query contains unknown nouns. The basic rules of the mapping are described below. These rules select multiple candidates, and each candidate is ranked by the rules. Finally, the highest ranked candidates are selected as the mapping result.

(a) Mapping without unknown words

The query is mapped as a whole to the user model according to the rules below. As the result, the nearest part of the user model is considered to be the meaning representation of the query.

rule a.1 A noun in the query is regarded as corresponding to a node, if the node name matches the noun.

rule a.2 Two nouns and the relationship between them are regarded as corresponding to two nodes and a link between them, if two node names and the link match the nouns and the relationships.

rule a.3 Two nouns and the relationship between them are regarded as corresponding to a node, if the node name matches both nouns.

These rules are not interpreted rigorously. That is, if there are no completely matched nodes or links, partially matched nodes or links are regarded as matched. If multiple candidates are matched, all of them are selected with their ranks.

(b) Mapping with unknown nouns

When an unknown noun is related to a known noun in the query, the rules below are used.

rule b.1 The unknown noun is regarded as matching a node which is linked from the node matched to the known noun. The link corresponds to the relationship.

rule b.2 The unknown noun is regarded as matching the same node as the known node, or the ancestor node of the known node.

As with the mapping through dialogues, hidden requirements are searched after the mapping.

3.5 Searching the Hidden Requirement

After mapping the query in both methods above, the hidden requirement which is not expressed in words is inferred. This is done for replacing the ambiguous nouns by more specific nouns automatically. At the same time, the user's requirement is transferred to keywords.

Starting from the mapped nodes of the previous method, links labeled "conscious" are traced and selected until reaching relevant keyword nodes. Traced and selected nodes and links, together with the mapped nodes and links, comprise the meaning representation. That is, the meaning representation is a sub-structure of the user model.

4 Evaluation of Query Understanding

4.1 Experiment System

The experiment system is built for examining the evaluation method by evaluating the two proposed understanding methods. In the experiment, "Artificial Intelligence" is selected as the domain of the documents. A typical domain model is represented by approximately 500 nodes as the initial state of the user models. This is constructed based on [8]. The database consists of approximately 800 documents indexed by the name of the keyword nodes.

The configuration of the experiment system is shown in Figure 3. The system is implemented on a SUN3/260 using ART, Lisp, and C. The document database is in ORACLE on SUN3/60.

4.2 Experiment Methods

The 4 subjects in the experiment are researchers in our laboratory. Each subject made three queries in his area of interest. Some of the queries are shown in Table 3. The experiment procedure is as follows:

(1) understanding through dialogues
Three queries were submitted to the system one by one, and repeated three times. After processing each query, the subject selected the target keywords within the 500 keywords of the domain model.

(2) understanding by analogy
After processing a query by understanding through dialogues, the query was processed by understanding by analogy using the same user model. In addition, queries which have the same request and are represented by other words are also processed.

(3) selecting documents
After processing queries, subjects selected their target documents, limited to 800, by referring to their abstracts.

(4) calculating the efficiency
Keyword efficiency is calculated according to the results of (1) and (2). Retrieval efficiency is calculated after retrieving the document database.

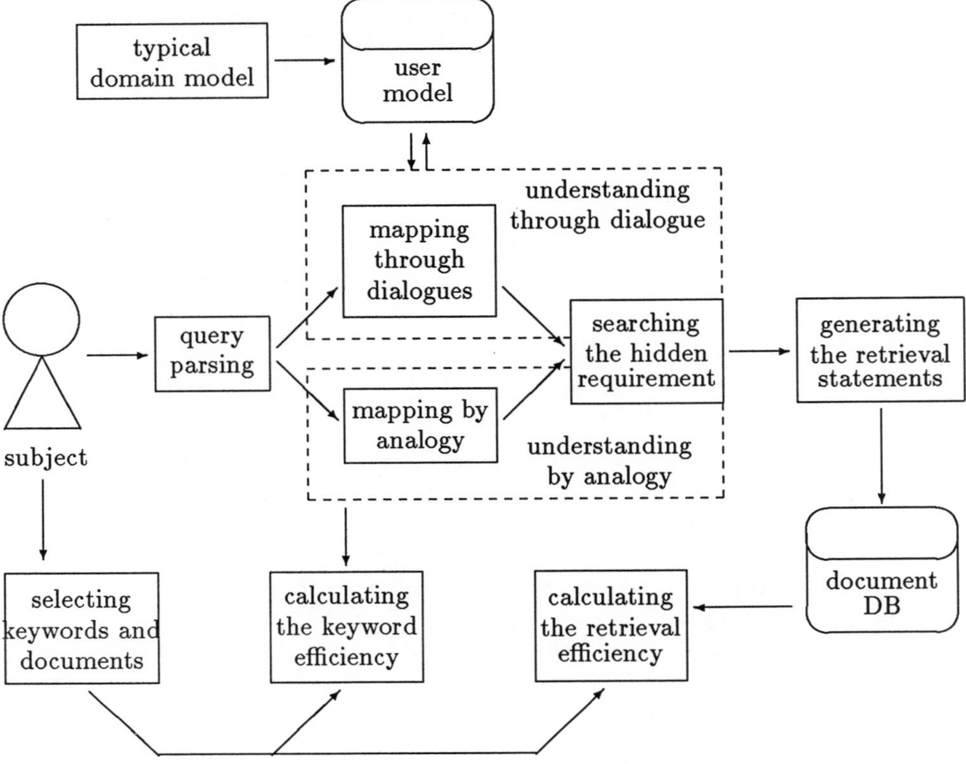

Figure 3: Configuration of the experiment system

4.3 Document Retrieval Methods

In phase 2, it is very difficult to get an optimum statement. Many methods for good retrieval were proposed. In our experiment, simple rules sufficient to evaluate the retrieval efficiency and analyze the co-relationships between phase 1 and 2 are used.

The retrieval method is called keyword matching. This method extracts keywords from meaning representation made by phase 1 processing, and matches the keywords to documents which have keywords as indices. Documents are ordered by number of matched keywords. Retrieval efficiency can be represented by the precision/recall curve as mentioned before. In this experiment, retrieval efficiency is represented by the mean value of the curve. This method is coincident with the vector method[9] of same weight values for every keyword.

4.4 Experiment Results

(a) Result of understanding through dialogue

Figure 4 shows the transition of the keyword and retrieval efficiency along with questions/answers of Q_1 of the subject b and Q_2 of the subject a. Table 4 shows the numbers of questions/answers of each query processing. These results show that, for keyword efficiency:

- The dialogues proceed as the keyword efficiency increases.

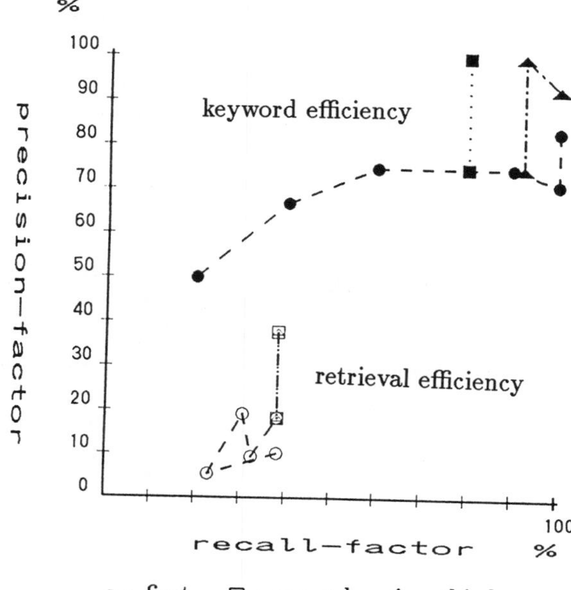

(a) Efficency transition of Q_1 of subject b

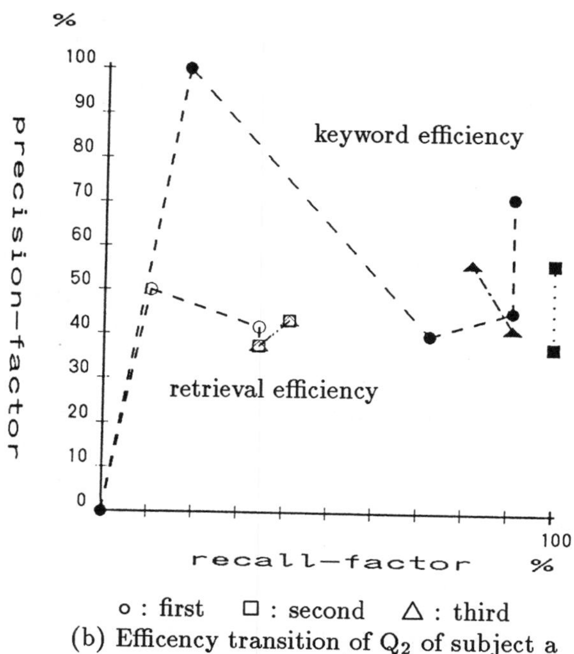

(b) Efficency transition of Q_2 of subject a

Figure 4: Keyword and retrieval efficiency of understanding through dialogues

Table 3: Sample queries made by the subjects

subject	query	statement
a	Q_1	*jiritsu-soukou-robotto niokeru shougaibutsu no ninshiki* (obstacle detection in autonomous robots)
	Q_2	*ninchi-chizu no sakusei* (making cognition maps)
	Q_3	*sizengengo-rikai niokeru mentarumoderu no riyou* (usage of mental model in natural language understanding)
b	Q_1	*user-interface niokeru gengo no yakuwari* (role of languages in user interfaces)
	Q_2	*kotoba no aimaisei no shori notameno suiron-housiki* (inference for processing language ambiguities)
	Q_3	*tukaiyasusa no koujou womokutekitosita user-interface* (user interfaces for increasing availabilities)

Table 4: Number of questions/answers in the understanding through dialogues

	subject a			subject b		
	Q_1	Q_2	Q_3	Q_1	Q_2	Q_3
first	8	7	4	13	6	6
second	3	3	2	3	5	3
third	3	3	2	5	2	3

- The numbers of questions/answers decreases with the processing of the same query.
- High keyword efficiency can be acquired after about 10 questions/answers in the case of a first processing, and about 5 questions/answers in the case of a second or third processing.
- Starting keyword efficiency of the second or third processing is high.

and for retrieval efficiency:

- The dialogues proceed as retrieval efficiency increases. However, the response to the retrieval efficiency of one question/answer is not particularly accurate. Moreover, the retrieval efficiency is saturated after several questions/answers.
- The final retrieval efficiency is not particularly good. The final keyword efficiency is approximately 90% of the precision and recall respectively, but the final retrieval efficiency is much lower.

In the second and third query processing, retrieval efficiency for each question/answer is almost the same.

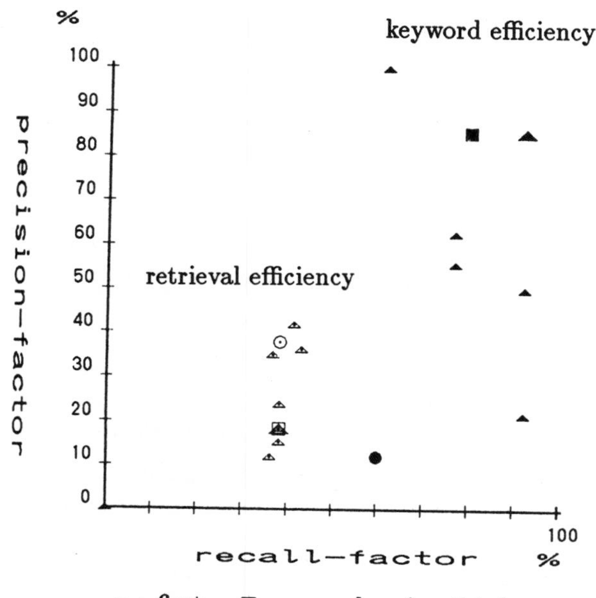

o : first □ : second △ : third
(small triangles show efficiency of alternative queries)

Figure 5: Keyword and retrieval efficiency of the understanding by analogy

(b) Result of understanding by analogy

Figure 5 shows the keyword and retrieval efficiency of understanding by analogy of Q_1 of subject b. Each point shows the final result of understanding by analogy. Figure 5 also shows the understanding result of alternative queries which are expressed in slightly different words but have the same requirement as Q_1 of subject b. Alternative queries are processed using the user model of third processing. These results show that, for keyword efficiency:

- High keyword efficiency can be acquired after constructing the user model (second and third processing). However, the keyword efficiency is not higher than the final point of understanding through dialogues.
- In the case of a query containing both known and unknown nouns, the keyword recall is approximately the same but the keyword precision is lower than a query containing the known nouns only.

and for retrieval efficiency:

- The final retrieval efficiency is particularly good.
- In Figure 5, retrieval efficiencies are not different than keyword precisions. Moreover, in Figure 5, the first efficiency is close to the second and third. This shows that the retrieval efficiency is mainly proportional to the keyword recall. The best retrieval efficiency in Figure 5 corresponds to the point of average keyword efficiency.

5 Considerations on the Experiment

5.1 Problems of the Experiment Results

The considerations on the experiment results are discussed. The experiment results show good keyword efficiency. However, from the point of retrieval efficiency or co-relationship between keyword and retrieval efficiency, there are some problems.

(1) Inefficiency of Retrieval

Retrieval efficiency is not particularly good in spite of the high keyword efficiency. The reason for that is as follows:

Lack of keywords
: Table 5 shows the keywords and their occurrences contained in the indices (multiple occurrences only) of documents selected by subject b with regard to Q_1. It also shows the extracted keywords of the third processing. Keywords which appear many times in the selected documents compared with all documents are considered to be important for the requirement. There are some important keywords unselected in the query processing. In Table 5, natural language processing or natural language understanding is regarded as important but not extracted. The lack of keywords seems to be caused because a user cannot imagine some important keywords. It is very natural because the user may pose the query before he arranges his requirement, or vagueness of his/her requirement prevent him/her to arrenge it.

Poor retrieval method
: As mentioned before, the retrieval method of the experiment is very simple. Some information in the meaning representation is not used in retrieving the database. Relationships between keywords is one piece of information. Keyword importance, that is, whether a keyword is a central concept or a qualifying concept, can be also extracted from the meaning representation. It is not so difficult to implement a retrieval method using the information. However, it is not our goal to implement a superior retrieval method.

(2) Saturation of Retrieval Efficiency

The experiment shows that the retrieval efficiency is saturated as keyword efficiency increases. One reason for the saturation is that the retrieval method proposed here is inefficient, and the other is that the understanding through dialogue forces a

Table 5: Keywords contained in the subject selected documents

occurrences		extracted	keyword
selected documents	all documents		
6	15	yes	Natural Language Interfaces
5	48	yes	Man Machine Interfaces
4	12		Natural Language Processing
3	18	yes	Information Retrieval
3	19		Natural Language Understanding
3	44	yes	Data Base
3	129		Knowledge Bases
2	30		General
2	51		Expert Systems
2	248		Modeling

user into detailed and unnecessary questions/answers to understand a query. This is because the understanding through dialogue try to extract all of the user's requirement from questions/answers.

5.2 Integration of Retrieval Methods by Feedback

To solve these problems, the feedback to understanding from retrieval result to find keywords which are difficult to extract by the previous understanding methods can be applicable. That is, retrieval output is shown to a user, and necessary keywords are extracted through dialogues with the user based on the output.

Figure 6 shows the results of hand simulation of the feedback for the previous results of understanding through dialogue (Figure 4). The retrieval efficiency is shown to be considerably improved by two or three times of feedback for both cases. They prove that the feedback works well. To decrease the number of times of the feedback, acquiring user models from retrieval result is applicable. Keywords which are extracted during the feedback can be acquired into the user model.

Efficient feedback mechanism for information retrieval was investigated to improve document retrieval[4][7]. However, no other feedback method constructs user models from retrieval results.

The feedback including constructing the user models from the retrieval result can integrate two proposed understanding methods. The outline is as follows:

(step 1) A query which contains more unknown nouns is processed by understanding through dialogue, and at the same time, the user model is constructed. Moreover, persistent questions/answers are not necessary. A query which contains less unknown nouns is processed by understanding by analogy.

(step 2) Retrieval output is shown to a user, and the user selects some target documents.

(step 3) Keywords are extracted from the selected documents, and his/her user model and meaning representation are modified based on the retrieval result.

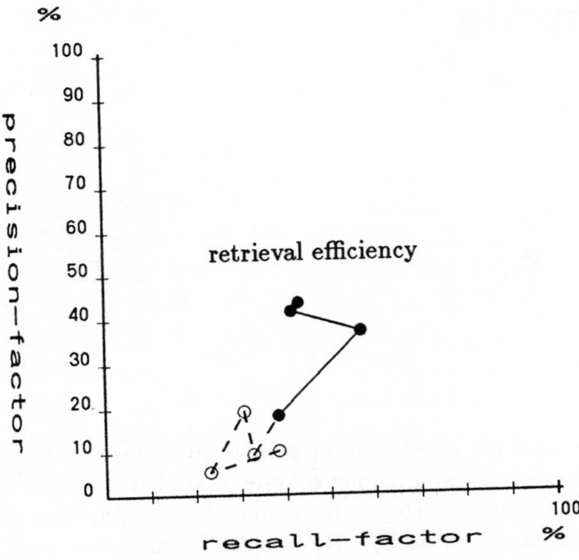

o : understanding through dialogue • : feedback

(a) Feedback after first dialogue of Q_1 of subject b

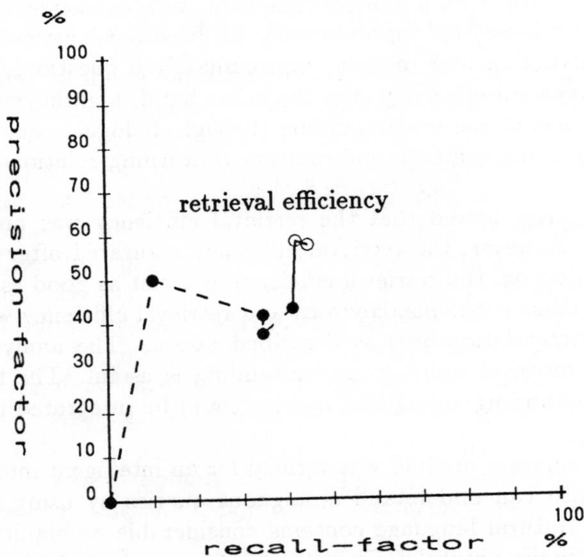

o : understanding through dialogue • : feedback

(b) Feedback after first dialogue of Q_2 of subject a

Figure 6: Transition of the retrieval efficiency by feedback

6 Conclusion

An evaluation method for intelligent interfaces to document databases which can understand incomplete or ambiguous queries stated in natural language was discussed. This method combined the performance of understanding queries (phase 1) and retrieving databases (phase 2). Keyword efficiency was used to evaluate phase 1, and retrieval efficiency was used to evaluate phase 2.

In addition, two approaches, understanding through dialogue and understanding by analogy, were proposed using user models. These approaches were evaluated by experiment using the evaluation method proposed here. The experiment showed that target keywords which each subject imagined were extracted (high keyword efficiency could be achieved) by approximately 10 questions/answers without user models. After constructing user models, approximately 5 questions/answers were sufficient for high keyword efficiency. On the other hand, high keyword efficiency, though lower than that of the understanding through dialogue, could be achieved without dialogue by using semantic information concerning relationships between nouns in queries.

The experiment also showed that the retrieval efficiency was proportional to the keyword recall. However, the retrieval efficiency saturated after several questions/answers. In addition, the retrieval efficiency was not as good as the keyword efficiency. To solve these problems, keyword and retrieval efficiency were analyzed together with their co-relationships as described above. The analysis suggested that feedback from retrieval result to understanding is useful. The two proposed approaches to understanding ambiguous queries could be integrated into the feedback framework.

The proposed evaluation method was verified for an intelligent interface to document database which can understand ambiguous queries by using keyword and retrieval efficiency. Natural language contains considerable ambiguity, vagueness, or redundancy. To make natural language interface more available and friendly, not limited to document databases, these properties of natural language must be allowed for. To examine such natural language interfaces, the evaluation indices and method proposed here must be widely applicable.

Acknowledgment

The authors wish to express deep appreciation to Dr. Kohhei Habara - Chairman of the board, Mr. Koichi Yamashita - President, Mr. Fumio Kishino - Head of ATR Communication Systems Research Laboratories for their helpful advice and encouragement of this work.

Acknowledgment of the collaboration of the members of our laboratory and their many useful discussions of our work is also due.

References

[1] G. Jakobson, et al. "An Intelligent Database Assistant", IEEE EXPERT, SUMMER, 1986.

[2] F. N. Tou, et al. "RABBIT: An Intelligent Database Assistant", in Proceedings of AAAI-82, 1982.

[3] I. Monarch and J. Carbonell, "CoalSORT: A Knowledge-Based Interface", IEEE EXPERT, SPRING, 1987.

[4] R. S. Taylor, "The Process of Asking Questions", American Documentation, Oct., 1962.

[5] N. J. Berkin, R. N. Oddy, and H. M. Brooks, "ASK for Information Retrieval: Part 1. Background and Theory", The Journal of Documentation, Vol. 38, No. 2, June, 1982.

[6] N. J. Berkin, R. N. Oddy, and H. M. Brooks, "ASK for Information Retrieval: Part 2. Result of a Design Study", The Journal of Documentation, Vol. 38, No. 3, Sept., 1982.

[7] J. Yen, et al. "Specification By Reformulation: A Paradigm for Building Integrated User Support Environment", in Proceedings of AAAI-88, 1988.

[8] David L. Waltz, "Scientific Datalink's Artificial Intelligence Classification Scheme", THE AI MAGAZINE, Spring, 1985.

[9] Gerald Salton (ed.), "The Smart Retrieval System Experiment in Automatic Document Processing", Prentice-Hall, 1971.

[10] S. Kinoshita, Y. Kanou, et al., "Deep Understanding of Japanese Queries in an Information Retrieval System", Proceedings of the 1988 International Conference on Computer Processing of Chinese and Oriental Languages, 1988.

[11] Y. Kanou, S. Kinoshita, et al., "Query Understanding Using User Modeling in a Document Retrieval System", ICCC Symposium '89, 1989.